THE MEDITERRANEAN WORLD

The Mediterranean World

From the Fall of Rome to the Rise of Napoleon

MONIQUE O'CONNELL & ERIC R DURSTELER

JOHNS HOPKINS UNIVERSITY PRESS | Baltimore

This book was brought to publication with the generous support of
the Gladys Krieble Delmas Foundation.

© 2016 Johns Hopkins University Press
All rights reserved. Published 2016
Printed in the United States of America on acid-free paper
9 8 7 6 5 4 3 2

Johns Hopkins University Press
2715 North Charles Street
Baltimore, Maryland 21218-4363
www.press.jhu.edu

Library of Congress Cataloging-in-Publication Data

O'Connell, Monique, 1974— author.
   The Mediterranean world : from the fall of Rome to the rise of Napoleon /
Monique O'Connell, Eric R Dursteler.
      pages cm
   Includes bibliographical references and index.
   ISBN 978-1-4214-1901-5 (pbk. : alk. paper) — ISBN 978-1-4214-1902-2 (electronic) —
ISBN 1-4214-1901-7 (pbk. : alk. paper) — ISBN 1-4214-1902-5 (electronic)
   1. Mediterranean Region—History—476–1517. 2. Mediterranean Region—
History—1517–1789. 3. Mediterranean Region—History—1789–1815.
I. Dursteler, Eric, author. II. Title.
   DE94.O27 2016
   909'.09822—dc23

                              2015018706

A catalog record for this book is available from the British Library.

Special discounts are available for bulk purchases of this book.
For more information, please contact Special Sales at 410-516-6936
or specialsales@press.jhu.edu.

Johns Hopkins University Press uses environmentally friendly book
materials, including recycled text paper that is composed of at least
30 percent post-consumer waste, whenever possible.

CONTENTS

CONTENTS

One of the great benefits of Mediterranean history as a field is that it allows us to step outside of traditional frameworks of nation-state and civilizational conflict and to offer alternative perspectives on how Europe, Asia, and Africa interacted in the premodern world. This process of challenging preexisting assumptions about the shape of the past can transform how we see ourselves and the world around us.

Any attempt to cover 1,300 years of history in 300 pages leaves out more than it includes, and experts on the various regions included here will be discomfited by the superficial treatment of many topics and themes essential to more specialized considerations. In fact, almost every paragraph of this book could be expanded into its own chapter. In our view, the benefit of such a general survey will be to hook a new generation of students and to engage enthusiasts of Mediterranean history, spurring their curiosity toward further investigation. Since this book is aimed at a more general readership, we have dispensed with footnotes and offer instead brief reading lists for each chapter that indicate our main scholarly debts and provide suggestions for further exploration.

We are deeply indebted to the Gladys Krieble Delmas Foundation for providing significant support for the research, writing, and publication of this volume. We both began our careers as students of Venetian history and benefited from the Delmas Foundation's generosity then, and we are profoundly grateful that the trustees and advisory board, especially George LaBalme, were willing to follow us on our journey out of the lagoon and into the larger cross-currents of the Mediterranean world. Indeed, Venice can be seen as a microcosm of the problems and themes of Mediterranean history in several ways. Scholars have often thought of Venice as a place that exhibited an unusual degree of religious diversity and religious tolerance as a result of its position as a point of exchange between east and west as well as north and south. Venice was also an agent of connection and economic exchange: Venetian merchants were prominent in Mediterranean ports, and the items they brought back created a richly diverse culture that drew on Byzantine, Islamic, and western models. Therefore, it is particularly appropriate that it was Delmas support that allowed us to include illustrations of the Mediterranean hybrid of artistic and material culture.

We are also thankful for the support and encouragement we have received from Johns Hopkins University Press. That this book exists at all is due to the vision and energy of longtime executive editor Henry Y. K. Tom, who perceived the need for such a volume, recruited us to write it, and worked closely with us to develop the proposal. His sudden death, in January 2011, left us deeply saddened that we were not able to show him the fruits of his labors. Suzanne Flinchbaugh showed extraordinary patience over the lengthy middle phase of our journey, and Matt McAdam and Catherine Goldstead helped us bring the project to completion. Marcia Underwood designed the maps that accompany the text.

Our respective universities, Wake Forest and Brigham Young, also supported this project in several ways. O'Connell received a yearlong Reynolds Research Leave from Wake Forest for academic year 2012–13, which allowed time for writing, and a Henry S. Stroupe Faculty Fellowship in History enabled her to travel to Istanbul and Cairo in 2010. The Wake Forest History Department sponsored Dursteler's 2009 visit to campus, where we received feedback on the proposal from colleagues and students. A 2011 invitation from the David M. Kennedy Center for International Studies at Brigham Young University allowed O'Connell to receive feedback on the Byzantine Empire in the Mediterranean. Dursteler also received research support from BYU's College of Family, Home, and Social Sciences; the David M. Kennedy Center for International Studies; and the Center for the Study of Europe.

We have also been fortunate to receive advice throughout the process of researching and writing the volume from colleagues at our own and other institutions. At Wake Forest, Charles Wilkins patiently and carefully responded to hundreds of questions about Islam and the Ottomans and read parts of the manuscript in draft, pushing us toward more accuracy and nuance. Jake Ruddiman read and discussed each chapter in the first part of the book, and the writing is much clearer as a result of his interventions. Lisa Blee also lent her perspective as a historian of Native Americans to multiple discussions of frontier societies, and Sharon DeWitte helped us understand the new research on the bubonic plague. While undergraduates at Wake Forest, Joseph De Rosa, Madeline Eckenrode, Brittany Forniotis, Joshua Garrett, Kara Peruccio, and Hillary Taylor all read, discussed, and commented on various pieces of this book as well, and their suggestions enhanced the final presentation, as did the comments from many other students who encountered pieces of this book in classrooms and seminars. Giovanna Benadusi, Palmira Brummett, Emrah Safa Gürkan, John Hunt, Benjamin Ravid, Brian Sandberg, Scott Taylor, and Francesca Trivellato all provided key feedback at various stages of the project. Edward Muir, as always, was a constant source of advice and encouragement. And, for Dursteler, Whitney Dursteler's support and encouragement were, as always, essential to every stage of the process. Finally, we would like to thank the two anonymous reviewers, whose many helpful suggestions and corrections at the final stage of the project were invaluable. It goes without saying that any errors that remain are our responsibility alone.

This coauthored volume reflects a long process of discussion, debate, and thinking together through the issues of Mediterranean history. We collaborated on the proposal and initial outline of the volume, and both the introduction and chapter 8, "A Renaissance Bazaar," are cowritten. O'Connell drafted the initial versions of chapters 1 through 7, covering the medieval period. Dursteler drafted the initial versions of chapters 9 through 12, covering the early modern period. We then collaborated on the process of revision for all of the chapters so that they reflect our shared vision of the Mediterranean.

A NOTE ON NAMES AND DATES

This book covers a wide geography and a long span of time, making a rigid consistency with regard to place names and personal names impossible. The names of cities and territories took different forms in different languages and names often changed along with political boundaries. We have used the place names most easily recognizable to nonexperts, for example Cairo rather than al-Qahira. We have tried to balance accuracy with clarity for the reader, using the name current in the period under discussion. Therefore, Byzantine Constantinople becomes Ottoman Istanbul in 1453.

A second issue comes with dates. As the book is aimed at a general audience, we have chosen a widely recognized system of dating. We use the modern adaptation of the Christian labels for dates, BCE (before Common Era) and CE (Common Era); all dates not labeled fall within the Common Era. Readers might rightly protest that in a book dedicated to the interaction of different religious traditions in a shared space, Muslim and Jewish dating systems should be included. Rightly or wrongly, we have sacrificed inclusiveness for clarity in the matter of dates.

THE MEDITERRANEAN WORLD

Introduction

The Idea of the Mediterranean

The Mediterranean is both very old and very new. As a geographical entity, it has existed for millions of years; once inhabited by humans, it became the center of some of the world's most ancient civilizations. But as an object of study, the Mediterranean has been the focus of intense and sustained scholarly investigation only since the last century. The idea of the essential unity of the Mediterranean Sea can be traced to antiquity: the Romans called it "Our Sea," while in English and Romance languages the term *Mediterranean* could be translated as the "Middle Sea" or the "Sea between the Lands." Located at the intersection of Asia, Africa, and Europe, the Mediterranean has connected the societies that surround the sea for millennia, creating a shared space of intense economic, cultural, and political interaction. A traveler to the region is immediately struck by the richly multicultural and layered nature of the ancient, medieval, and early modern histories of the societies that surround the sea. Greek temples in Sicily, Roman ruins in North Africa, Islamic palaces in Iberia, crusader castles in Syria, and Ottoman fortifications in Greece all testify that the Mediterranean has never been a place with fixed national boundaries or stable ethnic and religious identities. Rather, it has long been a contested space, one where different religions, polities, and ethnic groups have met, mingled, and clashed for thousands of years.

This book is intended to introduce readers to the contours of Mediterranean history in the medieval and early modern eras, the 1,300 years between the fall of Rome (c. 500) and the Napoleonic conquests (c. 1800). This chronological arc traces a time when no single power dominated the sea or the societies that surrounded it, meaning that the eras were characterized by complex patterns of accommodation, acculturation, fragmentation, and conflict. After the crumbling of the Roman Empire ended the political unity of the Mediterranean permanently, there were several new contenders for Mediterranean hegemony. Invaders from the north, south, and east—Visigoths, Vandals, Arabs, Bulgars, Vikings, Normans, and Turks—brought their own languages and cultural patterns to the region. These peoples established new states or took over older institutions, creating a patchwork of different political entities and a number of frontiers. In the early modern period, the Spanish, Ottoman, and Venetian empires emerged, creating composite states that consolidated governmental structures and contained considerable religious and cultural diversity. At the end of the period under consideration, another wave of contenders for power from the North arrived, this time in the form of Napoleon's armies and the Russians.

Significantly, the Arabs brought a new religion, Islam, which shaped the region's religious culture, together with Judaism and the varieties of Christianity that had taken hold in the waning days of the Roman Empire. Some historians and popular writers have seen the introduction of Islam into the Mediterranean as creating a fundamental division that persists into contemporary times, and they interpret Mediterranean history as the ground of a perennial clash of civilizations. This book takes a different approach to the question of religious division. While we recognize that religion played an important role in the medieval and early modern history of the region, we do not believe that religious belief was the only category that mattered in defining individual or group identities: gender, ethnicity, family ties, language, and regional and political ties all came into play as well. We thus see religious identity as part of a fluid and complex interplay, one among multiple factors. And while there were certainly moments of conflict, hostility, and violence with religious motivations or explanations, there were many more moments when coexistence, cooperation, or tolerance characterized events. It is often difficult to untangle the intertwined political, religious, and economic factors behind change and conflict, and throughout the book we have attempted to recognize the multifaceted nature of interconfessional interaction in the Mediterranean world.

We have structured the book around four interlocking themes. The first theme is the *mobility* of Mediterranean populations: people moved across the sea for a variety of reasons, and we discuss migration, slavery, commerce, pilgrimage, corsairs and pirates, and even travel for curiosity's sake. The second theme is *state development*: the events of conquest and territories won or lost, but also the methods and strategies of power and legitimation, including cultural production and court culture, religious ideologies, elite artistic patronage, and the development of urban centers. A third theme is *commerce* and economic development, including practices and innovations in trade methods, patterns of production and consumption, and interaction between merchants. The final theme is *frontiers* and borders: by tracing lines of demarcation and zones of contact, we highlight the complex reality in an environment without monolithic or static blocs of influence or identity: identity was multifaceted and situational, and cultural and political boundaries were crossed as often as they were created.

Since the early 2000s, there has been a wave of interest in the Mediterranean region. Scholars working in disciplines from anthropology to archaeology, from environmental studies to history, are producing a body of scholarship that is developed at research centers, presented at international conferences, and published in specialized journals and monograph series that are all devoted to the Mediterranean. This burgeoning interest can be attributed to several factors. First, the Mediterranean was, and remains, a unique contact zone in which a particularly diverse group of cultures intersected and engaged. The sea formed a liminal space where religious, ethnic, and political identities were contested and negotiated, and this interaction resonates in a multicultural contemporary world concerned with the formation of pluralistic societies. Second, the nature of Mediterranean studies has encouraged innovation through cross-disciplinary collaboration and dialogue. Finally, in this postnational, global age, scholars have become intrigued by transcultural and transnational histories (the Atlantic World, the Indian Ocean, world history) that move beyond the restrictive parameters of the nation-state, and the Mediterranean has been at the forefront of this development.

As a subject, Mediterranean history is the site of an almost infinite number of scholarly debates and controversies. We have outlined particular debates in the context of individual chapters. But what of the nature of the Mediterranean itself? Is it more important to focus on the fundamental qualities that unify the region, such as geography, nature, climate, and culture, or on the religious and political conflicts that at times divided it? Historians, anthropologists, literary scholars, art historians, and archaeologists have repeatedly returned to the question of whether the sea and its borderlands function and make sense as an analytical whole and, if so, what elements unite this diverse region and validate its study.

The genesis of Mediterranean studies in general, and the debate on Mediterranean unity in particular, dates back to the 1949 French publication of Fernand Braudel's *La Méditerranée et le monde méditerranéen à l'époque de Philippe II* (*The Mediterranean and the Mediterranean World in the Era of Philip II*), one of the great works of twentieth-century historical erudition and imagination. Braudel's monumental work emphasized a unified Mediterranean environment and economic structures that resulted in societies sharing a "common destiny." This vision was informed by his own experiences: born in northeastern France, Braudel taught secondary school in the French colony of Algeria from 1923 to 1932; there he became interested in the Mediterranean and chose as the setting for his university thesis the subject "Philip II, Spain, and the Mediterranean in the Sixteenth Century." From 1927 on he began devoting all his free time, particularly summer vacations, to research in Spanish, Italian, and Ragusan archives. During this research stage, Braudel stumbled on a tool that helped him gather and analyze the voluminous documentation that he collected. He purchased a used movie camera in Algiers, which he used to photograph documents (on some days, thousands of them) that he came across in the archives. This precursor to modern microfilming technologies allowed him to amass an unprecedented documentary base. After spending holidays gathering documentation, Braudel and his wife, Paule, whom he met while she was his student in Algiers, worked closely during the academic year to process these archival films. While one read from the filmed documents, the other took notes; working in tandem they were able process large quantities of data.

From 1935 to 1937, Braudel taught in São Paulo, Brazil. His time in North Africa and Brazil proved fertile for the genesis and development of what would be his masterpiece. Seeing the Mediterranean "from the opposite shore, upside down," shaped the way he conceived of the region; instead of approaching history from the narrowly nationalistic angle then common among historians, he envisioned a study with much broader horizons. Braudel abandoned his original topic of Philip II, inspired in part by the reaction of his adviser and, eventually, close friend and patron, Lucien Febvre: "Philip II and the Mediterranean is a fine subject. But why not the Mediterranean and Philip II? Isn't that an equally fine but different subject? For between the two protagonists, Philip and the interior ocean, the match is not equal."

The writing of Braudel's epic work on the early modern Mediterranean has become one of the great tales (some might say myths) of twentieth-century historiography. After years of research, when friends and colleagues despaired of him ever finishing what he admitted was his "overly ambitious work," in the summer of 1939 Braudel finally sat down in Febvre's summer home to begin writing. Very quickly, however, larger events intruded. As Europe rushed toward another war, Braudel, who had served previously in the military, was called back to active service. He saw limited action in the battles of spring 1940 and then was captured and shipped to Germany, where he spent the remainder of the war in a German prison camp. It was in this most unlikely of settings that Braudel returned to his thesis, carrying out much of the writing and significant revisions in detention. In describing this seemingly impossible task, his wife explained that just prior to the war's outbreak, Braudel went carefully through all his notes collected over the past 15 years and so was able to write the book "essentially from memory." His memory was supplemented, it must be said, by access to the university library in Mainz, where he was first imprisoned, a privilege he received because of the historical courses and lectures he offered fellow prisoners.

While some have doubted this feat, it seems quite clear that Braudel composed the majority of his thesis while in Germany. He sent several versions of the work by way of the Swiss embassy to Lucien Febvre. Following his release in 1945, Braudel and his wife spent the next two years checking the text against the research notes that he had preserved in a metal container in the basement of their Parisian home. Following the 1947 thesis defense, the manuscript underwent additional editing. The result of over two decades of work was published in 1949. Though not without its critics, the massive work was instantly recognized as one of the most innovative and significant works of twentieth-century historiography.

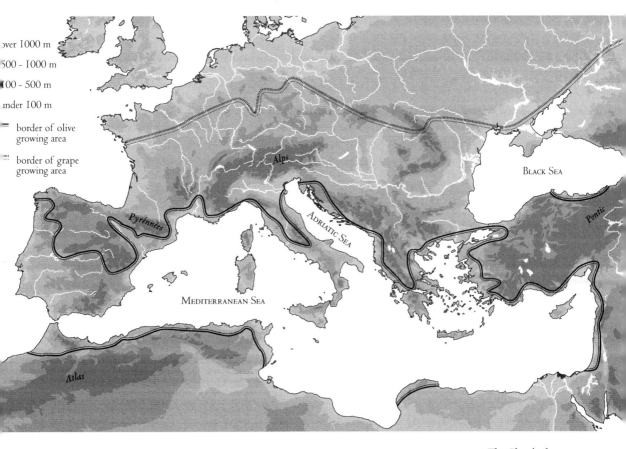

The Physical Mediterranean

 labels visible on the map: over 1000 m; 500 - 1000 m; 100 - 500 m; under 100 m; border of olive growing area; border of grape growing area; Pyrénées; Alps; ADRIATIC SEA; BLACK SEA; Pontic; MEDITERRANEAN SEA; Atlas

The book's protagonist is the Mediterranean itself: it is the story "of man in his relationship to the environment." Braudel divides his analysis into three layers, each of which approaches the early modern Mediterranean at a different level and builds on the preceding section. He begins with *la longue durée*, or *structure*, the nearly unvarying forces of geography and climate. This is followed by *la moyenne durée*, or *conjuncture*, which treats social and economic structures and forces that change only very slowly over time. He concludes with *la courte durée*, or *événement*, which is devoted to the political and diplomatic history of Philip II's reign. The work progresses logically and methodically, from geology and geography to social and economic structure to political narrative. The foundation of the book is the level of geography and climate, which Braudel describes as "a history whose passage is almost imperceptible . . . a history in which all change is slow, a history of constant repetition, ever-recurring cycles." This is geohistory: it is the tale of islands, mountains, deserts, land and sea routes, and climatic patterns. Braudel insists that these features, long studied by other social and physical scientists, cannot be divorced from or ignored in historical explanations; indeed, they are at its very foundation. He uses the limits of olive and grape cultivation to delimit the region of the Mediterranean, using these agricultural products as a rough measure of climatic similarity.

One of Braudel's most significant contributions is his insistence on seeing the Mediterranean as a whole, rather than broken into what he perceives as artificial divisions. He argues that societal trends within the Spanish west and the Ottoman east in many ways mirrored each other: in both areas the nobility consolidated its wealth and power, urban centers grew at the expense of the countryside, wealth became concentrated in fewer hands, and banditry and piracy arose as responses to this inequality. If the Mediterranean was rent in the military confrontation between the Spanish and Ottoman empires, there existed a deeper social and geographical unity that transcended these political events.

In the more traditional final section, Braudel provides a narrative of Spain's rivalry with the Ottoman Empire from 1550 to Philip II's death, in 1598. Despite its seemingly familiar focus, however, this section is not a canonical political history. While tracing the narrative, Braudel repeatedly emphasizes that the actors on the political stage of the Mediterranean are in most ways limited in their ability to act and control events. They are at the mercy of, and their actions are determined in many ways by, the much deeper and more immovable geographical and social structures described at length in the book's first two sections. In one of the book's most memorable images, Braudel describes the Mediterranean's wars, decisions, heroes, as but "surface disturbances, crests of foam that the tides of history carry on their strong backs." This image does not imply that political history has no importance; rather, Braudel wants to show that these forces have been emphasized at the expense of the equally real, and ultimately more important, structural forces that molded and controlled individuals and events. Braudel also uses the final section to try to break down the traditional nationalist boundaries of the history of his day—what he characterized as the "walled gardens" of history—by placing the events of the late sixteenth century in a much wider, even global, context. This global vision would become even more accentuated in the second edition of the book, published in 1966, in which Braudel significantly reworked, reorganized, and updated his original work in preparation for its translation into English in 1973.

Ironically, the breadth of Braudel's conceptualization of the Mediterranean for a time crowded out other historical voices. One notable exception was S. D. Goitein's six-volume study, *A Mediterranean Society* (1967–83), which used a trove of documents from the Cairo Genizah to reconstruct a picture of the rich and complex networks of Jewish merchants from the Indian Ocean to the Black Sea. The Mediterranean region also attracted the sustained interest of anthropologists, who identified what they perceived to be key elements of Mediterranean cultures: honor and shame, clientelism, sociability, food, the family, and symbolic systems.

Critics of Braudel's vision of Mediterranean unity fall into several camps. The anthropologist Michael Herzfeld argues that broad generalizations about Mediterranean-wide attitudes and values obscure significant diversity across time and place. Herzfeld and other anthropologists have resisted in particular claims that Mediterranean unity was not simply environmental but cultural, and that inhabitants of the region shared modes of thought and habits of mind. Herzfeld has also charged that scholarly views of the Mediterranean as a common cultural zone are based on northern European stereotypes of the region and on inhabitants' self-stereotyping and conscious fashioning of a Mediterranean identity. For scholars who take this perspective, the Mediterranean is the creation of academics and tourists, its unity manufactured only through self-serving discourses that emphasize broad patterns at the expense of local and regional differences.

Some scholars of politics and diplomacy have also challenged the idea of a unified sea, focusing on military conflicts and enumerating the multiple dividing lines that crisscrossed the region. Disagreeing with Braudel's conviction that politics and diplomacy were merely "surface disturbances," they give more explanatory weight to battles, generals, and politics in shaping the pattern of Mediterranean events. In the medieval period, these historians focus on the Crusades and on moments of open conflict between Christian and Islamic states, articulating a vision of the Mediterranean that acted as a staging ground for armies and battles between religious others. For the early modern period, Andrew Hess's *The Forgotten Frontier: A History of the Sixteenth-Century Ibero-African Frontier* (1978) is a systemic challenge to Braudel's conviction that the "Turkish Mediterranean lived and breathed with the same rhythms as the Christian." Hess argues that by focusing on what he sees as the sharp division between Iberia and North Africa in the western Mediterranean, religious and cultural divisions are thrown into stark relief.

Another critique of Braudel's vision of Mediterranean unity came from those who questioned his structuralist approach; reviewers charged that he had created a "history without humans," which limited the role of individual agency and choice. Critics noted that Braudel did not consider the attitudes, fears, and beliefs of the people of the Mediterranean, nor did he give religion any explanatory power or role. Some recent books have tried to redress this imbalance, placing cultural history at the forefront of their investigations. An example of this approach is Predrag Matvejević's *Mediterranean: A Cultural Landscape* (1999), which argues for the importance of religious, linguistic, culinary, and intellectual factors in shaping the history of Mediterranean. This highly impressionistic and descriptive work puts away the wide-angle lens employed by Braudel and instead focuses on the details: the sights, sounds, and smells common to the different peoples who surrounded the sea; travel literature and the experiences of crossing the sea; and the intense linguistic diversity of the region. More recently, David Abulafia's *The Great Sea: A Human History of the Mediterranean* (2011) emphasizes individual agency and change over time, presenting the Mediterranean as a stage for human interaction in which people shape their own destinies.

A further challenge to Braudel's vision of the unity of the Mediterranean comes from scholars who see Mediterranean space divided by religions in conflict. For the early medieval period, the Belgian historian Henri Pirenne famously stated that "without Mohammed there would have been no Charlemagne." He saw the arrival of Islam on Mediterranean shores as a rupture of Roman commercial and cultural unity and argued that Latin Christian Europe turned northward in the eighth century, developing its own economic, political, and religious trajectories. Pirenne's own life history in some ways anticipated Braudel's experiences: when the Germans occupied Ghent, where he was a professor at the university, Pirenne refused to continue teaching; as a result of this resistance, he was sent in 1916 as a prisoner to Germany, where he spent the remainder of the war. Like Braudel, Pirenne passed the time writing primarily from memory, in his case a history of Europe beginning with the fall of Rome and ending in the sixteenth century. After the the war, he sketched the outlines of his thesis on Mediterranean division in a 1922 essay entitled *Mahomet et Charlemagne* and in the first two chapters of *Medieval Cities: Their Origins and the Revival of Trade* (1925). He expanded on the same points in a short book published posthumously in 1935 and translated into English with the title *Mohammed and Charlemagne* in 1939. The details of the Pirenne thesis have been successfully challenged by later generations of scholars, but it remains an influential idea for interpreting changes in the Mediterranean economy and in European culture. Since 2000, two monumental works by the historians Chris Wickham and Michael McCormick relied on archaeological evidence not available to Pirenne to demonstrate that the transformation of the post-Roman world was much more complex and gradual than previously thought, refuting the idea that the rise of Islam and the expansion of the Arabs constituted a decisive or sharp break in Mediterranean patterns of interaction.

Other scholars and popular writers have pursed an oppositional approach to Mediterranean history, using binary antitheses such as east/west, Muslim/Christian, Spaniard/Turk, or Europe/Other as a shorthand for complex interactions. The continued currency and persistence of this "oppositional framework" among the general population as well as scholars is evident in Samuel P. Huntington's influential "clash of civilizations" model. Richard Bulliet has provocatively challenged the idea of a clash of civilizations, arguing that rather than being diametrically opposed, the histories of Christendom and Islam are so closely intertwined that the Mediterranean ought to be envisioned in terms of a shared "Islamo-Christian" civilization. *Europe and the Islamic World: A History* (2013), by John Tolan, Henry Laurens, and Gilles Veinstein, follows Bulliet's lead, challenging the "clash of civilizations" model by emphasizing the shared roots of Islamic and western cultures, looking at the medieval and modern periods and providing a wealth of detail that shows that the encounter between Islamic and Christian civilizations is not easily reduced to simplistic generalities. Similiarly, the recent *A Companion to Mediterranean History* (2014) includes a section on "religions in conflict and co-existence," but the other essays in the volume discuss climate, periodization, politics and power, settlement patterns, language and culture, and connections to the wider world, challenging the idea that religion is the defining or dominant force in shaping the region's history.

The publication of Peregrine Horden and Nicholas Purcell's *The Corrupting Sea* (2000), a weighty and ambitious reconsideration of Mediterranean unity and connectivity, revivified the debate on the Mediterranean. The work draws from a wide range of disciplines, including archaeological and ecological data, as well as relying on economics, geography, and anthropology. The authors see the history of the Mediterranean in terms of fragmentation and connectivity. They argue that the region is distinguished by its unusual ecological diversity, a diversity that creates a fragmented landscape of "microregions" that are defined both by their physical environment and by patterns of human interaction with that environment. In fact, they argue, each microregion is not just the sum of its parts but is defined by constantly changing interactions with other microregions. They describe this dense web of interaction as "connectivity," which they see as being driven by the need to manage risk through exchange. The authors conclude that "dense fragmentation complemented by a striving towards control of communications may be an apt summary of the Mediterranean past."

In Horden and Purcell's vision, the Mediterranean is unified chronologically as well as geographically. The authors see one of the benefits of their methodology as its resistance to efforts to periodize and divide the region's past; rather, they propose, "we must be prepared to see the events which we study on a smooth scale stretching into the distant past." This approach downplays the effects of climate change over time, and sharp breaks and discontinuities between historical eras are replaced by a more gradual waxing and waning of connectivity. As a result, the volume is organized thematically rather than chronologically. In the first section, the authors explain how they envision a "history *of* the Mediterranean" as something separate from "history *in* the Mediterranean." The methodology they propose is "historical ecology," meaning the study of the complex interactions between humanity and the environment across a broad period of time. The authors offer case studies of particular locations and themes, including the economy of food cultivation and the intersection of sacred geographies and the physical environment.

The Corrupting Sea has generated a great deal of discussion, debate, and renewed interest in the Mediterranean as an object of study. One area of vibrant and ongoing discussion is where the boundaries of the Mediterranean lie. The limits of Braudel's Mediterranean were defined by the cultivation of the olive and the grape, but where are the boundaries of a region defined by connectivity and dense networks of interaction? In a provocative essay, the historian David Abulafia asked how far the idea of the Mediterranean can be stretched in geographical terms. If "the Mediterranean" is simply a zone of exchange and connectivity, why not a Saharan Mediterranean? A Caribbean Mediterranean? A Japanese Mediterranean? Abulafia's own 2011 synthesis of Mediterranean history, *The Great Sea* situates the boundaries of the Mediterranean much more narrowly than Braudel did, focusing on the surface of the sea itself and the islands, shores, and port cities that acted as access points and way stations. *The Great Sea* offers a much more comprehensive chronology than most other works, providing a narrative history that sweeps from prehistory to the twenty-first century. Building on his past research in economic exchange in the western Mediterranean, Abulafia places much greater weight on the role of individuals and the influence of political, social, and religious factors than Braudel did.

To this point, Mediterranean historical studies have evolved in two primary directions, what Horden and Purcell have characterized as history *of* and history *in* the Mediterranean. Braudel, Horden and Purcell, and Abulafia are the chief examples of the first category with their sweeping, multimillennial, and interdisciplinary treatments. More common are works on some sector of the Mediterranean, or histories *in* the Mediterranean. These works are narrower and more monographic: generally they treat a specific region, city, or topic and rarely attempt to situate themselves within the broader question of Mediterranean unity. By focusing in an insular fashion on *convivencia* in Spain, conversion in the Balkans, or Ottoman monetary policy, these often excellent works are Mediterranean only in that their focus is geographically situated in the region. Despite their proximity, these two strands of Mediterranean research—histories *of* and histories *in*—often have informed each other only loosely.

APPROACHES AND THEMES

This book proceeds from a fundamental view of the Mediterranean as an integrated whole. We argue that Braudel's vision of Mediterranean unity, given greater clarity through Horden and Purcell's concept of connectedness, describes a historical situation characterized by great fluidity and complexity within the variegated religious, political, and cultural poles of the sea. From a geographical standpoint, we have taken a relatively broad approach, following the political, economic, and cultural influences that affected Mediterranean history far inland. Rather than proposing a rigid or constraining definition of where the borders of the Mediterranean begin and end, we have adopted a more flexible vision. The trading rhythms of the sea brought people and goods from Africa, Asia, and Europe, and the commerce of the Mediterranean was linked to the Indian Ocean, the Atlantic, and the Black Sea region. Immigrants and invaders have arrived on Mediterranean shores from these regions as well, and so while we have kept the overall focus on the sea itself and the societies that surrounded its shores, at times it has been necessary to wander a bit farther afield.

One of the main benefits of Mediterranean history is its ability to challenge the central role of the nation-state, but this does not mean that we have avoided the history of events. In many cases, an understanding of political developments provides an essential framework for the social and cultural experience of individuals. We have followed Abulafia in aiming to emphasize the human element of the Mediterranean, contending that individual experiences and life stories are an important method for understanding larger historical developments and patterns. Each of our chapters opens with a brief anecdote about one or two individuals or events that illuminate the main themes and patterns of historical development discussed. Many of the opening examples also highlight the sources available for reconstructing Mediterranean history, which are more fragmentary for the medieval period than for the early modern. Travel narratives are an important subset of these sources, and we describe individual journeys to Constantinople, the Levant, North Africa, Italy, the Iberian peninsula, and the Balkans that give a real sense of what it was like to travel across the Mediterranean for these particular people.

The book follows a primarily chronological organizational scheme. In order to balance descriptions of conflict and change with accounts of accommodation and interaction, the chapters alternate between narratives of political and military developments and depictions of movement across frontiers and religious, economic, social, and cultural developments. Chapter 1 offers a rapid overview of the ancient Mediterranean, tracing the rise and fall of the Roman Empire and its fragmentation into barbarian, Byzantine, and Latin Christian components. Chapter 2 examines the development of new Christian and Islamic societies that constructed new political structures from the remains of the Roman Empire in the early medieval era. Chapter 3 traces the economic, cultural, and religious contours of these new societies, identifying moments of commercial and intellectual exchange, shared experiences of the holy, and moments of tension and polemic between and among Christian, Muslim, and Jewish authorities.

Chapter 4 offers an account of Christian and Muslim holy wars in the high Middle Ages, placing the European Crusades and Muslim response in the framework of large-scale population movements from north, east, and south. Chapter 5 examines the frontier societies created by these newly formed polities, where religiously justified violence often gave way to intellectual, social, and artistic exchange, accommodation, and assimilation. Chapter 6 focuses on economic exchange in the high Middle Ages, looking at Latin European merchants' entry into Jewish and Muslim commercial networks and the changes wrought by the onset of the bubonic plague in 1348. Chapter 7 describes the demographic crisis, social and economic upheaval, and civil wars over the respective rights of rulers and ruled that ensued, surveying the gradual formation of regional states in Iberia and Italy, the rise of the Ottoman Turks as a serious contender for power, and the weakening Byzantine and Mamluk empires in the east. Chapter 8 turns to the cultural developments of the early modern world, considering the Renaissance in a Mediterranean context and examining changes in commercial patterns and in the circulation of luxury goods, as well as the articulation of a range of shared cultural practices.

Chapter 9 narrates the evolution of the Habsburg, Ottoman, and Venetian empires from their regional state predecessors, looking at how imperial politics and diplomacy shaped the early modern sea. Chapter 10 examines life on the early modern frontiers between empires, giving particular attention to those who crossed religious, political, and economic borders. Chapter 11 traces how global instability in climate, demography, and disease transformed Mediterranean culture, leaving aside traditional models of decline to recount ways that Mediterranean polities and people made serious attempts to adapt to the challenges and realities they faced in a variety of innovative ways. Chapter 12 acts as a conclusion, considering Napoleonic and Russian incursions in the late eighteenth and early nineteenth centuries as marking the transition from the premodern to the modern era in the Mediterranean.

CHAPTER ONE
The Waning of the Roman Mediterranean

S
tories of the Roman Mediterranean almost always begin in the city of Rome itself. At the height of its imperial splendor, all roads—and sea-lanes—indeed led to the capital city, which drew people, wealth, and culture from across the Mediterranean basin. But at the beginning of the fifth century, Rome lay in ruins, depopulated and stripped of its luxuries. In 410 a loose confederation of Germanic peoples known as the Visigoths had besieged and then sacked the city. Even before the sack, other capitals had replaced Rome as the seat of imperial government. Constantinople was home to the powerful ruler of the Eastern Roman Empire, while the emperor of the Western Roman Empire exercised what little remained of his authority from Ravenna, located in the marshes of eastern Italy. Real power in both cities lay with two powerful women of the imperial family, Galla Placidia and Aelia Pulcheria. Both ruled as regents for child emperors, Placidia in the west for her young son Valentinian III and Pulcheria in the east for her brother Theodosius II. The experiences of these two elite women illustrate the complex of factors that transformed the Roman Mediterranean in late antiquity: migrations and invasions from the periphery, the growing influence of Christianity on society and politics, and the fragmenting of Rome's unifying political control of the region.

Both Placidia and Pulcheria were part of the Theodosian dynasty. Theodosius I, from a wealthy Spanish family, became emperor in 379; he was the last to rule over both the eastern and western parts of the empire, which was divided between his sons on his death, in 395. When the Visigoths arrived outside the gates of Rome, Placidia's brother Honorius was safely ensconced in Ravenna. Placidia was taken captive during the siege and lived with the Visigoths for the next five years, first as a hostage and then, after her marriage to the Visigoth king Athaulf, in 414, as a queen. The marriage, which was celebrated with Roman-style festivities and magnificent gifts, was intended to stabilize Roman-Gothic relations, but it did not last long. Athaulf was assassinated in Barcelona in 415, and Placidia returned to Italy, where a second marriage made her, very briefly, an empress. After her husband's death, she fled to Constantinople, where her nephew, the eastern emperor Theodosius II, offered her and her children sanctuary. Placidia returned to Italy with Valentinian in 425, when he was proclaimed emperor; she ruled as his regent for the next 12 years and remained politically influential until her death, in 450. In Constantinople, Placidia would have met her niece Pulcheria, granddaughter of Theodosius. A devout Christian, Pulcheria publicly dedicated herself to perpetual virginity at age 14, acting as regent for her younger brother Theodosius. In 414, the same year Placidia married Athaulf, Theodosius gave his sister the title of empress, and she controlled government decisions until her death, in 453.

Coin with the image of Empress Galla Placidia. A richly dressed Galla Placidia is shown in profile, with the hand of God placing a crown or a halo on her head, illustrating a mix of sacred and secular power. *Museo Nazionale Romano (Palazzo Massimo alle Terme), Rome. Photo: Album / Art Resource, NY*

Placidia and Pulcheria lived in turbulent times. The early fifth century was a tipping point for the Roman Empire and for the Mediterranean. It encompasses both the end of the empire and the beginning of the medieval era. This period saw a growing influence of migrants and invaders from the north and east. Regular interchange between Romans and non-Romans on the frontiers of the empire had been under way for centuries. Roman literary sources often expressed hostility toward these so-called barbarians, imagining these people as the polar opposite of Romans: uncivilized while Romans were civilized, irrational where the Romans were rational. Archaeology shows that there was a contact zone along the borders of the Roman world, where Roman goods circulated widely and where Germanic peoples and Romans mixed. Some groups were invited into the empire as settlers or as federated troops; by the late fourth century the Roman army was becoming steadily more Germanic. This army fought other non-Roman groups who came as invaders. While Greeks and Romans believed "barbarians" existed in ethnically distinct groups that retained stable identities across centuries, modern scholars have advanced the idea of ethnogenesis, or the ability of a people to acquire a shared sense of ethnic origin. According to this view, both Romans and non-Romans exercised some choice in their statements of identity, through naming practices, dress, hairstyles, language, and material culture. Marriages between Romans and non-Romans, like that between Placidia and Athaulf, further added to the cultural fluidity of the era.

At the beginning of the fifth century, Rome still controlled the sea, but the long period of Mediterranean political unity centered on that city was drawing to a close. After sacking Rome the Visigoths tried to cross to Africa via Sicily but were stopped by winter storms as well as the death of their king, Alaric. A Roman law of 419 sentenced to death anyone caught teaching shipbuilding techniques to "barbarians," but this last-ditch effort was unsuccessful. A confederation led by the Vandals launched maritime raids on the Balearic Islands and crossed the Strait of Gibraltar in 429, conquering large parts of North Africa. Galla Placidia and Valentinian III were forced to cede this territory to the Vandal king, Gaiseric, and over the next 20 years Vandal fleets regularly raided Sicily, Italy, and the Greek coasts. The Vandal invasions began to fracture the political and economic unity of what Romans referred to as Mare Nostrum ("our sea").

The military threat Pulcheria and Theodosius faced in the east was quite different from the coalitions of Germanic invaders moving into the west. The Sassanian Persian Empire was highly centralized and rivaled Rome in cultural production as well as military might. The frontier between the two empires was generally peaceful in the fifth century, with the exception of two brief wars, in 421–22 and 440. But while the east was less affected by external invasions and migrations than the west, religious controversy and theological dispute destabilized society and government to a much larger degree. Christian communities around the eastern Mediterranean struggled furiously over theological questions, and the intersection of governmental and religious power structures often made these doctrinal disputes part of imperial politics.

By the end of the fifth century, the Roman emperor in the west had been deposed and the empire transformed into several smaller political units that were economically and culturally more self-sufficient. In the western Mediterranean, Roman provincial governors were replaced by Germanic kings and elites. The Eastern Roman Empire showed more continuity with Roman traditions, but it also changed character in this period, becoming more uniformly Greek in culture and language.

The waning of Roman political structures, or what the eighteenth-century historian Edward Gibbon proclaimed the "decline and fall" of the Roman Empire, has given rise to a great deal of scholarly debate. Some historians, labeled *catastrophists*, see a dramatic break with the Roman tradition in these centuries, pointing to a combination of internal weaknesses and the arrival of northern invaders as causes for the rupture of Roman order. Other historians, branded *continuists*, see the transformation of the Roman world in much more gradual terms, pointing to the slow and uneven pace of change in social and economic patterns. Recent scholarship has emphasized gradual transformation rather than decline or fall, although there remains a vigorous debate over why and how Rome's political dominance ended.

MARE NOSTRUM: THE MEDITERRANEAN UNDER THE ROMANS

Roman rule in and around the Mediterranean set into place patterns of society, culture, and exchange that shaped the next thousand years, and the ideological power of Rome deeply influenced the states that succeeded it. Rome did not become a sea

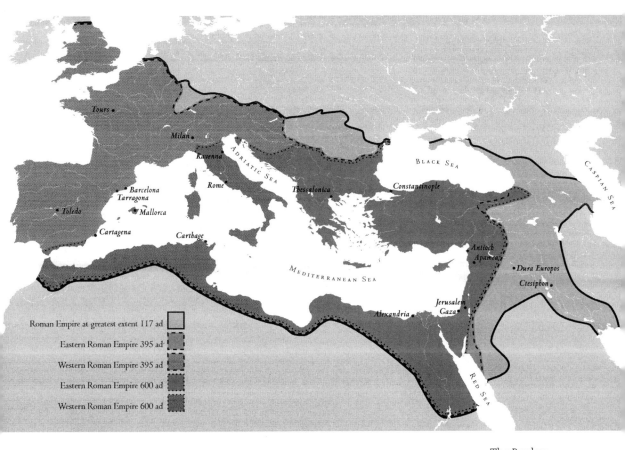

Roman Empire at greatest extent 117 ad
Eastern Roman Empire 395 ad
Western Roman Empire 395 ad
Eastern Roman Empire 600 ad
Western Roman Empire 600 ad

The Borders
of the Roman
Mediterranean

power until its struggle with the North African city of Carthage. In three separate wars, Roman forces gradually extended their authority in the western Mediterranean, conquering and destroying Carthage in 146 BCE. In the same year, Rome destroyed the Greek city of Corinth in punishment for an uprising, signaling its dominance over both the eastern and western parts of the sea and its trading network. Polybius, a Greek historian of Rome, wrote, "Previously the doings of the inhabited world were held together by no unity . . . but ever since this date history has been an organic whole, and all the affairs of Italy and Africa have been interlinked with those of Greece and Asia." Polybius's comment highlights the degree to which Roman rhythms drove the patterns of Mediterranean interaction.

During a phase of imperial expansion, Rome systematically expanded its dominance of the sea and the land that surrounded it. There is no evidence that the motives for Roman expansion were mercantile, but it is equally clear that the effect of Roman expansion was a rise in commerce. Under the rule of Octavian Augustus, Rome had unchallenged control of the Mediterranean. Fleets stationed at Ravenna, Naples, North Africa, and in the Black Sea ensured swift and safe passage from one end of the sea to the other, encouraging economic and cultural exchange. The Roman historian Pliny wrote, "Everyone is aware that as a result of the world being united under the majesty of the Roman Empire life has improved thanks to trade and the sharing of the blessings of peace." Maritime archaeology indicates that from 200 BCE to 200 CE sea traffic was two to three times higher than before or after.

Much of this traffic was in grain, oil, and wine destined to feed the city of Rome, which by 100 BCE had grown to more than a million people. Roman officials levied taxes in grain from North Africa, Sicily, and Sardinia, and the Roman aristocracy imported foodstuffs from their far-flung estates. There was no state-owned fleet to transport this grain—the trade relied on private shipowners paid by the government in money and in concessions such as the privilege of citizenship or exemptions from some laws. Smaller commodities and luxury goods traveled on top of the regular shipments of foodstuffs, facilitating active trade networks around the sea. There was also a small but significant trade in luxury goods from the Indian Ocean, facilitated by the Arabs of the Red Sea. Some Roman merchants traveled as far as India, trading wine, copper, tin, and silver coins and glass for spices and silks.

Where goods moved, people did as well. Rome drew Greek, Egyptian, Spanish, and Phoenician people and culture to the capital and exported its language, laws, architectural styles, and educational system throughout the empire. Roman intellectual culture was heavily indebted to Greek traditions, and Greek was as common as Latin in the eastern Mediterranean. Roman urban plans also drew on Greek models, as they were all centered around a forum—the Greek agora—a rectangular paved space with temples, meeting spaces, and markets. Roman city centers included baths and amphitheaters, and the regular street grid led to city gates, walls, and aqueducts. In the eastern Mediterranean there was an extensive urban culture before the Romans arrived, but in the western provinces the Romans built new cities, connecting them with a network of roads. Towns and cities were the focus of aristocratic life and the definition of *civilitas* (civility). Legal identity as a Roman citizen was one way for local elites across the empire to

Mosaic of Roman shipping in North Africa. This Roman mosaic from Tunisia was made in the third century and shows goods, probably iron ore, being unloaded. On the left, two men who are probably merchants are weighing the iron. *Bardo Museum, Tunis. Photo: Gianni Dagli Orti/Art Resource, NY*

THE MEDITERRANEAN WORLD

demonstrate their Romanness, but Roman identity could also be shown culturally, and local aristocrats from Spain to Syria adopted Roman styles of dress, read the same Greek and Roman literature, and sponsored entertainments in Roman-style amphitheaters.

At the center of the Roman cities were the civic temples, dedicated to the primary Roman gods, Jupiter, Juno, Minerva, and Mars (who had been adapted from their Greek counterparts Zeus, Hera, Athena, and Ares). Roman priests performed sacrifices for the communal good, and Romans attended public rituals and festivals in honor of local and imperial deities. Romans also had personal and household gods as guardians and protectors. As Roman territory expanded, so did its pantheon—some native gods found Greek or Roman equivalents, and a few won adherents across the empire. The worship of the goddess Isis began in Egypt, and devotion to the "Great Mother" Cybele began in Anatolia (modern-day Turkey), but cults dedicated to these goddesses sprang up across the Roman Mediterranean. The Persian god Mithras similarly gained adherents throughout the empire. The port city of Ostia, on the Italian coast, had temples dedicated to all three of these deities, as well as a synagogue.

The city of Dura Europos, on the eastern border of Syria, was abandoned after the third century CE and thus preserves an example of the religious and cultural complexity of a provincial Roman town. There were public temples dedicated to Greek and Roman deities—Artemis, Zeus/Jupiter, and Adonis—as well as to the Palmyrene god Bel. There were also more private spaces where Christians, Jews, and followers of the god Mithras gathered. Archaeological evidence from other parts of the Roman Mediterranean repeats this picture, indicating that by the second and third centuries CE, many individuals were turning from traditional Roman religious practice and looking for new forms of religious expression.

When the Romans conquered the eastern Mediterranean, they found themselves ruling over the Jews, who, unlike most Roman subjects, were strict monotheists, with their worship centered on the temple in Jerusalem. The Jewish refusal to sacrifice to Roman deities and to the emperor set them apart, and this religious difference merged with strong inclinations toward political independence. There was a major rebellion in the kingdom of Judea in 66 CE, which Flavius Josephus, a Jewish general turned Roman citizen and author, attributed to tensions between Greeks and Jews as well as Roman governors' rapacity. The future emperor Titus and the Roman army savagely repressed the revolt, taking Jerusalem in 70 CE and sacking the temple. After a second rebellion in 132–36 CE, the Romans banished all Jews from the city permanently, beginning what is called the diaspora, or the dispersal of Jews across the Mediterranean. There were Jews living outside of Syria and Palestine before the revolt, but this dispersal increased the Jewish populations in many Mediterranean towns and cities. The destruction of the temple also brought changes to the Jewish religion itself, as synagogues as became more important as meeting places and rabbis became more prominent leaders of community prayer. Archaeological remains of synagogues have been found across the Roman Mediterranean.

Like the Jews, Christians worshiped the God of the Hebrew scriptures, but instead of perceiving this God as an exclusive savior of the Jewish people, Christians saw him in the form of Jesus as a universal savior, the son of God sent to earth in human form to offer personal salvation to all who offered their loyalty. Accounts of Jesus's life and works, called gospels, were widely circulating by the end of the first century, partly as a result of the work of the apostles. The structure of the early church is revealed by the surviving letters of one of these apostles, Paul of Tarsus, who traveled through an eastern Mediterranean that was Greek in language and culture and Roman in politics. He made contact with Christian communities in the port cities of Greece and Anatolia. Paul described the Christian church as a social leveler "where there is neither Jew nor Greek, slave nor free, male nor female." Paul and other early Christian leaders wrote letters imagining Christians as members in a uniform and orderly community, led by bishops, priests, and deacons. Other early Christians, such as the Gnostics, saw the Christian community in much less hierarchical terms.

Scholars used to believe that Christianity spread first to those of low social status, but now they see a wide cross-section of Roman society among early Christian communities. Women were prominent in these communities, as believers and also sometimes as leaders, perhaps because of the increased protections Christian values offered to women and children. There were sporadic local persecutions of Christians and several more general persecutions initiated by emperors, notably in 65 by Nero and in 249–51 by Decius. It is difficult to know how many Christians there were in the Roman Empire at this time, but scholars estimate they represented up to 10% of population in the third century.

The Roman world of the second and third centuries CE was clearly centered on the urban, cosmopolitan world of the Mediterranean, but this zone was surrounded by long and very porous frontiers. Beginning in the third century, Germanic peoples in northern Europe formed federations of Goths, Franks, and Alemanni and began putting significant pressure on Roman frontiers, raiding across the frontier and several times penetrating to the shores of the Mediterranean. These same Germanic tribes also served as mercenaries in Roman armies and were sometimes invited to settle in imperial territory. The influx of new peoples on the northern frontiers was just one of the large-scale changes that affected the Roman world in what scholars often label the "Crisis of the Third Century." Political instability, near-constant warfare, and economic disruptions instituted profound changes in the empire. Between 235 and 284, there were more than 20 emperors, the majority of whom ruled for only a few months before meeting a violent end at the hands of a successor. In the east, the Persians presented a serious and ongoing military threat. The Roman army took on an important role in politics and grew in size, causing more and more of a draw on imperial coffers. This demand on the empire's resources was unsustainable, and there was a collapse in the silver coinage, price inflation, and a rise in the tax burden. In response to the new prominence of the army in politics and the threats along the frontiers, the practical center of administration moved northward, away from the Mediterranean, although Rome remained an important symbolic and ritual center.

The restoration of stability after the crisis involved significant and long-term changes. Diocletian, a soldier from Dalmatia, was proclaimed emperor by the army in 284, and he took direct action to restore political stability, control inflation, and reform tax administration and the legal code. As part of his restoration of Roman order, Diocletian demanded a return to traditional Roman values, including the worship of the Roman gods. When Christians refused to sacrifice to those gods, Diocletian ordered an empire-wide persecution that targeted churches, scriptures, and Christian leaders. Between 303 and 305, a number of Christians were executed for refusing to renounce Christianity; their deaths were narrated by Christian authors in stories that emphasized the martyrs' willingness to die for their beliefs and their repeated refusal to recant. The persecution strengthened Christian belief, and Christians revered those who had been executed and developed a cult dedicated to the martyrs and their remains.

Over the next decade, the Roman Christian community witnessed a dramatic reversal of their status in the empire. In the civil war that followed Diocletian's reign, Constantine was the ultimate victor. Under Constantine, the Roman Empire underwent significant and long-term changes, but the most obvious was Constantine's official policy of toleration for the Christian religion and his own eventual conversion to Christianity. Constantine was not formally baptized until 337, but it is his vision on the eve of the battle of the Milvian Bridge, in 312, that has come to symbolize his acceptance of the power of the Christian god. Constantine's biographer Eusebius related that on the eve of battle, Constantine had a vision of a cross with the inscription "Conquer by this." He and his soldiers carried Christian symbols into the battle and were victorious. The following year Constantine issued the Edict of Milan, restoring confiscated church property and permitting the public practice of Christianity. He subsequently exempted church property from taxation and clergy from the burden of public service, privileges priests of other religions already enjoyed. He also allowed the church to inherit property from its believers, a measure that led to its significant wealth in subsequent centuries.

Scholars have long disagreed about the intention and meaning of Constantine's conversion to Christianity. Some see him as a sincere reformer; others view him as a clever politician. There is no doubt that Christianity was useful for rulers; as Eusebius said, "As there was one god, so was there one king." Constantine took a measured approach, presenting himself as both a pagan and a Christian ruler. He still called himself Pontificus Maximus, the leader of the state cult, and used traditional Roman imperial imagery on his coinage. The triumphal arch he constructed in Rome commemorating his 312 victory contains no direct reference to Christianity, although he was a major patron of Christian churches in the city. Constantine also mixed old and new in his capital at Constantinople, founded on the ancient city of Byzantium in 324 and dedicated in 330. Constantine built or restored Roman public buildings such as the hippodrome and forum. At the center of the forum was a huge statue of him in the guise of the sun god, with rays of light emanating from his crown. He built the Church of Holy Sepulchre at Jerusalem, on what was believed to be the site of Jesus's burial and resurrection. Constantine's mother, Helena, founded other churches on the Mount of Olives and at Bethlehem, which became sites of Christian pilgrimage.

Constantine had no patience for the doctrinal disputes that divided the Christian church, particularly in the great cities of the east. He gathered the bishops of the empire at the Council of Nicaea in 325 with the goal of unifying Christian practice and dogma across the empire. The bishops were called on to regularize the dates of church festivals such as Easter, to ensure uniformity in the Christianization of time and space across the empire. The council also dealt with the nature of the Trinity, particularly the relationship of God the Son to God the Father. While there were a wide range of beliefs about the Trinity, Athanasius, patriarch of Alexandria, polarized the issue by accusing the Alexandrian priest Arius of heresy for his belief that God the Son proceeded from God the Father. The Council of Nicaea produced a statement of orthodox faith (the Nicene Creed) declaring that Father and Son were of the same substance, but there continued to be a great deal of intellectual debate and controversy over the precise meaning of this formulation. Two versions of Christian belief developed: the Nicene, also called Catholic, and the non-Nicene, called "Arian" by its detractors. Many northerners, particularly the Goths, converted to non-Nicene Christianity, making the difference in religious belief a marker of identity as well as a doctrinal difference. Nicaea set a precedent for councils to determine correct doctrine and for emperors to involve themselves in theological disputes.

Constantine's rule set in motion a tide of Christianization in the empire's administration and its population. Preference for Christians in imperial offices meant that the proportion of pagans in public bureaucracy decreased over the fourth century. The number of Christians in the empire increased exponentially during the same time, from 5 million to 30 million. Pagan civic and support systems—burial and retirement societies, banquets, and poor relief—were replaced with Christian ones, and from the fourth to the sixth centuries the Mediterranean landscape was gradually Christianized as well.

A CHRISTIAN MEDITERRANEAN

As the number of Christians in the empire grew, pilgrims traveled the roads and sea-lanes built for Roman commerce and military transport, layering a sacred Christian geography atop Roman imperial networks. Early Christian pilgrims traveled to Egypt and Jerusalem to directly experience the holy, contained not only in sacred spaces but in holy people. Egeria, a woman from the Atlantic coast of Spain, traveled to Egypt, Syria, and Jerusalem from 381 to 384 to see the holy places and to visit the living saints and monks of the Egyptian desert. She visited spots associated with individuals from the Old and New Testament, tombs of the martyrs, and the places of Christ's ministry and martyrdom, particularly those adorned by

Constantine in Jerusalem. Jerome, a Dalmatian monk educated in Rome who traveled to Syria, Constantinople, Egypt, Alexandria, and Jerusalem, described the dramatic reaction of the Roman pilgrim Paula in Jerusalem, saying that when she reached the Holy Sepulchre, "she fell down and worshipped before the Cross as if she could see the Lord hanging on it." Paula's reaction illustrates the intense emotional bond many of these early pilgrims felt with the holy dead as well as with the holy living, a connection that was enhanced by physical proximity.

Holy men and monasteries played a prominent role in these early pilgrim itineraries. The idea of achieving holiness through asceticism, or self-denial and separation from secular society, had deep roots in the ancient world, but in the Christian context the most prominent early monk was St. Anthony, a Coptic-speaking Egyptian farmer who abandoned family and property, retreated into the desert, and eventually became the model Christian hermit, known for his dramatic spiritual battles with demons. The appeal of ascetic holy men like Anthony spread rapidly. In Syria monks engaged in extreme and dramatic forms of ascetic practice, such as Simeon the Stylite, who prayed continuously standing atop a 60-foot-tall pillar. Historians explain the appearance of individuals or communities devoted to life of religious contemplation or service in multiple ways. Some see the appeal of self-sacrifice rising in a post-Constantinian world where martyrdom at the hands of public authorities was no longer an option. Others see

Arch of Constantine, Rome. Emperor Constantine erected this triumphal arch in the center of Rome to commemorate his victory at the battle of the Milvian Bridge in 312. Photo: Album/Art Resource, NY

it as a desire to withdraw from an unstable world, and still others see elements of flight from the growing tax burdens in Egyptian cities in economic crisis.

These highly individual forms of worship coexisted uneasily with more communal forms of monastic devotion. Pachominus, an Egyptian farmer press-ganged into Constantine's army, returned to Egypt and created a system for organized monastic life, linking cells of hermits into settlements. The settlements were directed by an Apa (abbot), father of the monks, and combined individual prayer and fasting with communal readings and meals. By the end of the fourth century, a network of monasteries across Egypt, Syria, and Palestine housed about 7,000 monks and nuns. This communal form of monasticism spread from its Egyptian and Syrian roots throughout the eastern and western empire, but the radical message of the desert ascetics was appropriated and adapted in different ways as it spread. In Anatolia, Basil of Caesarea used his authority as bishop to create and regulate monastic establishments, composing a shorter and longer rule that separated male and female monks and brought monasteries within the structure of the emerging church hierarchy. Basil saw charity as one of the overriding duties of monasticism, in addition to regular prayer and manual labor. Basil's rule became the standard for all subsequent monastic foundations in the eastern Mediterranean, and monasteries in the east were rooted in the life of great cities — monks allied with bishops and provided social services to the urban poor, working in hospitals, food supply centers, and burial associations.

The life of Basil's sister, Macrina the Younger, demonstrates the different pressures and expectations on women who desired to lead a monastic life. The majority of Christian and non-Christian traditions in the late Roman world perceived women to be intellectually and physically inferior to men, and while there were women among the early desert ascetics, they met with hostility and resistance. According to the *Life of Macrina*, written by her brother Gregory, Macrina struggled to avoid marriage, first forming a community of pious women within her mother's household and ultimately establishing a monastic community with herself as abbess on the family estates. Gregory's presentation of Macrina as an ideal virgin-philosopher was repeated in many other praises of holy women in the fourth century. Such women were believed to overcome the imperfections of their female bodies through ascetic practice and virtue and, as one male monastic writer put it, to "become, through their virtue, like men, to whom they are already created equal in their soul."

In Rome, neither Melania the Elder nor the Younger, wealthy and powerful women of the Roman elite, avoided marriage as Macrina did, but both were influential pilgrims and promoters of the monastic ideal in their own right. Melania the Elder, a widow from a affluent Roman senatorial family with roots in Spain, set out for Egypt in 370. After visiting the monks of the desert, she went to Palestine. There, she used her fortune to found monasteries for both men and women on the Mount of Olives, where she lived for over 20 years. Her granddaughter Melania the Younger followed in her footsteps. After marrying and bearing two children, both of whom died young, Melania and her husband, Pinian, renounced their worldly life, sold their extensive lands and possessions, and founded monasteries in North Africa and in Jerusalem.

The monastic ideal spread from east to west through bishops returning from church councils, pilgrims, and the *Life of Anthony*, a text that circulated widely. Some westerners, looking for an equivalent to the deserts of the east, established monastic communities on the tiny islands of the western Mediterranean. By the 370s there were both male and female monasteries in cities, but the extreme asceticism of the desert had to be modified before monasticism could be widely accepted in the west. John Cassian's works muted the desert ideal, reimagining dietary austerity as moderation and changing monks' dress to account for climate differences. Cassian wrote that monasteries should support themselves economically through manual labor, and he identified contemplation with scriptural study. By 600 there were at least 220 monasteries and convents in Gaul and about 100 in Italy; monastic institutions seem to have developed more slowly in Spain, however. Monasteries gradually became centers of education and literacy, although the content of a monastic education was far different from that of a classical one. Virginity for female monks also became more important, and nuns were seen as embodying sacred protection for an entire community.

Bishops had been an important part of the church since the first century, but their practical authority increased in the fourth and fifth centuries, particularly in the cities of the west. Constantine gave bishops judicial powers, and they were responsible for the defense of cities and distribution of supplies of food and clothing, previously the responsibility of the Roman state, turning the churches into a sort of public welfare system. By the fifth century there were approximately 2,000 bishops in the empire as a whole. There was no social uniformity among those who became bishops, although in Gaul and Spain there tended to be more landed aristocrats whereas eastern bishops were not as personally wealthy. Once in office, bishops in both east and west controlled the growing resources of the urban church; by 610 the patriarch of Alexandria had 8,000 pounds of gold in his church's treasury, supported 7,500 needy Alexandrians, and directed a trading fleet that sailed to Morocco and Cornwall.

The authority of bishops could take different forms, as the lives of the famous bishops Ambrose of Milan, Martin of Tours, and Augustine of Hippo demonstrate. Ambrose began life as a Roman administrator and was forcibly elected bishop of Milan by those who hoped he could end the local dispute between Nicene and non-Nicene Christians. Ambrose was not even baptized and certainly was not a priest, but once he became bishop, he was a fierce defender of Christian prerogatives in the public sphere. He influenced several emperors, urging them to adopt more aggressively Christian policies. When the pagan senator Symmachus petitioned the emperor to restore the statue of Victory to the senate, Ambrose warned against it; when the emperor attempted to take a church of Milan for his own purposes, Ambrose and his congregation blockaded it; when the emperor ordered a massacre in Thessalonica (Thessaloníki), Ambrose denied him communion until he performed public penance. Ambrose forcefully articulated the principle that even emperors were subject to moral correction and helped carve out a public and political role for Christian clergy.

Martin of Tours also began his career as part of the Roman imperial machinery, as a soldier, but became first a monk and then a bishop. He ruled the city of Tours from his riverside monastery, rather than the bishop's palace in the city, and waged a dramatic campaign against paganism in the countryside. He saw and fought demons, conversed with angels and saints, and exorcized evil spirits. Martin's parallel in the eastern Mediterranean was Gregory of Pontus, in modern Turkey, who was remembered as a visionary, a wonder-worker, and an effective agent of rural conversion as well as for his role as bishop. Bishops like Martin and Gregory drew their authority from their status as holy men, able to directly and physically manifest the power of the Christian faith.

The North African Augustine of Hippo began his career as a student and then a teacher of the Roman educational tradition. While he was teaching classical rhetoric in Milan, his reading of the *Life of Anthony* caused his dramatic conversion to a more dedicated form of Christianity; Augustine's description of his conversion experience in his *Confessions* was immensely influential in later centuries. He returned to North Africa and eventually became bishop of Hippo, where his authority derived from his education as well as his struggles against unorthodox Christian belief. He composed *City of God*, a significant contribution to Christian philosophy and history, in response to aristocratic Christians fleeing the sack of Rome and asking for an explanation of how the Christian God allowed this to happen. Augustine's many theological works on the justified use of force against heretics and the doctrine of original sin represented the continuing influence of classical culture and rhetoric on a newly powerful Christian literary tradition.

Ambrose, Martin, and Augustine were unusual in their influence and in the amount of evidence they left behind, but the different forms of religious authority they embodied—administrative, monastic, and intellectual—were typical. Bishops were located in cities, and the cities of the late Roman Empire were being transformed by the new social and religious patterns. Across the empire, construction of Roman public buildings—baths, amphitheaters, aqueducts, triumphal arches— slowed or stopped entirely. Regional elites instead used their wealth to build churches as physical testaments to their newfound faith. In the larger cities of the east, pagan temples were transformed into Christian churches, while church construction in the smaller western cities tended to cluster outside city walls. Private construction gradually encroached on the open space and broad thoroughfares of Roman cities, making them less uniform.

Bishops were often in the vanguard of the twin processes of Romanization and Christianization along frontiers, acting as agents of both church and state. Powerful bishops' claims to spiritual and secular authority brought them into frequent contact—and sometimes conflict—with Roman emperors and their families. These contacts were most intense in Rome and Constantinople. The bishops of Rome claimed a special authority based on the city's status and on the preeminence of the apostle Peter, believed to be its first bishop. Damasus, a Spanish-born bishop of Rome, deliberately set out to Christianize the city. Inside the walls, his new church foundations were located atop the traditional centers of Roman military and government authority—the Palatine and Esquiline hills and the Field of Mars—while outside the walls he encircled Rome with churches and chapels commemorating martyrs' tombs. He and his successors gradually claimed superior status and jurisdiction over other bishops and eventually took the title of pope, meaning father. In 445, Pope Leo I convinced Emperor Valentinian III to acknowledge papal authority over the rest of the Christian clergy. The end of Roman imperial authority in the west after 476 left popes more autonomy than their counterparts in Constantinople had.

The patriarch was the highest religious authority in Constantinople, but he shared power with the imperial family, responsible for creating much of the city's new sacred geography. In one telling incident, Pulcheria clashed with patriarch Nestorius, who alienated the population by banning the circus, theater, mimes, games, and dancers; more significantly, he refused Pulcheria entry into the church sanctuary and removed her portrait from over the church altar. Nestorius also challenged the theology of revering Mary as the Mother of God. In response, Pulcheria's ally Proclus preached an oppositional sermon and authored several works praising Pulcheria herself. In a clear demonstration of imperial control over the patriarch, Nestorius was deposed and excommunicated for heresy in 431, and Proclus was named patriarch in his place. Over time, imperial control over the patriarch and over theological matters grew even stronger, introducing a clear difference in the development of eastern and western Christianities.

On the level of daily life, it seems the vast majority of individuals in the Mediterranean were perfectly content to live in intimate contact with those of other faiths. People continued to celebrate many Roman festivals whatever their beliefs, and Christian clergy fulminated against their followers' attendance at those festivals with little effect. There was a shared world of magical beliefs and practices—amulets, spells, divinations, and prophecies—that united Christian, Jewish, and pagan believers. Some clergy denounced what they called "Judaizing" practices among Christians, criticizing individuals who went to synagogues, celebrated Jewish holidays, and generally did not respect the social or sacred boundary between the two communities. The attacks suggest the frequency of these behaviors.

Against this background of religious accommodation there was a rising tide of imperial legislation that first privileged orthodox Christians and then outlawed pagans altogether, leaving Jews as a protected but legally marginalized minority. There was growing perception that all forms of non-orthodox Christian belief were dangerous. Augustine wrote, "Heretics, Jews, and pagans: they have formed a unity over against our unity." Theodosius I in 380 issued an edict making Nicene Christianity the official religion of the empire and declaring other

Mosaic floor with zodiac, Israel. A sixth-century mosaic found in the Beth Alpha synagogue in the Jezreel Valley. Helios or the sun god is in the center, surrounded by zodiac signs and images of the four seasons, each accompanied by Hebrew captions. *Bibliothèque nationale de France, Paris/Art Resource, NY*

versions of Christian belief "demented and insane." In 381 Theodosius expelled non-Nicene clergy from their churches, and in 391 he issued a series of edicts confiscating and closing shrines and temples and banning the public or private practice of pagan sacrifices. The example of Gaza in Palestine shows that these orders were not immediately followed: a decade after Theodosius's ruling, Gaza had temples dedicated to the Sun, Aphrodite, Athena, and Zeus. Porphyry, the Christian bishop of the city, complained bitterly about this state of affairs—at one point, he so angered the non-Christian population of Gaza that he had to flee across rooftops to escape an angry mob. He eventually gained the support of the empress Eudoxia, and imperial troops sacked the pagan temples in 402.

In the fourth century, violence between pagans and Christians in the eastern Mediterranean increased, as monks, bishops, and the Christian masses led attacks on pagans and symbols of pagan worship and pagans defended themselves. Alexandrian pagans looted churches in 356 and lynched the actively antipagan bishop of the city in 361. In 386 the Christian bishop organized the destruction of the temple of Zeus at Apamea in Syria, and an antipagan riot in Alexandria in 392 led to the destruction of the Serapeum, the splendid temple of the city's patron deity. In 415 a Christian mob lynched and dismembered the renowned female philosopher Hypatia; contemporary sources report the mob was acting as part of a political dispute between the city's bishop and its Roman governor, while later sources describe the murder as motivated by antipagan sentiment. These outbursts of violence, in which the great pagan temples were deliberately violated and statues of pagan gods desecrated and broken, were aimed at wavering Christians as well as at pagans. By proving the pagan gods could not protect themselves and removing the temptation of familiar places of worship, violence forcibly Christianized the spaces of public worship.

Christian violence also targeted Jews and their places of worship. Such acts both policed the often blurry boundaries between Jewish and Christian identities and forced conversions to Christianity. Imperial legislation gradually banned Jews from the bureaucracy and from certain professions but allowed the continued practice of Judaism. Because Jews remained a legally protected minority, violence against them often precipitated conflict between imperial authorities and the Christian clergy and populace. When Christians burned a synagogue on the eastern borders of the empire at the orders of the local bishop, Theodosius I ordered that the perpetrators be punished and that the synagogue be rebuilt at Christian expense. Ambrose of Milan learned of the incident and castigated the emperor until he reversed his decision. In 414 the bishop of Alexandria expelled the Jews from the city and seized many synagogues. In 418 an argument between the Christians and Jews of Mallorca turned violent; the synagogue was burned, and the next day hundreds of Jews converted to Christianity out of fear for their lives. At the same time, however, archaeological evidence reveals sizable synagogues across the Mediterranean, indicating that the many Jewish communities were experiencing a period of quiet prosperity.

While violence marked the transition of the multifaith cities of the east to uniformly Christian spaces, the situation in the west was different. There, the form of pagan worship was rural and very diverse, and while there were certainly incidents of violence against pagan temples and sacred groves, the official stance toward pagan practice in the west was much less aggressive. Pope Gregory I laid out the more moderated principle of conversion in a letter of 601, recommending that pagan temples not be entirely destroyed but that pagan idols be replaced with crosses and festivals of sacrifice be replaced with Christian holidays. Gregory not only exercised papal influence through his voluminous correspondence to individuals across the Mediterranean, but he also made the papacy the largest landowner in

Italy, organizing Rome's defenses and rebuilding its walls. Gregory and his successors wielded secular power in Rome and central Italy as well as spiritual leadership in western Europe, pointing to the growing political divide between the eastern and western empire in the fifth and sixth centuries.

AN EASTERN AND A WESTERN MEDITERRANEAN

By the end of the fifth century, the principal mechanisms of the Roman state in the west had been dismantled. The tax structures that had funneled wealth to a centrally controlled army no longer functioned, and inhabitants of the Mediterranean recognized multiple law-giving authorities. While the end of a single Mediterranean-wide political order highlighted regional differences, it did not bring about complete fragmentation or disconnection. The large-scale systems of exchange driven by the Roman state ended, meaning a general drop in the frequency and scale of long-distance trade. Many Roman patterns of landowning, administration, and taxation remained largely untouched under new ruling elites, however. In the western Mediterranean, minor Vandal, Visigoth, and Ostrogoth elites ruled over large Romanized populations in North Africa, Spain, and Italy.

While the inhabitants of the eastern Mediterranean continued to call themselves Romans through the fifteenth century, historians call the Eastern Roman Empire "Byzantium" to indicate its transformation into a new kind of state. The timing of that transformation remains contested. The eastern Mediterranean certainly demonstrated more continuity with Roman traditions than the west did: while the cities of the west shrank dramatically, the east remained more urbanized and populated. Latin remained the language of the church and administration in the west. The eastern empire replaced Latin with Greek in its administration in the mid-fifth century, and Greek coexisted with the Coptic spoken in Egypt and the Syriac spoken in Palestine. Tax collection and state revenues declined sharply in the west, while emperors in the east continued to command a bureaucracy that efficiently collected taxes and funded public works and state armies.

The formal end of Roman rule in the west came in 476 with the deposition of the last Roman emperor, but even before that date Roman authority was fragile. The court at Ravenna was powerless to prevent the Vandals of North Africa from taking Carthage in 439 or to stop their advance into the central Mediterranean. The Vandal fleet raided Sicily and Crete and conquered Corsica, the Balearic Islands, and Sardinia. Rome's two attempts at retaliation were unsuccessful, and the Vandals destroyed Roman fleets in 460 and 468. The Vandals even sacked Rome in 455. The city had just avoided an attack from the north—the Huns, led by Attila, invaded Italy in 452, and Placidia's daughter Honoria rashly sent her ring to Attila, a gesture he chose to interpret as a marriage proposal. Attila and his army headed to Rome to collect his bride, but the invasion ended with his sudden death in 453. Pope Leo I had met Attila outside Rome; later chroniclers made much of Leo's apparent ability to convince Attila to leave the city unmolested, and the incident greatly increased papal influence. In 476 the Germanic troops in the Roman army proclaimed the general Odovacer as their king; Odovacer in turn forced Romulus Augustus, the young ruler of the western empire, to resign and sent the imperial regalia back to Constantinople, informing the eastern Roman emperor that there was no longer a need for an emperor in the west.

New regimes in Italy and Africa demonstrated continuity with Roman traditions. In Italy, Theodoric of the Ostrogoths replaced Odovacer; Theodoric had lived as a hostage in Constantinople as a young man and was exposed to the classical culture and Roman splendor on display there. His government relied on Roman bureaucracy, law and judicial procedures, and taxation structures. Despite legislation to the contrary, Theodoric's Ostrogoths became landowners, took Roman wives, adopted Latinized names for themselves or their children, and increasingly spoke Latin rather than Gothic. Vandal rule in Africa also continued some Roman traditions of government, and the Vandal elite quickly adopted many of the luxury consumption habits of the Roman nobility, enjoying imported silks from the east, bathhouses, banquets, Roman theater, and Latin poetry. The Vandal conquest of North Africa did not damage the local economy; there was an increase in imports from the eastern Mediterranean, and in the countryside there was little disruption.

The economic repercussions of the Vandal invasion were felt most severely not in North Africa but in Rome. The city had been supported by the tax shipments of grain and oil from the region, and when the Vandals broke this connection, Rome faced a fiscal crisis. The city, which had a million people in the first century and half a million at the outset of the fifth, by the sixth century had fallen to between 20,000 and 40,000 inhabitants, a population that could be supported by the region around the city itself. Despite this radical shrinking, Rome remained the largest city in Europe after Constantinople.

While the Vandal, Visigoth, and Ostrogoth elites that ruled Africa, Spain, and Italy soon adapted to the Romanized cultures of the Mediterranean, their adherence to the non-Nicene form of Christianity separated them from their subjects. The Vandals earned a reputation as particularly fierce persecutors of religious difference. The Vandal king Huneric executed individuals for heresy, exiled thousands of clergy and laypeople from Carthage, and in 484 ordered the closure of all Catholic churches. In Italy, Theodoric occupied the other end of the spectrum, adopting an attitude of toleration and insisting on peaceful relations between religious groups. His capital at Ravenna features both non-Nicene and Catholic churches and baptisteries, both decorated with splendid marbles and mosaics. Theodoric's religious toleration extended to non-Christians as well; when a group of Christians destroyed a Jewish synagogue in Genoa, he ordered that it be rebuilt, famously stating, "We cannot command the religion of our subjects, because no one is forced to believe against his will." Theodoric's attitude was unusual, as leaders across the Mediterranean used orthodoxy and unity of religious belief as a way of building their own legitimacy.

The Vandals and the Ostrogoths were swept away in the mid-sixth century by a resurgent Byzantine Empire that balanced continuity and innovation. Emperor Justinian rooted his authority in Roman traditions but also introduced significant changes in government, religious policy, and public works. Very soon after he took the throne in 527, he launched a major maritime offensive to restore Constantinople's control over the western Mediterranean. A Byzantine fleet, commanded by General Belisarius, conquered the Vandal kingdom in 534, capturing or killing the majority of the Vandal elite and imposing Byzantine rule on North Africa. Justinian and Belisarius then turned their attention to Sicily and mainland Italy. Sicily fell relatively easily, but a drawn-out and incredibly destructive war raged in the southern part of Italy for the next 20 years, ending not only Ostrogoth rule but a great deal of the Roman survivals in economic and landholding patterns. By 554, Byzantine Italy consisted of Rome, Ravenna, and a scattering of cities and fortresses in between. The invasion of the Lombards, a Germanic group from the Danube region, blocked further Byzantine conquest in northern Italy. Byzantine forces also conquered the southeastern corner of the Iberian peninsula from the Visigoths in the 550s.

With the exception of southern France and northern Spain, all of the Mediterranean coastline was united under a single political order once again, but it proved to be a fragile and short-lived unity. Byzantine conquests in North Africa and Italy were particularly destructive and did nothing to stop a slow economic decline, exacerbated by the devastating outbreak of plague that spread from Egypt to Syria and Asia Minor, reaching Constantinople by 542. The evidence on mortality is fragmentary, but historians estimate that between a third and a half of the population died in urban areas. New building came to a halt, and urban life declined in the west, although it remained strong in the east.

Like Constantine before him, Justinian wanted to rule a community of orthodox Christians but faced the reality of his subjects' widely differing beliefs. His religious policies tried to impose the uniform practice of orthodox Christianity on all his subjects. He closed the Platonic Academy in Athens in 529 and dismissed pagans from government and teaching posts. His law code had sections legislating penalties against Jews and heretic Christians. Justinian also intervened in a theological controversy over the nature of the Trinity, the question in this case being whether Christ had a single nature or if he united one human and one divine nature in a single person. Many Monophysites in Egypt, Syria, and Palestine emphasized Jesus's single divine nature, but the Council of Chalcedon in 451 had declared that Jesus had two natures, one human and one divine. Justinian called a church council in 533 that attempted to reconcile the dispute, but the council simply stirred up more controversy, particularly among African Christians looking for ways to resist Byzantine rule and among those who rejected imperial interference in theological matters. These theological disputes continued into the seventh century, alienating many Byzantine subjects and undermining the consolidation of Byzantine rule in the western Mediterranean.

In Constantinople a riot in 532 burned large sections of the city. Justinian and his wife, Theodora, seized the opportunity and undertook an ambitious building

program that proclaimed imperial and Christian power in the city. The riots ruined the Church of Hagia Sophia, or Holy Wisdom, and Justinian ordered it to be rebuilt on an unprecedented scale. The church is topped with a grand dome, soaring 180 feet above the ground and supported by four massive piers joined by arches. The interior of the church was decorated with golden mosaics, an architectural and decorative style that would characterize Byzantine building for almost a thousand years. The dome, pierced with windows at its base, appeared to be floating; it would remain the largest dome ever built until the sixteenth century.

Far to the west, Visigoth monarchs also relied on ceremonial splendor and religious orthodoxy to consolidate their rule in Spain, although they did so on a much smaller scale. King Leovigild established a capital city at Toledo and was the first Visigoth leader to sit on a throne and to wear royal garments. Leovigild was an adherent of non-Nicene Christianity, and he appointed his own bishops in the face of determined Catholic resistance; his successor, Reccared, formally converted to Catholicism under the influence of Bishop Leander of Seville at the

Rural life in North Africa. Late-fourth- or early-fifth-century mosaic from Carthage depicting the estate of Lord Julius. On the top, the lord and lady of the manor are shown among servants and peasants, and in the lower part of the image, servants are offering the fruits of the land. *Musée national du Bardo, Tunis.* © *Gilles Mermet / Art Resource, NY*

Third Council of Toledo (589). Visigoth legislation excluded non-Christians and was fiercely anti-Jewish. King Sisebut tried to forcibly baptize all Jews in Spain, and his successors forbid Jewish practices such as Passover, the Sabbath, and circumcision. In 694, King Eciga ordered the enslavement of all Jews in Spain, although it is unclear how much force any of these proclamations had in practice.

The idea of Rome, its ceremonial language and symbolism of power, and Roman culture retained a strong influence across the Mediterranean. But by the turn of the seventh century, the material and institutional transformation of Roman rule was well under way. Although the political unity of Roman Mediterranean was gone, the cultural and economic structures retained a good deal of continuity. This slow process of post-Roman cultural and economic transformation would result in changes that reverberated across the Mediterranean.

CHAPTER TWO

Forging New Traditions

Islamic and Christian Societies

In 621, a 51-year-old Arab man named Muhammad had a vision. He was awakened by the angel Gabriel and rode Burāq, a winged white half donkey–half mule, from his native Mecca to Jerusalem. On the way he met Jesus, Moses, and Abraham; on the Temple Mount in Jerusalem he found an assembly of prophets. After leading the prophets in prayer, Muhammad ascended a ladder to heaven, where he saw a vast number of angels and the torments of the damned in hell. On Muhammad's return to Mecca, many disbelieved his account of the journey, but when his friend Abu Bakr heard the story, he declared, "That's true, I testify that you are the prophet of God." The story of the Night Journey, briefly referenced in the Qur'an and given more precise shape by Islamic tradition, has caused much debate among scholars. Was it a physical or spiritual journey? Where precisely did Muhammad say he had gone, and how was the textual tradition narrating the journey constructed? Whatever its intentions and origins, the Night Journey illustrates the close relationship between the ancient monotheisms, Christianity and Judaism, and Islam, the new monotheistic faith of the Mediterranean world.

Sixteen years after Muhammad's visionary trip to Jerusalem, one of his companions, 'Umar, stood on the same Temple Mount in Jerusalem as the leader of a Muslim army. The area had been deserted after the Roman destruction of the Jewish temple in the year 70, and Byzantine Jerusalem had new sites of Christian religious devotion marking Jesus's death and burial. According to later accounts, when 'Umar arrived in the city, he cleared the ground by the rock and prayed there, indicating the future site of al-Aqsa Mosque. Over the next centuries, successive Muslim rulers constructed a series of buildings called Haram al-Sharif, or the Noble Sanctuary, including the Dome of the Rock marking the spot of Muhammad's ascension to heaven during the Night Journey. This site quickly became the third most holy place in Islam, superseded only by the desert cities of Mecca and Medina.

The changes Muhammad's followers brought to the city of Jerusalem were part of a much larger movement that transformed the political, social, and religious structures of the Mediterranean between the seventh and the eleventh centuries. By the ninth century, the new imperial capitals of Carolingian Aachen and Abbasid Baghdad had shifted these empires' centers away from the Mediterranean, leaving a porous frontier zone where people combined a shared Greco-Roman past with their new religious traditions. Byzantium consolidated around the core of Constantinople and in the tenth and early eleventh centuries emerged as a highly centralized state defended by regional armies, while the rest of the Mediterranean experienced waves of invasion and fragmentation.

As the Roman political order ended, elites across the Mediterranean searched for new ways to organize their states. The introduction of Islam proved to be a unifying factor for those who lived in the southern and eastern parts of the region, while the Byzantines and the Romanized Germanic elites of the north and west used Christian beliefs as a unifying force in their own realms. But while leaders in new imperial centers such as Baghdad, Aachen, and Cordoba relied on religious ideology as a tool for legitimizing their state-building efforts, there was no clear pattern of interfaith violence. Centralizing states fought to incorporate local and regional powers, and these internal struggles were exacerbated by sectarian religious divisions within Islam and Christianity. Christian and Muslim states contended with one another in frontier zones, but even there interfaith alliances were common. In this chapter, we focus on the transformations in state and society after the end of the Roman political order, and in the next chapter we examine the cultural and economic world of the early medieval Mediterranean.

AN ARABIC MEDITERRANEAN

Muhammad ibn 'Abdullah, the prophet of Islam, was born in Mecca at the end of the sixth century. Pre-Islamic Arabia was connected to the main centers of Mediterranean civilization by Red Sea trading routes, and Christian and Jewish monotheists practiced their religions alongside traditional polytheists. While Muslim tradition provides a rich and detailed account of Muhammad's life, there is a great deal of debate among scholars about the reliability of this material. A few scholars have provocatively questioned our ability to know anything at all about Islamic origins, given the lack of contemporary evidence and the clear bias of later sources. A more mainstream view acknowledges the problems with the early source material but finds the basic outline of Muhammad's life and career plausible. According to tradition, Muhammad was born into the Quraysh tribe in Mecca and orphaned at an early age. Raised by his uncle, he married a wealthy widow, Khadija, and managed her caravan trading business. Around 610, Muhammad began to receive revelations from the archangel Gabriel, and eventually his followers compiled these rev-

elations into the Qur'an, Islam's sacred scripture. Encouraged by Khadija, Muhammad began to preach publicly about his revelations, pointing to the essential unity
of God and the need for pious behavior. Muhammad saw himself as the seventh and
final in a line of divinely inspired prophets stretching back through Jesus to Moses
and Abraham. At first only a few Meccans recognized Muhammad as a prophet, and
his message provoked considerable opposition among the city's elite, so in 622 he
and his small band of followers traveled north to the oasis town of Medina (Yath-
rib). This *hijra* (emigration) marked the beginning of a politically independent
group, and within a few years of Muhammad's death, 622 would be recognized as
year one of the Islamic calendar.

Relations between Mecca and Medina soon deteriorated from occasional caravan raids to open warfare; at the same time, Muhammad continued to receive revelations that structured the community politically, socially, and religiously. In 630,
he marched on Mecca, took the city, and rededicated the Ka'ba to monotheistic
worship; by the time of his death, in 632, he had taken political control of all western
Arabia. Muhammad's revelations had been clear that he was the final prophet and
the Qur'an God's final word, so when he died, the community lost not only its political leader but its ongoing source of spiritual guidance. One of Muhammad's closest
advisers, Abu Bakr, emerged as the *amir al-mu'minin* (commander of the believers),
and he was followed in that position by two other close advisors of Muhammad,
'Umar ibn al-Khattab and 'Uthman ibn Affan. These three men led wildly successful
campaigns of conquest, extending their power into the urban centers of the Mediterranean as well as onto the plains of Mesopotamia.

Two key issues of historical interpretation arise at this point. The first question deals with the nature and definition of the faith community Muhammad created. The Qur'an does describe those who followed his message as Muslims (*mus-
limun*, or those who submit), but it much more often refers to them as Believers
(*mu'minun*). One scholar has proposed calling these early followers of Muhammad
Believers rather than Muslims, arguing that the category of "Muslim" as a distinct
faith identity did not coalesce until a century after Muhammad's death. According to this view, other monotheists, principally Jews and Christians, were part of
the "Believers' movement." While many scholars accept the idea that Islam gradually distinguished itself from rival monotheisms and a "classical Islam" distinct in
ritual and belief emerged in the eighth and ninth centuries, few accept the idea of
an ecumenical religious movement that included Christians and Jews on an equal
footing with Muslims.

Second, historians struggle to explain how and why Muslim forces conquered
Byzantine Syria, Palestine, and Egypt and Sassanian Iraq so swiftly and absolutely.
They controlled Mesopotamia by 638, Damascus and Jerusalem fell by 639, and
Egypt was conquered between 639 and 645. Moving into the Mediterranean, Muslim-
led armies took Cyprus in 649 and decisively defeated the Byzantine navy in 655.
Later expeditions besieged Rhodes in 672 and Crete in 674 and staged a series of
attacks on Constantinople itself from 674 to 680. These armies had established the

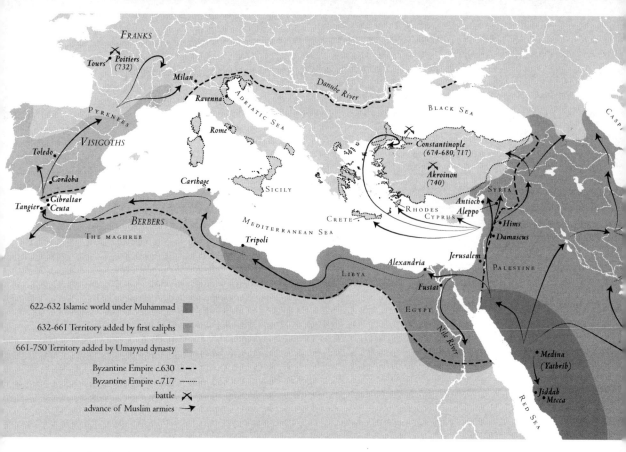

The Early Islamic
Conquests

garrison town of Qayrawan in North Africa by 670 and continued westward across
North Africa, allying with local Berbers and invading Iberia in 711. In order to
explain these conquests, historians have pointed to contextual and ideological factors. Both Sassanian Persia and Byzantium had been demographically weakened by
disease and decades of war. In North Africa, Italy, and Sicily, evidence suggests that
landowners resented and protested high Byzantine taxes and were thus not motivated to resist the change in rulers. Muslim armies were certainly motivated by the
promise of material rewards from conquest, but they were also driven by piety and
religious zeal. As one general explained his army's stunning success to a Christian
monk, "It is a sign that God loves us and is pleased with our faith, namely that he
gives us dominion over all religions and all peoples."

The Muslims' ideological focus had to do with the concept of *jihad*, a word used
in the Qur'an to indicate "striving" or "striving in the path of God." This striving
could take several forms: internal efforts to live up to one's religious duties, physical violence against unbelievers or in defense of Islam, or providing material support for those who are carrying out jihad. Some scholars have identified strong
similarities between the militant piety of the Christian martyrs of late antiquity
and the early practitioners of jihad; early Muslim authors themselves compared
jihad to Christian monasticism and its practitioners to Christian monks: "horsemen by day, monks by night." While later Muslim legal theorists developed
sophisticated definitions of jihad, in the initial decades of the Islamic conquests it

was a fairly open-ended concept that urged warriors to fight against unbelievers in the service of God.

Although past scholarship often viewed the Muslim conquest of the eastern Mediterranean as a major rupture in the region's history, the archaeological record has revealed a very different story. There is little to no evidence of destruction in the cities or in the countryside. In many cases, Byzantine towns and cities opened their gates and surrendered to the Muslim armies in return for lenient treatment. At least some Byzantine residents of Syria and Palestine expressed relief at the change in rulers, although many did not. An unknown number of Byzantines fled the Muslim invasion and resettled in the Anatolian provinces of the empire. After their conquests in Mesopotamia and in Egypt, Muslim armies lived in garrison towns, called *amsar*, which were next to but separate from cities, as at al-Fustat in Egypt. In Syria and Palestine the garrison towns alternated with Muslim occupation of abandoned quarters in existing towns. In North Africa, the inland garrison town of Qayrawan replaced Carthage, which was gradually abandoned. These garrison towns help to explain why the small number of Muslim conquerors did not assimilate into the much larger conquered populations but continued in an Arabic-speaking Muslim life with regular Qur'anic recitation and communal prayer. Non-Muslims came to the garrison towns to work, and eventually these became sites of conversion to Islam.

The Muslim success in conquest led to new challenges. The leaders of the state found themselves ruling over complex urban environments and large Christian and Jewish populations. The Qur'an refers to Christians and Jews as "People of the Book"—that is, monotheists with a scriptural tradition—and states that they should be allowed to continue in their faith while paying a special poll tax (*jizya*) (9:29). Early surrender treaties describe a simple exchange of protection and noninterference in local affairs in return for payment, but as Muslims gained experience in living alongside non-Muslims, the treaties were gradually consolidated into a single document, called the Pact of 'Umar, or more generally, the dhimmi pact. In addition to imposing a special tax on non-Muslims, dhimmi regulations restricted the public performance of Christianity and Judaism, which meant a particularly sharp change for the previously ruling Christians, who were required to remove crosses from public places, to wear a distinctive sash or belt to differentiate themselves from Muslims, and to refrain from ringing bells or loud chanting; they also were forbidden from trying to convert Muslims to Christianity. These restrictions on minority populations echoed Byzantine restrictions against Jews in the fifth and sixth centuries. Scholars disagree over the intended purpose of these regulations, with some pointing to the emphasis on enforcing subordinate social status for non-Muslims and others reading them as a way of protecting still-fragile Muslim identity.

In the half century after Muhammad's death, leadership of the new state remained in the hands of his close companions, but tensions over legitimate leadership and access to positions of wealth and power led to several civil wars among the Muslim Arab elite. The growing dominance of the Umayyad clan began with 'Uthman, who promoted many of his relatives to high office. His assassination, in

656, led to the First Civil War, between supporters of 'Uthman and 'Ali b. Abi Talib, Muhammad's cousin and son-in-law, who claimed the mantle of leadership after 'Uthman's death. Both Muhammad's widow, 'Aisha, and the Umayyad governor of Syria, Mu'awiya, opposed 'Ali's rule, and although 'Ali did defeat 'Aisha's forces in battle, the struggle for leadership split the Muslim faithful into several factions that had both religious and political significance. After 'Ali was assassinated while at prayer in 661, Mu'awiya emerged victorious in the civil war, taking the position of caliph, or *khalifat Allah* (deputy of God).

Mu'awiya established the Umayyad dynasty and brought significant changes to the new Muslim state. He and his successors moved the political capital from Mecca to Damascus, developed a more regular system of administering the newly conquered territories, and presided over the twin processes of Islamization and Arabization in the conquered lands. Divergent Islamic traditions coalesced under the Umayyads as well: the dynasty, and particularly the fifth caliph, 'Abd al-Malik, codified some elements of what would become known as the Sunni, or mainstream, form of Islam. Shia (from Shi'at 'Ali, or party of 'Ali) and the Khawarij developed their own visions of Islam in opposition to Umayyad rule. Shia contended that leadership of the Islamic community could only belong to a relative of Muhammad, primarily 'Ali and his descendants, while the basic principle of the Kharijites was that religious piety was the only qualification for leadership; many Berber tribes in North Africa converted to Kharijite Islam, acknowledging no state and paying no taxes.

'Abd al-Malik is credited with many religious and administrative innovations that together distinguished the tenets of classical Islam and the contours of the Islamic state. It was under his rule that the full *shahada*, or declaration of faith— "There is no god but God and Muhammad is the Apostle of God"—appeared on coins and was used increasingly on official documents. Stories about Muhammad's life and sayings, called hadith, were collected and took on an authoritative status second only to the Qur'an. The Dome of the Rock in Jerusalem, completed in 692, was a concrete statement of Islam's supremacy over Christianity and Judaism. The building used Roman Christian architectural forms, employed Byzantine crafts-people for its mosaic decoration, and was richly sheathed in marble. The interior dome was ringed with anti-Trinitarian inscriptions reading in part: "O People of the Book, do not exaggerate in your religion and speak of God, only the truth. The Messiah Jesus son of Mary was only the apostle of God and his Word . . . God is one deity only, He is above having a son." This clear critique of Christian doctrine atop Jerusalem's most sacred site is an expression of a self-confident Islam distinguishing itself from other Mediterranean faiths.

'Abd al-Malik also made changes to administrative and fiscal policies intended to emphasize the dynasty's Arab and Muslim character. The rapidity of early Muslim expansion meant that many Byzantine and Persian fiscal and administrative structures remained relatively unchanged in the century after conquest. The early Umayyad bureaucracy included many Christians, but 'Abd al-Malik began to change

this pattern when he decreed that state business should be conducted in Arabic instead of Greek, Coptic, or Persian. The gradual shift to an Arabic-language administration was followed by an even more gradual shift to Arabic as the spoken language of the population. Coptic, Greek, and Aramaic persisted in the port cities of the Mediterranean, but they were joined by Judeo-Arabic (Arabic written in Hebrew script) and Arabic written in Greek script. Byzantine gold and copper coins had freely circulated in the region into the early 680s, but ʿAbd al-Malik replaced Byzantine coinage with his own, creating a unified monetary system.

The Umayyads built or repaired a network of roads centered on Damascus and channeled surplus wealth into the construction of monumental architecture, new urban marketplaces, and rural agricultural-development programs. These initiatives directly and indirectly stimulated economic development. The archaeological and written evidence demonstrates growth in urban and rural production and trade during the first decades of the eighth century. Umayyad control of the Mediterranean coast meant control of shipping along it, as most maritime traffic remained in sight of shore. Port cities continued as trading centers

Byzantine and Umayyad coins. *Left,* Byzantine coin, 692–95. Justinian II changed the design of Byzantine coins to emphasize the link between the emperor and Christ. Christ is depicted holding the Gospel on one side, and the emperor is holding a cross on the reverse. *Top right,* early Umayyad coin, 695–96. In the same years, the caliph ʿAbd al-Malik changed Umayyad coinage as well. Instead of the Byzantine emperor, the coin features an image of the caliph drawing a sword, with a design modified from a Byzantine cross on the reverse and the shahada, the profession of faith, in Arabic script. *Bottom right,* Umayyad coin without images, 695. Soon thereafter Ummayad coins were decorated only with Qur'anic verses in Arabic script. Left: *British Museum, London. Photo: Art Resource, NY;* Top right, Bottom right: © *The Trustees of the British Museum / Art Resource, NY*

while taking on a new military function as defensive outposts on the frontier with Byzantium. Part of the Umayyad fleet was constructed in Alexandria, and an arsenal was built in Tunis between 705 and 714.

As the Umayyads consolidated their gains in territory and wealth, the Byzantine Empire struggled to adjust to its shattering losses. Byzantium had lost two-thirds of its territory and three-quarters of its wealth within a few decades, including the grain-producing province of Egypt, which had fed Constantinople for centuries. Byzantines were not only faced with Umayyad armies in the east but with Lombard attacks on their territory in southern Italy and Bulgar pressure on their borders in the Balkans. After a series of losses at sea, culminating in attacks on Constantinople in 674–80, the Byzantine state invested in a more permanent navy housed at the capital and in Anatolia. The Byzantines also reorganized their armies, dividing the empire into provinces called *themes* and distributing military land grants to soldiers charged with provincial defense. This reorganization stabilized the military situation to a degree, but the Byzantine state was further hindered by a crisis of leadership; there were seven rebellions between 695 and 717 that violently and swiftly raised and deposed one emperor after another. When Leo III took the throne, his was an empire shaken by civil war and on the brink of a massive Umayyad siege of Constantinople. The Umayyad army and navy reportedly had 120,000 men and 1,800 ships, and by the end of 717 this force blockaded Constantinople by both land and sea. The Byzantines broke the naval blockade using the recently developed Greek fire, a flammable liquid sprayed onto enemy ships and then ignited. A combination of an unusually cold winter and Bulgar raids broke the land siege. The retreating fleet was almost completely destroyed by Byzantine attacks, storms, and a volcanic eruption in the Aegean Sea, and Umayyad forces did not make a serious effort to retake Constantinople until the fifteenth century.

At the other end of the Mediterranean, Berber armies led by Arab commanders crossed the straits of Gibraltar and invaded Iberia in 711, overthrowing the Visigoth kingdom in a few short years. As was the case in the eastern Mediterranean, the conquest appears to have been based partially on violent military invasion and partially on treaties with local populations, but the early years of Muslim rule in Iberia left little direct evidence. Later Arabic and Latin accounts of the conquest point to civil war among the Visigoth elite and narrate King Roderick's betrayal of his vassal, Count Julian of Ceuta, through his rape of Julian's daughter. In revenge, Julian turned to the Muslim Berber governor of Tangier, Tariq b. Ziyad, encouraged him to invade Iberia, and helped Tariq's forces cross the straits. Although the story's elements of violated honor and revenge might not be true, Roderick, Julian, and Tariq were all historical personages, and it is clear that combined Arab-Berber armies defeated the Visigoth forces in a set of decisive battles in 711–12. Muslim leaders in Iberia made similar arrangements with their non-Muslim subjects as in Syria and Palestine, guaranteeing their safety and the right to practice their religion in return for their cooperation and the payment of the jizya tax. By the 720s, Islamic Iberia, known to its rulers as al-Andalus, was a province of the Umayyad Empire, ruled by governors from Damascus. Unlike other areas of Muslim expansion, the conquerors did not settle in garrison towns but became landowners themselves.

Scholars have disagreed sharply over the significance and long-term consequences of the Muslim conquest and rule of the Iberian peninsula. Some point to 711 as a time when Spanish history was set on a separate course from the rest of Europe. In the wake of the Western Roman Empire's collapse, these scholars argue, Visigoth Spain was following a process of ethnogenesis—the fusion of Germanic, Roman, and Christian traditions into a sense of a single people. According to this perspective, associated with the historian Claudio Sánchez-Albornoz y Menduiña, the Islamic invasion interrupted this process and took Spain "off track," until 1492, when the fall of the last Iberian Muslim kingdom of Granada restored Spain's Christian character. Another group of scholars, identified with Américo Castro y Quesada, see 711 as the beginning of the Spanish process of ethnogenesis and the subsequent fusion of Christian, Muslim, and Jewish traditions as the root of Spanish national identity. These divergent perspectives continue to shape the scholarship on al-Andalus.

In theory, Umayyad power stretched from one end of the sea to the other, but in practice continued conquests in the west stretched the connective tissue of the empire to the breaking point. By the 730s, the Umayyad dynasty faced challenges to their rule across their empire. Christian Copts in Egypt periodically revolted against high taxes. In 739–40, the Berbers of al-Andalus and North Africa revolted, apparently provoked by Arab domination, their own lesser social and economic position, and Kharijite Islamic teachings. The Umayyads sent Syrian troops to suppress the revolt, but tensions between Arabs and Berbers remained. Also in 740, Leo III led the Byzantine army to a decisive victory over Umayyad forces at the battle of Akroinon in western Anatolia. These difficulties coincided with significant religious and political resistance to Umayyad rule at home. In 750, the Abbasids, a family that claimed descent from Muhammad's uncle ʿAbbas b. ʿAbd al-Muttalib, defeated the Umayyads and replaced them as rulers of the Islamic world. The Abbasids ruled not from Mediterranean Damascus but from Mesopotamian Baghdad, a location that shifted trade and communication patterns in the Islamic world eastward.

BETWEEN NEW IMPERIAL CAPITALS

In the ninth and tenth centuries, new ruling dynasties consolidated their power in newly established imperial capitals at Baghdad, Aachen, and Cordoba. As the Abbasids consolidated their power in Baghdad, a Frankish dynasty established a center of power in northern Europe. Charles Martel (the Hammer) fought vigorously against other Frankish aristocrats and also defeated the Muslim governor of al-Andalus at a battle near Poitiers in 732, ending raids from the south. His grandson, Charlemagne, was crowned Holy Roman emperor at Rome in 800. Charlemagne's rule brought a new administrative, legal, and military unity to the Franks of northwestern Europe, but this emerging Latin Christian sphere was centered at Aachen, leaving real power in his Mediterranean domains to relatively independent local lords. Charlemagne did launch campaigns of conquest that temporarily extended Frankish rule to northern Italy, southern France, and northeastern Spain, particularly Barcelona, and he pursued naval actions around Corsica.

In al-Andalus, the only Umayyad prince to survive the Abbasid revolution, 'Abd al-Rahman, established a dynasty centered at Cordoba. Despite his claims to political independence, he did not take the title of caliph, ruling instead as emir of al-Andalus, and he and his descendants maintained close cultural and economic ties with the eastern Islamic world. Within al-Andalus, Umayyad rule from Cordoba was at times able to overcome deeply rooted localized tendencies, but at other times power devolved to the provincial lords. In addition to the longstanding tensions between Arab and Berber conquerors, native converts to Islam, called Muwallads, increasingly demanded equality in political and fiscal status with the Arabs and Berbers.

The only remaining center of imperial authority on the shores of the Mediterranean was the Byzantine capital of Constantinople. The city and the empire drew strength from its continuity with the Roman political order, but Byzantine government and military structures also transformed to respond to changing circumstances. After narrowly surviving the 717 siege of Constantinople, the Byzantine militia was reformed, and new, highly mobile regiments called *tagmata* were used to defend first the city and then along the frontiers. These troops helped Byzantium expand into the Balkans and Anatolia, creating a compact but resilient state in the northeastern Mediterranean.

As dynasties with imperial ambitions consolidated their regimes far from the shores of the sea, a number of independent regional polities emerged in the Mediterranean in the ninth and tenth centuries. Local lords claimed control in the interstices of more centralized states; while they often recognized the theoretical authority of distant dynasties, in practice these local lords operated quite independently. In North Africa, the Aghlabid family established their own dynasty in Tunisia, and the Tulunids did the same in Egypt; both offered nominal allegiance to the Abbasid caliph. In northern Spain and southern France, politics were organized through links of personal dependence forged through private warfare, and the most successful warriors rose to the top of the hierarchy. One chronicler described the process, saying that people gave themselves "kings born of their own entrails." In Catalonia, on the frontier between Carolingian and Cordoban power, Count Wifred "the Hairy" was the victor in these local contests for power. In 870 he received the title of count from the Carolingian dynasty to the north, but in practice he and his descendants arranged for defense, collected taxes, and oversaw what justice was on offer independently. In northern Italy, the city of Venice, founded in the marshes of the upper Adriatic by people fleeing the wars and invasions of the post-classical era, carved out a sphere of independent influence by playing Byzantine and Carolingian powers against one another.

These statelets were born in part of opportunity and in part from the need for protection from ongoing pirate raids and banditry. No political power exercised more than tenuous control over outlying regions, and as a result raiding and piracy in the Mediterranean increased dramatically in the ninth century. Muslim pirates had only loose affiliations with states and raided towns and coastlines regularly, temporarily conquering areas and using them as bases to raid farther inland. Berbers based in North Africa regularly raided cities and villages in Italy, southern France, and the Mediterranean islands. Pirates attacked Marseilles in 838 and Arles in 842 and 850, and they conducted further raids in southern France from their base at Fraxinetum, sometimes getting involved in local power struggles as mercenary troops. Andalusian sea raiders controlled Alexandria from 814 to 827 and took Crete in the 820s, successfully defending it against Byzantine counterattacks in the 840s. The Byzantine loss of Crete changed the strategic makeup of the eastern Mediterranean, as the island became a center for raids on other islands and ports in the region.

Andalusians were not the only pirates operating in the Mediterranean. Scandinavian traders and raiders, known as Vikings, penetrated from the north and launched expeditions that plundered al-Andalus and the central Mediterranean. In 859–60 a fleet led by Bjorn Ironside sacked Algeciras on the southern coast of Spain, the Moroccan coast, and the Balearic Islands. One part of the fleet then worked its way up the Ebro River in northern Spain, ravaging communities as far inland as Pamplona. They then turned west, sacking cities in southern France and Pisa in Italy. The Vikings next moved inland from Pisa and attacked the town of Luna, which they reportedly believed to be Rome. Unlike Sicilians and North Africans, the Vikings established no permanent bases in the Mediterranean, but their raiding contributed to the danger and insecurity of shipping and of life along coasts and rivers.

The ongoing struggle between Byzantine, Lombard, and local rulers in southern Italy created ample opportunities for pirates from Sicily and North Africa. These raiders were drawn to southern Italy not only by the possibility of plunder and the chance to participate in jihad against non-Muslims but also by invitations to work as mercenaries for competing Christian rulers. In the 830s, the independent duchy of Naples was under attack by the Lombard princes of Benevento and Salerno, and the Neapolitans hired a group of Muslim mercenaries from Sicily. The princes of Benevento and Salerno followed suit, hiring their own groups of Arab mercenaries. Later groups of Muslim raiders arrived in southern Italy on their own, plundering and then taking Taranto and Bari and using these cities as bases to raid the surrounding countryside. In 846, a force from Sicily raided Rome, plundering the pilgrim churches outside the walls, including St. Peter's. The shock galvanized the southern Italians to organize a defense. Three years later, a North African fleet approached Ostia but was beaten back by a Christian navy led by the Duke of Naples. The Neapolitan victory reduced but did not end the raids, which continued through the late tenth century.

The island of Sicily, with its strategic location along major sailing routes and rich agricultural hinterland, was the biggest prize in the western Mediterranean. Byzantine control of the island was extremely tenuous in the early ninth century, and the

χειντόναρμει | ικαικαταπαιω σινότινε πιζονωμιανκεκαμμένοϲ · τολαιωσιὸ πασιζοσ
ἐζωνιμ̂ζ αυτου · και περτακοσιοιω πεβοιο · αικδοι πτοϲωνιδρεσὰ ται μ̂εβωιυ
σον υπολησ̇δει ναιδερωιγκιεδ μαμεωσε υρολλομτηιιοσ · σογ τατορε σζ οιδιχνσιαδ σα
μεινοιεσιου σω πεσ· καιουμιμεζκογουκεδιγμυκορχαδοϲ σιν απεχτοντοισν με μνηντε τι
λιω περ δσριϲ τσν · ϲαρακκηνοσ

Τ ιωθοκλε σσιγσ τσο τωυ τυλδοι σ πειιπτιμε ρου · και με∫ γρα πεσ σιο σε κευ ησ πσϲ το ρεσ σο ∣ σι
μ̇νοδοκεικδε λι αισ πμει σγ κο τοσ · κατα νσ ρομγ πω πτουσιναικεσου · σιπεκωσ τ εκεκδσσγιγ
το · κσιγ κτοσ σκαι με τ μι ρει εργ επτολοκ σνλιοιικσικ οιειμιοτοσν · χηντγιαμω πρέ
λιασ̇εο πηγνι σίου με χλό ιπσιαυ σοτ σανυ · σν ινδε∫ ηπσι τα κατ σρε πειω τ σιμεν δ̇χ τι
λίωτσυ αι το ετγ τικοσ ου · κατα νσν σπσικεκου σν πρά μελεσ αρκοι σ σν μι αγ τισνιεσαρσ

Aghlabid dynasty of North Africa launched an invasion in 827. As was the case with the fall of Visigoth Spain, later chronicles try and explain the invasion in terms of a Christian ruler's dishonorable behavior: here, the Byzantine naval commander Euphemios allegedly carried off and married a nun and then, to avoid punishment, killed the Byzantine governor, set himself up as governor of Syracuse, and invited the Muslim Aghlabids to support his rebellion. In sharp contrast to the conquest of al-Andalus, however, the Sicilian campaign was slow and piecemeal. The coalition of Aghlabid troops gradually took the western part of the island, besieging Palermo in 831 and making it their provincial capital. Aghlabid and Byzantine forces struggled for control of eastern and central Sicily for the next thirty years. The stronghold of Syracuse did not fall until 878; the last Byzantine city, Taormina, fell in 902.

The battle for Sicily was part of a larger Byzantine war on its maritime frontier. By the second half of the ninth century, the Byzantines revived the imperial fleet to fight the Aghlabids and challenge pirates and raiders for control of the central Mediterranean. The Byzantine navy retook Crete in 946, reclaiming a dominant position in the eastern Mediterranean. In Dalmatia, the Byzantine fleet repelled a Muslim siege of Ragusa in 866, and in 870 the emperor, Basil I, established a new province in Dalmatia, with its capital at Zara, in order to coordinate the defense of the region. The Byzan-

Siege of Messina, illumination from a Greek history of the Byzantine emperors written in the eleventh century. The manuscript, the Codex Matritensis, was produced in Norman Sicily in the twelfth century. *Biblioteca Nacional, Madrid.* Photo: Album / Art Resource, NY

THE MEDITERRANEAN WORLD

tines allied with Frankish forces and waged a successful campaign in southern Italy, gaining control of the port cities of Otranto, Bari, and Taranto. By 890 the Byzantines also established two new provinces in southern Italy. A coalition of southern Italian rulers led by the Byzantines destroyed the Muslim colony north of Naples in 915 and offered the emir of Sicily an annual payment, ending the most destructive raids. This agreement redirected the corsairs' focus to Corsica, Sardinia, and the northern shores of the Tyrrhenian Sea, where Genoa was sacked and burned in 934. The Byzantines consolidated their hold in the region by rebuilding cities and populating them with freed slaves of Slavic origin and colonists from western Anatolia.

Farther to the west, the emir of Cordoba, 'Abd al-Rahman III, was also consolidating state power over the local lords, called *taifa* (party kings). When he began ruling Cordoba, in 912, provinces were ruled with almost complete autonomy by descendants of native converts (Muwallads) and Berber chiefs. 'Abd al-Rahman built an army made up of Slavic slaves brought from north-central Europe. In fact, the term *Slav* (*Saqaliba* in Arabic), originally referred to slaves of Slavic origin but then came to refer to all slaves brought to al-Andalus from the north. The emir first used this army to consolidate his control internally and then began a tradition of summer raids across the northern frontier. In 924 he personally led his army up the Ebro River valley and sacked the Christian city of Pamplona, using the campaign to affirm his status as the leader of all Muslims in al-Andalus. In 929 al-Rahman further claimed the mantle of Islamic leadership by taking the title of caliph. As caliph, he continued his northern campaigns against Christian sites as well as besieging the more independent Muslim cities of Badajoz and Toledo into obedience. He initiated a more active maritime policy, building a fleet, ports, and shipyards along the coast and recruiting formerly independent pirates to lead his navy against both Christians and a new Muslim rival to the south: the Fatimids.

At almost the same time that 'Abd al-Rahman III came to power in Spain, the Fatimids emerged as the dominant political force in North Africa, sweeping away the Aghlabids and incorporating many of the regional rulers under their banner. Like 'Abd al-Rahman III, the Fatimids used Islam to legitimate their rule, but unlike the Cordoban dynasty, the Fatimids were not followers of Sunni Islam. They were Isma'ilis, a branch of Shia Muslims who believed in a divinely inspired imam (the Mahdi) descended from 'Ali and Fatima, and ultimately the prophet Muhammad, whose imminent return would eliminate corruption, favoritism, and oppression in an overly materialist society based on trade in luxury goods and exploitation of the poor. Isma'ili missionaries spread this anti-Abbasid message throughout the Islamic world, and in 902 one of movement's leaders, 'Ubayd Allah, fled from Syria to Egypt and eventually to the edge of the Sahara, where he claimed to be the Mahdi. He gained adherents among the Berber tribes, and in 909 he and his followers overthrew the Aghlabids in Tunisia, took Qayrawan, and established a new maritime capital called Mahdiya.

When the Fatimids took control of Aghlabid territory and resources, they gained both a navy and theoretical control over Sicily, although in practice the island was much more difficult to hold. As the Aghlabids had done, the Fatimids sent a governor from North Africa to rule the island from Palermo, but resentment of Fatimid taxes and some resistance from Sicily's Sunni Muslims to their new Shia overlords soon led to open revolt. The rebels inflicted serious damage on the Fatimid armada in 913, but Fatimids destroyed the Sicilian fleet in 915 and in 916 sent a large fleet and Berber army to restore authority. A second uprising swept the island from 937 to 940, sparked in part by disagreements over land settlement, and despite rebel leaders' appeals to the Byzantine navy for aid, the Fatimid army eventually destroyed this rebellion as well. Thousands of Sicilians fled to Byzantine southern Italy, and thousands more were carried off to Tunis as slaves.

The Fatimid conquest of Sicily was a political and a religious challenge to the Sunni Muslim rulers of Cordoba and to the Abbasids of Baghdad. But the true target of Fatimid ambitions was the rich province of Egypt, ruled by clients of the failing Abbasid state. The Fatimids launched several campaigns in the first decades of the tenth century, but their advance was stalled in 943 by a massive Berber revolt in North Africa. Fatimid gains in the central Mediterranean also threatened the Byzantines; the Christian Byzantines and the Muslim rulers of Cordoba allied against the Fatimids and launched a coordinated maritime strategy. The Fatimids responded in 955 by sending a Sicilian fleet to sack and burn Almeria, an important Andalusian port. By 969 their armies had conquered Egypt and founded a new capital city, Cairo. Cairo became the capital of a Fatimid empire that, at its largest extent, ruled North Africa, Egypt, Palestine, and the upper Red Sea coast.

The era's frequent military conflicts offered swift paths to power for military men from a variety of backgrounds. The Fatimids relied on the skilled general Jawhar al-Siqilli (Jawhar the Sicilian), a former Greek or Armenian slave who created an army composed of Berber, Sudanese, Slavic, and Greek troops and began a campaign of conquest that first reached west and then east to Egypt. The Fatimids had ridden to success in Egypt with the support of Berber troops; the Fatimid caliph-imams tried to balance Berber influence and gain new military expertise by bringing in Turks from the east and Sudanese troops from sub-Saharan Africa. These troops entered the Islamic world as slaves: agents purchased non-Muslims and educated them in the principles of the Islamic faith and in the military arts. After completing their training, the young men were freed and began their military careers, with the possibility of attaining high military rank and office. The great advantage of these elite troops was that they brought with them no outside ties of kinship or loyalty, but they came to constitute an independent power in their own right.

The Fatimids paired the military strength of their multiethnic army with elaborate ceremonies and rituals that built the state through signs and symbols of power. Caliph-imam al-Mu'izz's ceremonial entry into Egypt was carefully stage-managed. Fatimid agents circulated coins with 'Ali and Fatima, emphasizing al-Mu'izz's legitimacy; artisans produced elaborate textiles with inscriptions praising al-Mu'izz, and the populace was given banners to unfurl upon his arrival. Subsequent caliph-imams continued to articulate their power through participation in processions, civic rituals, and festivals. While the Fatimids were themselves Shia, they adopted relatively benign religious policies toward Sunni Muslims as well as toward their Christian and Jewish subjects.

To the north, a militarized Byzantine state also saw the rise of a new class of military leaders, in this case from the provincial aristocracies of the Anatolian frontier, who pushed for changes in strategy, replacing annual frontier raids with territorial conquest and rule. The Phokas family of Cappadocia demonstrates the rise of this powerful military aristocracy. Nikephoros Phokas the Elder was a prominent general and led the Byzantine reconquest of southern Italy in the ninth century; his sons, Bardas and Leo, were also prominent generals involved in the machinations of court politics. Bardas's son Nikephoros continued in the family tradition, leading an assault on the island of Crete in 961, finally taking the island after earlier campaigns in 912 and 949 had failed. Nikephoros and his brother Leo led Byzantine armies against northern Syria, capturing more than 100 towns and fortresses in the border region. Using his military success as a platform, Nikephoros II Phokas claimed the imperial throne in 963; his armies then conquered Tarsus, the Abbasid base for raids into central Anatolia, in 965 and penetrated deep into Syria, taking Aleppo and Antioch in 969. Nikephoros also sent an expedition to take Sicily from the Fatimids in 964; that enterprise failed, but his forces did take the island of Cyprus in 965. These commanders moved from maritime to land frontiers and turned their success on the battlefield into power in the imperial court at Constantinople.

The Byzantine state expanded on both its mainland and maritime frontiers in the tenth century. Byzantine military success depended on a powerful navy and a reconfigured army. New heavy cavalry troops increased the army's offensive capabilities, and professional, disciplined heavy-infantry troops added power and flexibility to battlefield tactics. Politics in Constantinople was filled with assassinations, civil wars, and palace coups, but the imperial bureaucracy and administration kept the centralized machinery of the state functioning. Civilian and military elites were able to cooperate in the defense of the empire's borders and in campaigns of expansion.

The articulation of Byzantine state power relied heavily on elaborate rituals and processions that promoted imperial power. The imperial palace was expanded several times in the ninth and tenth centuries, functioning as a stage set for the elaborate rituals and processions that characterized court life. The tenth-century emperor Constantine VII Porphyrogenitus wrote or commissioned guides to the military and administrative ordering of the empire and to the increasingly elaborate court ceremonial. In his view the ranks of attendants, their ceremonial costumes, and the acclamations they delivered allowed the "reins of power to be held with order and dignity." Byzantine ceremonial drew on Roman hierarchy, Persian ritual, and Christian influence to display an image of imperial splendor and absolute power, and it influenced court ceremonies of the Fatimids in Egypt and the Umayyads in Spain.

As the Byzantines pushed south and east into Anatolian borderlands, they came into conflict with the Fatimids, who were extending their power north into Syria and Palestine. The independent rulers in Aleppo acted as a buffer state on the frontier between the two empires, briefly coming under first Byzantine and and then Fatimid control from 969 to 971. After repelling an invasion of the Rus from the north, the Byzantines won several significant victories over the Bulgars, and waged a successful campaign of conquest in northern Mesopotamia and Syria from 972 to 975. They conquered the cities and towns of the Syrian coast as far south as Sidon and Tyre but failed to take Jerusalem, their final objective. When Emperor Basil II fought his way to the throne in 976, he continued his predecessors' attention to frontier warfare, countering a renewed Fatimid offensive in Syria and Palestine in 995–98.

On the other side of the Mediterranean, new contenders for power in al-Andalus pursued their own frontier warfare against the Christian kingdoms of northern Spain and southern France. After al-Rahman's death, in 961, power in Cordoba was increasingly controlled by a small group of individuals who competed to control the caliph. One of these court officials, Ibn Abi Amir, systematically eliminated his rivals and eventually took complete control of the state. Taking the title al-Mansur (the Victorious) in 981, he consolidated his power by demonstrating his adherence to orthodox Islam: he built a massive extension to the Friday mosque in Cordoba, purged the caliph's library of unorthodox texts, and developed a policy of aggressive jihad on the northern frontier. Among the more than 50 raids under his reign, the 985 sack of Barcelona and the 997 sack of Santiago stand out as particularly destructive for those who suffered them and especially lucrative for the soldiers who participated in them. Al-Mansur was careful to publicize both his piety and victories; for instance, he displayed a hand-copied Qur'an on his campaigns and had prisoners of war carry the cathedral bells of Santiago de Compostela to Cordoba, where they were installed in the Great Mosque as symbols of Islamic triumph. His policy of frontier aggression was balanced by the kinship ties that crossed the religious and political lines. Al-Mansur married 'Abda, the daughter of King Sancho of Navarre, who was the mother of his son 'Abd al-Rahman, known as Sanchuelo.

Raids from the south only underlined the independence of the lords of Catalonia and Provence. Count William of Provence led a series of campaigns against the Muslim colony of raiders at Fraxinetum in the 970s. After the sack of Barcelona, Catalan appeals for aid to the Carolingian successor, King Lothair, and the newly elected king of France, Hugh Capet, went unanswered. Count Ramon Borrel was left to defend against continuing Muslim attacks on his own. When the caliphate at Cordoba collapsed, Ramon sent Catalan troops that participated in the 1010 sack of that city. The Catalans negotiated several treaties with the caliphs of Cordoba, making the region a nexus of exchange and interaction between Iberia and northern Europe.

CLIMATE CHANGE AND COLLAPSE

Around the year 1000, political shifts across the Mediterranean were complicated by the varying effects of a changing climate. Evidence from multiple sources points to a global shift in weather patterns, sometimes called the Medieval Warm Period, which peaked between 950 and 1100. This change brought a warmer climate to northern Europe; in the eastern Mediterranean, there were unpredictable weather conditions, including heavy, destructive rainfall and prolonged droughts. Central Asia suffered sharp cold snaps during the same time. These weather conditions coincided with a period of intense social and political upheaval across the Mediterranean. Centralized states in al-Andalus, North Africa, and Sicily fragmented into multiple statelets, and the Fatimid and Byzantine states were severely shaken. Migrations and invasions of nomadic peoples, perhaps fleeing cold or drought, further destabilized the region. Scholars searching to explain these events have pointed to political factionalism, particularly the power of blocs within multiethnic armies to direct the course of the state. More recently some have suggested climate change as a contributing factor in these developments, although research into the precise regional manifestations of changing weather conditions is ongoing.

The power of the caliphs of al-Andalus was centered on Cordoba. When that center foundered between 1002 and 1031, political life returned to a pattern of localized rule. During al-Mansur's regime, his campaigns of frontier warfare increased military strength, but the gradual demilitarization of the Muslim population of al-Andalus meant there was no counterweight to the caliphal armies. Al-Mansur's heirs had to balance the powerful Berber and Slav elements within the military, but disputes over succession meant that simmering tensions between the various court and army groups boiled over into uncontrolled violence. Slav and Berber factions in the army supported first one and then another claimant to the throne, and both factions called in aid from Castile and Barcelona to the North. A mixed army of Castilians and Berbers captured Cordoba in 1009, only to lose it to the Catalans and Slavs the following year. The Berbers returned in 1013, wrecking the palace, plundering Cordoba, and massacring its citizens. Disaster followed disaster until the final collapse of the caliphate in 1031.

In the aftermath of Cordoba's implosion, more than 35 independent statelets sprang up, each headed by a Berber, Slav, or Arab leader. One observer described the process, saying, "Every leader revolted in his own city and fortified himself inside his castle, after first taking thought for himself, and enrolling soldiers and storing up money, and they contended with one another for the world, and each of them was covetous of the rest." The Mediterranean coast was generally taken by Slav leaders, who established power bases at Tortosa, Denia, Murcia, and Almeria. Denia, for example, was ruled by a convert and freed slave, Mujahid al-Amiri, who conquered the Balearic Islands and sent an expedition to take Sardinia, in an effort to forge a maritime state in the western Mediterranean. A Pisan and Genoese coalition ousted the Denians from Sardinia in 1016. Even after this defeat, Denia continued its raids on Sardinia, southern France, and Barcelona, at the same time forging commercial connections in the region. Denia was annexed by its stronger neighbor Zaragoza in 1075; many of the smaller statelets were similarly absorbed by their neighbors, and by the mid-eleventh century there were six main dynasties with centers at Zaragoza, Toledo, Valencia, Badajoz, Seville, and Granada.

In North Africa and Sicily, the precipitating event for political decentralization was the Fatimid dynasty's move to Cairo in 970. The governors they left behind transformed their offices into semi-independent hereditary governorships. In Tunisia, the Berber Buluggin ibn Ziri founded the Zirid dynasty, and in Sicily, the Arab Abu al-Qasim established the Kalbite dynasty. The Kalbites reformed the island's tax system to pay for their elaborate court life in Palermo but were unable to mount an effective defense against the Pisan fleet that appeared in the Strait of Messina in 1005–6. These policies caused resistance and resentment among the Sicilian population, and there were several popular revolts. As in Iberia, ethnic divisions in the army fanned the flames of factionalism, and in 1015 the Berbers and sub-Saharan African regiments revolted as well. In the face of so much internal resistance, the two contenders for control of Sicily each turned to foreign allies, one inviting the Zirids of Tunisia and the other requesting Byzantine assistance.

Zirid and Byzantine armies took control of much of the island in the 1030s, and any semblance of central rule from Palermo vanished. The opposing armies were by no means monolithic: Byzantine forces included Greeks, Italians, Scandinavians, and Norman mercenaries from northern Europe. Their opponents, fighting under "Zirid" and "Kalbite" banners, included Arabs, Berbers, and sub-Saharan Africans, as well as the "people of Sicily." From this chaos five separate Sicilian statelets emerged. The two strongest contenders for power were Ibn al-Hawwas and Ibn al-Thumna. When their conflict turned to open war, Ibn al-Thumna recruited mercenaries from "the Franks" in southern Italy, opening the way for the Norman invasion of the island.

The Zirid dynasty in Tunisia itself experienced significant splintering in this period; as was the case in Iberia and Sicily, the army was heavily involved in politics. The dynastic founder, Buluggin, relied heavily on black soldiers from sub-Saharan Africa; after his death, in 984, these troops supported first one then another contender to the throne. Other members of the Zirid dynasty waged their own campaigns for power. One of these Zirids, Hammad, carved out an independent principality for himself along the coast to the west of Tunisia, stretching from modern-day Annaba to the west of Algiers. Another Zirid left North Africa entirely and forged a principality for himself in Granada, benefiting from the disintegration of the caliphate in Cordoba. Political disorder caused religious tensions in the capital; Sunni religious leaders provoked riots against Shia in Qayrawan and other cities and towns; large numbers of Shia were massacred. By the 1030s, the Zirid emir al-Muizz was considering a break with the Fatimids, and in 1048, he denounced them and pledged his loyalty to the distant Abbasids, rejecting Shiism and adopting Sunni Islam. During the same time, several famines were reported in North Africa, in 1004–5, 1018–19, 1022–23, 1033–34, and 1040–42. Many North Africans migrated to Sicily, and the Zirids depleted their gold reserves importing grain from Sicily to feed those who remained.

Fatimid attention was focused on difficulties in Egypt, which was hit hard by repeated droughts and famines. The Nile failed to rise to its usual levels from 1004–9

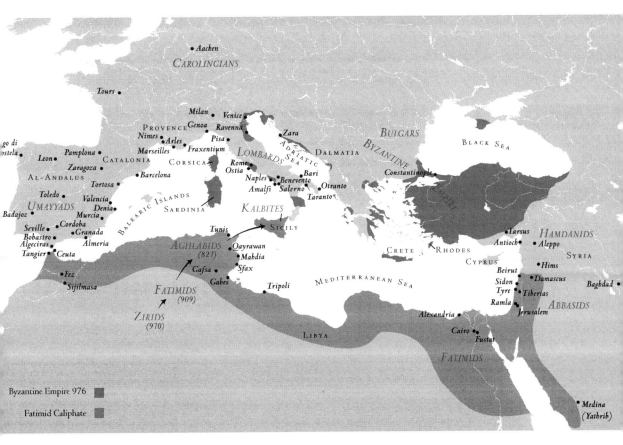

Byzantine Empire 976

Fatimid Caliphate

and again in 1023–26, leaving not only Egyptians but those who relied on Egyptian grain hungry. The second drought coincided with the difficult reign of the Fatimid caliph-imam al-Hakim, best known for his bizarre personality. Without warning, he ordered the execution of several thousand government officials and military leaders. He also issued strange dietary regulations, prohibiting the consumption of fish without scales or watercress, and instituted general social regulations such as forbidding chess and the killing of dogs. In 1003 he began the persecution of Christians and Jews: churches and synagogues were destroyed, and he ordered the destruction of the Church of the Holy Sepulchre in Jerusalem in 1009. While this demolition inspired no immediate retaliation by the Byzantines, it would become an important motivation for western European crusaders later in the century. Al-Hakim disappeared during one of his regular walks in the hills outside Cairo, most likely murdered at the order of his sister, Sitt-al Mulk, who then ruled as regent for her young nephew.

In this atmosphere of famine and political instability, there was unrest both in the army and among the population. The Turkish and Berber elements of the Fatimid military formed a coalition against the Sudanese troops, who rioted and burned the city of Fustat to the ground. There was an uprising against Fatimid rule in 1024–25 in Syria and Palestine, and intermittent factional fighting between the Turks and the Berbers broke out in Cairo several times during the next decades. These ongoing disturbances in Egypt meant that when the Zirids in North Africa declared their independence from the Fatimids, the caliph-imam al-Munastir was unable to respond with direct military action. Instead the Fatimid administration encouraged the Arab tribes of the Banu Hilal and the Banu Sulaym to migrate to North Africa. These nomadic pastoralists, resident in upper Egypt since the eighth century, had long been a source of instability and disorder. Alternately, the repeated droughts suggest the Banu Hilal left upper Egypt not simply for political reasons but in search of new pasturage for their flocks. The tribes moved into the Maghreb in 1050–51, and the Banu Sulaym settled in Cyrenaica, the region around Barce. The Banu Hilal continued on to Tunisia, defeating the Zirid armies in 1052 and sacking the city of Qayrawan in 1057. Several independent statelets emerged from the political disintegration of North Africa: the remains of the Zirids around Mahdiya and Sousse as well as the coastal towns of Tunis, Sfax, Gabes, and Gafsa.

Byzantium also experienced a period of great difficulty in the mid-eleventh century. Emperor Basil II led a campaign of conquest in Bulgaria, extending Byzantine control as far north as the Danube River. Basil never married, leaving the succession open on his death, in 1025, but he also left a full treasury and a consolidated state with stable borders. Over the next half century, the Byzantines lost control of southern Italy, debased the coinage, faced several tax revolts in the provinces, and cut back on military expenditures. They also faced nomadic invasions and migrations on two frontiers: the Pechenegs from the north in the 1020s and 1030s, and the Turks from the east. The Seljuk Turks, a nomadic people originally from Central Asia led by the Seljuk family, moved into Anatolia, Syria, and Palestine gradually during the tenth century.

The northwestern quadrant of the Mediterranean in the eleventh century faced the same shifts in weather patterns and political decentralization as elsewhere in the Mediterranean, but the long cycle of warmer conditions in northern Europe meant longer growing seasons, milder winters, and new agricultural technologies. The region could support a larger population, and waves of "Justinian's Plague" ended in 750, contributing to demographic growth as well. In northern Italy, southern France, and northern Spain, the decline of the Carolingian successor kings left a vacuum of centralized political power. Land, fortifications, and judicial and taxation rights devolved to the local landed nobility. What set northern and central Italy apart was its role as the main conduit for trade between Byzantium, the Muslim world, and northern Europe. Towns and cities played a much more important role in the emerging social order than was the case elsewhere in the Christian Mediterranean. Venice, Genoa, Amalfi, and Pisa all used their merchant fleets for both military and commercial purposes, participating in the political life of the Mediterranean as independent states. The profits derived from the region's commercial prominence boosted the civic and economic prominence of merchants and of towns generally. Independent, self-governing communes gave merchants a place in town government. This development had its roots in the late tenth and early eleventh centuries and fully blossomed in the twelfth and thirteenth centuries.

The experience of the Italian communes suggests a larger pattern: while the failures of centralized states to institutionalize power led to political fragmentation, that decentralization did not necessarily lead to economic or cultural decline. In fact, early medieval economic and cultural networks of exchange across the Mediterranean demonstrated a great deal of resilience and creative response to rapidly changing circumstances. Individuals and polities across the Mediterranean world drew on and reinterpreted the material, intellectual, and cultural traditions of the Roman world. The sea itself and the societies immediately surrounding it acted as a porous contact zone for cultural and economic transmission.

CHAPTER THREE

Early Medieval Economies and Cultures

In the tenth or eleventh century, a Jewish woman named Maliha wrote to her brothers, Mar Solomon and Abu Sa'id. Maliha had moved from the family home in Egypt to Byzantium, and possibly as a result of her husband's death, she now wished to return to Egypt. She wrote, "My soul is restless in my heart, my step has faltered, my bones tremble, and my strength has melted away. Great is my yearning to see you face to face, and I would run at the pace of a lion and rush to see you." She asked her brothers to come and escort her and her young daughter Zoë home, demanding, "Why does not one of you take his life into his own hands to come to me and take me back?" She also advised her brothers to bring merchandise on the journey, in order to profit from commercial opportunities on the way.

Maliha's letter was found in one of the most revealing collections of documents that exist for medieval Mediterranean history, the Cairo Genizah. When the Jewish community of Fustat rebuilt their synagogue in the eleventh century, they included a storeroom, or genizah, where they put discarded papers, letters, and any document with Hebrew characters, to avoid destroying the name of God. The collection came to light in 1896, and scholars have used it to reconstruct cross-Mediterranean trading networks and Jewish social and family life. The fragment of Maliha's journey across the Mediterranean also emerged from this storeroom: we do not know if her brothers went to retrieve her or if she ever made it back to Egypt. But from the letter we learn that a Jewish woman from Egypt traveled to Byzantium, where her daughter's Greek name suggests she married a Byzantine Jew. Her brothers' names, Solomon and Sa'id, illustrate the fusion of Hebrew and Arabic in the Egyptian world she came from. Her letter acknowledges the potential danger of travel but also points to the intertwined nature of commercial and family networks that linked the northern and southern shores of the sea.

We learn about a second, very different sort of journey across the Mediterranean from the life story of a saint, Elias the Younger. Saints' lives were written to demonstrate the holiness of their subjects, but they are a major source for cultural and social history, as well as religious history. Elias was born in Sicily around 823; as a boy, he had a dream that he would be captured and transported to Africa, indicating how common an occurrence this was for ninth-century Sicilians. On a trip outside the city walls, the twelve-year-old was snatched by slave hunters and sold to an African Christian slave merchant. Luckily, before the slave ship had gotten very far, a Byzantine warship chased it down, rescued the captives, and returned Elias to his parents. Three years later, events repeated themselves, except this time Elias was not rescued but sold to a Christian in Africa who worked as a tanner. Impressed by his character and piety, Elias's owner promoted him to head his household and manage his tanning business. After several decades, Elias was able to buy his freedom, and after becoming a monk he traveled widely in Syria, Palestine, and Egypt. He returned to Sicily and settled at a monastery, but soon he headed to Corfu, where Byzantine authorities arrested him on suspicion of being a Muslim spy. He founded a monastery in southern Italy, dying in 903 on his way to Constantinople. He moved first as a slave and then as a free man along the commercial and religious networks that joined Muslim, Christian, and Byzantine worlds.

Taken together, these two journeys illustrate the dangers of travel in the early medieval Mediterranean and the continued cultural, economic, and religious networks that linked separate parts of the region. The economy went from a low point in the eighth century to renewed growth in the ninth and tenth centuries, particularly in the Muslim world. Economic growth spurred the development of cities throughout the southern Mediterranean, and new cultural capitals emerged at Cordoba, Palermo, and Cairo. Scholars, artists, and diplomats traveled between these capitals and Constantinople, spreading intellectual and artistic styles and creating a shared culture of ostentatious display and learning among Mediterranean elites. While conversion to Islam shifted cultural and religious practices across the southern Mediterranean, there were still areas of shared sanctity, and Arabic became the dominant medium of communication for Christians, Muslims, and Jews. In the face of these changes, religious hierarchies and institutions struggled with questions of doctrine and sectarianism, especially the role of images and the balance of power between religious and political authorities.

SHIFTING ECONOMIES AND MERCHANT NETWORKS

The starting point for many scholarly debates on the transformation of the post-Roman world is the work of the historian Henri Pirenne, who saw the arrival of Islam on Mediterranean shores as the fundamental rupture of Roman commercial and cultural unity and the cause of Latin Christian Europe's turn northward

١٠٥

١٠٩

وكان خسيب شينط شرا وغلي السيد على اضا فاضى الحبث خلتفا ما اضا

ان قال الا العبد اذا رزق عبده وحفت موذ منزل مولاه مولاه واكن

A slave market, from an illustrated manuscript, executed by Yahya ben Mahmud al-Wasiti in Baghdad in 1237. Above, merchants are using scales to agree on a price, while slaves and buyers are represented below. *Bibliothèque nationale de France, Paris. Photo: Art Resource, NY*

لا وترجيب هذا الغلام البلد ان احفت ثمنه عليكم فان مائي ثمن

واشترى ماجيت فقلت فنه المبلغ مما انفذ ان الرخص الغال واا

in the eighth century. Pirenne pointed to specific economic changes in Carolingian Europe: the end of minting gold coins and the drop in the circulation of money, the prohibition of lending money at interest and the contraction of the merchant class, the decline in urbanization, and the end of importing eastern luxury goods such as papyrus, spices, silk, and African olive oil. While scholars generally agree that the eighth century was a low point in exchange between regions of the Mediterranean, they differ with Pirenne on the causes and the severity of the change in Mediterranean commerce. Chris Wickham and Michael McCormick have both used archaeological evidence not available to Pirenne to draw a different picture: Wickham argues that there was a decline in Mediterranean commerce before the Muslim arrival, with the end of the Roman taxation system that transported wheat and oil from North Africa to Rome and Constantinople. McCormick has demonstrated that many of the maritime trade networks of antiquity shifted inland during the early medieval age, but the travelers' accounts he analyzes show that regular and nonviolent exchange between Islamic and Christian worlds continued and even intensified in the ninth century.

While trans-Mediterranean trade waned in the seventh and eighth centuries, Muslim conquest opened the southern Mediterranean to the larger trading network of the Indian Ocean. The spread of the Arabic language and an Islamic legal framework facilitated merchants' travel and communication throughout the Muslim world. Islamic law recognized several types of business partnerships, one with the capital provided by sedentary investor and the management of trade by another merchant (*mudaraba*) and another with capital provided by both investor and merchant (*musharaka* or *inan*). Trans-Saharan gold trade with West Africa enabled the minting of gold and silver coins, and the gold *dinar* (from the Byzantine *dinarius*) and the silver *dirham* (from the Greek *drachma*) became the standard medium of exchange throughout the Muslim world.

Urban life boomed in the southern Mediterranean, both transforming former Roman cities and creating new ones. Under Islamic rule, Cairo, Cordoba, and Palermo grew to perhaps 100,000 people. In addition to luxury products such as silks, incense, and spices, trade was driven by the needs of newly established cities for food, building materials, and tools. The cities that evolved to service trade in the Muslim world had similar features: mosques, baths, marketplaces, accommodation for travelers, and Qur'anic schools. These Islamic cities looked very different from the urban centers of late antiquity. In a process of urban transformation that had begun before the Islamic conquests, urban industries and private building encroached on the clear public streets and squares that had characterized Roman cities, giving way to dense marketplaces and winding pathways. The large public plazas and wide avenues of Greco-Roman cities were gone; instead, the souk (marketplace), often near the main mosque, became the primary gathering place. The tenth-century traveler Ibn Hawqal gave a lively description of the market in Muslim Palermo, where there were sections for olive sellers, flour merchants, money changers, pharmacists, blacksmiths, grain markets, embroiderers, fish sellers, spice sellers, potters, bakers, rope makers, carpenters, and so on.

Travelers in the Islamic world brought new agricultural practices and edible plants from east to west, fundamentally transforming the productive landscape of the western Mediterranean. Muslim settlers in North Africa, Sicily, and Iberia drained malarial swamps and repaired and improved Roman irrigation systems, which had fallen into disuse, adding innovations such as the waterwheel. The result was an increase in agricultural productivity; new villages sprang up, and older farmlands were cultivated more intensively. New crops from India and Iran spread westward: the date palm, sugarcane, oranges, lemons, grapefruit, apricots, almonds, artichokes, rice, saffron, eggplants, and parsnips. These new foodstuffs were joined by cotton plants, mulberry trees, and silkworms. The overall effect was to make coastal agriculture more productive and profitable, and the new agricultural productivity stimulated lively trade between the western and eastern Mediterranean.

Although the trade between Christian Europe and the Islamic Mediterranean was not as intense as commerce within the Muslim world, there was a steady exchange between north and south. Christian elites bought luxury products like silks from the Islamic world. Large hoards of Islamic coins in northern Europe testify to these trade connections: northern Europeans sold honey, amber, and furs, but the main commodity exported from Europe to the Islamic world was slaves. All of the Mediterranean monotheistic religions—Christianity, Islam, and Judaism— forbade enslaving coreligionists, but the demand for slaves, particularly in the urbanized Islamic world, remained high. As a result, the slave trade was pushed to the peripheries of the monotheistic world, south of the Sahara desert in North Africa and north to the non-Christian populations of eastern Europe. Slaves were also taken captive in wars, or stolen from the shores of the northern Mediterranean and the Black Sea by violence or treachery, and sold south to Muslim world. The vast majority of these slaves' stories went unrecorded, but St. Elias the Younger's life offers a glimpse of one journey. Elias's experience is atypical in several ways, but it gives a face to the hundreds and thousands of young, male Byzantines, Italians, Franks, Slavs, Goths, and Jews who crossed the Mediterranean in captivity and contributed to the economic and demographic growth in the urban centers of the southern Mediterranean. Female slaves were employed in households as domestic servants, wet-nurses, and sometimes as concubines.

Venice, Naples, Almeria, and Cordoba developed as major centers of the slave trade. Venetian merchants in particular were active in the slave trade in the ninth and tenth centuries. In both the Byzantine and Muslim worlds, slaves worked as artisans, in agriculture, and in the households of the wealthy. A particular subset of slavery was the demand for castrated males to serve as eunuchs in the palace households of Constantinople and in the Muslim east. Muslim rulers also relied on slaves to fill the ranks of their armies, and there were thousands of Slavic slave-soldiers in Cordoba, Qayrawan, and Cairo.

Constantinople was one of the largest cities in the Mediterranean, with between 40,000 and 70,000 inhabitants and a preeminent position in the region's luxury trade. Because the Byzantine elites depended on imperial patronage for their positions, their lives and expenditures were centered in Constantinople, creating a booming market for luxury goods in the capital but hindering the development of more localized aristocracies that might have invested in the economy and society of provincial cities and towns. Even during the height of Byzantine-Muslim hostilities in the eighth century, luxuries from the Muslim world were available in Constantinople, and by the ninth century there was a well-established cross-border trade from Syria and Mesopotamia. There is evidence of a regular Muslim merchant presence in Constantinople from the tenth century, and Byzantine merchants traveled to the Black Sea region, Spain, and Egypt and exported a variety of products: pottery, metalwork, and glass produced in Constantinople, as well as commodities like cheese and timber. The Byzantine silk industry was famous for its quality of production and for the degree of state control over the guilds that produced it. The finished silk was so valuable that it was used as a form of pay-

Byzantine silk depicting a four-horse chariot. Made in Byzantium, this piece of silk was used to decorate Charlemagne's tomb at Aachen. Byzantine silks were often used as diplomatic gifts. *Musée national du Moyen Age, Thermes de Cluny. Photo: Erich Lessing/Art Resource, NY*

ment for Byzantine officials, and emperors sometimes sent silk as a gift to foreign rulers, but there were strict rules about the type and quantity of silk that could be sold to outsiders.

Adventurous, multilingual Jewish merchants played an important role in cross-cultural Mediterranean commerce. Jewish merchants had several advantages when it came to long-distance trade: there were Jewish communities along the shores of the Mediterranean, so travelers could rely on the hospitality and assistance of coreligionists. These communities were tied together through family, marriage, and commercial partnerships, making for easy communications and transfer of goods through a network of friends, family, and business agents stretching from al-Andalus to Sicily, Tunisia, and Byzantium. For instance, letters from the Taherti family partnership show that the head of the family, four sons, and eight grandsons were involved in trade between Cairo-Fustat and Qayrawan, and two Taherti daughters were married into other great trading dynasties. Because Jews as a group were not politically or militarily aligned with particular states, they could often cross political religious boundaries more easily than could Christians or Muslims.

Jewish and Muslim merchant networks overlapped through informal cooperation, sociability in the marketplace, and formal business partnerships. Jewish merchants tended to travel on Muslim-owned ships, and Jewish and Muslim merchants journeyed overland in caravans together. Jewish merchants generally followed Muslim commercial law in assigning risk to the sleeping partner at home rather than the traveling partner, and they used types of credit notes, bills of exchange, and cheques. Commercial matters were settled in both Jewish and Muslim courts, and legal opinions from rabbis and from Muslim kadis indicate that Jews and Muslims were business partners in shops and agricultural enterprises, and that they worked as artisans in the same workshops. One letter from the head of the Taherti family to another trading dynasty, the Tustaris of Cairo-Fustat, reveals an attitude of trust and frequent interaction with Muslim merchants: "Should a caravan set out in which trustworthy Muslims, who have given you sureties, will travel, let the merchandise of my brothers be sent with them as if it were yours. They would profit from this in many respects."

Christian merchants appear much less frequently in these networks of sociability and interfaith cooperation until the tenth century, when Italian merchants, particularly from the new towns of Amalfi and Venice, began to participate more actively in Mediterranean trade. These merchants adopted many of the commercial practices and much of the vocabulary already in use in the southern Mediterranean. Neither Venice, located in the marshy waters of the upper Adriatic, nor Amalfi, located on the steep cliffs south of Naples, could rely on agricultural hinterlands to fuel their growth, and merchants from both cities began to act as middlemen in the exchange of luxury goods from Byzantium and the Muslim world for timber, salt, amber, and, especially, slaves from northern Europe. Venice was a regional force in the Adriatic by the eighth century, and by the ninth century Venetian merchants had begun to specialize in trade with Palestine, Syria, and Egypt. The scale of this early trade is shown in the 829 will of one of the city's early rulers, Justinian Partecipazio, who had 1,200 silver pounds invested in overseas ventures. Amalfitans were active sailors and traders in Muslim Sicily and North Africa by the 830s. Merchants from Amalfi supplied the papal court at Rome, importing silks, gold, jewels, and other luxury goods; these merchants had ties to the court at Constantinople and signed a treaty guaranteeing commercial security for themselves and their successors in Cordoba in 942. Genoese and Pisan merchants entered into the markets of the southern Mediterranean in the late tenth and eleventh centuries, although their commercial relationships with Muslim states were markedly more hostile.

The booming commercial and agricultural sectors, together with the growing political fragmentation after the fall of the Umayyads in 750, stimulated urbanization, monumental construction, and elaborate court cultures in Cordoba, Palermo, and Cairo. These capitals of Muslim dynasties were influenced by memories of Umayyad court culture and the distant influence of Abbasid Baghdad, but they were also characterized by intense cultural interactions with Christian and Jewish cultures. These dynasties built palace quarters and ceremonial mosques in or near the expanding economic centers of the Islamic world, cultivating cultures of learning, elegance, and refinement. The most spectacular and significant of these ceremonial centers was Cairo, established by the Fatimid general Jawahar outside the older city of Fustat. A visitor in 1047 reported that the city had over 20,000 shops, in addition to bazaars, caravanserais (trading stations), and bathhouses. The demand for luxury goods at the Fatimid court drove the Red Sea trade in Indian perfumes, luxury textiles, and spices.

A key transformation in the urban and religious culture of the Muslim Mediterranean was the foundation of mosques, and new dynasties built or renovated Friday mosques in their capitals that visually represented their claims to legitimacy. Although destroying or appropriating Christian churches for mosques was actually not typical, several principal mosques were built on the sites of former Christian churches. The chief symbol of the Umayyad dynasty was the Mosque of Damascus, which al-Walid founded on the site of a church dedicated to John the Baptist, itself built atop a Roman temple to Jupiter. The Umayyads of Iberia founded their own Great Mosque in Cordoba, and there is a tradition that Caliph ʿAbd al-Rahman I purchased the existing church of St. Vincent and demolished it to begin construction of the mosque. There is no evidence for an actual church of St. Vincent, but the story evokes the history of the Great Mosque of Damascus and destruction of the Church of St. John, symbolically linking two buildings and making them sites celebrating Islamic victory. Dynasties in North Africa also rebuilt and enlarged Friday mosques, and the elites of these new Muslim polities established mosques and institutions of learning, ensuring for their perpetual upkeep through pious endowments called waqfs.

The capitals, particularly the competing caliphal courts, became centers of material and artistic culture. The caliphs, and the elites who emulated them, collected elaborately decorated metal and glassware, exotic birds and animals, ceramics, rugs, plants, jewels, and coins, and they recruited scholars and artists from across the Mediterranean. For instance, Ali ibn Zaryab, a musician, singer, astronomer, and geographer, arrived in Cordoba from Abbasid Baghdad in the 820s and quickly became an arbiter of elegance to the Cordoban elite, introducing new hairstyles, the practice of eating asparagus, and the use of deodorant. Another immigrant from the east, Ibn al-Haytham, known in the west as Alhazen, was drawn to Cairo by Fatimid patronage. He lived near al-Azhar Mosque, teaching

Al-Azhar Mosque, Cairo. Founded by the Fatimid dynasty around 970, the mosque is one of the oldest centers of learning in the Islamic world. Under the Fatimids it was dominated by Shia theology, but when Saladin replaced the Fatimids with his own Ayyubid dynasty, he reorganized al-Azhar as a center of Sunni learning. *Photo: Erich Lessing / Art Resource,* NY

and commenting on Greek texts in science, philosophy, mathematics, and physics; he also composed over 90 works on logic, ethics, poetry, music, and theology. He was only one of a host of scholars and artists who traveled between caliphal courts and transferred knowledge and styles.

These courts shared an attention to Islamic learning and to the arts of the book, and translators, copyists, and bookbinders were attracted to these new court capitals. One chronicler reported that the library of the Cordoban caliph al-Hakem II held 400,000 volumes, and that he had agents in major cities of the Islamic world to buy books for him and even to bribe authors to send him advance copies before they were generally available. Innovations in papermaking technology increased the bookmaking culture of al-Andalus; the earliest paper mill was located at Játiva, southwest of Valencia, to take advantage of the rivers there. Fatimid caliphs also founded libraries and maintained their own house of knowledge in Cairo that served as a meeting place for scholars of hadith, jurists, grammarians, doctors, astronomers, logicians, and mathematicians. By the end of the Fatimid era the library had as many as 1.6 million volumes. These courts learned, borrowed, and copied fashions from one another, creating a unified culture of learning and luxury consumption among the elites of the southern Mediterranean.

The strong Jewish presence in the political and cultural life of these courts has led some to refer to this time as a "golden age" for Jews in the Islamic world. In al-Andalus, the Jewish vizier Hasdai ibn Shaprut gained renown as a poet, physician, scientist, and diplomat, as well as a politician, and the Jewish vizier of Granada, Samuel ibn Naghrela, was also a renowned poet. The cross-cultural interaction between Hebrew and Arabic literary culture produced new poetic forms that borrowed and combined forms and words from classical Arabic and Romance languages. Muslim and Jewish scholars collaborated on projects of medicine, botany, and astronomy. The fall of centralized states and the fragmentation of the western Mediterranean into statelets did not ruin this culture of learning—in fact, courts competed to attract talented scholars and writers, improving their possibilities of patronage.

Constantinople was both a model for these Mediterranean caliphal courts and a competitor in the cultural world of ruling ceremonial, elite display, and scholarship. The intellectual culture of Constantinople, almost nonexistent in the difficult years of the eighth century, began to revive in the mid-ninth century. One of the early figures in this revival, known as Leo the Mathematician, encouraged the study of ancient mathematics and philosophy and came to the notice of the Byzantine emperor through the Abbasid caliph's repeated attempts to bring Leo to his own court. The emperor Theophilos gave Leo a position as a paid public teacher, and he eventually received the chair of philosophy in the palace school established in 855. The school ceased operation in the next century, but a revival of literary culture persisted from the ninth century on. Byzantine intellectuals in this period had a strong affinity for the Greek classics, which they copied and preserved. The standard script of Greek manuscripts changed from one using all capitals to a cursive minuscule, with spaces between words and sentences, fuller punctuation, and accent marks. Many of the ancient Greek classics and early Christian writings are known only in their transliterated ninth-century versions.

The material and intellectual culture of these courts circulated through diplomatic exchanges. In 840, Emperor Theophilos sent an embassy to the Umayyads in Spain, proposing they make common cause against their enemies the Aghlabids and Abbasids; 'Abd al-Rahman received the Byzantine ambassador and sent him back to Constantinople with two astrologers. The Cordoban ambassador Recemundo, or Rabi ibn Zayd, was in Constantinople in 949 and brought back with him carved and sculpted Byzantine basins as well as Greek mosaicists to work on the cupola and mihrab of the mosque in Cordoba. In the same year, a Byzantine embassy brought a Greek text of Dioscorides's treatise on botany and other manuscripts to Spain, but no one there was able to read Greek. So the Byzantine emperor sent a Greek monk who worked with a Sicilian Muslim and the Andalusian Jewish vizier Hasdai ibn Shaprut to decipher the text. The sometimes competitive nature of these exchanges is revealed in an exchange of gifts between the Byzantine emperor Constantine VII and the Fatimid caliph al-Mansur. Al-Mansur instructed his

ΜΑΝΔΡΑΓΟΡΑ   ἄρρεν

Ἡ   ΜΑΝΔΡΑΓΟΡΑ   ἄρρεν :–

οἱ δὲ · κιρκεον · οἱ δὲ · ζηρααθθη · οἱ δὲ · ἀντιμνιον · οἱ δὲ · ἀντίμιλι·

οἱ δὲ · βονβοχυλον · οἱ δὲ · μοινον · αἰγύπτιοι · ἀπεμουλα

πυθαγορας · ἀνθρωπομορφος · οἱ δὲ · ἀλοειτιν · οἱ δὲ · θριλαικιαν·

οἱ δὲ · καμμαρον · οἱ δὲ · ἀρχηρη · οἱ δὲ · βιαλεος · ζωροαστης · διαμονη

ἢ ἀρχηνη · προφηται · ἡμιονας · οἱ δὲ · γονογεωνας · ρωμαιοι · μλακνιμ

οἱ δὲ · μαλα · τερρεστρις ·

ἡ δ᾽ αὐτοῦ ὁ μὲν η τὸ θῆλυ· μέλαν ἥπερ δια λίαν ὑοσκύαμοσ· φύλλα ἐ
εμα σμικρότερα· καὶ μη μικρότερα· τριλαιμοσ· ὑπομάδη· καὶ μαρθα· καὶ αᾶ
τω ὁμιλω καὶ χυμὸρα· εστὶ γῆσ· καὶ παραπα μηλοιλδε λη θοιοχωω·
εμφερὴ ωχρα καὶ λη· ὁμοιο καὶ μαρ μᾶσ ὅσ απερ ατοῦου· ρίζαι δυμονη·
τθος· δύο· ἡ τρίφοσ· αρτεμποσ ολ δ μεραν αλληλω· μέλαιμ μαι·
ἐπιφαιραμ ἐπ δο· θερμ θευλιαμ φοι αλδσ· καὶ χωρ δέ οὐ φθορ
ρεμοσ καὶ μ θευλιού· ὁμ ετι οι πορι ορμ διαλθσαμ· φύλλα φθρ λ θευλια μ
γαραατω σπθας λ σαμ· τα δ ὁ μληα δ τπωλοιαμ· ἱερο λη ζ ομπ πτιλχροια·
δ ωλ δλη· μξαι μ ἄρους· ἀπρόσ· ἃ· καὶ ὁσθιουσιμ οἱ τωσιμ φορμπτοσ· τωσ
ὑπωλεροῦται· ρίζα αλ δὲ ὁ μοιαι πτπαρ ολιπττω· μαζορ δὲ καὶ θυλα τέρα
α ωλουλοσ δὲ καὶ αλ αυτη· χυλιζθαι δ ἔ ὁ φ λοιοσ· τπ ἡ ρίζα λα λωρος
λαι σφῖσ ις ὑπωποποσφσ· ω λαι λρ ειλω σδ ξαι μτ αυτο συαρ αφ θψαι απωπτ

treasurer to find more impressive gifts than those they had received, explaining that "we accumulate [treasures] only to rival our enemies in splendor, show the nobility of our sentiments, the greatness of our soul, and the generosity of our hearts in the gift of things of which one is envious."

Pairs or groups of scholars collaborated to translate philosophical, medical, astronomical, and mathematical knowledge from one language to another. Far from the Mediterranean, Jewish, Christian and Muslim scholars in Abbasid Baghdad copied and commented on Greek theological writings, medicine, astronomy, and philosophy. While no single location in the Mediterranean could match this enterprise, smaller translation centers emerged on the frontiers between Greek, Latin, and Arabic zones. In the ninth and tenth century, most of southern Italy was Greek-speaking, and Naples and especially Rome became sites for the translation of Greek theological works and saints lives' into Latin and vice versa. Scholars at Cordoba, in the generation after the translation of Dioscorides, continued to translate Greek science into Arabic, but al-Andalus was also a major site for the translation of the Arabic scientific corpus into Latin. The career of Gerbert of Aurillac is a good example of the way the intellectual and scientific culture of al-Andalus was transferred into a Latin Christian context. Born in south-central France, Gerbert became a monk and then traveled to Catalonia, studying in monastic libraries there and returning to France with the design for an abacus and an understanding of Arabic numerals taken from the Baghdadi scholar al-Khwarizmi's Arabic treatise *Kitab al-Jabr* (Book of Algebra). Gerbert spread his knowledge in his subsequent posts, as director of the cathedral school in Reims, tutor to the Saxon emperors, and archbishop of Ravenna, and finally as Pope Sylvester II (999–1003).

These translations in scholarly languages were happening at the same time as more gradual but profound changes in everyday linguistic cultures. In the south, the Arabic language spread to even those who remained Christian and Jewish, allowing them to participate in a common culture. In Syria and Palestine, Arabic became the language of ecclesiastical use even among some Christians who lost their ties to Constantinople and the Greek world and who articulated a Christian theological position in Arabic. Syriac remained an important literary and liturgical language among Syrian Orthodox (Jacobite) Christians as well. At the other end of the Mediterranean, there is substantial evidence that Andalusian Christians used Arabic in their daily lives, but only fragmentary Christian literature in Arabic from Spain survives, suggesting that Latin remained the predom-

Dioscorides, *Treatise on Botany*. Dioscorides was a Roman army doctor in the first century CE. His treatise, here shown in a Greek version from late-ninth- or early-tenth-century Constantinople, explains how to make medicines from over 500 plants. A copy was sent as a diplomatic gift from Constantinople to Cordoba in 949. This page depicts the mandrake root. Dioscorides's treatise was translated into Arabic in the ninth century and then into Latin. *The Morgan Library & Museum, New York*

inant language of the Christian church there. In the Byzantine Empire, the Greek language was disseminated among the general population in Anatolia, replacing local dialects by the ninth century. There were more and more Slavs living in Byzantine territories in these centuries as well, but it seems they gradually became Hellenized and began speaking Greek. The increasing dominance of Greek and Arabic contrasts sharply with the fragmentation of Latin in the west, where it remained the language of the church and of high culture but was replaced in daily life with proto-vernaculars: the forerunners of modern Spanish, Italian, and French.

RELIGIOUS LIFE: CONVERSION AND SHARED SANCTITIES

Between the eighth and tenth centuries, there were increasing numbers of non-Arab Muslims. There is extremely scant source material, but historians generally agree that the rate of conversion to Islam was slow in its first century and then rose rapidly in the second and third centuries of Muslim rule. The Qur'an formally forbids forced conversions; there were, however, examples of mass voluntary conversion to Islamic faith and governance, as was the case with the conversion of the Berbers in North Africa. In the eighth century, Christian sources in the eastern Mediterranean begin to lament large-scale conversions from Christianity to Islam, but even these sources admit that these conversions were voluntary. One Christian chronicler wrote, "For without blows or torture they slid down in great eagerness toward denial. Forming groups of twenty, thirty, and a hundred men, two and three hundred, without any kind of compulsion to this; they went down to Harran to the governors and became Muslims." Some regimes, particularly the Fatimids, encouraged conversion as part of a political strategy: in 962, Caliph-imam al-Mu'izz sent money and fine robes as presents for 14,000 Sicilian boys who converted and instructed the governor of Sicily to build a mosque and a minbar (pulpit) in each district. The connection between conversion, conquest, and economic interest was not limited to Muslim rulers: in 934, a Byzantine general in Anatolia set up two tents, one with a cross and one without. Those who were willing to convert to Christianity could register their movable property and families at the tent with the cross while those who "preferred Islam received a guarantee of safety for their lives and were taken away to a secure place. The greater number of Muslims went to the tent with the cross because they wished to recover their families and moveable property." Despite instances like these, the balance of conversion in the Mediterranean favored Islam. The surviving evidence of mosque construction, naming patterns, and hagiography indicates that the rate of conversion was most intense between 750 and 950 in the east, and between 800 and 1000 in Spain, with a peak rate of conversion occurring around 950. At the end of the process, as a rough estimate, between 75% and 90% of the population in Muslim-ruled territories had converted to Islam.

Conversion proceeded from social and economic pressure, from family ties and marriage relationships, and through captivity and enslavement. Non-Muslims had to pay additional taxes; in the first few centuries of Muslim expansion, many non-Arabs continued paying a higher tax rate even after their conversion, causing tension between Arab and non-Arab Muslims. In the first centuries of Islamic rule, Christians and Jews staffed the bureaucracies of the new polities, and many Christian accounts of martyrdom present their protagonists as tempted by offers of high office and wealth in return for conversion to Islam. One example is the first Fatimid chief minister Ya'qub ibn Killis, born a Jew in Baghdad around 930. He moved with his father to the commercial center of Ramla, in Palestine, where he served as the representative of the merchants until fleeing to Egypt to escape charges of mismanagement. In Egypt he converted to Islam and worked in the financial administration, eventually gaining the position of vizier, or chief minister, which he held until his death, in 991. Other administrators did not convert, such as Hasdai ibn Shaprut.

The life of ʿUmar Ibn Hafsun, a rebel against the caliphate in al-Andalus, illustrates the sometimes strategic uses of conversion as well as the interpretative difficulties questions of conversion can pose for scholars. Ibn Hafsun led a revolt against the caliph of Cordoba at a time when the caliphal government was regularizing tax collection, which triggered resistance and revolts. Ibn Hafsun, who claimed descent from a Visigoth count Alfonso and who was part of an indigenous family of converts to Islam, began as a bandit around Bobastro and won support from the region's Arab, Berber, and Christian populations. In the 880s he surrendered and was forced into the caliph's army, where he was reportedly mocked as a "neo-Muslim." He deserted and returned to Bobastro, where he rallied support by promising to protect the local population from Cordoba's excessive taxation and forced labor demands. He is said to have converted to Christianity in 899, but there is conflicting evidence, and scholars disagree not only as to whether he actually converted but also on what this possible conversion says about the larger significance of his career and rebellion. Some have seen Ibn Hafsun as a proto-Spanish Christian hero resisting the imposition of an Islamic society. Other scholars doubt the sincerity of the conversion or see him as a clever opportunist, a rebel against the forces of central government. Still others point to the 910 visit he received from Fatimid ambassadors as evidence he converted to Shiism. The difficulties historians have had in reconstructing the religious identity of this one well-documented individual point to the larger problems of generalizing about religious belief in a time of fluidity.

Interfaith marriages created religiously and ethnically mixed populations around the southern Mediterranean. When a Muslim man married a non-Muslim woman, she would be permitted to practice her own religion, although the children were considered by Islamic law to be Muslims. One traveler reported that in rural Sicily, boys were raised Muslim like their fathers and girls were raised as Christians like their mothers. Islamic jurists were asked to consider whether a Muslim could take his Christian mother to church, participate in funeral ceremonies for a Christian parent, or wear clothes previously owned by a Christian. In al-Andalus, the ethnic mixing was evident in the ruling dynasty, as many of the Iberian Umayyads married indigenous Spanish women. The emir Hisham I was described as fair with blue eyes; the first caliph, 'Abd al-Rahman III, had blue eyes and red hair that he reportedly dyed black.

The Christian communities of the southern Mediterranean gradually shrank through emigration and conversion. Christians moved northward: from al-Andalus to the kingdoms of northern Spain, from Sicily to Byzantine Calabria, and from Egypt and Syria into Byzantine Anatolia. In North Africa, Christianity appears to have almost completely died out by the ninth and tenth centuries, with only isolated communities remaining. Many Christians of the Muslim world were separated from their northern coreligionists by questions of doctrine, particularly over the nature of Christ. They were also distinguished by their adoption of Arabic language and culture. Scant evidence from Sicily suggests that the Christians there were bilingual in Arabic, and Christians in North Africa and Egypt were also fluent in Arabic. In al-Andalus, individuals who remained Christian but who accepted Islamic food restrictions, adopted Muslim dress, and spoke and wrote in Arabic were referred to as Mozarabs. One Spanish author, Paulus Alvarus, lamented, "My fellow Christians delight in the poems and romances of the Arabs; they study the works of Mohammadan theologians and philosophers not in order to refute them, but to acquire correct and elegant Arabic style." The Coptic Christian bishop of one Egyptian town, Sawirus (Severus) ibn al-Muqaffa, echoed Alvarus's complaint, explaining that he had to write theological treatises in Arabic because nobody understood Coptic, an indication that theological debate among both Jewish and Muslim communities was shifting to Arabic.

Small but well-documented groups of Christian martyrs violently resisted cultural and religious conversion. In the eastern Mediterranean, accounts of Christian martyrs become more common in the late eighth and ninth centuries. The accounts fall into two main categories: Christian Arab converts to Islam who return to Christianity and Christians who provoke Muslim retribution by publicly insulting Islam or by trying to convert Muslims to Christianity. In Cordoba, more than 50 Christians were executed for denouncing Muhammad as a liar and madman, openly preaching Christianity, and trying to convert others to Christianity. In the majority of these martyr accounts, the Muslim officials are presented as reluctant to proceed and as offering wealth and inducements. The stories performed the social function of strengthening the resolve and confidence of a Christian population that was rapidly becoming a demographic minority.

The complexities of religious and cultural identity created by large-scale conversions were eased by the common roots of Islam, Christianity, and Judaism. This shared religious culture encompassed similar practices, such as belief in the power of pilgrimage, relics, shrines, and saints, as well as reverence for the same holy places, texts, and people. While the evidence for shared participation in popular religious celebrations most often comes from the various religious authorities who denounced the practices, there was some interfaith participation in religious rituals and festivals. Religious authorities condemned the common behavior of "frequenting baths and taverns together, to attend one another's festivals, to marry, dine, and do business deals together," indicating that these practices were common enough to require censure. In al-Andalus, Muslims used the Christian calendar and observed Christian festivals like New Year and Easter. In Egypt, imams were known to visit churches and monasteries and to observe Christian festivals such as Epiphany and Coptic New Year; Jews invited Muslims to participate in their festivities. Christian priests in Islamic lands were unofficially permitted to give blessing of the saints to Muslims and pagans, to teach the children of Muslims and Jews, and to give communion to a Christian woman married to a Muslim.

Broadly speaking, there was a shared understanding in Christianity, Islam, and Judaism that certain places and objects were especially sacred and that believers would gain access to that holiness through physical proximity. Saints, or individuals recognized during their lifetime for holiness, were considered to have special powers of intercession after death, and the "holy dead" were important focal points for veneration in all three religions. In Latin and Byzantine Christianity this holiness was particularly attached to the bones of saints as well as to relics associated with their lives. Latin Christians were intensely interested in the physical remains of saints' bodies, while Byzantine Christians placed increasing importance on icons: images of Jesus, Mary, and the saints believed to provide access to the divine. Jews and Muslims visited the tombs of holy individuals respected for scholarship or piety, but they did not sanctify direct visual or physical contact with the remains of the dead as Christians did. Jews venerated biblical and post-biblical figures, as well as individuals known for piety during their lifetimes, although there was no formal theology of sainthood. There is no mention of "saints" or holy men in the Qur'an, but from the tenth century most Muslim religious scholars approved visiting tombs for *baraka*, or blessing, and Muslim saints were referred to as "Friends of God." While there were Muslim ascetics, who fasted, wore tattered garments, and participated in spiritual and mystical exercises, the majority of Muslim holy men tended to be more involved in society, as one commentator explained: "The true saint goes in and out amongst the people and eats and sleeps with them and buys and sells in the market and marries and takes part in social intercourse, and never forgets God for a single moment."

Visits to saints' tombs usually coincided with agricultural or seasonal festivals, and they offered opportunities for commerce and entertainment as well as religious devotion. Jewish, Muslim, and Christian participants in these festivities had similar objectives in visiting the holy dead: blessings, cures for themselves and their families, rain and plentiful harvests, or protection from evil. There was often tension between these popular religious practices and religious officials' conceptions of appropriate religious behavior. For instance, the synagogue of Moses at Dammuh was one of the most sacred places for Egyptian Jews, who would travel from all over Egypt to celebrate the holy days there. Jewish communal authorities in 1010 ordered the celebrants to desist from what was apparently their habitual merrymaking, beer brewing, playing games and musical instruments, and dancing during these festivals. One Jewish commentator, in the process of condemning what he saw as laxity, described common religious practices at tombs: "They sit by the graves, take up lodgings by the vaults, and speak to the dead, saying . . . 'cure me,' or 'impregnate me.' And they light candles at the graves of the saints, burn incense on bricks before them, tie bundles on the palm tree of the graves of the dead saints, make vows to them, call to them and ask them to grant their requests." Some Muslim religious scholars also criticized Muslims' devotional practices at tombs; one disapprovingly described practices of "kindling lights, kissing the tombs and covering them with fragrance, addressing the dead with needs, writing formula on paper with the message 'Oh Lord, do such and such for me.'" Such critiques demonstrate that despite the protests of religious officials, Muslims and Jews shared a culture of devotion at the tombs of their holy dead.

Pilgrimage, or religiously motivated travel, was important in all three religious traditions. Jerusalem had a central role for pilgrims of all faiths. Jews traveled to Jerusalem and focused their devotions on the remains of the Herodian temple walls. The primary destination of Muslim pilgrims was Mecca, but during the Umayyad period, pilgrims came to Jerusalem to visit Muslim holy places—the Dome of the Rock and al-Aqsa Mosque—as well as more general monotheistic sites commemorating Mary, Jesus, Zachary, and David. Christian pilgrims had been traveling to Jerusalem since the fourth century; these journeys continued in the eighth, ninth, and tenth centuries, although the typical pilgrim route gradually shifted from the north, through Byzantine territory, to the south, through Egypt. One Frankish pilgrim, Bernard the Monk, in 867 began his journey in Rome, where he joined a Spaniard and an Italian. The group traveled overland to Muslim-ruled Bari, where they embarked on ships packed with Christian slaves taken in raids on southern Italy and destined for the slave markets in Alexandria. The companions had to pay fees to the governors of Alexandria and Cairo and then proceeded overland to Jerusalem; Bernard praised the security of travel in the Islamic world and indicated that there was regular Christian pilgrim traffic through the southern Mediterranean. Rome and Constantinople's relic collections made them important secondary destinations for Christian pilgrims. Orthodox patterns of pilgrimage focused on great churches, relics, and icons in Constantinople, on the monastic settlements in Mount Athos or Meteora, and the tomb of St. John the Evangelist in Ephesus.

Muslims, Christians, and Jews did not just share the practice of pilgrimage; they venerated the same holy people and places in a shared sacred geography that stretched across the Mediterranean, with a dense network of holy sites in the east and relatively fewer in the west. John the Baptist, revered as one of the apostles by Christians, was also venerated as a prophet by Muslims, who called him Yahya b. Zakariya. The saint's shrine inside the Great Mosque of Damascus attracted both Christian and Muslim worshippers. Christian monasteries in Syria and Egypt attracted Muslim as well as Christian pilgrims; for instance, St. Catherine of Sinai had a special hostel for Muslim pilgrims. Abu Ayyub al-Ansari, one of the companions of the Prophet, died while accompanying a Muslim army to besiege Constantinople: he was buried under the walls of the city, and many authors reported his tomb became

a site of veneration for Greeks, who would pray for rain during periods of drought. Rarely, Christians and Muslims shared not just sites but actual spaces of worship. In the eighth and ninth centuries, there was a debate among Muslim scholars over the use of Christian churches as places of prayer; the debate indicates that it was not at all unusual for Muslims to visit and pray in Christian churches. In the Byzantine Church of the Kathisma, between Jerusalem and Bethlehem, archaeologists have tentatively identified a mihrab, or Muslim prayer niche, added in the eighth century.

RELIGIOUS INSTITUTIONS: MONASTERIES AND RIBATS

Islam and Christianity had similar types of religious institutions with the general purpose of spiritual retreat: monasteries and ribats. The first known ribat, constructed at Monastir in North Africa, was a converted monastery. There were strong similarities between the two institutions, but ultimately the monastery and the ribat served very different roles. Ribats began as a combination of frontier fortress, hostel, and religious retreat; their function shifted over time, but in the initial phases the military aspect predominated, and it only gradually took on the role of a sanctified site. Monasteries developed in a very different direction; what began in late antiquity as sanctified retreats from society became progressively more involved in the political and economic world around them. And whereas monks and nuns

Shrine of St. John the Baptist inside the Umayyad Mosque, Damascus. Muslims revered St. John the Baptist as Yahya b. Zakariya. Early traditions hold that the head of John the Baptist was unearthed during Umayyad caliph al-Walid's destruction of a Byzantine church. His shrine can still be seen inside the main prayer hall of the mosque. *Photo: Manuel Cohen / The Art Archive of Art Resource, NY*

took vows that bound them for life to their monasteries or convents, Muslim men would reside temporarily in ribats to fulfill religious duties; there were no parallel institutions for women in the Muslim world.

By the ninth and tenth century many monastic centers in western Europe had become economic and political powerhouses. Monasteries following the Benedictine rule spread widely; the majority were founded north of the Alps as part of the Carolingian religious revival, but there were also significant monasteries in southern Italy and Catalonia. The monks of these establishments took on public functions, their abbots were deeply involved in local and international politics, and the houses themselves controlled significant lands and resources. The monastic complexes were economically self-sufficient and had guest quarters to offer hospitality to visiting dignitaries. Latin Christian monasteries were also centers of learning; many monasteries educated secular children, and the great houses all possessed libraries and scriptoria, where monks studied and copied manuscripts. Beginning in the tenth century, the Cluniac reform movement tried to return these monasteries to their origins and to enforce the Benedictine rule, with varying success. Monasteries in Coptic Egypt kept the Coptic language and literature alive and provided the foundation for Christian intellectual activity in Egypt. Monasteries in Syria and Palestine continued to operate as well. In contrast, there is no evidence of Mozarabic monasteries in Muslim territory in Spain.

Monks and monasteries played a significant role in Byzantine society. The greatest numbers of monasteries were clustered in Constantinople itself, about 75 during the ninth and tenth centuries, and in the Holy Mountain regions of Olympos and Athos. Monasteries for women were overwhelmingly located in Constantinople itself. Byzantine monasteries were deeply influenced by mysticism; as in the west, some monasteries participated in reform movements. In one reform initiative, Theodore of the Stoudios monastery in Constantinople advocated a return to Basil the Great's idea of a working community of monks, with manual labor joined to prayer. He also reorganized the administrative structure of large monasteries, composing poetic verses describing the duties of each official. As was the case in the Latin west, monasteries began in the tenth century to acquire large tracts of land through purchase and through imperial and private donations, and they added hostels and houses for the poor to their complexes. Byzantine emperors several times tried to limit or forbid land acquisitions by monasteries, although these measures were eventually repealed. Unlike their western counterparts, Byzantine monasteries did not provide general education, although some monasteries did have scriptoria and libraries.

In contrast to the urban monasteries of Constantinople, ribats were typically located along Muslim-Christian frontiers and were concentrated along the North African coast, on the Syrian-Anatolian border, and around Sicily. In these institutions, Muslims performed their pious duty of standing guard on the borders in defense of Islam, the defensive counterpart to the offensive ideology of jihad. While on watch, the volunteers engaged in religious devotions, and they could earn spiritual merit by standing guard for their whole lives or for a few days. Like monasteries, ribats were autonomous economic concerns—supported by fields, mills, cisterns, income from rental houses, baths, and shops. Building or endowing a ribat was a pious act, and many wealthy merchants did so. In early ribats, volunteers practiced strict asceticism, living in cells furnished only with water skins and leather mats, but by the tenth century Ibn Hawqal recorded complaints that the early discipline had evaporated and that the Sicilian ribats in particular were full of hypocrites, not the truly pious. Ibn Hawqal's report is, of course, biased, as he was a Fatimid spy and the Sicilian ribats had become a place of refuge for Sunni opponents of the Fatimid regime.

Shared religious sanctities and parallels in religious life must be placed alongside frontier conflict between the Byzantine and Abbasid empires. Ribats on the Syrian-Anatolian border served as bases of operation for the Abbasids' regular raids on Byzantine territory. The frontier district housed resident soldiers settled in towns who received salaries from the government and small plots of land. Each summer and fall, volunteer fighters from across the Muslim world traveled to the district for the campaigning season, and their costs were supported by private charitable donations. Several Muslim scholars and intellectuals fought on the frontier in the ninth century and composed formal treatises that elaborated on the Qur'anic idea of jihad, developing it from something that served the state to an individual responsibility. The leading figure among these warrior-scholars was Abu Ishaq al-Fazari, author of the *Kitab al-Siyar* (Book of the Law of War), which treated practical questions such as the division of spoils as well as praising the merits of past generations of frontier fighters. Another influential warrior-scholar, Abdallah b. al-Mubarak, composed the *Kitab al-Jihad* (Book of Jihad), which considered jihad as a kind of ascetic practice that lay in the intention of the practitioner and was a responsibility for every pious Muslim. His book circulated in al-Andalus under the title *The Book of the Merit of Jihad*, spreading the ideas of holy war developed on the eastern frontier to the western Mediterranean as well.

On the Byzantine side of the frontier, there was a failed attempt by the great frontier warrior and then emperor Nikephoros Phokas to develop a Byzantine version of holy war. Nikephoros proposed that Byzantine warriors fighting Muslims should receive special religious merit, but this proposal was blocked by the ecclesiastical establishment because of their resistance to the sacralization of violence. Despite the church's official attitude that war was a necessary evil, ninth-century military writings and the popularity of military saints reflect beliefs that soliders were divinely protected and could recieve spiritual rewards for their actions in battle.

Ideologies of warfare against the unbeliever were developed along a stabilized frontier dotted with institutions of accommodation as well as war. In the ninth and early tenth centuries, the towns of the border regions were centers of commercial contact, and merchants used safe-conducts to travel back and forth. Slaves, renegades, and volunteers from each side filled the ranks of the other; many were bilingual in Arabic and Greek; and goods, ideas, horses, and women crossed borders in both directions. Even the armies that faced each other across frontiers were made up of heterogeneous groups. Both sides relied on mercenary troops for skills and tactics they did not themselves possess, incorporating Armenians, Slavs, Greeks, Bedouin, and Turks, who brought knowledge of particular skills and tactics.

One of the most institutionalized frontier exchanges was the ransoming or exchange of prisoners taken in annual land and sea raids. These exchanges took place along the three main frontiers: on the Syrian-Anatolian border, in Sicily and southern Italy, and in the north Iberian peninsula. Al-Maqdisi describes the regular redemption of prisoners at ribats along the coast of Syria and Palestine; as Byzantine ships arrived laden with captives, "Drums were beaten on the city keep, calling the populace down to the ribat on the shore, the people hurried out in force . . . and then the ransoming began." Ibn al-Athir describes a similar exchange in Anatolia in 830: "The Muslims and the [Byzantine] prisoners who were with them assembled at the river, and the Greeks arrived with their prisoners . . . When the Muslims set one prisoner free, the Greeks also released one Muslim prisoner to them; both met in the middle of the river and [then] each went to rejoin his own people." Exchanges involved large numbers of noncombatants: in 938 the Byzantines reportedly offered 6,300 men and women for redemption along the Syrian-Anatolian border, and al-Mas'udi lists 12 meetings where Muslims redeemed between 2,000 and 6,000 captives on each occasion. Not all of those captured returned to their original homes. Some disappeared into anonymity in the slave markets of Venice or Alexandria while others built new lives and careers. In 923, al-Mas'udi estimated that there were 12,000 Christianized Arab horsemen in the Byzantine military, and several high-ranking Byzantines, notably Leo of Tripoli and Damian of Tarsus, converted to Islam and had successful military careers in Muslim armies.

The redemption of captives was carried out by the state and also by individual religious communities. Bishop Nicolas of Myra traveled to Crete to redeem Christian captives there, and the bishop of Cyprus reportedly ransomed 16,000 Cypriots in 805–6. Jewish law held that it was a mitzvah, a charitable act, to redeem captive coreligionists, and the Cairo Genizah documents are full of references to redeeming captives. A Jewish historian and philosopher from Toledo, Abraham Ibn Daud, recounted a story of four Jewish scholars from Bari who were captured by pirates working for the Spanish Umayyad caliph 'Abd al-Rahman II. Each scholar was ransomed by a different Jewish community: the scholars spread to Alexandria, Tunisia, and al-Andalus. For Ibn Daud, the point of the story was to explain the transfer of Rabbinic authority from Babylonia to the west, but it also indicates the frequency of capture and redemption and the diasporic effects of these redirected journeys.

THE RISE OF RELIGIOUS ORTHODOXIES

While on a popular level there were shared elements, religious hierarchies and institutions struggled with questions of doctrine and sectarianism. Three broad issues caused contention within and among Christian, Jewish, and Muslim communities. First, the role of images in religious worship combined with politics in Byzantium to cause significant turbulence, which also affected Latin Christians, Jews, and Muslims. Second, each faith confronted controversies over religious and secular leadership of the community. The sharpest division over the right to lead the faith community was between Sunni and Shia Muslims, but disagreements over the authority of emperor, patriarch, pope, and rabbis divided Christian and Jewish groups as well. Finally, conversion and the role of religious minorities affected individuals from all three faiths in the increasingly Islamic southern Mediterranean and drove a competition between Orthodox and Latin Christians to claim the Balkans for their own particular branch of the faith.

Controversies over the use of images in religious worship, and over figural representation in art more generally, appeared throughout the Mediterranean in the eighth century. Jewish, Christian, and Islamic religious texts all contain passages discouraging or forbidding the production or display of figurative art in religious contexts. Attitudes to these prohibitions varied widely across time and place, but during the eighth and ninth centuries the use of figural representations in religious worship became a matter of great debate and struggle. The Islamic conquest of Syria and Palestine changed the balance of power, and as a new equilibrium between the three monotheisms shifted, the use or avoidance of religious images became a touchstone for redefined religious identities. In Islamic and Christian contexts, theological matters intersected with Byzantine and Umayyad state-building, particularly in attempts to assert state power over religious life. Early Islam firmly opposed idol worship, a principle that led some to oppose representations of all living forms.

In Byzantium there was a clear shift in ideas about images in religious worship around 680. Worshippers came to view images, and particularly icons, as containers of the holy. These representations of Christ, Mary, and the saints became as important as relics, and worshippers addressed prayers to these sacred portraits. While a tiny proportion of icons were thought to be miraculously or divinely produced, the vast majority were created by artists or artisans. A church council in Constantinople stated the matter plainly in 692 when it decreed that "Christ our God should be set forth in images in human form." Byzantines turned to these powerful works of art as protection against the many crises that beset the empire in the seventh century, including plague, earthquakes, and the attacks by the Slavs and Bulgars from the north and Umayyads from the east. These new ideas about the spiritual power of images caused a backlash among theologians, who struggled to distinguish between praying to an icon and worshiping a false idol. Questioning the idea that a representation painted on wood could transmit a believer's prayers to the saint portrayed, some churchmen contended that honoring icons was blasphemous.

In the decade after the failed Umayyad siege of Constantinople in 718, leaders in both the Byzantine and Umayyad world rejected established ideas about the role of images in sacred space. Scholars have frequently pointed out that the theological concerns that animated Byzantine and Umayyad concerns over images were

Mosaic floor with human figures removed, Church of St. Stephen, Umm ar-Rasas, Jordan. Originally there were donor portraits below the Greek inscriptions in this eighth-century floor, but human figures were later removed. About 60 churches in Syria-Palestine have floors with changed or removed human and animal figures, but the reasons behind these alterations remain obscure. While the images are within the sacred space of a church, they are not icons—images of Christ, Mary, or the saints—and thus are distinct from anti-icon sentiments in the Byzantine Empire. The same destruction occured to images in synagogues. *Photo: Jane Taylor/Art Resource, NY*

quite different, but the timing suggests the entangled nature of state and society in both regions. Historians traditionally date the beginning of the iconoclasm movement in Byzantium to 726, when Emperor Leo III reportedly had his soldiers tear down a golden icon of Christ from the main ceremonial entrance to the imperial palace and issued edicts against displaying icons. More recent research has cast doubt on the incident, which is only recorded in later sources composed in defense of the pro-icon position. Nonetheless, it is clear that by the 730s there was growing sentiment against icons and some instances of clergy physically removing icons from churches had been reported. The Umayyad caliph Yazid II is also said to have issued an edict in 721 that targeted Christian symbols and images of living beings.

Struggles over icons were deeply intertwined with Byzantine imperial politics, and Leo's son Constantine V combined iconoclastic policies with a series of successful campaigns in western Anatolia, consolidating the link between military victory and iconoclasm. At the Synod of 754, more than 300 bishops and Constantine himself agreed to ban sacred images outright. Some figural representations were replaced with mosaic crosses in Byzantine churches, but ultimately iconoclasm was a complete failure. The ban on icons lasted until 787, when the empress Irene came to power and reversed imperial policy, condemning iconoclasm and restoring icons. Iconoclasts returned to power and revived the ban on icons, in a modified form, from 815 to 842. The Synod of 843, supported by the empress Theodora, restored icon worship, which then became a characteristic piece of eastern Christian spirituality. The result of these struggles was that after the mid-ninth century the sacred spaces of Byzantine Christianity and Islam were easily distinguished from one another.

Controversies over religious imagery were intertwined with disputes over the balance of sacred and secular authority. In banning and then restoring icons, Byzantine rulers exercised what they perceived as their right to direct the spiritual course of the empire. When Germanos, the patriarch of Constantinople, disagreed with Leo's opposition to icons, Leo deposed him, installing another, more-agreeable patriarch in his place. The emperor claimed the power to depose not only patriarchs but also the pope in Rome, and in 649 Emperor Constans II had Pope Martin I abducted and deposed because of a theological controversy. Subsequent popes relied on the growing political loyalty of Italians and Romans; when the emperor Justinian II tried to impose eastern church practices regarding clerical marriage, fasting, and representations of Christ in 691, a Roman mob defended the pope against imperial officials. In the 730s, Pope Gregory II, already enmeshed in a protracted struggle over Byzantine taxation of papal lands in Italy, not only rejected Leo's position on icons but also refused to recognize the new patriarch and insisted that Christian doctrine could not be determined by a layman. Subsequent popes continued to protest Byzantine emperors' involvement in doctrinal matters, arguing that secular, political forces should not legislate theological issues or call church councils. While emperors deposed and appointed patriarchs virtually at will, the Roman pope acted as an independent political and religious force in these years, turning to the Frankish Carolingians rather than to the Byzantines for military protection.

Even after 843 and the final restoration of icons, contests over religious authority continued to divide Rome and Constantinople. When Emperor Michael III deposed Patriarch Ignatios in 858 and replaced him with Photios, Pope Nicholas I convened a council and deposed Photios. In the subsequent exchange of threats and insults, Michael complained about the barbarity of Rome while Nicholas made expansive claims for the reach and precedence of papal power and denounced imperial interference. The controversy was exacerbated by the ongoing competition between Latin and Greek missionaries to convert the Balkans and central Europe. Mutual excommunications flew between pope and emperor, and while the matter was formally resolved, it highlights the growing cultural and theological divide between eastern (Greek) and western (Latin) Christian realms.

In Islam, the caliph was the theoretical embodiment of both religious and secular authority, but strong disagreements over who was eligible for the position divided the Muslim faith community from an early stage. Shia believed leadership of the Islamic community could only belong to ʿAli and his descendants and thus rejected the legitimacy of the Umayyad caliphs. Furthermore, the Umayyads were not theologians but political and military leaders. From the eighth and ninth centuries, a group of religious scholars, called the ulama, gradually came to hold religious authority in Islamic society. The ulama were sometimes employed by the state as counselors, ambassadors, or judges, but their authority came from their knowledge of law, theology, and above all the hadith traditions. The ultimate source of guidance for Muslims was, of course, the Qurʾan, but as it was silent on many important matters, Muslims turned to the hadith, or the sayings and actions of Muhammad. These traditions about the prophet were at first transmitted orally, and the ulama were experts not only in what this large and sometimes inconsistent body of material contained but in the chains of transmission that traced the story back to its originator, usually one of the Prophet's wives or companions. The Abbasid caliph in the ninth century briefly attempted to assert his right to intervene in doctrinal disputes, but he failed in the face of determined resistance from religious scholars. From that point on, the ulama, not the caliphs, were the ultimate source of religious authority in Muslim society.

In the ninth and tenth centuries, scholarly opinion crystalized into several separate "schools" or approaches to Islamic law. The differences between the schools arose from the differing balance each assigned to the Qurʾan, the hadith, customary practice, and judicial reasoning. The earliest "founders," Malik b. Anas and Ibn Hanbali, were the most influential in North Africa and al-Andalus, where a majority of jurists were Malikite. Egyptian jurists were strongly influenced by al-Shafiʾi, who moved to Egypt in 814 and wrote influential legal commentaries there. The real division lay not between these various law schools, who all gave a role to sunna, or practice of the community, but between these "Sunnis" and the Shia, who relied on a divinely guided individual, the imam. This division was made most clear in the Mediterranean by the rise of the Fatimids, whose leader claimed to be not only the caliph but the imam as well. The Sunni ulama in North Africa played an important role in resisting Fatimid rule, and the ulama as a group were generally active in politics, with the exception of al-Andalus, where they acted as civil servants or remained aloof from politics entirely. The political disintegrations of the tenth and eleventh centuries in the Islamic world helped to consolidate the power of the ulama. Dynasties of religious specialists developed and joined the urban elite in organizing and governing cities in the absence of ever-changing dynasties.

There was also a debate within Judaism over correct doctrine and leadership of the community, although the division affected a fairly small number of people. The majority of Jews looked to rabbis as community leaders and as arbiters of law. The rabbis were experts in the Mishnah, collections of oral commentaries on the Talmud, the Hebrew sacred scriptures. The Kararites, originally from Iraq, rejected the authority of the rabbis and the oral law, instead looking to the Talmud alone as a source of religious guidance. The Kararites arrived in the Mediterranean world in the early ninth century, and they had small but significant communities in Jerusalem and Egypt. Kararites and Rabbinites differed on the ritual calendar, on dietary laws, and on the details of synagogue worship. There were moments of open hostility between the two groups, particularly during the Feast of the Tabernacles on the Mount of Olives in Jerusalem, when, according to Abraham Ibn Daud, Rabbinites and Kararites would encamp opposite one another, "like two little flocks of goats." The Rabbinites would then take out a Torah scroll and excommunicate the Kararites by name. But there was also a great deal of social contact: Rabbinite and Kararite Jews intermarried, lived side by side, and collaborated on the redemption of captives and the collection of taxes.

The religious diversity of the Mediterranean led to shared religious practices, but it also led to hostility and violence between representatives of different religious groups. On an intellectual level, this hostility can be seen in the polemics between religions, which in this period occurred most often in the Muslim world. Christian-Muslim polemics were concerned with a few key issues: the Trinity and the incarnation of Jesus, Muhammad's status as a prophet, and the Qur'an as a legitimate book of revelation. John of Damascus, the defender of icon veneration, also wrote against Islam, which he categorized as a heresy rather than as a new religion. He castigated Muhammad as a false prophet, ridiculed Islamic doctrines or practices, and told scurrilous stories about Muhammad, selectively quoting from the Qur'an. At the other end of the Mediterranean, the anonymous author of the *Ystoria de Mahomet*, composed in southern Spain, also portrayed Muhammad as a perverter of Christian doctrine while at the same time demonstrating familiarity with the Qur'an and with the doctrines of Islam. These polemical texts aimed to critique and convert rather than to inform or to spur open-minded intellectual exchange.

Polemical debates between defenders of orthodoxy unfolded in person as well as in texts. In Egypt the converted vizier Ibn Killis held weekly interconfessional discussions where Muslim, Jewish, and Coptic Christian theologians debated religious matters. The prominent place of Jewish advisers in Muslim government gave rise to real resentments among Muslim populations, and intellectual debate sometimes gave way to scurrilous literary attacks and physical violence. Abu Ishaq, who lost his official position in Granada and blamed the Jews for his fall, wrote a bitterly anti-Semitic poem against Samuel's son Joseph and the Jewish community, saying, "I came to live in Granada and I saw them frolicking there. They divided up the city and the provinces with one of their accursed men everywhere. They collect all the revenues, they munch and they crunch." The poem, which was widely circulated, charged that the Jews had broken the dhimmi pact and thus could and should be killed. In 1066, Joseph and other Jews of Granada were murdered in a popular riot that turned into a massacre. Across the Mediterranean, another eleventh-century Jewish adviser, Abu Sa'd Ibrahim ibn Sahl al-Tustari, served the Fatimids in Egypt before his assassination. His downfall was preceded by popular anti-dhimmi agitation, apparently sparked by a popular verse that criticized Jewish influence: "The Jews of this time have attained their utmost hopes and have come to rule. Honor is theirs, wealth is theirs too, and from them come the counselor and ruler." In these cases, it is difficult to distinguish resentment over religion from economic and social tension.

By the beginning of the eleventh century, the Mediterranean was linked together by economic and cultural networks of exchange that crossed political and religious frontiers. Against this background of regular cross-cultural interaction, there were moments of conflict and hostility between adherents of different faiths, although disputes within religious communities were just as common. In the later eleventh and twelfth centuries, new groups arrived on the shores of the Mediterranean from the north, south, and east, bringing with them new approaches to religious identity and ushering in an era of warfare justified in religious terms.

CHAPTER FOUR

Reshaping Political Communities

Christian and Muslim Holy Wars

I n 1080 the Norman noblewoman Matilda married Raymond of Toulouse, a warrior and nobleman from the south of France. The wedding, celebrated with elaborate rituals on the bride's home island of Sicily, brought together two families that were part of the Latin Christian elites who became increasingly dominant in the eleventh-century Mediterranean. Matilda's father, Count Roger of Sicily, was a member of the Hauteville clan, a Norman family whose ancestors had come from Scandinavia. At the moment of the marriage, Roger had been fighting for 20 years to extend Norman rule over Muslim Sicily; nearby, in southern Italy, Matilda's uncle Robert was battling Lombards, Muslims, and Greeks to extend his dominion there. The Normans were relative newcomers to the Mediterranean region; the groom's family, however, had deep roots in Languedoc, in the south of France. The marital ties of Raymond's extended family crisscrossed southern France and northern Iberia, bringing the counties of Barcelona and Toulouse into close contact. Matilda and Raymond's marriage was part of a larger assimilation strategy that connected the recently arrived Normans to trans-Mediterranean structures of local power.

The marriage was short-lived. By 1094 Raymond had remarried, this time to Elvira, the illegitimate daughter of Alfonso VI of León-Castile. The male kin of both of Raymond's brides, Matilda and Elvira, were deeply involved in warfare justified through religious motives. Alfonso alternately allied with and fought against his Muslim neighbors to the south. In 1085, he took the city of Toledo, ushering in a new era of Christian conquest in Iberia. Raymond, Matilda's cousin Bohemond of Taranto, and many other southern French and Norman warriors all led contingents of crusading armies to Syria and Palestine to fight against Muslims there. Over the next two centuries, violence in the name of religion would repeatedly reshape the political landscape of the Mediterranean.

Since the eleventh century, people have debated the nature, motivation, and significance of the Crusades, and there is a vast body of literature on the subject. The disagreements begin with definitions. Some historians, called traditionalists, consider only campaigns fought to recover or defend Jerusalem as crusades, while others, labeled pluralists, think of the Crusades as a particular type of Christian holy war, thus including campaigns in Iberia, the Baltic Sea region, and Anatolia as well as Palestine and Syria. Leading historians also hold widely differing views on what motivated the crusaders. Was it genuine religious fervor, hope for material gain, anti-Islamic sentiment, political considerations? Islamic states and Muslim individuals also fought in the name of their faith during this period. The ideology of jihad was revivified by the crusaders' conquests in Syria and Palestine, and twelfth- and thirteenth-century Islamic leaders used this concept of holy violence to motivate conquest of Christian-ruled territories.

In this chapter we take a broad approach to the phenomenon of religiously motivated warfare in the medieval Mediterranean, considering Muslims and Christians who fought in the name of their faiths between 1050 and 1220. Whether within the framework of Christian crusade or Muslim jihad, the potent combination of religion and military power played a significant role in state formation. The changes were most intense at the two ends of the sea, in Iberia and the Levant, where Islamic and Christian political realms came into contact with one another. The long-term outcomes of these two encounters were very different. In the east, along the Byzantine-Islamic frontier, armed pilgrims from the Latin west arrived and established crusader kingdoms in Syria and Palestine. These kingdoms gradually gave way to Islamic states—first Ayyubids, then Mamluks—that relied on jihad ideology to mobilize their armies to conquer crusader-held lands. In the west, along the Iberian frontier, conflict between Islamic and Christian states initially took place within a framework of political and cultural familiarity, where aggression alternated with alliance. By the early thirteenth century, newly powerful Christian states deploying the rhetoric of crusade and reconquest had permanently expanded their rule through almost all of Iberia, leaving the kingdom of Granada as the last Islamic outpost north of Gibraltar. In all these frontier societies, armed struggle against a religious other coexisted with accommodation, alliance, and cooperation across religious boundaries, which is the subject of the next chapter.

NEW CONTENDERS FOR POWER FROM THE PERIPHERIES

Norman adventurers from northern Europe arrived on the shores of the Mediterranean ready to find a fragmented political space; like other new arrivals from the peripheries of the classical world, they combined mercenary service with military campaigns fought on their own behalf. The Seljuk Turks, a nomadic people originally from Central Asia and led by the Seljuk family, had been moving into Anatolia, Syria, and Palestine gradually over the course of the tenth century. Turks were often employed as mercenaries by the Fatimids and Byzantines, and by the early part of the eleventh century, Turkish frontier-raiding parties reached eastern Anatolia and northern Syria. In 1071 the Byzantine emperor Romanos Diogenes, needing a military victory to secure his shaky hold on the throne, led an army to the fortress of Manzikert, located at one of the main entry points to eastern Anatolia. The Seljuk sultan Alp Arslan was in the region, and the two armies met in battle. The Byzantine army, composed of foreign mercenaries as well as Byzantine troops under the command of generals opposed to Romanos, fragmented during the battle, and the emperor was captured. The Byzantine defeat led to a widespread civil war in which the various contenders for power each called on Turkish troops for support, hastening Turkish penetration into Anatolia. By the 1090s, a branch of the Seljuks was established at Nicaea; other Turkish leaders took control of Smyrna, and Turkish troops dominated a patchwork of Anatolian territories. These conquests were followed by Turkish migration and settlement in the region.

The Seljuks did not immediately press their advantage in Anatolia because their chief military target lay to the south. As Sunni Muslims, they saw the Shia Fatimid dynasty as the principal threat to Muslim orthodoxy and aimed their attacks at Syria rather than Byzantium. The Seljuks commanded support among the Muslim populations of northern Syria and Palestine. Aleppo surrendered to the Seljuks in 1071, and sultan Alp Arslan's successor, Malikshah, took Damascus and Palestine in 1078 and Antioch in 1084. The conquest involved pillaging and massacres of local populations, including but not limited to Christians and Jews. Under Malikshah and his powerful vizier Nizam al-Mulk the Seljuk realm was relatively unified, but after his death, in 1092, principalities began to assert their independence.

The Seljuk attacks hit the Fatimid dynasty just as it was struggling with natural disaster and political instability. Drought caused intermittent famine in the 1060s, followed by a devastating civil war between Turkish and black troops in the Fatimid army in the late 1060s and early 1070s. In 1073, Caliph al-Mustansir called on Badr al-Jamali, a freed slave of Armenian origin, to restore order. As vizier, Badr used his personal army of Armenian Christians and Turks to restore order, and he became the de facto ruler of the Fatimid state, introducing a period of conflict over succession and resulting weaknesses in border defense.

Like the Turks, the Normans had a reputation as fearsome warriors and were much in demand as mercenaries. The historian Robert Bartlett has argued that western European elites, including the Normans, had several mutually reinforcing advantages: military technologies like the use of heavy cavalry, archers, and castle building combined with the social importance of knighthood to drive an aristocratic diaspora that spread western European influence far beyond the old Carolingian heartlands. In southern Italy, Norman mercenaries benefited from the deep divisions among Byzantine, Lombard, and independent powers. By 1059 much of southern Italy was under Norman rule. Pope Nicholas II recognized

الجاهل من ظن العلم هما شاملا بلدة الرزف واخرى مل الى السواد ولخد الهما انظر الى الجوى واخرى الى اسفل وكان اسنانه دقيقة حاذة الرؤس وكار وجهة كوجه الاسد وكان شجاعا عاجرا على الحروب مناصله بنرس الله الرودة

Seljuk manuscript illustration, thirteenth century. A miniature from al-Mubashshir's *Mukhtar al-Hikam* depicts a Turkish sultan on his throne. *Topkapi Palace Museum, Istanbul. Photo: Bridgeman-Giraudon / Art Resource, NY*

بأب لكتاب الاسكندر الملك الحكيم ملك طول دنيا

Robert Guiscard as the duke of Apulia, Calabria, and Sicily, giving papal sanction to continued Norman expansion at the expense of Greeks, Lombards, and Muslims and exacerbating the growing rift between the Latin and Orthodox churches. Robert's brother Roger, whom one chronicler described as "avid for dominion," began the conquest of Sicily in 1061. The initial Norman advance was as military support for the emir of Catania, Ibn ath-Thimnah, and the Normans relied on their Muslim Sicilian allies for support through most of the conquest. After establishing a bridgehead near Messina in 1061 and defeating a defending army sent from Tunisia in 1063, Roger and his Normans proceeded slowly across the rest of the island. Palermo fell in 1072, and Roger spent the next 20 years conquering the rest of the island.

Norman ambitions stretched from southern Italy and Sicily to the Byzantine east. Robert Guiscard had pursued a strategy of alliance with Michael VII Doukas, one of the contenders for power in the Byzantine civil wars that followed Manzikert, and Michael VII's 1078 overthrow gave Guiscard and his son Bohemond an

84

THE MEDITERRANEAN WORLD

excellent excuse, buttressed by a papal blessing, to launch an attack on Byzantium's Balkan territories. In 1081 the Normans took the city of Dyrrhachium (Durazzo or Durrës) in Albania, followed by the island of Corfu in 1084. Dyrrhachium, at the head of the main road across the Balkans to Constantinople, was a key strategic position, and the new Byzantine emperor, Alexios I Komnenos, rushed to defend it, suffering a serious military defeat at Norman hands. In order to induce the Venetians to offer naval assistance against the Normans in the Adriatic, Alexios I granted them a commercial quarter in Constantinople and trading concessions, a precedent for later commercial treaties in the Mediterranean. The immediate Norman threat to Byzantium ended with Robert Guiscard's death, in 1085, but Normans and Turks continued to be employed as mercenaries in Byzantine armies.

Byzantium suffered a serious reversal of its fortunes in the eleventh century. At the death of Basil II, in 1025, the empire controlled southern Italy, the Balkans, and Anatolia. By 1080 the empire had lost all of Italy, part of the Balkans, and most of Asia Minor. There was clearly a failure of leadership, as one imperial contender followed another after Basil II's death. Historians continue to debate the underlying structural causes for this crisis: some have pointed to struggles between civilian and military aristocracies and growing instability among the empire's elites; others have looked to the increased control of great landowners over peasants and their property. These shifts in state and society coincided with near-simultaneous attacks on Byzantine frontiers from the Seljuks in the east, the Normans in the west, and the Turkic Pechenegs from the north. After 50 years of difficulties, Alexios I slowly pacified the Balkans and restored stability in state and society, a process his successors continued into the twelfth century.

In the west, Alfonso VI of León-Castile conquered Toledo in 1085, marking the beginning of widespread political change in Iberia. Alfonso was already quite familiar with the city: during a brief period of exile, he had lived in Toledo under the ruler al-Mamun's protection. In a turn of the tables, after returning to power in León-Castile in 1072, Alfonso took the new ruler of Toledo, al-Qadir, under his protection. Al-Qadir commanded little support from his own elites and was under constant pressure from rival *taifa* (party or faction) states; in 1085, Alfonso and his troops occupied the city with the consent of at least a portion of the city's elite. While it was more the outcome of practical politics than ideological commitment to holy war against the infidel, Alfonso's capture of Toledo sent shock waves through al-Andalus. 'Abd Allah, the exiled king of Granada, wrote in his memoirs that the city's fall "filled the inhabitants with fear and despair." Al-Qadir of Toledo was not alone in his dependence on Christian military and political aid, and many Andalusians were increasingly critical of the taifa kings' willingness to form alliances with Christians and their payment of huge tributes (*parias*) in return for security. In the earlier eleventh century, the poet Ibn Hazm caustically denounced these taifa kings: "By God, I swear that if the tyrants were to learn that they could attain their ends more easily by adopting the religion of the cross, they would certainly hasten to profess it!" The flow of gold from south to north weakened the taifa states at the same time it strengthened the fledgling kingdoms of the north, setting the stage for the Christian kings' incursions into al-Andalus from the second half of the eleventh century on.

Like Byzantines, Lombards, and Sicilians, the taifa kings relied on mercenary troops rather than expanding local military participation to fight in their wars. By the eleventh century those mercenaries were often Christians from the northern kingdoms. By far the most famous of these mercenaries was Rodrigo Díaz de Vivar, known as El Cid. Like the Normans in southern Italy and Sicily, Díaz benefited from the political fragmentation of the region. He began his career fighting for the kings of León-Castile, but Alfonso VI exiled him in 1081 for his too-enthusiastic raids on Toledo. Díaz then entered the employ of the Muslim king of Zaragoza, where he fought against the Christian count of Barcelona and the king of Aragon. After a decade of shifting alliances, Díaz won the taifa state of Valencia for himself in 1094. His career demonstrates the possibilities for individual mercenaries to make their fortunes fighting for both Muslim and Christian rulers and the unstable nature of political and military allegiance in this period.

After the fall of Toledo, the taifa kings realized they were in a vulnerable position and looked to other powers in the Muslim world for help. Directly across the Strait of Gibraltar, the growing strength of the Almoravid Empire seemed to offer a solution. The armies of the Almoravids, a confederation of Berber tribes from the Saharan borderlands, had won a series of victories that spread their empire from Ghana to Algiers and Oran in northwestern Africa. The name Almoravids is derived from al-Murabitun, "people of the ribat," a reference to the armed monasteries on the frontiers of the Islamic world (see chapter 3). The dynasty traced its roots to the legal scholar Ibn Yasin, who was invited by the Almoravid leadership to act as a sort of missionary of orthodox Islam in North Africa, a project he wanted to pursue through jihad as well as preaching. Ibn Yasin and his followers condemned using secular justice rather than religious law, collecting taxes not sanctioned in the Qur'an, and employing Jews and Christians in senior administrative posts. A series of Almoravid leaders used Ibn Yasin's spiritual authority to unify their subjects and to justify their territorial expansion into North Africa.

For the Almoravids, political motives and religious explanations for violence were deeply intertwined. In response to the taifa kings of al-Andalus's request for help, the Almoravid leader Yusuf ibn Tashfin crossed into Iberia in 1086. He summoned the Andalusian Muslims to join his armies in a holy war and defeated a Christian army at the battle of Zallaqa, in the west of Iberia. Unfortunately for the taifa kings, the strict and legalistic religious outlook of the Almoravids caused them to judge the taifas' alliances with Christians and other transgressions of Islamic law as harshly as the poet Ibn Hazm had. Ibn Tashfin returned twice more to al-Andalus, but his subsequent expeditions were aimed at the taifa kings themselves, whom the Almoravids systematically deposed and exiled. At the turn of the twelfth century, the Almoravids dominated the Mediterranean coast of Iberia as far north as Zaragoza, conquered in 1110, and reached over to the Balearic Islands in 1116.

CHRISTIAN IDEAS OF HOLY WAR
AND THE FIRST CRUSADE

In 1095, Pope Urban II issued a call to crusade at the Council of Clermont. Urban was not the first to propose justifications for holy war against infidels, nor was the First Crusade the first armed expedition that relied on faith to justify violence. Urban followed the reform policies of his papal predecessors Leo IX, Alexander II, and Gregory VII, all of whom promoted the belief that armed service to the church was spiritually beneficial and that fighting itself could be a penitential act for a warrior. In the decade preceding Urban's call, theoretical discussions on the Christian use of violence were spread to the laity during campaigns against Muslims in Iberia and Tunisia. The 1087 Pisan and Genoese attack on the Tunisian city of Mahdia, for instance, combined piety with hopes of plunder and commercial advantage. In 1089, Urban himself told Catalans that colonizing Tarragona, on the frontier south of Barcelona, was a penitential act equivalent to the Jerusalem pilgrimage, declaring, "It is no virtue to rescue Christians from Muslims in one place, only to expose them to the tyranny and oppression of the Muslims in another."

At Clermont, Urban merged these ideas of spiritually beneficial violence with an appeal to liberate the city of Jerusalem, as well as eastern Christians, from Muslim rule. By adding Jerusalem as the goal, Urban linked the enterprise to the penitential power of pilgrimage. The numbers of western Christian pilgrims to Jerusalem increased in the eleventh century. Several pilgrim groups fell afoul of the state of lawlessness and political disorder in the Muslim east, and news of these attacks exacerbated Christian shock and dismay at the Fatimid caliph Hakim's destruction of the Church of the Holy Sepulchre in Jerusalem, in 1009. While the Byzantines had partially rebuilt the church by 1050, there remained a strong sense that the sacred sites of Jerusalem were under threat. In a letter to Flanders, Urban wrote, "We believe that you, brethren, learned long ago from many reports, the deplorable news that the barbarians in their frenzy have invaded and ravaged the churches of God in the eastern regions." Western sources also recount Byzantine emperor Alexios I's appeals to Urban for military aid against Turkish invaders; some scholars have questioned whether Alexios actually asked for aid, but Urban certainly urged western elites to help Alexios against the "pagans."

Western Europeans responded in large numbers to Urban's proclamation of crusade and the promise that they could atone for their sins through participation. Individuals who took vows affirming their intention to liberate Jerusalem had crosses stitched onto their clothing, and crusading was referred to as "taking the cross." A series of armies left for Constantinople, the rendezvous point, over the course of 1096 and 1097. The armies included nobles and knights but also many noncombatants who had responded to Urban's call to armed pilgrimage with enthusiasm. The earliest forces, associated with the charismatic preacher Peter the Hermit, proceeded to Constantinople and were massacred in their first engagement with the Turks. The second wave, with more effective military contingents, arrived at Constantinople in the winter of 1096–97. The Byzantines were surprised and threatened by the larger-than-expected numbers of the western armies and offered a lukewarm welcome. Estimates vary, but historians calculate that the army included between 30,000 and 80,000 fighting men; noncombatants raised the total number to 70,000–100,000. Alexios I extracted oaths of loyalty from the leaders of the armies and then encouraged them to cross into Anatolia individually, so the first time the various armies coalesced was under the walls of Turkish-held Nicaea in June 1097, where the crusaders had their first victory.

Historians continue to debate what motivated these crusaders. Urban II's declaration at the Council of Clermont highlighted the importance of religious intent: "Whoever for devotion alone, not to gain honor or money, goes to Jerusalem to liberate the Church of God can substitute this journey for all penance." Anna Komnene, a Byzantine historian, argued, "The simpler folk were in very truth led on by a desire to worship at our Lord's tomb and visit the holy places, but the more villainous characters . . . had an ulterior purpose." Some critics of the crusaders found crusading piety to be false, a cover for material ambitions. While crusaders did compete for the spoils of sacked cities, the historian Jonathan Riley-Smith has pointed out that crusading was an expensive enterprise, and many crusaders had to sell property to finance their expeditions, so it is unlikely that profit was the sole motive. Other historians have pointed to the prospect of gain from precious goods, slaves, or ransoms, or the more intangible benefits of glory and prestige. Individuals who took the cross did so for a complicated mix of reasons: compelled by conscience, religious leaders, or peers and family members or drawn to seek privilege and power.

The crusaders, knowingly or not, had arrived at a moment of extreme political disarray in the Islamic world. In addition to the ongoing struggle between the Seljuks and Fatimids for control of Syria and Palestine, all of the region's major political leaders had recently died. In 1092 the powerful Seljuk vizier Nizam al-Mulk was murdered by Nizari Assassins, and a month later the Seljuk sultan Malikshah died under mysterious circumstances, closely followed by the rest of his immediate family. In 1094 the 58-year reign of the Fatimid caliph al-Munastir ended with his death, and his powerful vizier Badr al-Jamali died the same year. These disruptions in rule allowed local powers to gain independence, so the crusaders' arrival was met with concern but no unified defensive effort.

The majority of the crusader forces were led by aristocrats from northern France, but Godfrey of Bouillon, Robert of Flanders, and Stephen of Blois were joined by the Mediterranean lords Raymond of Toulouse and Bohemond of Taranto, who had briefly been linked by marriage a decade earlier. The Byzantine emperor offered financial and military assistance to the crusading army as it fought its way across Anatolia and into northern Syria in 1097. While Godfrey's brother Baldwin of Boulogne and Bohemond's nephew Tancred veered off to conquer the inland city of Edessa, the main body of the army proceeded to Antioch and placed the city under a prolonged siege. Acute food shortages and disease threatened the army's survival, and the withdrawal of Byzantine forces caused hostility and feelings of betrayal between Latins and Greeks. The city fell on June 3, 1098, but was almost immediately besieged in turn by Kirbogha of Mosul. At this low point in crusader fortunes, visions of Christ and the discovery of the Holy Lance revived the crusaders' morale, and bolstered by religious fervor they defeated the besieging army and consolidated their hold on the city.

The crusading forces remained at Antioch for months, at first to avoid the summer heat and then paralyzed by disagreements among the leadership. Finally, pressure from the rank-and-file crusaders forced the march to resume in the early spring of 1099. The armies moved quickly down the coast, turned inland at Jaffa, and overcame water shortages and divisions among the leadership to take Jerusalem on July 15. The crusaders sacked the city and massacred its Jewish and Muslim inhabitants, and the sources testify to the enthusiastic pillage and the religious exultation of the victors. Raymond of Toulouse's chaplain recounted that "in the temple and the porch of Solomon, men rode in blood up to their knees and bridle reins. Indeed, it was a just and splendid judgment of God that this place should be filled with the blood of the unbelievers, since it had suffered so long from their blasphemies." Another author said, "Our men rushed round the whole city, seizing gold and silver, horses and mules, and houses full of all sorts of goods and they all came rejoicing and weeping from excess of gladness to worship at the Sepulcher of our Savior Jesus, and there they fulfilled their vows." Sources also recounted that even those who sought sanctuary in synagogues and in the al-Aqsa Mosque were killed. By the thirteenth century, Muslim historians were recounting the desecration of the Temple Mount and al-Aqsa Mosque in lurid terms, some saying that the Franks had killed between 70,000 and 100,000. Historians now believe that while thousands of Muslim and Jewish men, women, and children were killed, the actual number of dead was much lower than these sources reported. On August 12, the crusaders defeated a large Fatimid counterinvasion at Ascalon, consolidating their hold on the region.

The crusaders had achieved their goal of liberating Jerusalem, and in the winter of 1099–1100 many began to return to western Europe. Those who stayed found themselves in a vulnerable position: the two enclaves of Antioch and Jerusalem were separated by hundreds of miles. As the chronicler Fulcher of Chartres observed, "There were not enough people to defend it from the Saracens if only the latter dared attack us." But fleets from Genoa, Pisa, and Venice soon began to attack coastal cities, conquering Jaffa, Haifa, Caesarea, and Acre. In 1123 the crusaders won a naval victory over the Fatimids off Ascalon, and Tyre fell soon thereafter. The victory marked a turning point for Christian naval supremacy, as the Fatimids lost access to the forests of Lebanon as well as ports to resupply their ships. It is important to note that Italian trading posts in the Levant predated the Crusades; some older scholarship attributed the maritime republics' assistance to the crusaders to a desire to force open new markets, but it is much more likely that the Italians were motivated by the same mix of piety and self-interest that applied to other crusaders.

The Venetians, Genoese, and Pisans did receive trading privileges and commercial quarters in the coastal cities, which became centers of exchange as well as bases for the arrival of new troops and supplies from western Europe.

The crusaders who remained established four separate states: Tripoli, Antioch, Edessa, and the Latin Kingdom of Jerusalem. Following Bohemond of Taranto, Norman leadership dominated in Antioch, while the southern French following Raymond of Toulouse established the coastal principality of Tripoli. The northerner Godfrey of Bouillon was the first prince of Jerusalem, although he refused the title of king; after his death, in 1100, his brother Baldwin came from Edessa to take the position and the title. Baldwin began the process of establishing the institutions of rule in the kingdom, including a chancellery, a legal system, and an ecclesiastical hierarchy. The crusade leaders in each principality embarked on massive building programs of port facilities, town fortifications, monasteries, and churches. They generally took over preexisting institutions of government such as tax collection and customs offices. Outside the towns, the crusaders built castles that acted as kernels for new rural settlements. These kingdoms, collectively known as Outremer (over-the-sea), were frequently riven by factionalism, power struggles between elites, and the kings of Jerusalem's difficulty in establishing a clear line of succession.

Two particular religious orders with a military focus emerged from the needs and circumstances in the Latin east. The Hospital of St. John, a monastic complex that offered assistance to the holy poor, existed in Jerusalem before the crusaders arrived. While the process by which the Hospitallers acquired a military branch is unclear, by 1136 the organization had a constable and brothers-at-arms and were able to staff the castle of Behtgibelin. A second military order, the Templars, began in 1119–20 as a military brotherhood with the aim of securing the pilgrim roads to and from the holy places. The knights were recognized in 1129 as an official order of the church, although there was some resistance to the idea of an order of monks who prayed and then rode out to kill their enemies. Both Hospitallers and Templars grafted the idea of holy violence onto monastic organization: the knights took vows of poverty, celibacy, and obedience and lived and prayed as part of a community. In contrast to most crusaders, their crosses were not the sign of a temporary undertaking but a lifetime vocation. While their origins lay in the crusader kingdoms, the two orders quickly spread across the Mediterranean and into western Europe. The actual numbers of Templar and Hospitaller knights was very limited: each order had about 300 at any given time. To fulfill their purpose of defending roads and settlements, the orders employed mercenary soldiers. For instance, at the Hospitaller castle of Krak des Chevaliers there were as many as 2,000 fighting men but only 60 brother knights. Castles and mercenaries were enormously expensive, so the Hospitallers and Templars developed networks of convents in Europe that produced wealth and transferred it east.

Both military orders and the ideal of crusading spread to Iberia in the early twelfth century, where it was used to legitimate and justify Christian kings' wars against Muslim neighbors. A Pisan-Catalan expedition, sailing under a papal crusading indulgence, attacked the Muslim Balearic Islands in 1114. Alfonso I of Aragon, relying in part on the assistance of French knights returning from crusading ventures in the east, attacked and conquered Zaragoza in 1118, also with a papal crusading indulgence for those who died in the conflict. In addition, Alfonso organized military orders for frontier defense. Members of the Confraternity of Belchite swore to "never make peace with the pagans, but let them strive for all their days to harass and insult them, except for those who are under the lordship of the Christians." Alfonso's crusading zeal was reflected in his last will: since he died in 1134 without heirs, he left his kingdoms of Aragon and Navarre to the Hospitallers, the Templars, and to the Order of the Holy Sepulchre. These orders had given up their claims to the Spanish kingdoms by the 1140s, but they had acquired significant property in Iberia as a whole. While scholars disagree on whether there was any direct influence, Christian military orders bore some similarities to the Muslim ribat: both institutions combined the idea of religious war and rewards in the afterlife with an ascetic, prayerful common life, and both were used to garrison frontier regions.

Iberian monarchs used crusading rhetoric and institutions in order to promote their own campaigns of territorial expansion, but historians continue to debate the relationship between Iberian and Near Eastern enterprises. Many Iberian monarchs deployed the idea of the Reconquista (reconquest), or taking back the Visigothic heritage lost to Muslim invaders centuries earlier. Some clerics explicitly connected the fight against Iberian Muslims with the fight to recapture Jerusalem. Archbishop Diego Gelmírez of Santiago issued this passionate call to arms in 1125: "Just as those soldiers of Christ and faithful sons of the church opened up the road to Jerusalem by much toil and bloodshed, so we should become soldiers of Christ and after defeating his enemies, the evil Saracens, let us with his grace beat a shorter and much less difficult path through the regions of Spain to the same Sepulcher of the Lord." Spain's patron, St. James, was depicted as a knight of Christ slaying Muslims, in keeping with a more aggressive and militant vision of Christianity that characterized the mid-twelfth century. But Christian monarchs alternated antagonism with alliance in their dealings with Muslims.

A SECOND WAVE OF HOLY WARRIORS IN THE EAST AND WEST

By the mid-twelfth century, the descendants of the first waves of conquerors had settled into their new homes, assimilating to some local social and cultural practices and engaging in local political struggles. But both Iberia and Syria-Palestine saw a second influx of religiously motivated invaders who sought to emulate the successes of their predecessors. Almoravid power in southern Iberia and in North Africa was challenged and eventually replaced by the religiously fundamentalist Almohads, while the Second Crusade pulled crusaders from across northwestern Europe and sent them to the Slavic regions in the north, southern Portugal, and the Holy Land.

St. James of Compostela. In this thirteenth-century relief from the cathedral of Santiago di Compostela in Spain, St. James has been transformed from his earlier depiction as a pilgrim to a more militarized saint, sword in hand. *Photo: Album / Art Resource, NY*

The Almohads in the Maghreb were led by the charismatic Ibn Tumart, who united the Berber tribes into a common enterprise, legitimating political and military domination through religious authority. Like the Almoravid founder, Ibn Yasin, Ibn Tumart condemned North African Muslims' departures from Islamic norms and customs, but Ibn Tumart was influenced by the Persian philosopher and mystic Abu Hamid al-Ghazali rather than by strict legalism. In 1125, Ibn Tumart was acknowledged as the Mahdi, the "rightly guided one" responsible for bringing God's order and justice into the world. His supporters, the Almohads, followed his calls for religious and political reform and his declaration of jihad against Jews and Christians as well as the Muslim Almoravids. Ibn Tumart's successor, 'Abd al-Mu'min, led the Almohads to victory over the Almoravids in Marrakesh in 1147. In Iberia, Andalusian support for the Almoravids was rapidly waning and many regions were in open rebellion. In this atmosphere of political unrest, the Almohads pressed their advantage and took many western Iberian territories. In eastern Iberia, an adventurer named Muhammad ibn Mardanish, known as El Rey Lobo (King Wolf) to the Christians, rose to power in Murcia and Valencia in part through alliances with Castile and Aragon. Christian subsidies, clever diplomacy, and military skills kept his principality intact until 1172.

THE MEDITERRANEAN WORLD

A Second Crusade, motivated by the fall of Edessa in 1144, began recruiting armies in 1146–47, but this endeavor lacked the single-minded unity of purpose that the First Crusade had shown for Jerusalem. Armies traveling under crusading banners attacked a variety of targets. Genoese, Catalan, and Norman forces won victories in the western Mediterranean. English crusaders captured Lisbon, and the Genoese captured Almeria in 1147. The port brought clear commercial advantages for Genoese merchants, but the Genoese described their mission in terms of holy war, saying they were "advised and summoned by God." Genoese and Catalan armies also besieged Tortosa, south of Barcelona. While not formally part of the Second Crusade, Normans from Sicily captured the Fatimid city of Mahdia in 1148, with the help of the Muslim renegade admiral George of Antioch. The Sicilians governed the port, benefiting from the Saharan trade and the Fatimid textile factories, until the Almohads conquered the city in 1160.

The French and German crusading armies that did make it to the eastern Mediterranean arrived in Constantinople in 1147–48 and proceeded separately across Turkish Anatolia. The German army was shattered by Turkish attacks and massacred; survivors joined the French army, which also sustained heavy casualties but made it to the Latin states, where they found a civil war brewing between Queen Melisande of Jerusalem and her son Baldwin III. In a decision historians still find puzzling, the crusaders chose to besiege Damascus. Poor military preparations and strategy, and factional politics between supporters of Melisande and Baldwin spelled disaster for the expedition, which retreated in July 1148 after a siege of only four days. The outcome was truly disastrous for the Christian forces, causing a significant breach in trust between western powers and the leadership of the Latin states.

How did the Islamic world react to the crusaders? Their initial success was certainly shocking, but only a few isolated voices called for immediate unified Muslim action against the Christians. The most prominent of these was the Syrian jurist al-Sulami, who preached in the Umayyad mosque in Damascus that the Muslims had suffered defeat at the hands of the Christians because they had abandoned their religious duties. Al-Sulami's *Book of Holy War* laid out the necessity for Muslims to engage in the "greater jihad," repentance and spiritual struggle against one's baser self, before undertaking the "lesser jihad," physical struggle against the enemies of Islam. He had a clear understanding, unlike many of his contemporaries, of the differences between the western Europeans (Franks) and the Byzantines, and he also perceived the Crusades as part of a larger pattern of Frankish movement from Spain to North Africa to the Levant: "A group [of Franks] pounced on the island of Sicily in a moment of discord and mutual rivalry and they conquered in like fashion one town after another in Spain." These views did not have a widespread effect on his fellow Muslims, and campaigns against Frankish crusaders in Syria and Palestine remained individual initiatives or temporary coalitions for the first decades of the twelfth century, as it served Seljuk and Fatimid authorities well to have buffer states along their principal frontier.

Council of Acre and siege of Damascus, twelfth-century miniature from William of Tyre's *Histoire d'outre-mer*. Above, the leaders of the Second Crusade and the kingdom of Jerusalem debate strategy at the Council of Acre (1148); below, crusader heavy cavalry heads toward the Muslim city of Damascus. *Photo: HIP / Art Resource, NY*

Nur ad-Din (Nurredin), a Turkish leader based in Aleppo, revived the idea of jihad in order to legitimate his conquest of the region and to motivate a unified response to the Frankish states. His father, Imad ad-Din Zengi, had been responsible for the 1144 conquest of Edessa. Nur ad-Din embarked on a campaign of conquest and unification in northern Syria, combining aggressive political strategies with the skillful use of religious propaganda emphasizing his role as the leader of a jihad against the enemies of Islam. The failure of the Second Crusade allowed him to take Damascus in 1154. Nur ad-Din patronized religious scholars and used mystics, lawyers, Qur'an readers, and preachers in his armies to highlight the religious aspects of fighting. At his request, Ibn Asakir composed the popular treatise *Forty Hadiths for Making Jihad*. Nur ad-Din built and endowed madrasas, hospitals, and mosques; these monuments included inscriptions describing him as a fighter of jihad. He had an elaborate pulpit (minbar) made in Aleppo, covered with jihad inscriptions that, among other things, declared his intention to relocate the pulpit to Jerusalem. The rise of Zengi and Nur ad-Din threatened the other Muslim states of the region as well as the Latin states, and the Muslim elites who ruled Damascus signed a treaty of alliance with the Latin Kingdom of Jerusalem, demonstrating that political pragmatism could trump religious unity even in the Latin east.

The power of the Fatimid dynasty was rapidly failing. Attacked in the east by Normans and in the west by the Latin Kingdom of Jerusalem, which took the stronghold of Ascalon in 1153, the dynasty also suffered from schisms at its center. After al-Mustansir's

Minbar from Almoravid Spain. Every congregational mosque has a minbar (pulpit), where the imam preaches his Friday noon sermon. Most were elaborately carved and decorated, as is this example from a mosque in Cordoba. *Badia Palace, Marrakesh. Photo: Erich Lessing/Art Resource, NY*

death, in 1094, the powerful vizier made his younger son, al-Mudtanir, caliph, passing over the elder son, Nizar. This action contradicted previous Fatimid practice and Shia understandings of the legitimate succession of imams. A breakaway group called the Nizaris actively resisted the new Fatimid caliphs, relocating to Iran and adopting a practice of murdering prominent political and religious figures in Mesopotamia and Syria. By the early twelfth century, the Nizaris were operating in Aleppo and Damascus, and their leader established a mountain stronghold at Alamut. The so-called Assassins killed the next Fatimid caliph-imam, al-Amir, in 1130; in the ensuing turnover of leadership, rival viziers came to dominate Fatimid politics. In 1163–64 one vizier asked for Nur ad-Din's assistance while his rival called on King Amalric of Jerusalem, and by 1168 both Frankish and Muslim armies were headed for Egypt.

Nur ad-Din's army was under the command of the Kurdish Shirkuh, who blocked the Frankish invasion. Shirkuh's nephew Salah al-Din (Saladin) took over for his uncle in 1169, taking control of the Fatimid state and abolishing their caliphate in 1171. Following Nur ad-Din's example, Saladin pursued the political objective of Muslim unity through a strategy of Sunni religious orthodoxy and the promotion of jihad ideology. At great cost to himself, Saladin eliminated all unlawful taxes; while removing Shia from power, he also patronized mosques, religious schools, and Sufi establishments. In 1174, Nur ad-Din's death left the way clear for Saladin to establish his own dynasty, the Ayyubids, over both Syria and Egypt, creating a united front against the Latin states. The Latin states, meanwhile, were worn down

eratur treuge ad
t ad certamen: Quod
m de populatur.
mandatur.
exin est felix. dus een
nouebit. hurc de nunciar
cest

fto qiunto feilicet & quarto nonar tulit infra
octauar aploz petri & pauli. euafit etiam ab
hac clade theodoricuf magifter milicie templi.

The Horns of Hattin. Saladin and the king of Jerusalem, Guy de Lusignan, struggle over the true cross in a depiction of the battle at the Horns of Hattin (1187) from a thirteenth-century Latin Christian manuscript. *Courtesy of Master and Fellows of Corpus Christi College, Cambridge*

by constant Muslim military pressure, financial difficulties, and ongoing dynastic conflicts and factional tensions among the different rulers of the region.

Saladin won a series of important victories against the crusader states. Using Egypt as a base, he began construction of a fleet to challenge Christian naval dominance; the navy was defeated at Tyre in 1187, but that defeat was more than balanced by Saladin's stunning victory at the Horns of Hattin in the same year. Saladin's attacks on Tiberias pressured the new king of Jerusalem, Guy of Lusingnan, to rush to that city's aid across an arid plateau in the height of summer. The vast majority of the Christian force was killed or captured, including King Guy and the master of the Templar Order. Saladin ordered all of the Templars and Hospitallers executed, although other crusader barons were offered for ransom. The thousands of soldiers who could not afford the price of redemption were sold into slavery, leaving the Latin states almost completely bereft of fighting men. In the weeks following Saladin's victory, city after city surrendered—Ascalon, Acre, and finally, in October 1187, Jerusalem itself. The Latin states were reduced to the three vulnerable coastal enclaves of Tyre, Tripoli, and Antioch.

Saladin's conquest of Jerusalem caused delight throughout the Muslim world and despair in western Europe. According to the Iraqi historian Ibn al-Athir, a picture circulated in the west showing Christ being struck in the face by an Arab. In response to what they saw as a devastating loss, three of the most powerful monarchs in Europe—the Holy Roman emperor Frederick I Barbarossa, Philip II Augustus of

France, and Richard I the Lionheart of England—set out on the Third Crusade in 1189. Frederick's army left Constantinople and traveled overland, skirmishing with Byzantines and Turks but getting as far as Christian Armenia before Barbarossa drowned in a bizarre accident while crossing the river Saleph. Deprived of leadership, the German crusading contingent crumbled, and many returned home. The French and English forces arrived by sea, stopping at Sicily to retrieve Richard's widowed sister Joan and, after some struggle, her dowry. When a part of Richard's fleet was shipwrecked on Cyprus, the Byzantine rebel ruling there seized the ships and imprisoned the survivors. In retaliation, Richard's troops mounted an assault on the island; meeting little resistance, they established direct crusader rule, to the consternation of the Byzantines. The capture of Cyprus in 1191 initiated almost four centuries of Latin rule there, creating a useful food source, military and naval base, and eventual refuge for the crusader states.

When the French and English contingents reunited outside of Acre, they discovered that leadership in the Levant was divided between Guy of Lusignan, who had been released from captivity after his devastating defeat at Hattin, and Conrad of Montferrat, who had organized a heroic defense of Tyre. In July 1191 the combined Christian forces retook Acre and, crucially, captured Saladin's fleet, crushing his attempt to develop maritime power. Philip and the French crusaders departed soon after the victory, leaving Richard to attempt the reconquest of Jerusalem. While his forces won several victories and recovered part of the coast for the Latin Kingdom, Jerusalem remained out of his grasp. Before departing, Richard signed a truce with Saladin that guaranteed Christian pilgrims protected access to the holy sites of Jerusalem. Richard also attempted to resolve the persistent factional infighting among the Latin elite over the kingship by recognizing Conrad of Montferrat as king while giving Guy of Lusignan Cyprus as a consolation prize. The Lusignan dynasty quickly took root on the island, while Conrad's victory was cut short by two Assassins, who killed him in the streets of Tyre in April 1192.

Both Richard the Lionheart and Saladin developed reputations as outstanding examples of medieval chivalry. From the thirteenth century, Saladin became a heroic figure in western European literature, representing an idealized noble adversary for the crusaders in general and for Richard in particular. Crusade epics and romances praised Saladin for his clemency, generosity, hospitality, and justice. He appears alongside classical heroes in Dante's *Inferno* as a "good pagan." In the Arabic tradition, Saladin's reputation was carefully curated immediately after his death; unusually, two of his close advisers, Imad al-Din and Baha al-Din ibn Shaddad, wrote biographical accounts of his career. But by the thirteenth century, the Iraqi historian Ibn al-Athir questioned Saladin's commitment to fighting the Franks, and in the Islamic world his reputation paled in comparison to Nur ad-Din and the Mamluk sultan Baybars.

The Third Crusade had achieved significant victories and assured the continuing survival of the Latin states, which also benefited from the competition that erupted among the Ayyubids after Saladin's death, in 1193. Rather than pressing their military advantage, the sons and successors of Saladin treated the Franks as potential allies, signing commercial and political treaties with some Christians and engaging in border skirmishes with others. Over the next decades, Christian forces headquartered at Acre were able to regain some of the territories lost to Saladin, and their control of commerce in Mediterranean port cities meant a continued economic relationship with the Muslim hinterland. By the mid-thirteenth century, the Franks of the Levant were fully integrated into the political map of Syria and Palestine, dominated by several competing factions of quasi-indigenous ruling elites vying for power.

NEW MONARCHS, NEW STATES

Significant changes in the structure of religious and political authority occurred in both the Christian and Islamic worlds at the turn of the thirteenth century. The Abbasid caliph al-Nasir, who began his reign in 1180, wanted to reestablish the caliphate as the religious and political focus of the entire Islamic world. He developed an integrative vision of Islam that brought together Sunni and Shia under the umbrella of Sufism, arguing for the importance of religious unity among Muslims. In order to create a greater sense of social solidarity, he unified and reorganized the system of the *futuwwa*, groups of men bound by a common honor or moral code and following a single master, sometimes but not always acting as urban gangs or militias. Al-Nasir reformed the organization and placed himself at the head, using the futuwwa as a means of political power in service of the caliphate. The Ayyubids never fully accepted al-Nasir's innovations, but they provided a competing focus for Muslim loyalty and allegiance.

In the Latin west, Pope Innocent III made expansive claims for the administrative and legal reach of the papacy, as well as for its spiritual authority over all Christians. Crusading was part of this program: in addition to his 1198 call for a new crusade to retake Jerusalem, he also offered crusading indulgences to fight against heretics and secular lords who displeased him. In response to Innocent's proclamation, a group of French and Flemish barons committed to the eastern crusade and sent envoys to Venice to negotiate passage for an estimated 33,500 soldiers. The Venetians duly constructed a fleet to transport the crusading army east, but the force that arrived in Venice in 1202 was two-thirds smaller than had been anticipated, and the crusaders were not able to pay the Venetians what had been promised for their transport. What happened next is the subject of intense controversy among historians; what is clear is that Pope Innocent had lost control of the crusade's progress. When the fleet carrying the crusaders arrived at the Christian city of Zara, which had rebelled against Venetian rule, the crusaders bowed to Venetian pressure and agreed to sack the city in return for partial forgiveness of their debts. Then Alexios, a Byzantine prince claiming to have been wrongfully excluded from the throne, appeared and offered payments and aid to the crusading army in return for help regaining his position. The army's leaders agreed to help and sailed to Constantinople, but when Alexios was unable to pay what he had promised, the cru-

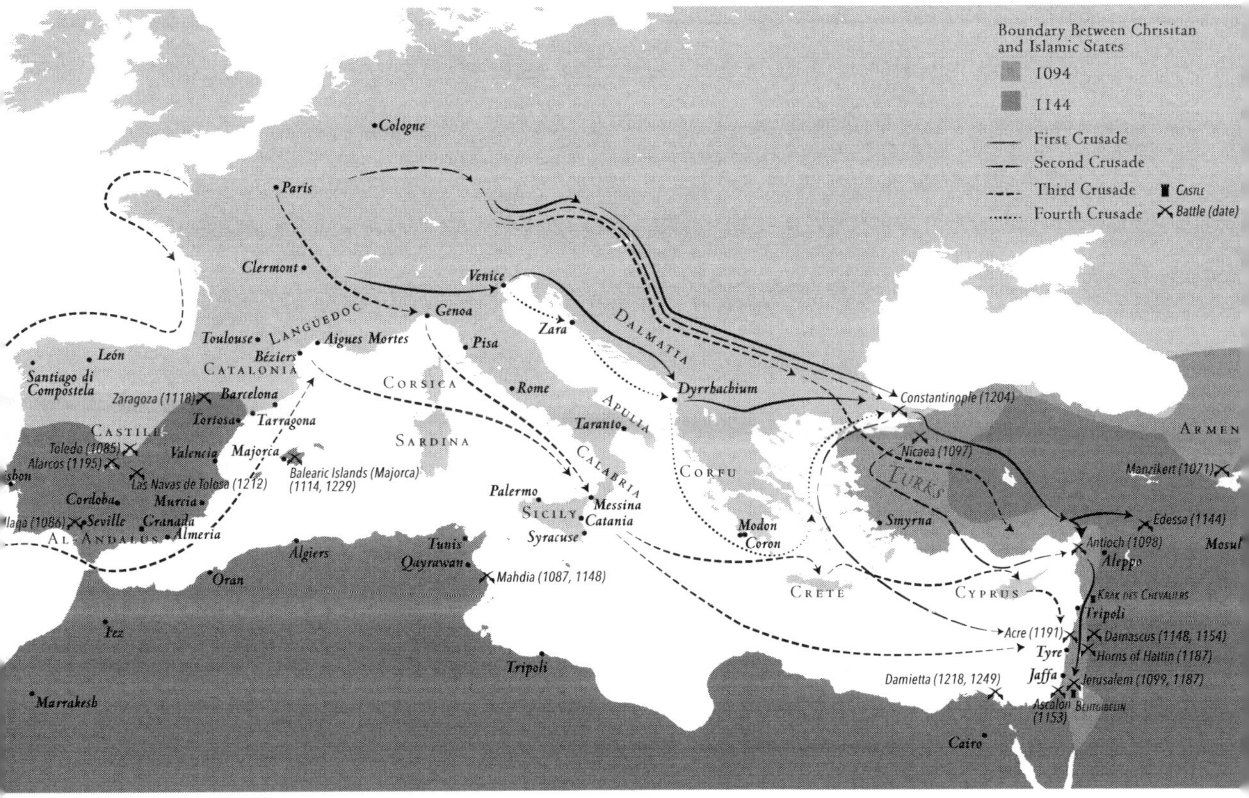

Boundary Between Chrisitan and Islamic States
1094
1144
First Crusade
Second Crusade
Third Crusade
Fourth Crusade
Castle
Battle (date)
Cologne
Paris
Clermont
Venice
Genoa
Zara
Dalmatia
Toulouse
Languedoc
Aigues Mortes
Béziers
Catalonia
León
Santiago di Compostela
Zaragoza (1118)
Barcelona
Pisa
Corsica
Rome
Apulia
Dyrrhachium
Constantinople (1204)
Tortosa
Tarragona
Castile
Toledo (1085)
Alarcos (1195)
Valencia
Majorca
Balearic Islands (Majorca) (1114, 1229)
Sardina
Taranto
Calabria
Nicaea (1097)
Turks
Manzikert (1071)
Las Navas de Tolosa (1212)
Murcia
Cordoba
Seville
Granada
Almeria
Al-Andalus
Palermo
Sicily
Messina
Catania
Syracuse
Corfu
Modon
Coron
Smyrna
Edessa (1144)
Antioch (1098)
Aleppo
Mosul
Algiers
Tunis
Qayrawan
Mahdia (1087, 1148)
Oran
Crete
Cyprus
Krak des Chevaliers
Tripoli
Acre (1191)
Damascus (1148, 1154)
Tyre
Horns of Hattin (1187)
Jaffa
Jerusalem (1099, 1187)
Damietta (1218, 1249)
Ascalon (1153)
Beitgibelin
Cairo
Fez
Marrakesh
Tripoli

Holy War in the Mediterranean

saders and Venetians sacked the city and established themselves as rulers of Constantinople and its territories. Some scholars see in these events a series of difficult decisions and accidents while others find evidence of a prearranged conspiracy.

The Latin army pillaged Constantinople with shocking savagery. Niketas Choniates, a Byzantine eyewitness and civil servant, narrated the horrific events of the sack, describing the crusaders' smashing of icons and holy relics and assaults on the city's population: "There were lamentations and cries of woe and weeping in the narrow ways, wailing at the crossroads, moaning in the temples, outcries of men, screams of women, the taking of captives, and the dragging about, tearing in pieces, and raping of bodies heretofore sound and whole." There had been growing estrangement between Latin and Greek Christians over theological issues and the Latins' perception of Byzantine indifference or treachery toward Latin crusaders and Latin states. On the Byzantine side, Emperor Andronikos II had risen to power on a wave of anti-Latin sentiment that erupted in riots in Constantinople in 1182. The outcome of the Fourth Crusade poisoned relations between eastern and western Europe for centuries and demonstrated the transformation of the crusading ideal into a weapon to be used against Christian enemies.

The Fourth Crusade completely reversed the political pattern of the northeastern Mediterranean. Long the only unified state in a politically fragmented region, Byzantium was shattered by the fall of Constantinople, leaving a disjointed frontier divided between remnants of Byzantium, Frankish crusader lords, and Venetian colonial possessions. One of the leaders of the crusade, Boniface of Montferrat, gave his claims over Crete to the Venetians in return for Thessalonica, in central Greece, where he established an independent kingdom. Venice took the ports of Modon (Methoni) and Coron (Koroni) in addition to Crete, and individual Venetians and crusaders seized territories in the Peloponnese and Aegean islands. Byzantine aristocrats also set up competing successor states centered at Trebizond (Trazbon), Nicaea, and Epirus. At Nicaea, the Byzantine noble Theodore Laskaris gained the support of both the Orthodox clergy and many of the old elite; he was crowned Byzantine emperor in 1208. His successors pursued the reconquest of Constantinople at the same time that Byzantine government in exile underwent structural changes and simplifications. By the time that Michael VIII Palaiologos retook Constantinople, in 1261, and reestablished it as the capital of a Greek-speaking, Orthodox state, the Byzantine Empire had been irreversibly changed. No longer an expansive multiethnic empire, it was now a compact Balkan state with only a few Anatolian outposts.

The reputation of crusading in Europe suffered another serious blow with the disastrous Fifth Crusade. Pope Innocent imagined an expedition under papal control with a bureaucratic and centralized organization, carried out in close cooperation with secular powers; he also expanded the spiritual benefits of crusade, asking those who could not physically travel east to contribute through fasting and prayer. Proclaiming that those who paid to outfit and supply a crusader could share in the crusading indulgence, crusade preachers spread out across northern Europe, and many monarchs as well as common people took the cross. Hungarian, Austrian, and German leaders all answered the call, but many contingents only stayed for a single season, meaning that the army of the Fifth Crusade was highly changeable, growing and shrinking seasonally with departures and arrivals.

In the summer of 1218, the crusading army arrived on the Egyptian coast and began to besiege the port of Damietta. The Ayyubid ruler of Egypt, al-Kamil, beset by internal dissent and competition with his brothers in Syria and Mesopotamia, offered the crusaders a deal: leave Egypt and he would return the kingdom of Jerusalem. They rejected the offer, and by the fall of 1219, the blockade of Damietta had weakened the city enough for the crusaders to seize it. Once the crusading army was in possession of the port, dissension within the leadership and conflict over the spoils of victory weakened the army's cohesion. While the crusaders remained in Damietta for more than a year, al-Kamil constructed a fortress at Mansurah, blocking the route south to Cairo. It was not until the summer of 1221 that the army left Damietta to confront Egyptian troops, not taking into account the flood patterns of the summer Nile. Disastrously, the army was bogged down between two branches of the river and had to accept al-Kamil's terms for surrender. In exchange for their lives, the crusaders handed back Damietta and left Egypt in disgrace, bringing the Fifth Crusade to an ignominious end.

The transformation of Christian crusade into a politicized enterprise can be seen in the different ways three long-reigning thirteenth century European monarchs used crusades as part of their own state-building efforts. The count-king James I of Barcelona-Aragon conquered a significant swath of the western Muslim Mediterranean, including the Balearic Islands and the kingdom of Valencia. Frederick II, king of Sicily and Holy Roman emperor was both a successful crusader and an excommunicated heretic, illustrating the complex problems created by papal use of crusading indulgences against religious and political enemies. King Louis IX of France benefited from the outcome of the Albigensian crusades, which extended royal power to southern France, and went on two separate expeditions to North Africa in 1248 and in 1270. Each of these examples demonstrate the difficulty of disentangling religious and political motivations in thirteenth-century crusading.

James I of Barcelona-Aragon mixed crusading rhetoric with mercantile motivations in his western Mediterranean expansion. Only a few decades before he came to the throne in 1213, Almohad power in Iberia had been at its height. Taking advantage of deep divisions among the principal Christian powers in the region, the Almohads defeated Alfonso VIII of Castile at Alarcos in 1195 and took the Balearic Islands in 1203. But Almohad fortunes collapsed as quickly. Aided by Pope Innocent III's recruitment efforts for the Fifth Crusade, Alfonso's Castilian army was reinforced by French knights at the battle of Las Navas de Tolosa, in 1212. The outcome of that battle was a resounding Christian success and a crippling blow to Almohad military power, shattering the fragile unity the Almohads had imposed on southern Iberia and western North Africa. In addition to the military consequences of the defeat at Las Navas de Tolosa, the Almohad leader Yusuf II's death in Morocco in 1224 led to a succession crisis that the Christian rulers of Spain exploited to the hilt.

It was in the post-Almohad collapse that James launched the Catalan conquest of the Balearic Islands. In 1229 a fleet of Catalan and southern French ships attacked Majorca and quickly took the main city of Mayurqa, renaming it Palma. The other Balearics soon fell into Catalan hands as well: James I convinced Minorca's Muslims to surrender in return for the right to govern themselves and to practice Islam freely, while Ibiza was captured in 1235 by a private expedition led by the archbishop of Tarragona. In mainland Iberia, James used a combination of diplomacy and force to take the coastal towns and tighten the noose around Valencia. Valencia was ruled by Zayyan ibn Mardanish, who had taken control in the post-Almohad confusion. James used a combination of sea and land forces to besiege the city into surrendering in 1238 and then continued his march south, taking Murcia in 1266 but then ceding that city to Castile.

Aragonese, Castilian, and Portuguese conquests in al-Andalus meant that by 1250 the kingdom of Granada was the lone remaining outpost of Muslim rule in Iberia. The dynasty that ruled there was known as the Nasrids, after the kingdom's founder, Muhammad ibn Yusuf ibn Nasr. The kingdom survived through a combination of diplomacy and military strength. Granadan rulers were formally vassals of the kings of Castile and paid an annual tribute, but the approaches to the kingdom were well fortified. The Granadans also looked to their southern neighbors, the Marinid dynasty. When the great Almohad confederacy of the mid-twelfth century began to falter, the Marinids had broken away and established their own capital at Fez, and they established close diplomatic, military, and economic ties with the Nasrids of Granada.

In the central Mediterranean, Frederick of Hohenstaufen, heir to both the Holy Roman Empire and the kingdom of Sicily, brought a sense of diplomatic pragmatism to his crusading ventures. Frederick took a crusading vow but repeatedly delayed his and his troops' departure. In 1225 he gained a claim to the crown of Jerusalem through marriage but continued to delay his venture, which angered the pope so much that in 1227 he excommunicated Frederick for reneging on his crusading vow. The excommunication did not stop Frederick from sailing for Syria in 1228. He received a mixed reaction there, as many suspected he had only arrived to pursue his own claims to kingship rather than to assist in the defense of the crusader states.

To the shock of many in the Frankish Levant as well as in Latin Europe more generally, Frederick pursued his crusading aims through negotiation rather than military campaigning. He reached a deal with Sultan al-Kamil of Egypt that returned the cities of Jerusalem, Bethlehem, and Nazareth to Christian control, although the Temple Mount and al-Aqsa Mosque remained under Muslim control. Frederick's methods of diplomacy, negotiation, and compromise outraged many observers, some of whom charged him with being overly sympathetic to Islam and lacking in sincere crusading motives. The treaty appalled many in the Muslim world as well, who accused al-Kamil of betraying Saladin's legacy. Political trouble between Frederick and Pope Innocent IV in the 1240s caused the pope to allege that Frederick was a heretic as well as a traitor to the Christian cause, excommunicating him and declaring an anti-Hohenstaufen crusade that lasted for decades. This struggle broke centralized rule in southern Italy and Sicily and opened the way for continued conquests by foreign invaders. Nonetheless, Jerusalem remained under Christian control until 1244, when Muslim Turkish troops from central Asia conquered and sacked it.

When the young king Louis IX came to the throne of France in 1226, two decades of bloody crusading wars against internal enemies were coming to an end in the country's south. Latin Christians were increasingly concerned about heretics at the turn of the thirteenth century, and in 1208 Pope Innocent III had called a crusade against Count Raymond IV of Toulouse, in southern France. Raymond was accused of not prosecuting or impeding the activities of the heretics, called Cathars or Albigensians, who resided in the region. Thousands of northern French warriors, eager to reap the spiritual benefits of crusade and the material rewards of the wealthy south, responded to the call. Raymond saw the error of his ways and joined the crusading army, which viciously sacked the coastal city of Béziers and continued through southern France. A northern Frenchman who had participated in the Fourth Crusade, Simon de Montfort, took leadership of the army and deployed it for political and territorial gains, as well as in the defense of religious orthodoxy. Bloody power struggles divided the region for the next 20 years, until

King Louis VIII marched into the region at the head of a crusading army in 1226. The peace treaty of 1229 broke the independent power of the southern French lords and brought royal control, as well as northern French bishops, laws, and military elites, to the Mediterranean coast. The French monarchy began construction on the city of Aigues Mortes, to give the newly enlarged kingdom a Mediterranean port and a jumping-off point for future crusading ventures.

Louis IX left much of the kingdom's government in the capable hands of his mother, Blanche of Castile, while he won the reputation of a pious and saintly king through his crusading ventures. In 1244, Louis organized a primarily French expedition aimed at defeating Muslim power in Egypt as a prelude to taking and defending Jerusalem. The expedition repeated both the strategy and the disaster of the Fifth Crusade. They seized the port of Damietta in 1249 and then began to march inland; the Egyptians captured Louis and all of his army in 1250. In return for his release, Louis had to pay a huge ransom and return Damietta.

The French defeat was all the more remarkable because the Ayyubid sultan Malik al-Salih died just as the crusaders attacked, leaving the Egyptian state without an official leader. Malik's widow, Shajar al-Durr, attempted to promote her son as the next sultan, but after his murder in 1250 a faction of Turkish Mamluk troops placed Shajar al-Durr herself on the throne. She married and ruled in conjunction with one of the Mamluk generals but arranged his murder when she discovered his plan to marry an Iraqi princess. The new Mamluk ruler, al-Muzaffar Qutuz, had to face a new wave of Central Asian invaders: the Mongols, who had swept into Anatolia and northern Syria in the 1240s, demanding that the Seljuk sultans of Rum, as well as the crusader principality of Antioch, acknowledge their overlordship. Qutuz led his troops into battle against the Mongols at Ayn Jalut in 1260 and won a resounding victory. The Mamluks were the first power to defeat the Mongols in battle, leaving them with no real competitors for control of the region and strengthening their claims to be the legitimate protectors of Islam. Almost immediately after the battle, Qutuz was assassinated and al-Zahir Baybars, regarded by many as the real founder of the Mamluk state, was chosen as the new sultan.

The Mamluk governmental order that emerged under Baybars and his successors created a long-lasting and stable Muslim state that gradually established its hegemony over the southeastern quadrant of the Mediterranean. Baybars was determined to remove the last remnants of the crusader kingdoms from Syria and Palestine for both religious and strategic reasons. The Frankish presence threatened the lines of communication between Egypt and Syria, and to the Mamluks, Syria was a province to be governed, not a separate piece of a federated principality as it had been for the Ayyubids. Baybars's propagandists also portrayed him as a warrior for Islamic purity, cleansing his realm of infidels and bolstering his image as a protector of the Muslim faith. Baybars himself directed many campaigns against the remaining Christian cities, and his successor led the destruction of the last Frankish city, Acre, in 1291.

Fighting justified by faith had radically reshaped the political and military

Church door in Mosque of Sultan al-Nasir Muhammad, Cairo. This doorway from a Gothic church in Acre was brought to Egypt after the city's 1291 conquest by Mamluks. *Photo: Monique O'Connell*

boundaries of Mediterranean societies between the mid-eleventh and mid-thirteenth centuries. These realignments caused major upheavals not only in the borders between regions but in individuals' lives. The displacements of Ibn Hamdis, an Arabic poet, exemplified the experience of many. Born in Islamic Sicily, near Syracuse, Ibn Hamdis left during the Norman takeover and settled in the taifa king-dom of Seville in 1078. When the fundamentalist Almoravids took the city, he left again and traveled through North Africa, dying in Majorca in 1132. His poems are full of nostalgia for his Sicilian homeland; he wrote, "The land of others is not your land, nor are its friends and neighbors your friends and neighbors . . . Chain your-self to the country which is your beloved homeland, and die in your own abode." The dislocation of exile life and the accommodations, upheavals, and adjustments experienced by those living under new rulers show the complexities of individual experience in a Mediterranean where religious, social, and cultural boundaries were constantly being created, crossed, and renegotiated.

CHAPTER FIVE

Crossing Boundaries

Medieval Frontier Societies

I n the 1130s, two elite warriors crossed the religious and political frontiers created by crusading states. In Iberia, the Almoravids captured a Catalan baron
known as Reverter, and he built a career serving them as a mercenary soldier
in North Africa. After his death, his widow returned to Catalonia; she is buried in
the Gerona cathedral with a tomb inscription in Latin and Arabic. One of their
sons became a Muslim and served the Almohad regime, while the other, a Christian
named Berenguer, returned to Spain and served as a solider for the count of Barcelona. Berenguer signed documents in Arabic and reportedly joined the Knights
Templar before his death. Reverter's family demonstrates the often unexpected allegiances and survival strategies, including religious and cultural conversion, that
developed along the frontier.

Across the Mediterranean, the Syrian warrior and diplomat Usama ibn Munqidh
negotiated political alliances within the fragmented Muslim world and between
Muslim powers and the rulers of the newly established Kingdom of Jerusalem. During his career he served the emirs of Aleppo and Damascus, the Fatimids in Cairo,
and the new Ayyubid dynasty of Nur al-Din and Saladin. A poet as well as a diplomat, Usama was part of the learned circle surrounding Saladin. He remained firmly
within the religious and cultural sphere of Islam, but in his memoirs he recounted
numerous friendly encounters with Franks in Jerusalem as well as recording severe
judgments against their lack of honorable jealousy, cleanliness, and judicial practices. Usama's frequent interactions with Christians across a crusading frontier resulted in familiarity, if not necessarily respect.

Both of these men lived in medieval Mediterranean frontier societies, characterized by frequent and complex interactions across religious and political boundaries.

From Iberia to Sicily and southern Italy to the Levant and Anatolia, different religious and cultural communities lived side by side, ruled over by newly powerful rulers from outside the region. Despite the rhetoric of religious purity and holy war that many of these rulers used to justify their rule, it was impossible to separate individuals and communities into neat cultural categories, as the experiences of Reverter and Usama demonstrate. It was common for Christians to fight for Muslim rulers or vice versa; shared aristocratic values smoothed diplomatic relationships between these powers. Renegades, apostates, and converts from one religion could be found in the courts and palaces of the other faith, either temporarily or more permanently.

The shifting political boundaries of the medieval period created opportunities for elite men like Reverter and Usama to move between poles of influence, but the formation of "frontier societies" also shaped the lives of individuals who never traveled at all. Many medieval Mediterranean frontier societies were established by Latin Christians from western Europe, who came during or after the Crusades and imposed their rule on majority Muslim populations. The gradual ascendancy of Turkish frontier emirates in Anatolia offers the example of Muslim rulers moving into a Christian region. The idea that the existence of a frontier created a particular type of society was articulated most influentially by Frederick Jackson Turner, historian of the American West, who argued that the character of the United States was shaped through the ongoing process of westward expansion. Critics of Turner's thesis have pointed out that American frontiersmen were not expanding into vacant territory but conquering land inhabited by Native Americans. For these scholars, the frontier is inevitably tied up with conquest and colonization. Many historians of medieval European society have found "frontier societies" a useful way to discuss the expansion of Latin Christianity in the tenth–thirteenth centuries, when western Europeans expanded not only into the Mediterranean but also to northeastern Europe. Unlike the Latin Christian frontier in northeastern Europe, Mediterranean frontiers were formed in urban, cosmopolitan, and religiously and culturally diverse societies. When Latin Christian conquerors arrived in al-Andalus, Sicily, or the Levant, they found societies ruled by Muslims but with flourishing Christian and Jewish minorities. These Mediterranean communities had developed strategies for practical coexistence. When western European newcomers conquered and began to rule these regions, there was a great deal of tension between attempts to impose a Latin Christian society and acculturation of the conquerors to existing traditions. Unlike the newly established Latin Christian states, Byzantine imperial power was distinguished by its continuity, at least before 1204. The Fourth Crusade's capture of Constantinople and the subsequent fragmentation of power meant that in many places, Latin Christians imposed their rule on former territories of the Byzantine Empire, creating a sort of frontier society between Latin and Greek Christians.

Medieval Mediterranean frontier societies were zones of contact, where different cultural and religious identities overlapped and there were regular exchanges of intellectual and material culture between different groups of people. The framework of these interactions, however, was conquest and colonization of territories and the gradual but deliberate imposition of a particular type of society. This process also caused a great deal of mobility, both voluntary and forced, as people were forced into exile, migrated to more hospitable regions, or arrived on the frontier in search of new opportunities.

INDIVIDUAL AND COMMUNITY LIVES ON THE FRONTIER

The political fragmentation of the medieval Mediterranean makes it especially difficult to generalize about the experience of Jewish and Muslim populations subjected to Latin Christian rule. Policies changed from city to city and from one ruler to the next. There are some basic commonalities that structured the experiences of many on Mediterranean frontiers. The circumstances of conquest affected the way the residents were treated after the battle ended. When a fortress, town, or city was brought under Christian rule by forcible assault, the victors were more likely to kill the defenders and enslave or exile the survivors. When a place came under Christian rule by negotiated surrender, terms could be more generous: the defeated population was sometimes allowed to leave with their movable goods and sometimes allowed to stay, under regulations that legislated protection, rights, and duties. The examples of Aragon-Catalonia, Sicily, and the Frankish Levant provide contrasting models of how conquest, colonization, and acculturation could proceed.

The conglomeration of territories loosely allied under the crown of Aragon, where the surviving source material is richest, demonstrates the diverse possibilities even under a single ruler. The feudal and rural kingdom of Aragon, joined dynastically to the urban and commercial county of Catalonia, in the thirteenth century was ruled by the count-king James I, who also ruled the southern French commercial entrepôt of Marseilles. The kingdom of Aragon had a high number of mostly rural Muslims who cultivated and irrigated farmlands and worked as artisans; historians estimate there were about 100,000 Aragonese Muslims in the thirteenth century. In contrast, there were a relatively small number of Muslims living permanently in Catalonia but a larger number of Muslim merchants, particularly in the port of Barcelona. James treated the Majorcan Muslims as an economic asset after the conquest and guaranteed their rights to practice their own laws and religion. In Valencia, the city itself was emptied of Muslims and the principal mosque was transformed into a cathedral, but Muslims in the surrounding countryside were allowed to practice their own religion, live under their own laws, and administer their own communities. James's combination of economic pragmatism and the language of religious war was not unusual; many ruling elites in medieval frontier societies justified themselves by pointing to their crusading successes while at the same time promoting practical cultural and religious coexistence.

Surrender treaties generally guaranteed remaining Muslims the right to practice their own religion and live under their own laws, but they also imposed an obligation to pay a special tax. Jewish communities, who had lived as *dhimmi* people

The "Giralda" belltower in Seville, Spain. Originally part of the Great Mosque of Seville, the structure was transformed into a belltower when the rulers of Castile changed the mosque into a church. *Photo: Album/Art Resource, NY*

under Muslim rule, continued as a protected minority under Christian rule, paying a special tax as well. Where populations were large enough, particularly in Aragon and Valencia, both Jewish and Muslim community life was institutionalized through the *aljama*. The aljama, from the Arabic word *al-jama'a* (assembly), was both the governing council and the community as a whole, which operated under the direction of its own leaders. The magistrates and judges in Muslim aljamas represented the community to Christian rulers and organized taxation, military obligations, mosque activities, and schools. Jewish aljamas were governed by an elected council of elders that regulated taxation, synagogue activities, and schools. In urban areas, Jews and Muslims often had a separate quarter or streets that were the center of the community, but there was not the strict physical separation and state control typical of early modern ghettos.

The model of separate religious communities regulated by their own laws and living in their own quarters at times extended to non-Latin Christians as well. After

Alfonso VII conquered Toledo, he issued a charter of privileges to the local Christians (Mozarabs). In the Latin east, the crusaders found distinct Christian communities with their own languages, liturgical traditions, and customs: Greek Orthodox, Syrian Orthodox (Melchite), Armenians, and Jacobites (Arabic speakers with the liturgical languages of Syriac and Greek). In Jerusalem, these people lived in their own special quarters of the city and had their own marketplaces. An older generation of scholars argued that the Franks remained distinct from non-Latin Christians, but more recent research has shown that Latin and non-Latin Christians were fairly integrated, living in the same villages, worshipping at the same churches, and respecting local laws and religious traditions.

Although there is comparatively little evidence for the experience of rural Muslims and Jews under Christian rule, it is clear that their labor was economically necessary for the conquerors, at least initially. Latin Christian rulers wanted to attract settlers to their new territories and offered land and other incentives to encourage migration, but the process was gradual and differed significantly in Iberia, Sicily, and the Latin east. The Norman and Hohenstaufen rulers of Sicily were the most immediately successful at attracting Christian settlers; the process was more gradual in Aragon and Valencia, and limited in the Latin east.

Historians debate how to interpret the status of Muslims under Christian rule; all agree that the imposition of Christian rule was a significant change, but some emphasize the continuity in daily life and privileges and protections guaranteed in surrender treaties while others focus on the Muslims' subordinate status and pressures on the community. The traveler Ibn Jubayr, born in Muslim Valencia and who served as a courtier in Granada, set out for Mecca in 1183 via the Balearics, Sicily, and Alexandria; in his account of the journey, he comments on Muslim life under Christian rule in both Sicily and the Frankish Levant. In the Latin east, he reports that Muslims dominated the rural districts and were "living comfortably with the Franks," although they surrendered half their crops and paid a poll tax for each person. Mosques had been converted to churches, but in Acre a part of the principal mosque remained open for Muslim worship, and in Tyre a mosque remained as well. On his return journey, Ibn Jubayr stopped in Palermo and reported that Muslims there had their own quarter of the town with mosques, schools, and judges. He went on to say that the Muslims did not mix with Christians and had no security of goods. Ibn Jubayr's account depicts an uneasy accord between Muslim and Christian populations, a Mediterranean where trade and travel flourished but where certain communities held themselves apart.

Ibn Jubayr looked critically on the Muslims living in the Latin east, saying, "There can be no excuse in the eyes of God for a Muslim to stay in any infidel country, save when passing through it." His comment reflected an Islamic legal opinion that ruled it wrong for Muslims to live under Christian rule, but not all Muslims had the resources, the ability, or even the desire to leave their homes and resettle elsewhere. In Iberia, many of the wealthy and the intellectual elite of al-Andalus did emigrate to Granada and to North Africa, so as the thirteenth century wore on,

Muslims under Christian rule were increasingly artisans, farmers, and unskilled laborers. Conversely, the population of Muslim Granada grew exponentially, and the large Andalusian population in North Africa rose to economic and political importance there. In Sicily the Muslim elite was eventually ousted by the Norman expropriation of land and revenues and the gradual transformation of the countryside into the domain of a Latin Christian feudal nobility. The evidence from the Latin east is more fragmentary, but it also suggests that many of the intellectual and political elites left, leaving rural Muslim society in place.

Expulsions and deliberate transfers of populations were not limited to moments of conquest; while it was not the general pattern, both Christian and Islamic states tried to eliminate religious minorities through expulsion. In 1125, Alfonso I of Aragon mounted an expedition into eastern al-Andalus; in addition to besieging Granada, he took many Andalusian Christians back to Aragon with him and resettled them on Aragonese lands. The following year, the Almoravid regime expelled Christian populations from Granada, Cordoba, and Seville and deported them to Morocco. Two decades later, the fundamentalist Almohads revoked dhimmi status for all non-Muslims, and Jews and Christians had to choose between conversion, death, or going into a hasty exile. In the early thirteenth century, the Muslims of western Sicily rebelled against the increasingly severe restrictions on their lives. At the end of a military campaign to repress the rebellion, Frederick II deported the survivors to Lucera in southern Italy between 1223 and 1246. Frederick's Angevin successors disbanded the colony in 1300 and enslaved over 9,000 Muslims, bringing a brutal end to the protected enclave.

There were also moments when tensions between religious communities or resentment against new rulers exploded into violence. In Sicily, political struggles combined with popular Christian resentment of Muslim courtiers in 1160–61: Sicilian barons stormed the palace, massacred Muslim administrators, raided the treasury, and burned landholding records. When the violence spread outside the court, Christian crowds sacked and destroyed Muslim businesses and seized land, pushing the Muslim population farther into the west of the island. Beginning in 1189, and continuing through the 1220s, the Muslims of western Sicily revolted and established autonomous enclaves with independent leadership. In Castile, Muslims revolted in 1264 with help from Nasrid Granada; in response, James of Aragon subdued the city of Murcia. In James's own territory of Valencia there was a series of Muslim rebellions in the 1260s culminating in a large revolt from 1275 to 1278. Gradually, the Muslim populations of Sicily and of Iberia contracted through voluntary and forced migration as well as conversion.

CONVERSION, PERSUASION, AND INQUISITION

Increased mobility, pressure from political and religious elites, and social forces all led to individual and collective conversion. The choice to change from one belief system to another is a complicated one, and individuals on Mediterranean frontiers had a wide variety of motivations for doing so: sincere religious seekers, victims of war, colonized populations, and opportunists had different incentives and pressures to change their religious identity. Unlike the early medieval wave of conversion to Islam in the southern Mediterranean, in the high medieval period conversion went in all directions, although it is difficult to generalize from fragmentary evidence. In the frontier societies of Valencia and Sicily the general trend was for conversion from Islam, or less often, Judaism, to Latin Christianity. In Anatolia converts were more likely to switch from Greek Orthodox Christianity to Islam. Christian and Jewish conversion to Islam, at least externally, spiked in Iberia under Almohad rule, and the more gradual trend of conversion from Christianity to Islam continued under Ayyubid and Mamluk rule.

The desire many rulers and religious authorities expressed for their subjects' conversion was complicated by suspicion of converts' sincerity, popular distrust and hostility toward new converts, and economic incentives. Forced conversions were particularly worrisome to both Christian and Muslim religious authorities, who doubted the new converts' genuineness and adherence to the faith. Almohad authorities suspected the honesty of Jewish converts: "Jews in our midst behave outwardly as Muslims: they pray in the mosques, they teach their sons the Qur'an. They behave like our coreligionists and adhere to our tradition, but God alone knows what they hide in their hearts and what they do in their houses." Some Christian rulers and clergy expressed similar fears, and new converts to Christianity were sometimes met with suspicion from their new coreligionists. Municipal law codes regularly forbade insulting converts: James I issued a law in 1242 prohibiting anyone from calling converted Jews renegades, turncoats, or apostates.

Rulers and landlords sometimes resisted the conversion of Muslims and Jews under their rule because these groups were more profitable than their Christian subjects. Pope Innocent III complained to the Catalan clergy in 1206 that many Muslims desired baptism but were blocked by greedy lords. The bishop of Acre, Jacques of Vitry, reproved the Frankish elite for the same reason. In 1237, Pope Gregory IX attempted to end the struggle between missionaries aiming for conversions and landholders who blocked their efforts by decreeing that slaves who converted would not automatically be freed. This principle was adopted in Iberia and the Frankish Levant.

The pope and religious orders campaigned for Jewish and Muslim conversion with increasing fervor in the twelfth and thirteenth centuries. Newly founded mendicant orders — Franciscans and Dominicans — actively attempted to convert Muslims and Jews. Franciscans followed the example of St. Francis of Assisi, who in 1213 set out to convert the Almohad caliph in al-Andalus but fell ill; in 1219 he traveled to Egypt in the wake of the Fifth Crusade and tried to convert the Ayyubid sultan al-Kamil. As Christian proselytizing was forbidden in the Islamic world, Francis risked death; accounts say he charmed the sultan and escaped unharmed. Later Franciscans in the Islamic world adopted confrontational tactics like aggressive public preaching in mosques and medinas that resulted in martyrdom. When two Italian

Franciscans went to Almohad Valencia and tried to preach in the central mosque, the ruler there, 'Abu Zayd, had them executed. These missions met with resistance and hostility from local Christian communities too, who resented disturbances in the rough tolerance they depended on for survival.

The thirteenth century was the high point in Latin Christian belief that conversion was best accomplished through dialogue and persuasion. Peter the Venerable, who commissioned the first Latin translation of the Qur'an, urged winning Muslim allegiance "not by force but by reason, not by hate but by love." Peter's polemical works against Islamic belief portrayed Islam as a Christian heresy, a common approach in Christian refutations of Islam. In the Frankish Levant, Jacques de Vitry preached to Muslims as part of his larger evangelization and reform efforts. Raymond Llull, a troubadour poet and courtier turned mystical Franciscan tertiary, believed the main block to conversion was ignorance and composed 243 works in four languages, including Arabic, and established an Arabic language school for missionaries on Majorca.

Dominicans were specialists at conversion through rational argumentation, and they founded Arabic language schools to give missionaries the ability to engage in polemical philosophical conversation. Based in Barcelona, these schools were located where there were large concentrations of Muslims, notably in Játiva, Murcia, and Valencia. Some schools also began to teach Hebrew in order to convert Jews. The Catalan Dominican Raymond Penyafort was the architect of a whole program for the conversion of Jews and Muslims. The career of another Catalan Dominican, Raymond Martí, illustrates the shift in attention from Muslim to Jewish conversion. Martí first studied Arabic and composed a treatise against the Qur'an and then turned to the study of Hebrew and the censorship of Jewish books in the 1280s. His most famous work was the 1278 polemic *Dagger of Faith against Muslims and Jews*.

These campaigns of conversion show a thirteenth-century Latin Christian church increasingly concerned with instituting spiritual reform, enforcing orthodox belief and practice, and policing the boundaries between Muslims, Christians, and Jews. Religious authorities tried to forbid close, particularly sexual, contact between individuals of different faiths. The first such regulations, instituted in the Frankish Levant at the Council of Nablus in 1120, regulated adultery, sodomy, and theft among the Franks and forbade sex between Christians and Muslims, ordering equal punishment for transgressors. The council also prohibited Muslims from wearing "Frankish dress" so that religious identity would be immediately apparent. The Third Lateran Council in 1179 tried to limit social and economic contact, ruling that Christians could not sell war matériel to Muslims or captain their ships and that Jews and Muslims could not own Christian slaves. These regulations against the religious "other" fit with campaigns against heretics within Christianity itself. Heresy was defined as a public and deliberate denial of an article of Christian faith, and in the eleventh and twelfth centuries there were several large-scale religious movements the church judged heretical, including the Cathars and the Waldensians of southern France and northern Italy.

Francis of Assisi preaching to Mamluk sultan al-Kamil. Attributed to Giotto, Basilica of San Francesco d'Assisi, Italy. *Photo: Scala/ Art Resource*

The Fourth Lateran Council, convened and led by Innocent III in 1215, was the most important of these efforts to reform the church, restrain heresy, and regulate interfaith relationships. Innocent saw crusade as a crucial part of his program of church reform, which he hoped would serve to "uproot vices and implant virtues, to correct abuses and reform morals, to eliminate heresies and to strengthen faith." Among its 71 decrees were condemnations of specific heretical doctrines, a summary of basic Christian beliefs, and demands that secular powers actively root out heresy in their domains. The council banned Jews from building new synagogues, owning slaves, and holding office, and it introduced a requirement that Jews and Muslims "at all times shall be marked off in the eyes of the public from other peoples through the character of their dress." Innocent explained this regulation by pointing to the prohibition on interfaith sexual relations, arguing that these relationships were arising through errors and mistaken identity. While the regulation itself aimed simply at segregation, its implementation emphasized Jewish inferiority in the eyes of Christian society. Pope Gregory IX continued Innocent's program of church reform and antiheretical action, and in 1233 he instituted the papal inquisition, a court to inquire into heretical belief. The inquisition was intended to bring order and legality to the process of identifying and punishing heretics.

In Anatolia there was a gradual yet profound and permanent transformation of the region from Greek Orthodox to Turkish Muslim. Scholars continue to debate the balance of voluntary versus forced or pressured conversion in causing this transformation, but the overall pattern is clear. From the early twelfth century onward, Orthodox cultural and political institutions disappeared and were gradually replaced with Islamic ones: churches became mosques, Sufi lodges rather than monasteries served as communal religious organizations, and caravanserais provided shelter and protection to merchants who traveled the countryside. There were also increasingly large numbers of Greco-Turks, born from mixed marriages between Muslim and Christian parents. Charitable foundations, or waqfs, actively supported the process of conversion from Christian to Muslim by providing funds earmarked for converts to Islam to pay for instruction in religious principles and new shoes, clothes, and food. Institutions funded by waqf endowments were effective instruments for local governments and elites to spread their influence and gain political legitimacy and popular support, demonstrating the balance of political, cultural, pious, and private motivations that surrounded conversion efforts in Anatolia.

Sufism, a mystical and inward-looking method of practicing Islam, and Sufi lodges played a key role in this conversion effort. The lodges—called *khanaqah* in the Arabized Persian of the east and ribats in the west—began as frontier institutions and gradually became associated with Sufi masters and disciples. These lodges functioned as centers of charity as well as piety, and many offered shelter to travelers and had public kitchens. By the thirteenth century they were institutionalized into hierarchical ranks, with initiation procedures, set rituals, rules of conduct, and links with other brotherhoods dedicated to same master. There is some evidence for lodges for female Sufis in Cairo and farther east. Ibn Jubayr visited a Sufi lodge during a music recital and reported that "sometimes, so enraptured do some of these absorbed ecstatics become when under the influence of a state that they can hardly be regarded as belonging to this world after all." Mendicant dervishes, members of Sufi orders dedicated to poverty and asceticism, wandered the countryside and were very effective in the conversion of rural Christians to Islam. One of the most famous Anatolian Sufis was Jalal al-Din Rumi. Rumi's poetry expressed the soul's ecstatic journey to union with the divine. His followers were more prominent in urban centers and spent time in marketplaces discussing mystical love with merchants and artisans. Rumi had a wide appeal even among those who remained Christian, and his funeral, in 1273, was attended by Christian and Muslim mourners alike. Islamic religious scholars sometimes expressed suspicion of the more extreme forms of Sufism, but there was no reaction comparable to Latin Christian anti-heretical actions.

Conversion was also at issue in the experience of captivity, which was common on the frontier. As was the case in the early medieval era, defeated warriors and the populations of conquered territories and cities could be captured and enslaved, but some were usually set aside for ransom and prisoner exchange. Outside of formal warfare, warriors and pirates raided across land and sea, taking men, women, and children. State and individual efforts to redeem captives for political, religious, and charitable motives also continued, as restoring liberty to a captive coreligionist was seen as a pious act in all three of the major faiths. Bequests for ransoming captives were common in the wills of Mediterranean Christians. In the Islamic world, there were waqfs that did the work of ransoming, and Jewish trading networks were also used for individual and communal ransom of coreligionists.

When the crusaders arrived in Syria-Palestine, they initially broke with this practice, not taking captives themselves or trying to ransom other crusaders who were captives. Over time, the crusaders learned that ransoming captives could be a very lucrative activity, and their exposure to local practices of ransom made it more common for them to participate in networks of prisoner exchange. At the same time, Franks often benefited from the labor of enslaved captives: in 1263 the Mamluk sultan Baybars offered to exchange Christian for Muslim captives, but the military orders of Acre rejected the proposal, citing the great profit they earned from Muslim craftsmen. Not all captives were ransomed—some converted to the religion of their captors and assimilated into local societies, sometimes permanently and sometimes only temporarily.

In the Latin Christian world, thirteenth-century concerns about conversion in captivity led rulers and religious orders to institutionalize the practice of ransoming. In Iberia, royal ransomers were operating as early as 1126. Families and town militias also relied on the services of these intermediaries, who were often merchants and Jews accustomed to border crossing. In 1198, Pope Innocent III approved the creation of the Trinitarian Order, dedicated to ransoming captives, as a response to the massive number of Christian captives created by Saladin's victory over Jerusalem (1187) and the Almohad victory at Alarcos (1195). The Trinitarians established centers in Syria-Palestine, France, England, and Iberia. A Catalan ransoming order, the Mercedarians, began in the 1220s, during King James's conquests of Majorca and Valencia. Both the Trinitarians and the Mercedarians solicited donations to support their ransoming efforts, often playing on popular fears of conversion and the rape of female captives and emphasizing the charitable nature of ransoming. Merchants contributed heavily to the ransoming orders because their frequent travels made them vulnerable to capture. The orders redeemed captives from all social classes, liberating fishermen, shepherds, and militiamen as well as women, children, and warriors. One historian has estimated that more than 2,300 people were redeemed annually in Aragon alone, suggesting the massive scope of the enterprise.

Regulations that strictly delineated and separated religious communities described an ideal world in the eyes of many religious authorities, but the realities of life on the frontier often encouraged cross-cultural contact. The frequency of rules banning Muslims, Christians, and Jews from eating together, wearing similar clothing, or sharing municipal ovens, mills, and bathhouses suggests that these practices were in fact quite common. It is clear that newly arrived elites gradually experienced a degree of acculturation, particularly on the level of material culture — adopting local styles of dress, eating local foods, and building with local artistic and craft traditions. Scholars debate how to interpret the complexities of these interfaith social relationships. In the Spanish context, the scholar Américo Castro's conception of *convivencia*, or "living together" in toleration and harmony, has given way to more nuanced understandings of pluralistic societies where different faiths lived side by side, worked together, exchanged goods, ideas and artistic styles, but where conflict and competition could break into violence and hatred as well. Brian Catlos has suggested the analytical framework of *conveniencia*, or the principle of convenience. In this view, mutual interests caused by economic interdependence and shared political frameworks shaped the bonds that connected Muslim and Christian societies. For relationships between the different Christians of the Frankish Levant, Christopher MacEvitt has proposed the idea of "rough tolerance," which depended on individuals' willingness to overlook doctrinal and cultural differences.

Mediterranean frontier societies fell on a spectrum between mutual acceptance, grudging toleration, and open hostility and violence toward religious others. The constant feature of all these societies was the mobility of their populations, particularly among elites. Migrants acculturated to the customs of their new homes to different degrees. Mobility could take the form of permanent migration or more temporary sojourns; it led to greater familiarity with other societies, although that familiarity did not always translate into friendly regard. Mobility also functioned to spread ideas across the Mediterranean; knowledge was carried by individuals but also introduced into institutions of learning.

As the examples of Reverter and Usama suggest, there was considerable mobility across frontiers among military, political, and intellectual elites, and they have left traces in Mediterranean archives, allowing historians to reconstruct their experiences in relatively greater detail than is the case for other individuals. Given the crusader ideology that animated the establishment of the Latin states in Syria-Palestine, scholars have been especially interested in understanding the degree of acculturation among the Frankish elites over time. Fulcher of Chartres, a chronicler of the First Crusade, wrote, "For we who were occidentals have now become orientals. He who was a Roman or a Frank has in this land been made into a Galilean or a Palestinian." According to Fulcher, this fusion took place through the development of a common language and intermarriage with local populations: "Some have taken wives not only of their own people but Syrians and Armenians or even Saracens who have obtained the grace of baptism." Usama reported a similar process, describing a Frankish knight of his acquaintance who employed an Egyptian cook and ate no pork; by contrast, "It is always those who have recently come to live in Frankish territory who show themselves more inhuman than their predecessors who have been established among us and become familiarized with Muslims." An earlier generation of scholars used reports like this to argue for elite assimilation, particularly on the level of material culture: crusaders wore eastern garments, lived in Syrian-style houses, took baths, used soap, and ate sugar. A later generation depicted the Franks as a separate ruling class, removed from their Syrian subjects by language and religion and maintaining their dominance over local populations through force. Most recently, scholars have distinguished between the Franks' relationships with eastern Christians and Muslim populations, pointing out that while Franks did live in the countryside and intermarry with eastern Christians, they did not do the same in Muslim-dominated regions.

On an elite level, physicians, courtiers, and mercenary soldiers readily sought and found employment with rulers and regimes of different religious faiths. The Fatimids, except for brief periods of persecution under al-Hakim, employed Jewish and Christian administrators, and the rulers of Norman Sicily followed the Fatimid example. Roger II maintained an administration staffed by bilingual Greek and Arabic speakers. George of Antioch, born in Syria and experienced in the financial administration of Byzantine Antioch and in Zirid Mahdiyya, is the most brilliant embodiment of the multiplicity of cultural influences that characterized Roger's court. George spoke both Greek and Arabic and was the patron of the Greek-rite church Santa Maria dell'Ammiraglio, which featured Byzantine mosaics and a Byzantine hymn transliterated into Arabic letters around the base of the cupola. After Roger's death, the administration of Sicily was increasingly influenced by Latin European bishops and clerics, and Norman French and Latin began to be used alongside Greek and Arabic in the kingdom's administration. In Anatolia, Christians served in the Seljuk administration, and the Seljuk chancery had a special section of Greek scribes. In Valencia, Jews acted as diplomats and administrators for the monarchs, notwithstanding legislation to the contrary. In the Frankish Levant, Muslims played a negligible role in the administration, but Arabic-speaking eastern Christians served as notaries and customs officials.

Frontier armies reflected the religious and linguistic diversity of the medieval Mediterranean. Seljuk armies had special contingents of local Greek troops with their own officers and uniforms. Valencian armies had units of Muslim warriors; Muslim troops defended the town of Gerona from French attack in the 1280s. Sicilian Muslim soldiers in the Norman army fought in southern Italy. Many Christians fought in Almoravid armies in North Africa, either because they had been captured or because they had hired out their services as mercenaries. The Nasrid sultans of Granada employed Christian bodyguards and militias. Even the fundamentalist Almohads employed Christian mercenaries at times. One historian estimates that

The multilingual character of the Mediterranean has left traces in polyglot inscriptions that offer tangible evidence of the flexible nature of lived experience. *Top,* Sicilian tombstone with Hebrew (above), Latin (left), Greek (right), and Arabic (below). *Bottom,* trilingual manuscript of the Psalms in parallel Greek, Latin, and Arabic versions, from the mid-twelfth century. Top: © Nico Traut/Shutterstock.com. Bottom: © The British Library Board

there were several thousand Christian mercenaries in al-Andalus in the twelfth and thirteenth centuries.

Political and military elites moved easily and frequently across borders, either as exiles, rebels seeking a temporary refuge, or in search of opportunity. Defections in both directions played an essential role in the diplomatic and political process on the Byzantine-Turkish border in the twelfth century. Some defectors stayed temporarily and waited for political circumstances at home to change in their favor, while others converted, married into local aristocracies, and attained high positions in new homes. Because of a conflict with his brother, Emperor John II, Isaac Komnenos fled from Constantinople in the mid-twelfth century to the Danishmend court in northeastern Anatolia and remained there for over a decade. Isaac's son John converted to Islam and married the sultan's daughter. Another Byzantine prince, Andronikos Komnenos, after several romantic entanglements in Armenia and the Frankish kingdoms, fled to the court of a Turkish emir with Theodora, the widow of King Baldwin III of Jerusalem. When Theodora was kidnapped and brought to Constantinople, Andronikos was forced to return as well and submit himself to imperial authority. When the Seljuk sultan sent an ambassador to negotiate a treaty with Byzantium, the emperor persuaded the messenger, who had a Turkish father and Georgian mother, to switch sides; the man was baptized and made a duke.

There was a similar dynamic along the Christian-Muslim frontier in the western Mediterranean. King James of Aragon-Catalonia quarreled with one of his barons, Blasco of Alagon, who fled to Islamic Valencia. Another member of the same family, Artal, served in Muslim Murcia, and a third Alagon, Giles, converted to Islam, took the name Muhammad, and served the ruler of Majorca. Mahomet Abenadalill, courtier and warrior from Muslim Granada, served one king of Aragon-Catalonia as soldier and acted as an envoy to his successor. The last ruler of Almohad Valencia, 'Abu Zayd, became a client of James I and by 1236 had converted to Christianity; some of his sons remained Muslim and others converted to Christianity. As conquest pushed the Christian-Muslim frontier south and Almohad rule collapsed, Valencian, Castilian, and Portuguese nobles continued to enter the service of the Nasrids of Granada and the Hafsids of Tunis, and the son of the last Almohad caliph fled to Barcelona. In the 1250s, James of Aragon agreed to send a Catalan militia to serve the Hafsids, and he made a similar agreement with the Marinids in 1274. These organized legions joined the other Christian mercenaries in North Africa, independent individuals seeking their fortune and Catalan, German, and Italian refugees from political struggles at home.

The tensions between pragmatic strategies of accommodation and ideologically motivated warfare can be seen in epic literature about frontier warriors, which migrated from oral to written form in the twelfth century. Authors writing in Old French, Occitan, and other Romance languages as well as Greek and Arabic all contributed to medieval Mediterranean romance literature; a subset of that genre related the adventures of fighting heroes, although they only sometimes used their military skills against the religious other. In these poems, converts and renegades mix easily with warriors fighting holy wars; Muslim and Christian warriors share a culture of restrained aristocratic violence, and interfaith romances abound. *The Song of Roland*, set along the Muslim-Christian frontier in France and Spain, looks back to the eighth century but is imbued with the spirit of religious zealotry, chivalry, and concern for honor French knights brought to twelfth-century battlefields. In the poem, Charlemagne's army is fighting Muslims in northern Spain, and "King Marsile" of Zaragoza offers to convert to Christianity if the Franks will leave. The knight Roland, due to the machinations of his villainous stepfather, Ganelon, and King Marsile, is ambushed as he leads the rear guard of Charlemagne's army across the Pyrenees. Claiming that it would be dishonorable to call for help, Roland refuses to sound his horn until the last moment. Summoned by Roland's dying breaths, Charlemagne's army then defeats the Muslim force at Roncevalles, takes the city of Zaragoza, and rides back to France with Marsile's wife, Bramimonde, captured and converted at the siege. Also on the Iberian frontier, the adventures of the Castilian nobleman Rodrigo Díaz de Vivar were related in *The Song of My Cid*. While the historical Díaz worked as a mercenary for the Muslim king of neighboring Zaragoza before conquering and ruling over Muslim Valencia, El Cid of the poem is presented as an independent warrior who often revels in anti-Muslim violence and declaims his Christian beliefs. El Cid also entrusts his wife and daughters to one of his Muslim allies.

The story of the Byzantine hero Basil Digenis Akritis has a complex mix of militancy, romantic love, and shifting alliances. As his name indicates, the hero is literally Di-genis, or double born. The story unfolds on the Byzantine-Arab frontier and begins with an Arab emir's raid into the region. Though the would-be rescuers find the captured Greek Christian girls murdered and mutilated in a ditch, these Greek brothers discover one sister had been spared after the emir had fallen in love with her. That girl's brother then defeats the emir in single combat and forces him to convert to Christianity. Vanquished by honor and love, the emir marries the girl and goes over to the Byzantine side of the border. Their son, Digenis, is renowned for his strength and speed—he also steals a bride, in this case from another Byzantine castle, and then settles down to a life as an Akritis, a border guard on the Byzantine-Arab frontier near the river Euphrates. There, his main task is not to repel Arab incursions but to fight against Greek Christian irregular troops who had turned to banditry.

In the Arabic tradition, the epic poem *Ḏāt al-Himma*, or *Delhemma*, relates the adventures of the warrior princess Delhemma. Set along the Arab-Byzantine border of the eighth and ninth century, the poem follows Delhemma as she fights rival Arab tribes and Byzantines. All of the protagonists experience multiple rounds of captivity, and conversion is one of the principal plot points: Delhemma's husband, al-Harith, goes over to the Byzantines and converts to Christianity, while the Byzantine emperor's chamberlain and Yanis, lord of a border fortress, are both secret Muslims. The poem indicates a general uncertainly about the sincerity and motiva-

Manuscript illustrations from the *Cantigas de Santa Maria* from thirteenth-century Castile. These images depict a military campaign in Morocco. Both of the opposing armies include Christian and Muslim troops, suggesting the prevalence of mercenary or renegade troops. *Real Monastero de San Lorenzo. Photo: Album / Art Resource, NY*

tion of conversions. Taken together, these epic poems reflect the intricate balance between religious, military, and family allegiances in frontier experience, as well as the complex identities that developed there.

MOVEMENT OF IDEAS AND INTELLECTUALS

There was also a high degree of connection in the intellectual life of the Mediterranean, particularly in Spain, Sicily, and Egypt. A small elite traveled across boundaries both physically and intellectually; the structure of their thought and their conclusions were shaped by their prolonged and intimate exposure to other religious traditions. While not all of these thinkers were friendly toward individuals and ideas of other faiths, they did demonstrate an intimate knowledge of works from other linguistic and religious traditions. The reception of Aristotle's works, for instance, with their focus on reason, logic, and the laws of nature, posed a theological problem for Muslims, Jews, and Christians: was God best understood through revelation and faith or through reason? One of the most prominent Mediterranean thinkers to engage with this problem of reason and revelation was Maimonides—known in Hebrew as Moshe ben Maimon and in Arabic as Mussa bin Maimun. Maimonides was a rabbi, a physician, and a pioneer of speculative philosophy within the Jewish tradition. He was born in 1135 in Almoravid Cordoba, where he read Greek philosophy in Arabic translation as well as Jewish law. When the Almohads replaced the more tolerant Almoravids in 1148, Maimonides and his family fled Cordoba. Eventually, the family settled in Fez and likely lived as Muslims; there, Maimonides studied Islamic law and philosophy. Around 1165 the family crossed the Mediterranean to crusader Acre and finally settled in Cairo, where Maimonides lived through the Ayyubid conquest of the Fatimid dynasty. In 1174 he was appointed head of the Jewish community in Cairo and became court physician to the Ayyubid sultans. He wrote a wide variety of medical, philosophical, and religious works in Arabic, Judeo-Arabic, and sometimes in Hebrew.

One of the central tenets of Maimonides's philosophy is that it is impossible for the truths arrived at by human intellect to contradict those revealed by God. Maimonides argued that God had created a rational world and given humans reason in order to perceive divine order. To demonstrate the rationality of Jewish law, he wrote the *Mishneh Torah*, a codification of Jewish oral laws still seen as authoritative today. His *Guide for the Perplexed*, written in Arabic for an audience of educated Jews, suggested that philosophy and rational inquiry were not only compatible with faith but in fact enhanced a soul's capability for divine love. While Maimonides may not have been directly influenced by the writings of Ibn Rushd, known in the west as Averroës, the two men operated in the same intellectual milieu. Ibn Rushd, born in 1126 to a family of prominent jurists in Almoravid Cordoba, wrote extensively on Islamic law, Arabic grammar, medicine, mathematics, and astronomy, but is best known for his commentaries on Aristotle. Like Maimonides, Ibn Rushd was forced to leave Cordoba by the Almohads, who objected to his rationalist stance.

One of his works, *The Decisive Treatise Determining the Nature of the Connection between Religion and Philosophy*, argued that philosophy, while best limited to a learned elite, was a legitimate topic for Muslims.

Maimonides and Ibn Rushd's rationalism existed in dialogue with the other major intellectual and philosophical trend of the medieval Mediterranean: mysticism. The Persian Abu Hamid al-Ghazali spread the mystical approach of Sufism across the Mediterranean through the popular guidebook *Bringing the Religious Sciences to Life*. Al-Ghazali began as a theologian and professor of law. Dissatisfied with legal formalism and faith in authority, he aimed at a sweeping reform of scholarly Islam, including Sufism as an element that would offer a genuine spiritual grounding. He attacked Aristotelian rationalism in a treatise entitled *The Incoherence of the Philosophers*, arguing that philosophy was not compatible with religious faith. Ibn Rushd refuted al-Ghazali's points and defended the rationalist approach in a treatise called the *Incoherence of Incoherence*. Following al-Ghazali, scholar-sufis continued to engage in Mediterranean-wide controversies, indicating the existence of widespread networks of intellectual connection and correspondence.

Almohad persecution as well as intellectual curiosity motivated some scholars to travel from Spain to the Islamic east in this period, making Cairo and Damascus centers of learning. The journeys of two Spanish mystics, philosophers, and poets, the Jew Judah Halevi and the Muslim Ibn al-Arabi, are examples of this trans-Mediterranean intellectual experience. Early in his life, Halevi lived alternately in Christian Toledo and in al-Andalus and was a renowned poet—while he wrote in Hebrew, he drew on the rhythms, patterns, and themes of Arabic poetry. Halevi later experienced a deepening of his faith and came to believe that religious fulfillment was possible only in the land of Israel. He sailed for Alexandria in 1140 and died in Syria-Palestine in 1141. Ibn al-Arabi was born in Murcia and moved to Almohad Seville; he was deeply influenced by Sufi mysticism. In 1201 he made the pilgrimage to Mecca and then continued his travels through Syria, Palestine, Iraq, Turkey, and Egypt. His poetry expressed the transcendent power of the soul's union with the divine. He wrote, "My heart has become capable of every form / it is a pasture for gazelles and a convent for Christian monks / and a temple for idols and the pilgrim's Ka'ba and the / Tables of the Tora and the book the Qur'an. / I follow the religion of Love."

Judaism was also influenced by mystical approaches to religion, particularly in the development of kabbalah, an esoteric lore with connections to Aristotelian philosophy and Sufi mysticism. Kabbalah appeared in the closely connected Jewish communities of southern France and northern Spain at the turn of the thirteenth century; it comprises a vast and complex literary and intellectual tradition but generally emphasized mystical and contemplative approaches to faith. Like Sufism, kabbalah stressed the personal relationship between master and disciple. Maimonides's son Abraham drew on Sufi mystical traditions to promote a Jewish-Sufi form of piety that gained followers in Cairo and elsewhere. Kabbalah gained its classic form with the compilation of the *Zohar*, a multivolume work produced at the end of the thirteenth century that offers a comprehensive system that mystically interprets Judaism through complex symbolism. The *Zohar* has been attributed to the Castilian Moses de León; scholars disagree on whether the book is his own work or a compilation of older traditions.

Mystical approaches to faith encouraged some unusual individuals to highlight the commonalities among different religious faiths. Abraham Abulafia, the founder of an ecstatic and prophetic type of kabbalism, studied in Tudela and Barcelona and traveled to southern Italy, Greece, and Acre in order to disseminate his belief that letters of the Hebrew alphabet could be combined in complex patters that would reveal a spiritual path to God. Abulafia attempted to convince both Jews and Christians of the truth of his prophetic message, even trying to convert Pope Nicolas III in 1280. The Franciscan missionary Raymond Llull brought the common beliefs of Jews, Christians, and Muslims together with his own mystical and theological doctrines. In one of his many books, he argued that "just as we have One God, one creator, One Lord, we should also have one faith, one religion, one sect, one manner of loving and honoring God, and we should love and help one another." While neither Llull's nor Abulafia's ideas gained many followers, their journeys demonstrate the flow of intellectual currents and new religious ideas around the medieval Mediterranean.

Ideas did not only travel via the movement of individual intellectuals; they also were diffused through the translation of texts. Teams of translators worked in Barcelona, Toledo, southern France, and Sicily to translate Arabic works on philosophy, medicine, mathematics, physics, astronomy, and geography (both translations of Greek and Syriac works and original works by Islamic authors) into Latin and Hebrew. Jewish communities and individuals were particularly important for the translation movement. Judah ibn Tibbon, born in Granada, emigrated to southern France to avoid Almohad persecutions and translated numerous works from Arabic into Hebrew; his son Samuel translated, among other things, Maimonides's *Guide for the Perplexed* from Arabic into Hebrew. Jacob Anatoli, Samuel's son-in law, translated Ibn Rushd's commentaries on Aristotle into Hebrew, winning such fame as a translator that Frederick II invited him to Naples. There, Anatoli collaborated with Michael Scot and translated other works of Ibn Rushd, as well as Ptolemy's *Almagest* and al-Farabi's treatise on the syllogism. In Barcelona, Plato of Tivoli collaborated with Abraham bar Hiyya al-Nasi to translate texts on practical geometry, algebra, and astronomy from Arabic and Hebrew into Latin.

These centers of translation, intellectual discourse, and interfaith collaboration drew Latin Christian scholars from northern Europe interested in the acquisition of Arabic scientific knowledge. Adelard of Bath, one of the leading figures in the Latin translation movement, traveled first to southern France then to Salerno, Sicily, Syria, and probably to Palestine and Spain, where he likely learned Arabic and translated mathematical treatises. Gerard of Cremona traveled from northern Italy to Toledo, learned Arabic there, and translated 71 Arabic scientific works, including texts by Ptolemy, Galen, Ibn Sina, al-Kindi, and al-Khwarizmi. Gerard's contemporary in Toledo was the Jewish poet, astronomer, mathematician, and philosopher Abraham ibn Ezra, who traveled to southern France, Italy, Egypt, Syria-Palestine, and Paris and England, bringing Andalusian Judeo-Muslim learning to northern Europe. Michael Scot also learned Arabic in Spain and collaborated with the Jewish scholar Abuteus Levita; Scot then worked at Frederick II's court in southern Italy.

At the same time that individual philosophers and religious thinkers wrestled with problems of faith and reason, institutions of knowledge in both the Christian and the Muslim worlds grew and spread. Madrasas, schools of instruction in Islamic law usually attached to a mosque, were founded throughout the Muslim world. In the regions around the Mediterranean, the Seljuks, Ayyubids, and Mamluk states used madrasas as institutions to spread a Sunni consensus and fight against radical forms of Shia learning. The transmission of religious knowledge was a fundamental part of Islamic tradition and was passed from teacher to student. Madrasas did not replace the importance of this personal relationship, but by the twelfth century, the construction of madrasas had become a popular form of philanthropy, and many Muslim elites established charitable foundations for their support. In addition to the construction of madrasa buildings, including living quarters and libraries, these waqf foundations subsidized teachers' salaries and offered student stipends. In its most typical form, a madrasa consisted of teacher and student rooms arranged around a central courtyard, where instruction and discussion took place. Madrasas did not formally enroll students, and the schools and study circles were open to all believers. One scholar explained this practice by saying, "To lock the door of a madrasa is to shut out the masses and prevent them from hearing the [recitation of] knowledge . . . and being blessed by it." Women could attend lectures and study groups, and in Damascus women took particularly active roles as patrons, scholars, and sometimes teachers. By the end of the twelfth century, there were more than 30 madrasas in Damascus and a similar number in Cairo.

In western Europe, universities founded in the late eleventh and twelfth centuries began to institutionalize and regularize intellectual life, in some ways replacing the more individual exchanges of scholars and texts that had characterized Mediterranean intellectual life in earlier centuries. Universities, like madrasas, began as corporations of masters and students and were based around colleges, residential foundations that offered groups of students housing and support. Students and teachers in Latin universities enjoyed a set of legal rights that instructors and attendees of madrasas did not, and the Islamic schools had no fixed curriculum as Latin universities did. Finally, madrasas did not offer formal degrees. In Mediterranean Europe, Bologna provides an example of the development of a university organized around a corporation of students. There were famous teachers in Bologna throughout the twelfth century, and students from all over Europe traveled there to study civil and canon law in particular. In 1155 the emperor Frederick I Barbarossa issued a document protecting the rights of foreign scholars, and these economically, socially, and politically prominent students banded together into corporations to safeguard their interests against both the town government and

teachers. In universities patterned on Bologna, teachers did not form corporate bodies with the power of fixing statutes; it was only the student corporations that could regulate courses of study and punish deficient teachers. These student universities contrasted with the institutional organization found in the northern European universities of Oxford and Paris, where the university was defined as a single corporation including schools of masters and students. In Iberia and southern France, a mixed type of university predominated, where students were in control of certain university offices but colleges of doctors were incorporated as well. Schools at Montpellier and Salerno emerged as leading centers of medical learning, and they incorporated Greek and Arabic works into the study of medicine.

Teaching in Islamic and Christian contexts. *Opposite:* manuscript illustration, executed by Yahya ben Mahmud al-Wasiti in Baghdad in 1237, depicting a teacher addressing a group of male and female students. *Right:* fourteenth-century Italian manuscript illustration showing a professor teaching in a medieval Latin university. Opposite: *photo, bpk, Berlin / Bibliothèque nationale de France / Art Resource, NY.* Right: *Bibliothèque municipale, Cambrai. Photo, Erich Lessing / Art Resource, NY*

INTELLECTUAL AND ARTISTIC CULTURES AT COURT

After their territorial conquest, rulers faced the problem of how not only to govern what they had conquered but also to justify their rule in terms that all of their subjects could understand. New dynasties in Iberia, southern Italy, and the Levant deliberately promoted court cultures that drew on multiple traditions and sponsored cross-cultural artistic and intellectual endeavors. Elite patrons of artistic and intellectual endeavors wanted to demonstrate that they had access to luxury goods and to participate in common Mediterranean displays of power and legitimacy. This cross-cultural artistic and intellectual patronage was least intense in Valencia. The kings of Aragon-Catalonia did not become patrons of Islamic intellectual culture in the same way the kings of Castile did. Toledo and Seville remained the centers of Latin translation and assimilation of Arabic and Hebrew artistic, literary, and scientific traditions.

The literary and scientific achievements of the Latin east were relatively low compared to other regions, and scholars have pointed out that few of the first rulers of Jerusalem patronized intellectually creative men; additionally, religious zeal was prized more than scholarly achievement among the clergy who chose to emigrate to Jerusalem. William of Tyre, the major historian of the crusader states, is certainly an exception, but he needed to go back to France and Italy for an education as there was no Latin university in the Levant. When he returned to Jerusalem in 1165, King Amalric I made him an ambassador to Byzantium and asked him to write a history of the Muslim world (now lost.) In the twelfth century, Stephen of Antioch did translate Arabic medical treatises into Latin, but he was not part of a larger culture of intellectual inquiry and exchange.

Not surprisingly, architectural patronage in the Latin east focused on building or restoring Christian churches. Crusader artistic styles did not deliberately use Islamic forms, but did demonstrate a creative mixture of Italian and Byzantine traditions. Melisande, the queen of Jerusalem in the 1140s, showed through both her personal history and her artistic patronage that the main cross-cultural influences in the Frankish Levant traveled between different Christian communities. The daughter of an Armenian princess and a Frankish king, Melisande extended her support to Armenian, Jacobite, and Greek and Syrian Orthodox churches. She commissioned the convent of St. Lazarus and possibly the new mosaic decorations and Latin inscriptions in the Dome of the Rock. Byzantine influence grew over the course of the twelfth century: after the 1130s, for instance, bilingual Latin and Greek inscriptions replaced the Latin inscriptions in the Church of the Nativity in Bethlehem.

The rulers of Sicily created an elite court culture that relied heavily on Islamic intellectual, artistic, and ceremonial influences, but at the same time they actively crusaded against Muslim states abroad and restricted the lives of their Muslim subjects at home. Under Roger Guiscard's ruthless and talented son Roger II, the island had become both an economic powerhouse and a military force in the central Mediterranean. Roger II gained control of much of southern Italy and won the title "king of Sicily" from the pope in 1130. Sicilian fleets raided the Balkan possessions of the Byzantine Empire and briefly established an outpost at Mahdia on the North African coast. The Capella Palatina (Palatine Chapel), built by craftsmen from Fatimid Egypt under Roger's reign, exhibits its hybrid influences: its ceiling is composed of painted wooden panels joined together in recessed arches and connected to the surrounding walls by *muqarnas*, arches in a typically Islamic manner. The ceiling, which sits atop walls covered with Byzantine mosaics, is decorated with images of a prince surrounded by court officials, jugglers, musicians, and dancers in addition to birds, plants, and animals. Roger's coronation robe conveys the same blend of cultural influences: made of Byzantine silk and decorated with precious gems, it has Arabic (Kufic) script around the border. Roger patronized the geographer and cartographer al-Idrisi, who was born in Ceuta, studied in Cordoba, and traveled widely in Morocco, Spain, and southern France before settling in Palermo and producing maps and geographical texts. Roger and his family also patronized the many Greek orthodox monasteries on the island as well as Islamic and Byzantine craftsmen. Under Roger's grandson, King William II, Sicilian fleets attacked Ayyubid Alexandria and Byzantine Thessalonica. William II oversaw the construction of the Zisa of Palermo and the church at Monreale, built by Arabic craftsmen and decorated by Byzantine mosaicists.

In the 1190s a dynastic crisis meant that the Normans on Sicily were replaced by another northern European dynasty, the German Hohenstaufens. Like his Norman predecessors, Frederick II created a court culture that drew on multiple cultural currents, but like other Mediterranean frontier societies in the thirteenth century, the practical, rough tolerance of the immediate post-conquest period had given way to a more stilted cross-cultural exchange. Both Latin and Arabic sources portray Frederick as intensely interested in Greek and Arabic science and philosophy, but as the historian David Abulafia has pointed out, his cross-cultural exchanges were carried out in large part by letter and thus do not represent ongoing and personal intellectual exchanges. There were translators working at Frederick's court, but in this case the translation of Greek, Arabic, and Hebrew texts into Latin, rather than indicating a vibrant cross-cultural life, demonstrates the increasing Latinization of court culture. In contrast to Roger's administration, Frederick had no Arabic scribes or Muslim administrators, and the Greek elements at court were also on the wane. Frederick's interest in Arab science must also be seen in the context of his increasingly restrictive policies toward Muslim communities, culminating in the mass relocation of 15,000–20,000 Sicilian Muslims to Lucera in 1223.

Medieval frontier societies created vibrant and complex cultural realms that were often multiconfessional, multilingual, and multiethnic. Relationships between individuals who lived in these frontier zones were not always harmonious but neither were they shaped entirely by ideologies of religious opposition or intolerance. The individuals, ideas, and cultural forms that traveled from one society to another were transformed and adapted to fit local needs. Of course, one of the engines driving the mobility of both people and culture in this era was cross-cultural economic exchange. New political and social configurations would reshape the commercial patterns of the Mediterranean in the twelfth and thirteenth centuries, creating new possibilities and dangers for merchants, pirates, pilgrims, slaves, and other Mediterranean travelers.

CHAPTER SIX
Commerce, Conquest, and Travel

Benedetto Zaccaria was a naval adventurer whose career spanned the medieval Mediterranean. Born to a wealthy and powerful Genoese family in 1248, he entered the service of the Byzantine emperor and won control of the port of Phocaea, a main source of the limited supply of alum. Alum was essential to leather tanning and textile dying, and the Zaccaria family sold it to western cloth-producing centers for an immense profit. Their galleys sailed as far as Bruges, trading not only alum but grain and textiles as well. Far to the east, the family maintained its own set of merchant lodgings and storehouses, called a *fondaco*, in the Genoese colony of Kaffa on the Black Sea. Zaccaria's prowess at naval combat complemented his merchant successes: he was the victorious admiral of the Genoese fleet in the war against Pisa, and he also defended Tripoli, one of the last crusader states in the eastern Mediterranean. Unable to prevent the fall of Tripoli, Zaccaria turned to piracy, attacking and seizing Egyptian shipping. These actions caused trouble for other Genoese merchants trading in Egypt, but Zaccaria avoided censure at home by entering the king of Castile's service in 1291, attacking Muslim shipping in Morocco. From 1295 to 1300 he commanded the French navy; he then returned to the eastern Mediterranean as an independent agent and won the island of Chios, the sole source of mastic gum, from Byzantium in 1304. Although the scope and success of Zaccaria's career was certainly unusual, his combination of commerce, state-directed naval combat, and piracy demonstrates the permeable lines between these activities.

Zaccaria lived during a large-scale economic reorganization of the Mediterranean, which unfolded between 1150 and 1350. Unlike earlier centuries, when Jewish and Arab traders based in the eastern Mediterranean had been the prime agents of commercial exchange, Mediterranean trade in the twelfth and thirteenth centuries came to be dominated by Latin merchants, especially those from the Italian maritime republics of Genoa, Venice, and Pisa. In the thirteenth century, the Latin merchants consolidated their gains, and the Mediterranean economy was increasingly directed by "national" communities of Latin merchants supported by their states. Venetian and Genoese merchants predominated, and Catalan merchants had a presence in the markets of the Levant as well. The relationship between a city-state and its merchants was different in each case, but all of these merchants had an advantage because of the close connection between their commercial endeavors and the willingness of Latin states to use violence to protect their traders and their trade routes.

These large-scale transformations were affected by changes within the Latin, Byzantine, and Muslim worlds that surrounded the Mediterranean, as well as by shifts in the relationship between Muslim and Christian merchants. Within Europe, population growth and an increased appetite among elites for prestige goods raised the demand for commodities and luxuries that could not be provided locally: spices, primarily pepper, but also things like perfume, incense, medicines, sugar, precious stones, silk and other cloth, paper, soap, ceramics, rugs, and decorated metals. Within the Muslim world, the Crusades' destruction of Mediterranean ports and arsenals weakened states' capacities for both naval warfare and commerce, and the spread of Islamic trading networks to the south and east drew Muslim merchants away from the Mediterranean. Finally, the Italians and Catalans had gained significant commercial advantages in Byzantine and Muslim societies through their cooperation with the crusaders, and these tax exemptions and legal privileges gave the Latin merchants a competitive edge over locals.

In addition to these economic and political factors, scholars have offered contrasting cultural explanations for the development of a particular commercial culture in western Europe, especially in the northern Italian city-states. Their debates have focused around two main themes: the role social, religious, and political institutions played in shaping commercial culture and the development of networks of trust in business relationships. It is clear that Italian merchants relied on an increasingly complex set of business practices, a favorable legal climate in their city-states, and military protection to construct international commercial enterprises. Scholars have explored these questions to expose the "roots of capitalism" and to explain the long-term divergence in the economic paths of western Europe and the Muslim Mediterranean. A handful have controversially pointed to the role of Islamic law, charitable institutions, and relatively hierarchical political structures as factors that discouraged investment and commercial innovation in the Muslim world. Others have vigorously refuted these claims, pointing to the vibrancy of trade within a larger Islamic world that stretched to the south and east and the relative poverty of resources in western Europe as factors that made Muslim merchants less interested in actively pursuing trading opportunities in the Mediterranean. What is certain is that few Muslim merchants traveled to Latin

Europe, and that Christian Europe was generally more hostile to non-Christians than the Muslim world was to non-Muslims.

When Italian and then Catalan merchants entered the marketplaces of Byzantine Constantinople, Ayyubid and then Mamluk Alexandria, and Hafsid Tunis, they did so under treaties guaranteeing commercial protection and privilege. In twelfth-century Byzantium, first Pisa and Venice and then Genoa negotiated treaties that traded military support for semiautonomous merchant quarters in the city of Constantinople and drastically reduced customs duties. European merchants had been actively trading in the port cities of the Muslim Levant before the Crusades, but as part of the Latin colonization of the east, Genoese, Venetian, and Pisan merchant communities consolidated their privileged positions there as well. After the Ayyubids conquered these Levantine port cities in the late twelfth and thirteenth centuries, Italian merchants quickly negotiated treaties and agreements that guaranteed them their continued possession of urban properties, privileged status, and tax reductions or exemptions. In contrast, the Ayyubid, and then the Mamluk, rulers of the region taxed the local Muslim and Jewish merchants heavily, making it more difficult for them to compete in the trans-Mediterranean trade. The rapidly shifting political circumstances of the medieval Mediterranean meant that these treaties were often renegotiated or abrogated, but more often than not western merchants operated at a distinct advantage, allowing them to edge out their rivals.

COMMERCIAL EXCHANGE AND INNOVATIONS

The increased presence of Latin Christian merchants in Mediterranean commerce can be explained in part through large-scale changes in Europe's society and economy between the eleventh and the fourteenth centuries. In a process historians often refer to as the Commercial Revolution, the European economy transformed from one that was primarily local and agrarian to one marked by an urban orientation and commercial dynamism. Several factors led to this change: between about 1050 and 1300, the climate was exceptionally mild: average temperatures rose several degrees, and rainfall was more regular; agricultural yields grew, and Europe's population nearly doubled, from less than 40 million in 1000 to around 75 million in 1340. This demographic growth was most dramatic for northern Europe, which saw its number of inhabitants triple. The population of southern Europe, already more densely settled and urbanized than the north, also grew, from 17 million to about 25 million. The overall demographic change in Europe increased demand for commodities and luxury goods, and Italian merchants stood ready to supply what these expanding markets demanded.

In northern Italy, people lived in growing towns and cities, and the need to feed these expanding towns led to a thriving regional trade in foodstuffs: grain, wine, and olive oil. In 1288 the Milanese friar Bonvesin della Riva marveled at his city's booming population and its insatiable hunger for cereals, fruits, vegetables, beans, chickpeas, and lentils from the surrounding territory. In the 1330s the chronicler

Giovanni Villani estimated that his native Florence, with a population of about 100,000, needed 700,000 bushels of wheat annually, in addition to 4,000 oxen, 60,000 sheep, 20,000 goats, 30,000 pigs, and 25 million quarts of wine. The largest Italian cities imported grain from southern Italy, Sicily, and the eastern Mediterranean. After defeating Pisa in 1284, Genoese merchants dominated this trade in commodities, using heavy ships to import grain from the Black Sea region.

While wheat, wine, and olive oil fed Europe's growing population, a smaller but extremely profitable trade in luxury goods provided for the demands of European elites. Merchants from the Italian maritime cities of Amalfi, Genoa, Pisa, and Venice, as well as competitors from southern France and Catalonia, traveled in increasing numbers to the great cities of Byzantium and to the Muslim world in search of luxury products. Spices, a category that included seasonings, perfumes, dyestuffs, and medicines, were the most important of these luxuries. Spices played a role in European cuisine, but they also were used medicinally and as symbols of social status, taste, and beauty. Merchants traded the raw materials of northern Europe—wood, metals, slaves, wool, and furs—for these luxuries. This exchange stimulated European manufacturing, and by the fourteenth century many northern Italian city-states were producing cotton and linen cloth, glass, ceramics, soap, metalwork, and paper that imitated and competed with imported luxuries. Italian manufacturing enterprises depended on Mediterranean commercial networks for their supply of raw materials. For instance, silk weavers in Lucca bought raw silk that Genoese merchants imported from Sicily, Calabria, and Asia Minor and turned it into finished textiles. The Venetian glass industry dominated the trade in soda ash from Syria and by the early fourteenth century was producing luxury glass for export to Egypt, Constantinople, and Syria as well as for markets in northern Europe.

In order to undertake long-distance voyages and safely transport merchandise, the Italian and Catalan city-states invested in shipbuilding. Venice established an arsenal as early as 1104, an industrial complex capable of turning out multiple ships at once. Italian mariners relied on two types of ship to build their fleets: long ships, called galleys, with oars and one or two masts, and round ships, propelled solely by the wind. The galley's great advantage was its large cargo space: by the thirteenth century such ships could hold up to 500 metric tons of goods, and the average galley grew in size during the thirteenth century, reaching 130 feet in length. Their maneuverability made galleys flexible in function, and they moved between duty as warships, pirate ships, and merchant vessels carrying small and precious cargos. The smaller round ship, most commonly known as the *nef*, also came into widespread use. Ships' crews often had a variety of origins, making life onboard a mix of languages and cultures. Italian mariners also began to use new sailing technologies such as the compass and portolan charts. In order to provide protection from hostile Latin powers and endemic piracy, the Genoese and Venetians began to form convoys, state-organized fleets that sailed at regular times and included military as well as merchant ships. The Genoese fleet began to sail in convoy from 1277, and the Venetian fleet followed suit in 1314.

Portolan chart. Navigational map, based on compass directions and detailed observation of the coastline, showing the cities of Marseilles, Genoa, and Venice. *Museo Correr, Venice.* © *DeA Picture Library / Art Resource, NY*

The construction and outfitting of ships capable of long sea voyages was an expensive proposition that required significant outlays of capital. Profits could be considerable, but it was difficult for any one individual to finance a voyage. Merchants needed reliable mechanisms for investing capital and distributing the risk among the pool of investors. By 1200, merchants regularly used contracts that divided ships into shares, or parts, distributing the cost of outfitting the ship, pooling the risk, and dividing the profits from the voyage. Italian merchants drew on existing Roman, Byzantine, and Islamic legal traditions for these contracts. Merchants could form a *societas*, or basic partnership, pooling their capital and labor and sharing in the profit and in the risk. The *commenda* was the most commonly used type of contract; it was a flexible instrument and took a number of forms, but generally one partner entrusted capital to another partner, who used it for an overseas commercial venture and returned the original capital plus a share of the profits to the first partner. Italian merchants perfected a series of commercial practices that contributed to increased merchant activity: double-entry bookkeeping, maritime insurance, postal systems, and bills of lading that cataloged a ship's cargo, all of which helped long-distance voyages run more smoothly and profitably. Latin Christian merchants also began to use more sophisticated banking and credit techniques, such as letters of credit and letters of exchange. Some Italian communes began to mint their own gold coinage: the Florentine florin, first minted in 1252, and the Venetian ducat, first minted in 1284, quickly came into common usage in Mediterranean trade.

The rise in banking, business, and accounting also led to the widespread use of "Arabic" numerals. While mathematicians in the Islamic world had been using these numbers for centuries, Italian merchants were the first to consistently use Arabic numerals for business. Leonardo Fibonacci of Pisa visited Provence, Sicily, Egypt, Syria, and Constantinople and wrote in the introduction to his *Book of the Abacus* (1202) that he had first learned the art of calculating in North Africa and had met with Latin, Greek, and Arabic mathematicians across the Mediterranean. Fibonacci's treatises on mathematics both synthesized and added to this knowledge, contributing to the rapid adoption of Arabic numerals among European merchants.

TRADE, COLONIZATION, AND THE STATE

Merchants from northern Italian city-states, particularly Venice, Genoa, and Pisa, and to a lesser extent merchants from Catalonia, were able to parlay their wealth not only into increased social status but, more importantly, into political power as well. From the eleventh century on in northern Italy, the struggle for spiritual and secular superiority between the pope in Rome and the Holy Roman emperor in Germany opened a space for cities to seize autonomy. Communal associations of nobles and urban elites wrested administrative and legal control of their cities from counts or bishops and began to develop town institutions, regulate town law, organize town defenses, and appoint town officials. The northern Italian communes were not precisely democratic, as they were ruled by a restricted elite, but they were a novel political form in medieval Europe that allowed for more social mobility than was the case elsewhere. The German chronicler Otto of Freising, who visited Italy with Emperor Frederick Barbarossa in the twelfth century, was struck by the inclusiveness of this form of government, saying that the communes did "not disdain to give the girdle of knighthood or the grades of distinction to young men of inferior status and even to some workers of the vile mechanical arts whom other people bar like the plague from the more respected and honorable pursuits." Gradually, influential and wealthy merchants claimed political power, sometimes through guild structures, and enacted legislation favorable to their own commercial interests. Otto saw the results of this openness: "From this it has resulted that they far surpass all other states of the world in riches and power." The possibility of ascending the social ladder offered merchants incentive for undertaking risky overseas ventures, and the strong merchant presence in the governments of trading capitals like Genoa and Venice meant that the city-states were willing and able to protect mercantile interests. The flourishing economy led to civic embellishment: new churches, arsenals, bridges, and other buildings beautified the growing merchant cities, and new law codes consolidated and organized their governments.

The situation in Barcelona was slightly different, as the city was governed first by a count and then, from the mid-twelfth century, a count-king of both Catalonia and Aragon. Beginning in the mid-thirteenth century, the citizens of Barcelona had a representative assembly, but the true engine of Barcelona and the Catalan merchants' rise to prominence in Mediterranean exchange was the convergence of the count-king and the urban patrician interest in naval campaigns and in overseas trade. In 1228, Pere Martell, a prominent shipowner in Catalonia, gave a banquet for the count-king James I; there they formalized their plans for the invasion of Majorca. Muslim Majorca was already a Mediterranean trading station with communities of Genoese and Pisan merchants, and its key strategic position on the sea route to North Africa made it a desirable target. After the conquest, territory was divided among James's armies, and the merchants of Barcelona, Marseilles, and Montpellier were also rewarded with urban properties and lands. In hopes of increasing Majorcan trade, James also invited Jews from Catalonia, southern France, and North Africa to settle on the island. Jewish merchants active in trade and finance networks in North Africa helped make Majorca a central node in the network that connected southern France, Catalonia, and Islamic North Africa.

The Catalan conquest of Majorca was not unique: there are several examples of Latin Christians conquering and then colonizing key commercial locations in the Mediterranean. These groups of Catalans, Genoese, and Venetians used a combination of private enterprise and state power to wrest territories from the fragmented Byzantine Empire. The precise relationship between state structures, merchants, and military power was different in each instance, but the overall pattern was one where violent conquest and Latin settlement were employed for commercial as well as political advantage. During the dismemberment of the Byzantine Empire in the wake of the Fourth Crusade, Greek territories were divided between the Frankish crusaders and the Venetians. In addition, many enterprising individuals conquered islands or port cities and held them as semiautonomous vassals of the Latin emperor in Constantinople.

Venetian and Genoese experiences provide two different models of the relationship between state centralization and merchant enterprises. After the Fourth Crusade, Venice received the port cities of Coron and Modon and a partial claim to Negroponte (Euboea) in Greece, but its greatest colonial undertaking was the island of Crete. Venice came away from its participation in the Fourth Crusade with title to Crete, and in 1211, Venetian forces conquered Genoese pirates and then the Cretans themselves, imposing their rule by force. Venice replaced the Greek Orthodox nobles with its own settlers, introduced Venetian law, and replaced the Greek Orthodox religious hierarchy with Latins, although they did not ban the practice of Orthodoxy on the island. Venetian colonists were given confiscated land, called fiefs, in return for military service. Merchants and other immigrants from Venice and elsewhere in the Latin Mediterranean followed, and Candia (Heraklion), the capital city, became one of the main commercial entrepôts of the eastern Mediterranean. Venetians also exploited the island's agricultural resources, producing wheat, wine, and cheese for export. Venetian territorial administration overseas was relatively centralized, with governors elected in Venice for two-year terms and Venetian state resources dedicated to their control and defense.

Genoese colonies, by contrast, were acquired and governed in a much more decentralized manner. In the west, Genoa dominated the political and economic life of Corsica and struggled with Pisa for predominance on Sardinia. The Fourth Crusade and Latin empire in Constantinople blocked the development of a strong Genoese position in the region, but the Genoese did benefit from the 1261 restoration of the Byzantine Empire. Michael VIII Palaiologos offered them substantial commercial privileges and a trading quarter of their own in Pera in return for naval support. In the late 1260s the Genoese also established a trading outpost in Kaffa, on the Black Sea. At the same time, the Genoese adventurer Benedetto Zaccaria won an imperial concession to the port of Phocaea, and in 1304 acquired the island of Chios as well. Phocaea and Chios briefly returned to Byzantine control in 1326, but in 1346 a Genoese society of investors armed a fleet and retook these islands. While the city-state of Genoa had sovereignty, the revenues from the islands' alum, mastic, and dried fruit went to the corporation, called the Mahona. The Genoese also had a commanding commercial presence in Famagusta, on Cyprus, from 1291, and in 1373 a squabble over precedence between Venetian and Genoese representatives on Cyprus led the Genoese to invade and take control over the city. Unlike Venetian Crete, the Genoese presence in its colonies was limited to castles and port cities and did not involve agricultural settlement of the interior. Although Genoese merchants attained exceptional prosperity from these enterprises, Genoa itself did not necessarily benefit to the same degree.

The value of these ports and islands lay not only in their status as ports of call and points of commercial exchange but in their productive capacities. Cyprus, for instance, became one of the most important Mediterranean centers for sugarcane production in the fourteenth century. Western Europe had been importing sugar since the eleventh century, and farmers cultivated sugarcane in Syria, Egypt, Sicily, and southern Spain. Sugarcane could be planted on lands that were too poor to produce grain, but it required irrigation works, mills, and machinery for processing the raw cane into sugar. During the Crusades, the crusader states as well as Italian merchants and the military orders began to produce sugar as a market commodity; after the fall of the these states, producers shifted to Cyprus, which first exported sugar in 1301. The island's Lusignan dynasty, the Hospitaller military order, and several individual families, notably the Corner of Venice and the Ferrer of Catalonia, produced sugar for export, in some cases relying on Syrian immigrant labor skilled in sugarcane production.

Genoese, Venetian, and Catalan colonies were often founded at the expense of the Orthodox Christian Byzantines. Even after the restoration of the Byzantine Empire, in 1261, Byzantine merchants remained in a weak position relative to their western counterparts. Byzantine merchants exported food and raw materials as well as acting as middlemen in the luxury trade from the east, and they imported manufactured articles from western Europe. But it was the Venetians and the Genoese in their protected merchant quarters that took the lion's share of the profits from the trade. Emperor Andronikos II Palaiologos's 1285 cost-cutting measure to dismantle the Byzantine fleet was a disastrous decision, as it left Byzantine territories prey to both Latins and Turks and allowed piracy in the Aegean to go unchecked. There is some scholarly debate on the degree to which the advent of Italian merchants damaged the Byzantine economy—some economic historians have argued that the arrival of foreign merchants acted as a motor for more dynamic commerce in the urban coastal regions, linking town and country more closely.

In Anatolia, where the Byzantines struggled to maintain a foothold in the western part of the peninsula, first the Seljuks and then other Turkish principalities actively promoted trade and engaged in patterns of Mediterranean commerce. The Seljuk sultans fostered trade by constructing a network of caravanserais (trading stations) to provide shelter and security for merchants and their goods along the journey from central Anatolia to the southern port cities of Antalya and Alanya. The Seljuk rulers also settled rich merchants in these port cities to ensure the development of exchange networks. The Mongol invasions of the 1240s temporarily disrupted these trading systems and fatally weakened the Seljuks of Rum, but the small principalities, or emirates, that arose from the Seljuk disintegration continued to support and foster commerce in their territories. The Venetians concluded trade agreements with the emirates of Menteshe and Aydin in south Anatolia, and Genoese traders remained a frequent presence in these ports as well. When the Ottoman Turks began their campaigns of conquest in Anatolia and the Balkans, they took care to ensure that the towns and markets they conquered flourished under their rule. Immediately after conquering a town, the new Turkish ruler would establish a market, along with a mosque and bathhouse, and appoint officials to impose order and combat mercantile fraud.

In Mamluk Egypt, the European demand for luxury products from the east shaped the patterns of commercial traffic within the realm. Trade in the Red Sea region rose significantly from the twelfth century onward, and Muslim merchants became wealthy as a result of this trade, in particular the Karimi merchants. The Karimi were a close-knit group of predominantly Muslim merchant families who benefited from their close alliance with first the Ayyubid and then the Mamluk rulers and used the sultans' protection to dominate the Red Sea trade in spices and luxuries from India. Some of the Karimi achieved vast fortunes and acted as bankers for the sultans, extending credit for building projects, fortifications, and armies. But unlike their Italian counterparts, the Karimi took part in politics only indirectly, remaining dependent on the ruler's favor and vulnerable to taxation changes. The rise of the Karimi merchants, together with the increasing importance of Italian merchants in the Mediterranean, meant a contraction in the trans-Mediterranean trading activities of the Jewish genizah merchants. By about 1200, the commercial letters in the genizah rarely refer to trade matters outside of Egypt.

In northwest Africa, Almohad rule gave way in the mid-thirteenth century to oscillating control between the Hafsid regime centered in Tunis and regional emirates at Bougie (Bijaya), Mahdia, and Algiers. The Almohads, though hostile to their Christian and Jewish minority populations, welcomed foreign merchants as sources of revenue. Pisan and Genoese merchants visited the ports to acquire leather, wool, fine ceramics, and gold dust that arrived via trans-Saharan caravan. The Hafsid dynasty also welcomed foreign merchants, although it took a more assertive attitude toward taxation and expanded oversight over merchants and markets. Merchants from Pisa and Genoa were joined by traders from Marseille and Catalonia. The Genoese in particular had large and vibrant trade outposts in the North African ports. There were also many Muslim Andalusi merchants who had fled Christian and Muslim wars in Iberia, resettled in North Africa, and become wealthy and powerful through trade. These Andalusis made alliances with regional rulers and thus exercised political influence, although they were vulnerable to periodic expropriations. Numerous North Africans practiced piracy, and these pirates came to play an important role in Hafsid politics from the mid-fourteenth century, when the emirate was weakening.

COMPETITION, CONFLICT, AND CRUSADE

Conflict intermittently disrupted the Mediterranean trading networks of the twelfth and thirteenth centuries. Intense competition between the Italian maritime cities several times led to open war. Individual European monarchs launched crusades targeting the Islamic world, and the pope issued embargoes on trade in war materials between Christians and Muslims. Even when there was not open warfare, pirates and corsairs were a continual danger. Despite all of these difficulties, trans-Mediterranean trade remained frequent and profitable.

The Italian maritime cities competed for predominance in the commercial worlds of the eastern and western Mediterranean. Genoa and Pisa struggled to control the islands of Corsica and Sardinia, which were agricultural producers as well as key ports on the shipping routes from southern France to North Africa. The Genoese fleet, led by Benedetto Zaccaria, inflicted a crushing defeat on Pisan forces at the battle of Meloria (1284). Pisa never recovered, declining to a second-rate power at the same time that Catalan merchants were becoming more prominent in the western Mediterranean. The Genoese and Venetians fought bitterly for supremacy in the eastern Mediterranean. As a result of the War of St. Sabas (1256–70), begun as a dispute over possession of a monastery in Acre, the Genoese lost their merchant quarter in that coastal city. Although both sides agreed to a peace in 1270, tensions simmered for the next 20 years. The War of Korčula (Curzola) (1293–99) was fought at sea and also by raids on colonies and coastlines. Venetian admirals burned the Genoese colony at Pera in 1295 and attacked Kaffa; in return, the Genoese slaughtered Venetian representatives in Constantinople. Both sides sustained heavy losses in the main battle of the war, off the island of Korčula, in the Adriatic. A corsair fighting on Venice's behalf, Domenico Schiavo, raided Genoa itself, raising the banner of St. Mark over the port and, to add insult to injury, struck a Venetian ducat in Genoa's harbor. The pope forced a peace between the combatants in 1299, but the two cities remained hostile.

The Mamluk conquest of the remnants of the crusader states in the later thirteenth century, combined with the Mongol expansion in central Asia, caused a northward shift in patterns of exchange and enriched ports in and around the Black Sea region at the expense of the Levant. The Latin barons of the crusader states felt this economic contraction even before the final Mamluk conquest and sold their estates to Italian merchants and to the Templar and Hospitaller orders, who became the real powers in the kingdom. Divisions between Templars, Hospitallers, and the Italian merchant communes made it difficult for the port cities of the Levant to withstand Mamluk military campaigns. Caesarea, Arsuf, and Haifa fell in 1265, Jaffa and Antioch in 1268, and Ascalon in 1270. Sultan Baybars's strategy was to destroy the harbors and port facilities of these towns, eliminating the possibility that assistance would come from the west, although few western European powers made such an effort. The last crusader outpost, Acre, fell in 1291. These conquests did not end trade in the eastern Mediterranean by any means: Baybars resumed traditional Egyptian-Sicilian trade relations, made commercial agreements with Castile and Aragon, and continued to do business with Marseilles, Venice, and Genoa. Alexandria became an important trade entrepôt in the fourteenth century.

The fall of the crusader states in the Levant did not mean the end of European crusading overall, although fourteenth- and fifteenth-century crusading efforts existed in a complex relationship with trading relationships. After the fall of Acre, the pope tried to forbid Latin Christian trade in commodities that could have military uses: primarily wood, metal, and slaves. There is little evidence that the restrictions actually stopped Latins from exchanging these goods with their Muslim counterparts, and from 1291 to 1344 the bans on trade in war material were often flouted. After 1344 the papacy relaxed its restrictions and gave wide-ranging exemptions from the ban. The targets of crusade in these centuries also multiplied: some had as their ultimate goal the recapture of Jerusalem, but many aimed to secure control of shipping lanes or port facilities, and several resulted in new trade agreements between Christian and Muslim states. After Mamluks expelled the Hospitallers and Templars from Acre, the Hospitallers seized poorly defended Byzantine territories for themselves, taking the island of Rhodes in 1310. Their crusading reach was greatly amplified by the 1302 fall of the Templars, accused of heresy and dissolved by papal order in 1312. The Hospitallers received much of the Templars' property; some of the revenues went into the fortification of Rhodes, which became an attractive port of call for merchants looking for a safe harbor in the eastern Mediterranean. They also used Rhodes as a base for piracy, ostensibly targeting Muslim shipping as a part of their crusading efforts but in reality taking all sorts of ships.

In the early fourteenth century, Europeans employed the idea of crusade to prosecute warfare on Muslim-Christian frontiers. In Iberia the complexity of these frontier relationships even resulted in Pope Clement V granting a crusading license in 1308 to a joint Christian-Muslim expedition against Granada in which Aragon was to take the port of Almeria, Castile was to seize Algeciras, and the Marinids of Morocco were to seize Ceuta. The Marinids abandoned the alliance after regaining Ceuta, and the Christian sieges were failures. Aragon thereafter pursued its interests in North Africa by diplomatic and commercial means. In 1344, Pope Clement VI allied with Venice, Cyprus, and Rhodes to form a Holy League that sailed against the emirate of Aydin in western Anatolia. The crusaders captured the port city of Smyrna, which they held until 1402.

The variety of effects of later fourteenth century crusades on trading relationships can be seen in the different outcomes of the Cypriot attack on Alexandria in 1366 and the joint French-Genoese expedition against Mahdia in Hafsid Tunis. King Peter of Cyprus dreamed of leading a crusade to recapture Jerusalem, but he had difficulty securing Venetian support for his enterprise, as they were concerned that his plans would interrupt their trade with the Mamluks and instead wanted to send an expedition against the Turks. The Cypriots did take and sack Alexandria, resulting in reprisals against the Christian merchants in the city and damage to the fortifications and harbors. In 1390 the Genoese proposal for a crusade against Mahdia was at least partially inspired by their desire to stop Hafsid pirates from damaging their shipping in the region, although the Genoese themselves had garnered a reputation as fearsome pirates as well. The French joined the enterprise enthusiastically, but after a three-month siege of the city, the Genoese negotiated a renewal of their earlier treaty with the Hafsids, and trade with the port resumed, channeling leather, wax, coral, and ostrich feathers from the trans-Saharan trade to Mediterranean merchants.

The line between state-sponsored violence and piracy was often difficult to determine, as individuals like Benedetto Zaccaria moved back and forth between piracy and merchant activity. Piracy provided motivation and legitimation for crusading efforts, and both Christian and Muslim commentators aimed their ire at pirates of other faiths, some painting piracy itself as motivated by religious fervor. The North African historian Ibn Khaldun wrote, "When the Christian Franks came to be ruled by many kingdoms, the desire to raid their lands grew among many Muslims on the coasts of Ifriqiya. The people of Bijaya (Bougie) had started to do so prior to 1390, gathering those who were eager to fight among the pirates, building up the navy, and choosing for it the best men. They then sailed to the coasts of the Franks and their islands, [attacked them] by surprise and kidnapped as many people as they could. They also fought the unbelievers' ships, often taking them away from them, and returned with booty, slaves, and captives." Against Ibn Khaldun's Muslim pirates attacking "unbelievers" we might place the 1381 example of the Genoese pirate Onofrio di Piccamiglio, who was accused of going into business with the vizier of Bougie with the purpose of arming pirate galleys and seeking to benefit from the sale of Christian captives. Both the Muslim Hafsids and the Christian Genoese had identifiable economic and political motivations for piracy, making it difficult to characterize pirates' activities as solely an outgrowth of a crusading mentality or religious hostility.

MOBILITY OF PEOPLE

The rising volume of international trade in the Mediterranean was accompanied by an increase in individual and collective mobility. From the twelfth to the fourteenth century, countless thousands of men and women crossed the Mediterranean involuntarily, as captives or slaves. A smaller number of travelers moved to and fro voluntarily, as merchants, migrants, pirates, or pilgrims. In the mid-fourteenth century, the Italian poet and humanist Giovanni Boccaccio composed the *Decameron*, a collection of 100 short stories that give a vibrant picture of Mediterranean travel in this period: full of danger but also offering opportunities to the bold, the resourceful, and the lucky traveler. Boccaccio presents a world where interaction across religious boundaries was common, if not always free of hostility. As a whole, the stories encompass the erotic, the humorous, and the tragic; a subset recount the adventures of merchants who win and lose fortunes in the markets of the east, pirates who rise to high social position through plunder, and men and women who are shipwrecked, captured, enslaved, converted, and ransomed. In one story a Muslim princess of extraordinary beauty, Alatiel, sets out from Alexandria to marry a North African king but is shipwrecked on Majorca. A lord of the island, entranced by her beauty, tricks her into becoming his mistress; from there, she is kidnapped by a succession of love-struck merchants, princes, and emirs, traveling from Corinth to Athens to Chios to Smyrna. After escaping Smyrna for Rhodes with a servant of the Turkish lord of Smyrna, Alatiel accompanies a merchant back to Cyprus, where, with the connivance of her father's old servant, she is restored to her previous position, claiming to have spent her time away from Alexandria in a southern French convent.

Individuals could be enslaved through several mechanisms. Beyond the Mediterranean region, slave traders captured or purchased people on the Russian steppes or the Sahel and savanna zones of sub-Saharan Africa and transported them to the booming markets of the Mediterranean. Eastern Europe and central Asia were the major sources of slaves for the Mediterranean world as a whole; the Muslim societies of North Africa also looked to the trans-Saharan slave trade to supply its slave markets. Only a small number of these black Africans were sold farther north, to the European colonial societies on the islands and to the port cities of Latin Europe. From the fourteenth and fifteenth centuries, Portuguese slavers brought West Africans to Mediterranean markets; they were a small minority of enslaved people in Italy, although they made up larger numbers in Iberia. Within the Mediterranean, people were enslaved through war and conquest, piracy, and frontier raiding. The courts sentenced some individuals to slavery, and in other cases people sold themselves or their children into slavery out of desperate poverty.

In the late medieval era, the religious identities of the slaves who moved across geographic and religious boundaries became an increasingly fraught issue for Latin Europe in particular. Scholars used to believe that slavery had faded away in Europe as a whole by the eleventh century, but now it is apparent that the institution remained significant in eastern Iberia, southern France, and Italy through the fifteenth century. In Byzantium, slavery declined after the eleventh century but was never formally abolished. By the fifteenth century, the enslavement of Greek Christians by Latins was on the decline in Iberia and in the Italian peninsula, but Greek slaves did remain part of the society and economy of Venetian Crete, Frankish Cyprus, and Genoese Chios. Christian merchants were less likely to buy Christian captives and Muslim merchants less likely to buy Muslim captives, but slave traders did not inquire too closely into the religious identities of the enslaved men and women they purchased. In a small number of unusual cases that have emerged from archives in Italy, Crete, Majorca, and Valencia, individuals challenged their enslavement via the courts. In the cases from Italy and Crete, judges set the women plaintiffs free on the basis that they had been Latin Christians before their enslavement, and therefore were illegally enslaved. In fifteenth-century Valencia a man named Johan successfully won his freedom by demonstrating he was a Latin Christian originally from Hungary. Given the extraordinary difficulty the average slave would have had in accessing such a judicial remedy, it is likely these cases represent a much larger pool of Christians illegally enslaved by their coreligionists.

Pirates aimed to capture goods, but they also wanted to capture people for ransom or sale, and coastal raiding was a common feature of life near the sea. Maria, a young Greek woman originally from Nicosia in Cyprus, described to a fifteenth-century court in Valencia how she had been playing with other little girls in the town when she was kidnapped by Genoese pirates. Christian merchants from Catalo-

Manuscript illustrations from the *Cantigas de Santa Maria*, thirteenth century, Castile. *Top,* a merchant galley pursued by pirates. *Right,* merchants from Spain selling their wares in the Levantine city of Acre. *Biblioteca Real, Escorial, Madrid. Photo: Album / Art Resource, NY*

nia and from Italy raided the coastlines of Greece for captives to sell in southern Mediterranean markets. In the east, Turks raided Latin territories regularly and sold their captives to Catalan and Venetian merchants in Thebes, Naxos, and Asia Minor. The chronicler Marino Sanudo Torsello reported that the Turks took 25,000 people prisoner in 1331–32. In the early fifteenth century, Cypriot raids on the shores of their Muslim neighbors took 1,500 subjects of the Mamluk sultan to work on the island's sugar plantations, provoking a Mamluk attack on the island in 1426.

Raids and redemption were a common part of the frontier economy on land and at sea, and the principal goal of many raids was often the capture of people for profit, either through sale or by ransom. The frequency of ransoming by the state or religious orders made piracy a predictably profitable enterprise; it also meant that some fortunate individuals eventually returned to their homes, while the unlucky and unransomed were sold. States sometimes redeemed their subjects through diplomatic means: in 1358, for instance, the Venetian Duke of Crete convinced Emir Musa of Menteshe, in Anatolia, to return 24 Cretans who had been kidnapped. Others were redeemed by their coreligionists or relatives, as was the case for six enslaved Jews on Cyprus who were redeemed by a Jew from Palermo.

Slavers bought and sold enslaved men and women at markets throughout the Mediterranean. Even though the nature of the evidence is fragmentary and does not allow for statistical overviews of

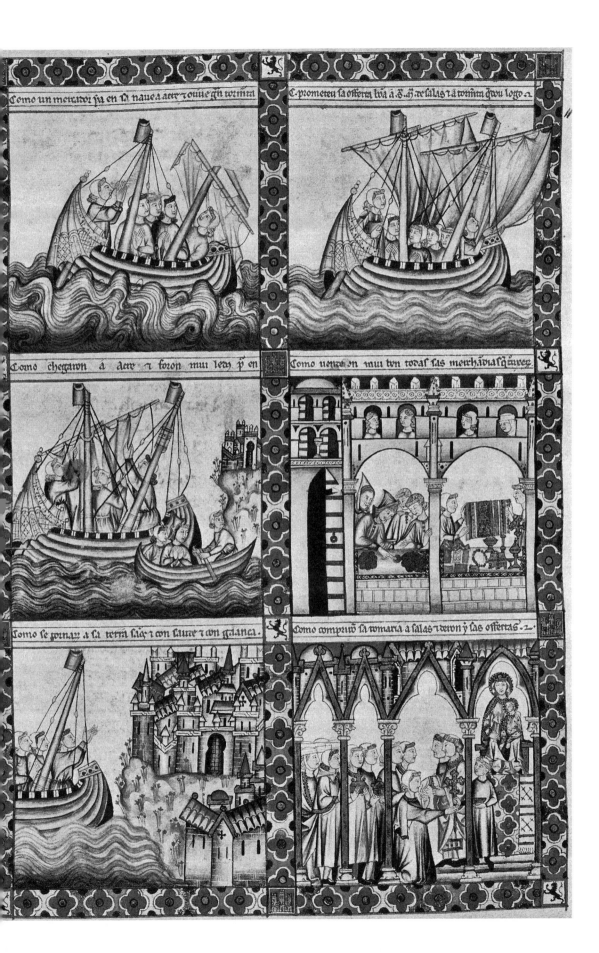

Como un mercador ja en sa naue a aerz rouue en tormta

E prometeu sa offerta bõa a S.ãa de salas e a tormta chou logo

Como chegaron a aerz e foron mui leds p en

Como uenzron mui ten todas sas merchãdias quirez

Como se pornar a sa terra saoz e con sauer e con ganca

Como compriu sa romaria a salas e deron y sas offertas

medieval slavery in the region as a whole, the general patterns of the trade are clear. Venice and Genoa were major centers of the slave trade in Italy; first Barcelona and then Valencia were centers of the Iberian trade. The islands of Majorca, Sardinia, Sicily, Crete, Rhodes, Cyprus, and Chios functioned as international slave emporia as well, although their relative importance shifted with political and economic changes. For instance, the fall of the last crusader outposts in the 1290s led to the rise of Famagusta as a center of commerce in general and the slave trade in particular. From these centers, merchants either sold slaves on the domestic market or reexported slaves to meet demand elsewhere. The Genoese were likely the most active, but merchants from all Mediterranean societies participated in this trade: Venetians, Hospitallers, Catalans, Anconitans, merchants from Marseilles and southern France, and Turks.

Across the Mediterranean, slaves were most commonly employed in the households of the elite; less frequently, they were used in agricultural enterprises or as business agents. Slaves formed a very small percentage of urban populations, probably 2–5%; the figures were likely slightly higher in Venetian Crete, Genoese Chios, and Cyprus, where the enslaved worked alongside dependent and free laborers in the vineyards, fields, and sugar mills of these colonial societies. Young women commanded the highest prices in Latin European slave markets, reflecting their desirability as domestic servants. Women also worked in the households of the Muslim elite, and they could also be trained as entertainers or end up as sex objects in the harem system. In Latin Europe, women were sexually exploited within the confines of the household, and the children they bore to their masters were free. There are frequent records of manumissions of domestic slaves; freed and Christianized, these individuals assimilated into the mass of the urban populations.

A particular feature of slavery in the Muslim world was the use of young men as slave soldiers, called mamluks. Islamic rulers from the ninth century had relied on these military slaves for state maintenance, but the armies of the Mamluk rulers of Egypt, as their name indicates, were entirely made up of such slave soldiers. The great advantage of these elite troops was that they brought with them no outside ties of kinship or loyalty. The experience and status of the young men brought into this system through enslavement was different from that of other slaves: Mamluk agents purchased non-Muslims and educated them in the principles of the Islamic faith and in the military arts. After completing their training, the young men were freed and began their military careers, with the possibility of attaining high military rank and office. Their children were born as free Muslims and were thus ineligible to follow their fathers into the army. As a result, the Mamluk demand for young male slaves remained extremely high: the dynasty imported as many as 10,000 slaves per year in the late thirteenth and early fourteenth century.

In addition to the involuntary mobility of captives and slaves, many people moved from place to place of their own accord. Merchants, pilgrims, and other travelers moved along the same routes and relied on the same sorts of institutions to ease their journeys. In almost every Mediterranean port, travelers could find an inn or hostel, sometimes combined with warehouses or storage sheds for merchant goods. These flexible yet ubiquitous accommodations for travelers, known as a *pandocheion* in Greek, *funduq* in Arabic, and *fondaco* in Italian, had deep roots in Mediterranean port cities. In the Islamic world, the funduq took the late antique pandocheion's hostelry service and added a commercial function, meaning that funduqs came to be associated with particular types of merchants and merchandise and were regulated by the state. The large trading cities of the Mediterranean had dozens or even hundreds of these institutions, each providing particular communities of visiting merchants, pilgrims, and travelers access to their own laws, religion, and foodways. There were also interpreters and translators to facilitate business dealings, chapels, and baths. Christian funduqs in the Muslim world often had permission to sell wine, which was forbidden to practicing Muslims. Within the Christian and Byzantine worlds, fondacos also offered storage, lodging, and protection for communities of foreign merchants. These fondacos were important sites not only for negotiating business deals and exchanges but also for mediating cross-cultural interactions in general.

Merchant communities abroad were often represented by a consul, part of the institutional framework that helped mediate between merchants and the state. Consuls acted as diplomats when necessary and also as internal arbiters and judges. Venetian, Genoese, and Pisan consuls often offered protection not only to their own citizens but to other groups of western merchants from cities without independent representation.

Several long-distance travelers left accounts of their trans-Mediterranean voyages in this period, and their tales give a sense of the wide variety of travel experiences as well as the commercial, political, and religious motivations for these journeys. Benjamin of Tudela, a rabbi from northern Spain, undertook a pilgrimage to Jerusalem and back between 1165 and 1173. On his outward journey, he went overland via southern France, Rome, and Constantinople, describing the lands he visited and the number of Jews in each town where he stopped. On his return journey, he went by sea, sailing from Alexandria to Sicily and home. Tudela described the diversity of Christian merchants in Alexandria: "Alexandria is a commercial market for all nations . . . each nation has an inn of its own." At almost the same time, the Spanish Muslim pilgrim Ibn Jubayr set out for Mecca in 1183 via the Balearics, Sicily, and Alexandria. Although he visited Syria and Palestine during a time of crusading warfare, he reported that the Christian customs clerks wrote and spoke Arabic and that trade between the two communities went on unabated. Ibn Jubayr also described the alarming experience of arriving in the port of Alexandria, where Ayyubid customs officials boarded the ship, recorded the names and destinations of all the passengers, and sent them off to the customs house, where they were searched for goods. "The Customs House was packed to choking. All their goods, great and small, were searched and confusedly thrown together, while hands were thrust into their waistbands in search of what might be within." His account of his voyage leaves a vivid picture of life on board a ship. Buffeted by storms on the outward and return passage, the Muslim and Christian passengers on the Christian-owned ship remained separate but suffered the same hardships.

The Venetian merchant Marco Polo is famous for leaving the Mediterranean for China, following in the footsteps of his father and uncle. His trip offers some hints at the routes of western merchants who traveled widely in search of the fabled riches of the east, as well as demonstrating the way Mediterranean trading networks connected to more global patterns of exchange. From Venice, Polo traveled to Acre and from there to Ayas, where he accompanied a caravan crossing Anatolia for the Black Sea region. He then joined the traffic crossing the silk roads, newly opened by the unification of central Asia under Mongol rule. At around the same time, the French Franciscan William of Rubruck left on his mission to convert the Mongols to Christianity via Constantinople and the Black Sea. Marco Polo spent many years in China; when he returned, he was caught up in Venice's war with Genoa and captured at the battle of Curzola, in 1298. He narrated the account of his adventures to a fellow inmate in the Genoese prison, and the manuscript spread through Europe, circulating the tales of China's fabulous wealth. Polo himself returned to Venice and spent the rest of his life as a merchant investor.

Like Ibn Jubayr, Ibn Battuta set out from the far west of the Islamic world on a pilgrimage to Mecca. He proved to be as much a wanderer as a pilgrim, and between 1325 and 1354 he walked, rode, and sailed an estimated 75,000 miles, the longest known journey undertaken by any single person before 1500. Like Marco Polo, Ibn Battuta's travels took him far from the shores of the Mediterranean, but his detailed account of his voyages offers rich evidence of the conditions of travel in the Muslim world. He observed the many caravanserais and fondacos intended for merchants in Alexandria and the Mamluk realms, and he traveled within a network well provisioned with stopping places, where "travelers alight with their beasts, and outside each *khan* is a public watering place at which the traveler many buy what he requires for himself and his beast." He himself depended on the hospitality of fellow legal scholars as well as Sufi mystics. Although Ibn Battuta's travels spanned an age of crisis in the mid-fourteenth century, his account presents the Mediterranean lands of Islam as generally peaceful, profitable, and orderly.

THE BUBONIC PLAGUE

In the mid-fourteenth century, several interconnected crises beset the Mediterranean world. By the late thirteenth and early fourteenth centuries, the favorable climate of the "medieval warm period" was ending, bringing colder winters and less predictable rainfall. While in northern Europe colder temperatures meant a contraction of available cropland, individuals living in the Mediterranean experienced rainier summers and localized flooding rather than widespread crop failure. Heavy rains could be very destructive: in 1345, rain fell constantly through Italy, the major rivers all flooded, and Villani estimated that 4,000 people died of hunger. While this figure is likely inflated, it accurately points to the specter of starvation that

stalked the crowded cities of the early fourteenth century. Famine also struck Catalonia in 1333 and 1347.

In 1348 the same connectivity that allowed merchants, luxury goods, and travelers to cross the sea with ease brought devastating disease: bubonic plague, from the nineteenth century referred to as the Black Death because of the subcutaneous hemorrhages leading to skin discoloration in its victims. The region had not seen a large-scale epidemic since the time of Justinian's plague in 542, but beginning in

A Muslim traveler arrives in town. Manuscript illustration, executed by Yahya ben Mahmud al-Wasiti in Baghdad in 1237, showing some typical features of a Muslim town: the mosque and minaret are visible in the upper left, and the arched doorways are the town's marketplace. *Bibliothèque nationale de France, Paris. Photo: Art Resource, NY*

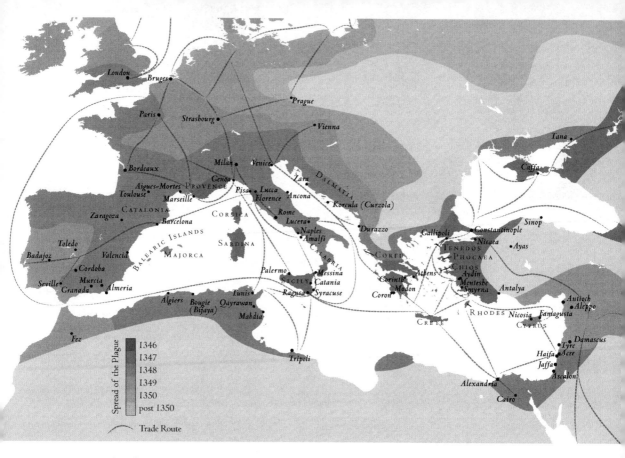

London Bruges
Prague
Paris Strasbourg
Vienna
Bordeaux Milan Venice
Zara DALMATIA
Aigues-Mortes PROVENCE Genoa
Toulouse Pisa Lucca Ancona
Marseille Florence
CATALONIA Korcula (Curzola)
Zaragoza Rome
CORSICA Lucera Sinop
Barcelona Naples Durazzo Gallipoli Constantinople
BALEARIC ISLANDS Amalfi Nicaea
Toledo SARDINA TENEDOS Ayas
Badajoz Valencia MAJORCA PHOCAEA
Cordoba CALABRIA CHIOS
Seville Murcia Palermo Messina Corinth Aydin Menteshe
Granada Almeria SICILY Catania Athens Smyrna Antalya
Algiers Tunis Ragusa Syracuse Modon Antioch
Bougie Qayrawan Coron RHODES Aleppo
Fez (Bijaya) Mahdia CRETE Nicosia Famagusta
CYPRUS
Damascus
Tripoli Tyre Acre
Haifa
Jaffa
Ascalon
Alexandria
Cairo

Spread of the Plague

1346
1347
1348
1349
1350
post 1350

Trade Route

Tana
Caffa

Networks of
Exchange and the
Spread of Disease

1347 and reaching its peak in 1348, plague ravaged Mediterranean societies. While the evidence of the plague's effects is uneven, it is clear that this was a demographic disaster everywhere. Approximately 35 million people died in western Europe, and the mortality rate was equally high in the Byzantine and Islamic worlds. It first reached the shores of the sea at Kaffa, where Mongol armies were besieging the Genoese trading colony. Merchant ships fleeing Kaffa stopped at Constantinople, where plague was reported in July 1347, and in Sicily, where plague was reported in November. The disease spread like wildfire along the bustling commercial routes that crisscrossed the sea. Mamluk Egypt imported Russian and Tatar slaves, horses, furs, and wax from the Black Sea region; the plague took the same route, arriving in Alexandria in September 1347. The Egyptian chronicler al-Maqrizi reported that a ship from the Black Sea region set out for Alexandria with 32 merchants and 300 slaves and crew members; when it arrived in Alexandria, 4 merchants, 1 slave, and 40 crew members were still alive.

The plague spread swiftly along commercial routes. Merchant ships brought the infection to Genoa in December 1347 and Venice in January 1348. In the western Mediterranean, Majorca and the Catalan world were infected by the spring of 1348, and the disease reached Almeria and the Muslim kingdom of Granada in May. By the spring of 1348 the disease was reported in the majority of the major Mediterranean ports, and from there it spread inland, to the cities' hinterlands and into rural areas. Mortality rates were highest in the crowded cities, where between 50 and

75% of the population died. Scientists disagree over the medical profile of the disease: the traditional explanation, that the disease is endemic in rats and spread to humans by infected rat fleas, has been challenged by genetic evidence strongly suggesting that transmission was airborne. Chroniclers across the Mediterranean commented on the disease's swift progress: the Byzantine Nikephoros Gregoras wrote, "Several homes were emptied of all their inhabitants in one day or sometimes in two," and al-Wardi, a judge in Aleppo, commented that among a family, "one of them spits blood, and everyone in the house is certain of death."

Mediterranean doctors, who shared a framework of understanding of the human body and disease based on the work of the Greco-Roman physician Galen, were helpless to stop the painful and terrifying progress of the disease. Islamic, Christian, and Jewish physicians all accessed Galen's work through Ibn Sina (Avicenna)'s influential translations and commentaries. Galenic medicine was based on the theory of humors, the four basic elements that constituted everything: water, fire, air, and earth. Each element had its accompanying quality—wet, hot, cold, and dry. In terms of health, each element also corresponded to a humor—blood, phlegm, choler (yellow bile), and melancholy (black bile)—and these humors determined one's temperament: sanguine (passionate), phlegmatic (sluggish), choleric (bad-tempered) and melancholic (sad, depressed). For Galen and other thinkers, health was determined by the balance of humors. Doctors attributed widespread illnesses like the plague to miasmas, or bad air, which unbalanced the body's humors. Some saw astrological influences in the widespread and fatal imbalance of the humors. In the Islamic world, astrological explanations were more popular with the lower classes while many educated European authors also gave astrological influences a large role. Medical practitioners thus approached the onset of the plague with an arsenal of treatments that attempted to rebalance the humors: bloodletting, purging, sweating, vomiting, drugs, and diet. None of these treatments was effective.

A second strand of explanation focused on contagion. Observers of the plague's progress often commented on the way the disease seemed to spread from person to person. Boccaccio, describing the onset of the plague in Florence, wrote, "Whenever those suffering from it mixed with people who were still unaffected, it would rush upon these with the speed of a fire racing through dry or oily substances that happened to be placed within its reach." Two Muslim physicians in Granada, Ibn Khatima and Ibn al-Khatib, wrote medical treatises on the plague that acknowledged contagion, although this theory directly contradicted the orthodox Islamic belief that plague was a mercy and a martyrdom from God for the faithful Muslim and a punishment for the infidel. As a result of this belief, the normative Muslim response to plague was to neither enter nor flee a plague-stricken land. While Ibn Khatima upheld the belief in contagion only indirectly, his friend and colleague Ibn al-Khatib's treatise openly supported the theory of contagion and directly contradicted Islamic belief. He wrote, "The existence of contagion has been proven by experience, deduction, the senses, observation, and by unanimous reports." About 20 years after the first onset of plague, in 1371, al-Khatib was accused of heresy and

Allegory from a fifteenth-century Italian book cover. The bubonic plague appears as a dark horseman of the apocalypse, trampling over dead bodies in the street and shooting arrows at other victims. *Photo: bpk, Berlin/ Kunstgewebemuseum/Saturia Lake/Art Resource, NY*

forced to flee Granada; he was lynched by a mob in Fez while awaiting trial.

Latin Christians looked for the source of the infection in the heavens and within their own society. Many Latin Christian commentators attributed the appearance of the plague to divine wrath, sent to punish humanity for its sins. Gabriel de Mussis, a lawyer in northern Italy, described the onset of the plague as divine justice: "The quivering spear of the Almighty, in the form of plague, was sent down to infect the whole human race, aiming its cruel darts everywhere." Christians turned to God, to local saints' cults, and to public ceremonies of atonement and penance. Latin Christians also scapegoated minority communities for the disease. When the plague struck Cyprus in 1348, the Egyptian al-Maqrizi reported that the Cypriots assembled all Muslim slaves and massacred

THE MEDITERRANEAN WORLD

them for fear that the Muslims would gain control of island. Jewish communities suffered terribly; there were pogroms in southern France and in Catalonia in spring 1348 based on accusations that Jews were causing the plague by poisoning the wells. Pope Clement VI tried to stop the persecution of the Jews by issuing an order of protection that pointed out that the plague was afflicting Jews as well as Christians, but despite his efforts pogroms and anti-Jewish violence spread northward into Germany, where many thousands of Jews were killed.

The sudden arrival of the plague, its swift and seemingly inevitable mortality, and the lack of explanations or cures all contributed to a profound sense of social disconnection and despair among its survivors. Boccaccio commented on the disease's capacity to rend the traditional ties of kinship and obligation: "This scourge had implanted so great a terror in the hearts of men and women that brothers abandoned brothers, uncles their nephews, sisters their brothers, and in many cases wives deserted their husbands." Fear even frayed the seemingly unbreakable bond between parent and child: "Even worse, and almost incredible, was the fact that fathers and mothers refused to nurse and assist their own children, as though they did not belong to them." The emperor of Byzantium, John Kantakouzenos, described the discouragement caused by the lack of any remedy: "Whenever people felt sick there was no hope left for recovery, but by turning to despair . . . they died at once." Al-Maqrizi wrote, "Everywhere one heard lamentations, and one could not pass by any house without being overwhelmed by the howling." Cities were overwhelmed by the number of dead bodies; al-Maqrizi went on to explain that in Cairo, "cadavers formed a heap on the public highway, funeral processions were so many they could not file past without bumping into one another." Civic authorities struggled to organize the removal of the dead and to preserve public order.

The initial onslaught of the plague had run its course by 1350, but the Black Death had come to the Mediterranean to stay. Recurrent outbreaks of plague in the late fourteenth century depressed population growth. Persistent labor shortages followed, and those who survived demanded higher wages and greater privileges. The plague also had dramatic effects on commercial exchange and on economic relationships. Venetian and Genoese merchants continued to visit the ports of the Muslim Mediterranean in search of luxuries, but the European demand for foodstuffs contracted sharply. The social and demographic upheavals also caused political change and upheaval. Plague was just one of a host of crises that beset the Mediterranean in the fourteenth century, crises that led to a major realignment of politics and society.

CHAPTER SEVEN

Crisis and Consolidation in State and Society

The Mediterranean travels of Ciriaco Pizzecolli, also known as Cyriac of Ancona, have earned him the title "Father of Archaeology." Born in Ancona in 1391 and trained as a merchant, Cyriac voyaged throughout the eastern Mediterranean, including to Alexandria, Constantinople, the Aegean islands, Greece, and Anatolia. Like many of his contemporaries, he was fascinated by the classical past as well as by more recent Italian writers like Dante, Petrarch, and Boccaccio. But where other Italian humanists were interested in texts inherited from the Greco-Romans, Cyriac focused on the material remains of that world. His travels were increasingly motivated by his desire to visit and document the crumbling and often abandoned ruins scattered throughout the region, and his letters, diaries, and notebooks document his quest for antiquities. Addressing the Holy Roman emperor in Rome, Cyriac decried the way Roman monuments were being despoiled for their marble, declaiming that the buildings "are the shining witnesses the ancients left behind them and they possess particular power to fire the minds of noble men to the greatest deeds and to the pursuit of undying glory." Cyriac's intellectual interests placed him at the center of the cultural movement known as the Renaissance, which drew on literary and physical remains of the classical past in the Italian peninsula as well as in a larger Mediterranean context.

In addition to being an antiquarian, Cyriac was a politician and a diplomat, and he observed or participated in important changes to the Mediterranean political framework. By his day the Ottomans, Turkish warriors from Anatolia, had crossed into the Balkans, where they had established a new capital at Byzantine Adrianople, renaming it Edirne. Cyriac's business took him to that city in 1429, where he witnessed the pageantry of the Ottoman sultan's court and the misery of Greek prisoners of war taken during the Ottoman siege of Thessalonica. While buying leather, carpets, and wax for Italian markets, Cyriac actively collected intelligence for his Roman patron Pope Eugenius IV on the possibilities of church union between Greeks and Latins and a crusade against the Ottomans. Acting as a diplomat, he lobbied the Byzantine emperor to come to Italy and participate in a church council; it took the emperor seven years to agree and to travel to Italy for the Council of Florence, but when he did, Cyriac was by his side during the negotiations.

While Cyriac's travels aimed to recover fragments of the Roman Empire, a time of Mediterranean unity, he moved through a world being reshaped by new contenders for power. The Ottoman expansion that he and his Italian patrons found so threatening in the early fifteenth century had begun more than a century earlier, when legends relate that a Turkish Muslim lord on Byzantium's Anatolian frontier had a dream. Osman, who after his death would be revered as the first sultan and founder of the Ottoman dynasty, saw a moon arise from a holy man's chest and sink into his own; "a tree sprouted from his navel and its shade encompassed the world." Under the tree's shade, streams flowed through a land of plenty. Osman's dream was not recorded until the later fifteenth century, after his successors had built the foundations of an expansive domain that ruled a large portion of the eastern Mediterranean, but it then became a foundational myth for a divinely sanctioned empire.

The Ottoman rise to power was perhaps the most dramatic example of a larger pattern in fourteenth and fifteenth century political life in the Mediterranean: upheaval, demographic crisis, and civil wars gradually led to new ways of structuring political and social space across the region. In much of the Mediterranean, the religiously motivated warfare of the eleventh and twelfth centuries had allowed new dynasties and social groups to seize territory and claim privileges and rights. The late thirteenth and early fourteenth centuries were characterized by consolidation of these gains. Almost every major polity faced demographic crisis, social and economic upheaval, and civil wars over the respective rights of rulers and ruled. These trends were exacerbated by natural disasters: a changing climate, and epidemic disease. In the western Mediterranean, a consolidated Castilian-Aragonese monarchy gradually asserted control over most of the Iberian peninsula, the islands, and southern Italy. In northern Italy, cities conquered their neighbors and formed regional states. In the east, the restored Byzantine Empire engaged in a drawn-out struggle against foreign encroachments until 1453, when an expanding Ottoman state took Constantinople and much of the Balkans. The Mamluks dominated the southeastern Mediterranean but faced internal challenges to their rule.

NEW CONTENDERS FOR POWER

The issues Cyriac confronted in the early fifteenth century—church union as a condition of Byzantine survival and alternating diplomacy and aggression against Muslim neighbors—had roots in late-thirteenth-century political struggles. Charles of Anjou, the younger brother of the French king, was one of the new contenders for power. At the invitation of the pope, Charles invaded and conquered the kingdom of Sicily in 1266, establishing Angevin French control over both southern Italy and Sicily. His ambition did not end there; in 1271 he seized control of Durazzo and claimed the title king of Albania, as a first step in a trans-Balkan expedition to retake Constantinople for the Latins. The French crusade to Tunis in 1270, led by the king of France and Charles's brother, Louis IX, can be seen as part of the same effort to create an eastern Mediterranean empire.

Angevin ambition ran up against the restored Byzantine Empire in the east. After 60 years of Latin rule, Byzantines managed to retake Constantinople in 1261, which had repercussions throughout Mediterranean politics. Latin European powers were not willing to let Constantinople return to Orthodox rule without a fight, and Charles of Anjou was determined to extend Angevin rule to Constantinople itself. The new Byzantine emperor, Michael VIII Palaiologos managed to neutralize the Angevin threat by skillful diplomatic maneuvering. In 1274, at the Second Council of Lyon, Michael agreed to a treaty that offered the possibility of union between the Latin and Orthodox churches. He promised to recognize papal primacy and to accept the Latin solution on two theological points, temporarily removing the religious motivation for Latin attacks on Constantinople.

Michael's foreign policy of rapprochement with Latin powers clashed with his domestic agenda. Finding the city's infrastructure close to ruin, he embarked on a major campaign of restoration and refurbishment that asserted both his own legitimacy as ruler and the Greek Orthodox character of the empire. He restored several monasteries and the Blachernae Palace and reconstructed the city's defenses and its markets, streets, baths, and harbors. He refurbished Hagia Sophia in Orthodox style, erasing evidence that it had been a Latin cathedral for the past 60 years. In hopes of gaining Mamluk support for his new regime, he subsidized the construction of a new mosque to replace the one the Latin crusaders had burned in 1203. Byzantine elites also patronized monasteries, churches, and palaces, contributing to the city's revival in Orthodox style. Michael's subjects rejected his attempts to forge a union between the Greek and Latin churches, viewing him as a traitor to the faith. The proposed union was also rejected by later popes, who demonstrated the still-simmering Latin suspicion of Orthodoxy by excommunicating Michael in 1281, condemning him as a "patron of the Greeks who are inveterate schismatics and fixed in the ancient schism." Later Byzantine rulers also attempted to trade religious compromise for political benefits with little success.

The island of Sicily was the flash point for several Mediterranean powers in the late thirteenth century. Large numbers of northern Italians, used to civic traditions of self-government, had settled on the island in place of the Muslim population displaced by Frederick II, and they deeply resented Angevin rule, taxes, and foreign officials. Both the Byzantines and the Aragonese took advantage of Sicilian discontent to remove the Angevins from the island. Peter III of Aragon pressed his wife's claim to the island, and the Byzantines supported his efforts, dispatching generous financial subsidies to the Aragonese and Sicilians. Sicily was simmering

Giuliano Sangallo's drawing of Cyriac of Ancona's now-lost sketch of Hagia Sophia, Constantinople. *Vatican Apostolic Library*

with resentment when, at a vespers mass near Palermo in 1282, some Angevin soldiers insulted a young Sicilian wife. The ensuing struggle soon turned to slaughter, as Sicilians crying "Death to the French!" massacred Angevin garrisons across the island. After some dynastic struggle, a branch of the house of Aragon ruled Sicily, while the southern Italian mainland was governed by an Angevin dynasty. The central Mediterranean was politically divided between these foreign dynasties, the papal states, and the autonomous communes of northern Italy.

The Aragonese and the Angevins both had ambitions for a pan-Mediterranean empire, and the two remained locked in a struggle for preeminence in the early fourteenth century. The Aragonese monarchy was fragmented into several regions ruled by separate branches of the royal dynasty: Aragon itself, Majorca, and Sicily each had its own king. Within the Iberian kingdom of Aragon, the regions of Aragon, Catalonia, and Valencia shared a single monarch but were distinct in law and administration. Each region had its own parliament, or *cortes*, responsible for local privileges and matters of taxation. During the course of the fourteenth century, Aragonese control of Sicily weakened, leaving the Sicilian barons with nearly independent fiefdoms and little centralized control to stop private disputes between barons from turning to civil war. The barons allied and fought under the factional labels of Latin and Catalan, indicating the powerful foreign influences that controlled the island.

The Angevin king of Naples, Robert "the Wise," managed a series of diplomatic and marital alliances that reached outward in all directions. To the east, the Albanian Thopia family supported Angevin claims there, and in the Peloponnese, the Angevins enforced their authority in Achaia. Robert's granddaughter and heiress, Joanna, married Andrew of Hungary, building a trans-Adriatic alliance. To the west, Robert's own marriages to Yolanda of Aragon and Sancia of Majorca were intended to consolidate the Angevin position in Sicily and the western Mediterranean. Robert mounted multiple expeditions against Sicily, in 1314 and again from 1330 to 1343, but none of these short-term victories turned into long-term occupations.

Robert was deeply involved in the political struggles of northern Italy due to three factors: the papacy's absence from Rome, Neapolitan financial dependence on Florentine banking houses, and the factional rivalries that divided and defined political life in Italian towns. The permanent residency of the popes in the southern French city of Avignon began with Clement V, elected in 1305, whose close relationship with the king of France and poor health kept him from ever visiting Rome. In the pope's absence, Robert became the de facto leader of the papal party in Italy, called the Guelfs. The opposing faction, the Ghibellines, supported the German Holy Roman emperor's claims to authority on the peninsula. Guelfs and Ghibellines battled for control of civic institutions across northern Italy, and Robert was often drawn into these disputes, as the example of Genoa demonstrates. Conflicts between Genoa's noble families were extraordinarily bitter and constantly threatened to undermine the city's overseas trade. In 1311 the strife-weary Genoese handed themselves over to the Holy Roman emperor Henry VII, enraging the Guelfs among the population and sparking a civil war after Henry's death, in 1313. By 1317 the Genoese Guelf faction was in control and gave the city to Robert's protection, a lordship that lasted until 1335.

Robert's involvement in Tuscany was driven not only by factional conflict but also by culture and by his connections with the Bardi and Peruzzi banking houses of Florence. Without the grain resources of their Sicilian holdings, the Angevins needed money. Robert borrowed significant sums from Florentine bankers in return for export rights over wheat from southern Italy, an arrangement that gave the banks a great deal of control over the region's economy. Robert, concerned with his kingly image and appearance of legitimacy, also patronized Tuscan art and literature. Giotto, the most famous Florentine painter of the time, worked at the Angevin court, and Robert awarded the Laurel Crown to Petrarch in 1341 for his Latin poetry. A young Giovanni Boccaccio, an apprentice of the Bardi bank in Naples, also spent time among the Neapolitan nobility and learned some Greek.

Byzantine entanglements in the west meant that the emperor neglected the remaining provinces in Anatolia, which were heavily taxed and subject to constant Turkish attacks. Western Anatolia was controlled by a shifting constellation of independent Turkish principalities called emirates or beyliks. In 1300 the Ottomans were one among several competing emirates in the region; the Ottoman leader Osman alternately attacked Byzantine territory and made a series of strategic alliances with more powerful neighbors, including key diplomatic marriages with the Byzantines. The Ottomans expanded quickly in the early fourteenth century, beginning with Osman's victory over the Byzantines near Nicomedia in 1302 and continuing to the conquest of the former Byzantine capital of Nicaea in 1331.

Historians have struggled to understand what motivated Ottoman expansion; there is little contemporary evidence from the Ottomans themselves. What gave the Ottomans legitimacy? Were they motivated to conquest by commitment to holy war against unbelievers? The historian Paul Wittek influentially argued that this was the case: in his framework, often called the "gazi thesis," religious zeal and the ethos of frontier warfare were key to Ottoman success. Other scholars have criticized this explanation, pointing to the ethnic and religious inclusivity of Turkish nomadic traditions and arguing that the Ottomans benefited from the fluid nature of the frontier and their strategic position closest to the poorly defended Byzantine border. Cemal Kafadar has offered a convincing reworking of the gazi thesis, showing that early Ottoman successes were a product of the sultans' creative and flexible combination of a variety of traditions, practices, and beliefs from their frontier environment. The Ottoman leaders successfully fused Islamic, Byzantine, Central Asian, and Persian institutions and customs into a resilient political and military culture, often forging coalitions that ignored religious identity in order to further dynastic objectives.

The Ottomans were the most successful polity on the western Anatolian frontier in the long term, but other contenders for power, Christian as well as Muslim, combined economic and political self-interest with religious ideology. The Byzantines, who relied on mercenary troops for border defense, introduced a destabilizing force when they hired the Catalan Company, a group of mercenary adventurers under the command of a renegade Templar, Roger de Flor. The Catalans were so successful that the Byzantines, fearing his ambition, arranged for Roger's assassination in 1305. The leaderless company, allied with some Turkish forces, then began a campaign of pillage within Byzantium, beginning in Gallipoli and continuing through Thrace and Macedonia, finally arriving in the Duchy of Athens in 1310. After a brief stint in the duke's service, the Catalans turned against him, defeated him in battle, and took the duchy for themselves. For the next 60 years, all attempts to dislodge them from Athens failed, and they ruled the region for their own benefit. The emirate of Aydin, based in the port town of Smyrna, also became a naval power in the region, raiding and trading in the Aegean and lending naval aid to Byzantine factions during their civil wars.

In the southeastern Mediterranean, the overall Mamluk governing system remained relatively stable in the first part of the fourteenth century, although the sultanate changed hands numerous times. The Mamluks consolidated their hold on Egypt, Syria, and Palestine. Mamluk rule was characterized by regular factional struggles between the leading emirs. The Mamluk sultan's legitimacy depended on the support of the dominant emirs, whose position and economic interests were based on the *iqta* system, which the Mamluks had inherited from earlier polities. Iqtas, or land grants to governors and officials, bore some resemblance to European fiefs in that their revenues were intended to pay soldiers' salaries, but holders of iqta estates had no political or legal rights over the peasants who worked the land, nor were these estates hereditary. Sultans' attempts to reform or redistribute the iqtas met with violent resistance from the emirs. Mamluk urban and rural financial administration was dominated by Coptic Christians; the Muslim masses, encouraged by religious scholars, deeply resented the power, wealth, and influence of these Copts.

The Mamluk elite, linguistically and culturally separate from the Egyptian people, relied on scholars and Sufis for religious and political legitimacy. Sultans' and emirs' patronage of madrasas and Sufi lodges transformed the urban fabric of Cairo. Madrasas supplied the scholars responsible for the orthodoxy of educational and judicial systems, while the lodges of Sufi orders promoted popular Islam and provided a bridge between the elites and masses. As the Mamluk system was generally a nonhereditary one, both male and female Mamluk elites combined their patronage of orthodox religion and learning with funerary monuments for themselves; these mausoleum-mosque complexes were supported by waqf endowments. Over the course of the later fourteenth and fifteenth centuries, Mamluks promoted cross-fertilization between madrasas and Sufi lodges by appointing Sufis to teach in madrasas and ulama to teach in lodges, lessening the difference between the two institutional types. Early Mamluk architecture also commemorated individual sultans' military victories over crusaders, incorporating marble columns and decorative elements taken from conquered Latin buildings.

At the other end of the Mediterranean, in Nasrid Granada, the sultans held on to their independence through a diplomatic strategy that played Iberian and North African powers against one another. The Alhambra palace complex, enlarged and expanded by Yusuf I and Muhammad V in the mid- to late fourteenth century, lent the dynasty an impression of dignity and strength. The audience halls, private dwellings, towers, and gates were set among luxurious gardens with water features that evoked Islamic ideas of paradise. The interior was covered in stucco designs and draped with silken wall hangings whose austere geometric patterns were designed to match the stucco. Unusually, the interior was covered in inscriptions—some pious invocations from the Qur'an or invocations to God, and poetry written by court literati, principally the vizier Ibn Zamrak. While the actual policies of the sultans favored cooperation and alliance with their Christian neighbors, particular buildings and inscriptions praised the sultans' military victory over non-Muslims, as in this poem extolling Muhammad V's 1369 victory at Algeciras: "How many infidel lands did you reach in the morning only to become the arbiter of their lives in the evening! You put on them the yoke of captives so

Court of the Lions at the Alhambra, Granada. The central courtyard of the fourteenth-century Nasrid dynasty palace of the Alhambra shows a mix of Islamic and Christian influences. *Photo: HIP / Art Resource, NY*

that they appear at your doorstep to build palaces in servitude." The plague halted Castilian attempts at conquest for more than a century, allowing Granada to survive as a fragile frontier polity.

THE FOURTEENTH-CENTURY CRISIS:
SOCIAL AND ECONOMIC UPHEAVAL

Scholars often invoke the four horsemen of the apocalypse to symbolize the interlocking disasters that turned the fourteenth century into an age of crisis. The unpredictable rainfall and flooding that accompanied a cooling climate led to intermittent famines. War and conquest destroyed crops and pushed governments to raise taxes; peasant revolts and urban insurrections demonstrated popular resistance to this development. The most dramatic disaster was the massive mortality of the 1348 plague. Historians continue to debate the effect of the plague on society: while all agree that the dramatic drop in population was part of a more general crisis in medieval society, they disagree on its role in causing that change. Some see the plague and attendant depopulation as the primary factor behind the subsequent agricultural depression, peasant revolts, and the fall of feudal aristocracies; others point to population decline, agricultural stagnation, and peasant discontent as trends that existed before 1348.

The plague's overall economic effect differed widely across the Mediterranean. In Latin Europe it stimulated already widespread monetization and commercialization of society, but its effect on wages and the status of laborers was inconsistent. In the immediate aftermath of the plague's mass mortality, tenants and laborers demanded improvement in their leases and wages. Iberian rulers attempted to reverse this development through ordinances or laws that placed a ceiling on wages and fixed prices: in Aragon in 1349, Zaragoza in 1350, and Castile in 1351. These restrictions were ineffective, and the general trend was rising wages and prices for several decades after the onset of the plague. There were exceptions: in Valencia, the declining population caused landlords to tie Muslim peasants more tightly to the land, and the Cortes of Valencia banned all emigration in 1403. In Catalonia there was a sharp deterioration in the status of the peasantry. Italian city-states enacted legislation to restrict laborers' mobility and limit demands for higher wages, but they also tried to attract immigrant labor with tax relief and the promise of good treatment. In Egypt the effect of the plague was general depopulation, peasants' flight from the land, and economic decline.

At least partially in response to the demographic crisis caused by the plague, there was a rise in the number of insurrections across Europe from the 1350s to the 1370s. Historians have proposed several models for understanding these revolts: the "traditionalist" revolt was primarily local in scope, often prompted by a lord violating custom and practice, and called for the restoration of just order; "radical" rebellions, by contrast, envisioned a transformation of society into a new order. An older body of scholarship saw these revolts as led by social superiors and generally unsuccessful. The historian Samuel Cohn has challenged this view, using a wide range of examples to argue that revolts were almost always led by workers, artisans, and peasants themselves and that the rebels' motivations were primarily political, aiming for greater inclusion in local governing structures and an expansion of their personal and communal rights. Italy saw several protests and revolts in the post-plague era. For instance, during the Ciompi revolt in Florence, between 1378 and 1382, wool carders excluded from the Florentine guild system protested with increasing violence, eventually gaining control of the city government for a brief period. Within four years the old elites had regained influence and restored oligarchic control. In Rome, the popular leader Cola di Rienzo overturned the aristocratic regime in 1347 and took the classically inspired title of Roman tribune, but his government quickly collapsed.

Factional disputes and wars in Italy were exacerbated by the 70-year absence of the papacy from Rome. Pope Gregory XI returned to Rome in 1376; when he died there two years later, the Roman mob exerted pressure on the cardinals in conclave to elect the next pope, shouting, "A Roman! A Roman! Or at least an Italian!" The cardinals gave way and elected a Neapolitan, who took the name Urban VI. Urban proved an unhappy choice, refusing to return to Avignon and attempting to demote the cardinals from princely co-governors of the church to obedient courtiers. The French cardinals withdrew from Rome and elected a new pope, Clement VII, who returned with his own supporters to Avignon. The two popes excommunicated one another and the various European political powers chose sides, beginning the Great Schism in Latin Christianity. The division would last until 1415, when the Council of Constance elected a Roman aristocrat as Martin V. Martin spent his next years attempting to win back control of Rome and reestablish papal authority in his territories.

With the exception of a failed coup d'état by the doge Marin Falier in 1355, Venice avoided the civic unrest and popular revolts that convulsed other Italian city-states. Venice did face uprisings in its commercial colonies in the Adriatic and Aegean; in these cases, resentment over taxes and labor demands were complicated by resistance to foreign rule. The Dalmatian city of Zara (Zadar) rebelled against Venetian rule in 1344, and it took Venice two years to regain control. At the head of the Adriatic, Capodistria (Koper) rebelled unsuccessfully in 1348. In 1363, in Candia (Crete), the lynchpin of Venetian dominion in the eastern Mediterranean, a group of discontented Veneto-Cretan feudatories joined with Greek citizens there to imprison the Venetian duke of the island and raise the flag of San Tito, the local patron saint. This was not the first revolt against Venetian rule on the island, but it was the most serious threat to Venetian control, as it involved local elites as well as the Greek peasantry. A large mercenary army put down the revolt and executed the leaders, but there were further incidents of unrest in the fifteenth century.

The Venetians and the Genoese fought two long and costly wars over commercial supremacy, from 1350 to 1355 and 1378 to 1381. The Venetians generally dominated Egyptian markets and the Genoese predominated in Constantinople and the Black Sea region, but the two states turned to war in hopes of unseating the other. During the first conflict, the Genoese allied with the Hungarians, who resented Venetian dominance along the eastern Adriatic coast. Venice was unable to resist both powers, and in 1358 signed a peace treaty ceding all of its Dalmatian territories to Hungary. The loss of Dalmatia was a serious blow: Venice lost its control of the Adriatic salt markets and access to the overland routes of the Balkans, as well as the sheltered ports and manpower for its fleets. In 1378 war broke out again over control of the Aegean island of Tenedos (Bozcaada) and with it access to the Black Sea; the Venetians repelled a Genoese attack and regained control of Adriatic shipping.

In southern Italy, the 1340s saw an era of dramatic decline for the Neapolitan crown. The Bardi and Peruzzi banks, mainstays of the Neapolitan economy, collapsed in 1343–45. After King Robert's death, in 1343, his granddaughter Joanna was

Distribution of grain outside the church of Orsanmichele in Florence during the famine of 1335. From the Florentine codex of Domenico Lenzi, fourteenth century. *Biblioteca Laurenziana, Florence. Photo: Scala / Art Resource*

crowned queen; her unfortunate husband, Andrew, was murdered and flung out a castle window, provoking two Hungarian invasions of southern Italy by his revenge-seeking relatives. Joanna was acquitted of any involvement in his death, but her reign was characterized by factionalism and instability. That reign ended with her imprisonment and murder in 1382, and rival Angevin princes claimed the throne of Naples. During this turbulent time, the Neapolitan barons exploited royal weakness to expand their own local authority, eroding centralized control of the provinces.

In sharp contrast to the decline of centralized royal power in southern Italy, Aragonese royal power became stronger and more consolidated during the later fourteenth century. During his long reign (1336–87), Peter the Ceremonious asserted a coherent vision of Aragonese territories unified by political loyalty as well as commercial connections. In 1343 he reconquered Majorca from a cousin and celebrated his victory by offering generous grants and trade privileges to the island's inhabitants. Peter met considerable opposition from the barons and towns in Valencia and Aragon, who defended their own liberties and privileges, but aided by the onset of the plague, Peter scored a decisive victory over these protesters in late 1348. He was drawn into a long war for control of Sardinia, fighting both the Genoese and the Sards themselves for footholds on the island. Aragon also became involved in the civil war that roiled Castile from 1355 to 1369 and which eventually put the Trastámara dynasty on the Castilian throne.

Peter's second son, Martin I, continued the drive to political unification in the western Mediterranean, mounting a successful expedition to Sicily in 1392 that returned the island to effective Aragonese control. Catalan nobles began to acquire extensive estates on the island and Catalan cultural influence dominated. But the kingdom of Aragon's commercial fortunes did not follow its political and military success. Barcelona in particular suffered a sharp economic decline in the late fourteenth century. The Aragonese debasement of its coinage was certainly damaging: by 1365 the gold florin of Barcelona was devalued by 75%, and in 1381–83, there were several bank failures in the city. The volume of trade passing through Barcelona fell fivefold between 1350 and 1450. Even before the plague hit, Catalonia had been suffering from problems of depopulation, but after 1340 the Catalan population shrank by about half. In 1340, Barcelona was the largest city in Iberia, at 50,000 inhabitants, but by 1480 it had shrunk to only 20,000. Catalonia's losses were Valencia's gains: the province's population tripled between 1340 and 1490, and the city had 70,000 residents by 1489, making it the largest on the peninsula.

These economic difficulties form the backdrop to the explosion of anti-Semitic violence and pogroms that swept across Iberia in the summer of 1391. Violence against Jews had been a part of post-plague social unrest in many locations, and during the Castilian civil wars of the 1360s, crude anti-Semitic propaganda circulated widely, claiming that Jews had ritually murdered Christian children or repeating the accusation that Jews had caused the plague. Jewish aljamas had several times been attacked in Castile during the civil wars. In June 1391 the virulently anti-Semitic preaching campaign of Ferran Martinez exploded into violence, first in Seville, where as many as 4,000 Jews were massacred, and then in the rest of Andalusia. By July the pogroms had spread to Valencia and Barcelona. In Valencia a Christian mob broke through the walls of the Jewish ghetto and massacred its defenseless inhabitants, offering the choice between death and forced conversion. Synagogues were transformed into churches, and Jewish property was despoiled. The violence against Jews spread as far as Majorca and Sicily.

Social grievances overlapped with religious sentiments in the violence of 1391. In Gerona resentment of the Jews was mixed with anger over fiscal and social issues. In Barcelona the artisans and peasants who attacked Jews also demanded tax concessions and made threats against rich Christian citizens, the town government, and even Christian clerics. A chronicler of the event related that the mob "threatened to kill all clerics and forced them to pay taxes and other contributions as if they were laymen. Silversmiths, merchants, and other rich people were threatened with death." These types of demands have led some historians to interpret the events of 1391 as primarily social and fiscal revolts, similar in type to other uprisings in Latin Europe demanding lower taxes and increased representation on municipal councils. Other historians have emphasized the peasants' and artisans religious motivations, pointing to the way Jews were targeted in cities across Spain as evidence of a deep-seated anti-Jewish hatred. These resentments were likely exacerbated by the small minority of great Jewish financiers, doctors, and administrators, who despite regulations to the contrary, served in elite and royal households. The combination of religious and social grievances resulted in Jewish communities across Iberia being nearly wiped out: according to Rabbi Hasadi Crescas, an observer of the massacre in Barcelona, the Jewish community there was completely destroyed through murder or forced conversion.

The many thousands of Jews who had been forcibly baptized were not welcomed into the Christian community with open arms. Spanish Christians suspected that these conversos had accepted baptism externally but remained Jewish in their hearts; furthermore, they feared that secret Jews might tempt sincere converts to return to their old faith. In order to make the boundaries between Christian and Jew clear, rulers introduced strict segregation of the two communities, forbidding converts to live, dine, or interact with Jews, who were required to wear obvious badges and hats marking them as Jewish. The Dominican friar Vincent Ferrer, a popular and influential preacher, pursued Jewish and Muslim conversion through mandatory disputations critiquing the Jewish faith as well as discriminatory legislation that would move Muslims and Jews to segregated neighborhoods and restrict their economic activities. These draconian restrictions, enacted between 1412 and 1415, caused a second wave of mass conversions. Overall, the period 1391–1416 saw the death of about a third of Spain's Jewish population and the conversion of another third to half. Tension and suspicion over crypto-Jewish religious identity continued through the fifteenth century and played an important role in the expulsion of the Jews in 1492.

Social and economic difficulties in Mamluk Egypt also formed the backdrop to

Interior of a synagogue in Barcelona, from a fourteenth-century manuscript illustration. *British Library, London. Photo: Album / Art Resource, NY*

anti-Christian and Jewish sentiment and brief outbursts of violence, although there was nothing comparable to the massacres and forced conversions seen in Iberia or western Europe more generally. Egyptian religious leaders were sometimes hostile to non-Muslims, particularly those in positions of authority, and anti-dhimmi propaganda circulated throughout the fourteenth century. The instructions to a market regulator around 1300 make this stringent attitude clear: "Know that any show of leniency toward the Ahl al-Dhimma in matters of religion is extremely dangerous . . . The purpose of differentiating between them and Muslims is so that they shall not be shown any dignity." Mamluks in general took sumptuary laws very seriously, forbidding all non-Mamluks to dress like Mamluks or to ride horses. Laws requiring Jews and Muslims to distinguish themselves through dress also were enforced with increasing vigor. This general atmosphere of hostility turned violent several times. In 1301, vigilante mobs tore down the upper stories of dhimmi homes and shops, vandalizing or razing some churches or synagogues. In response, the sultan adopted discriminatory policies against Coptic Christians, and many individuals converted to Islam to retain their offices. In 1321, anti-Christian riots broke out, and the situation for minorities became so bad that Christians began converting to Islam in large numbers. Another wave of rioting swept the country in 1354, in the aftermath of the plague's mass mortality: 25,000 acres belonging to Coptic churches were confiscated, and even Christians who had converted to Islam were dismissed from their administrative posts. Egyptian Copts converted to Islam on a large scale, shrinking the Coptic population to a small minority.

A 1442 incident illustrates Mamluk officials' attention to enforcing the letter of the law when it came to religious minorities, something that had both positive and negative consequences for dhimmi communities in Egypt. During an inspection looking for signs of illegal repairs in a Cairo synagogue, Muslim officials came upon an almost illegible inscription of the Prophet's name on the stairs of the minbar, or preacher's platform. The officials concluded they had found an example of Jews deliberately defacing Muhammad's name and launched an investigation of all non-Muslim houses of worship. The officials pursued a legal case against the three Jews found responsible for the inscription and destroyed the minbar, though not the entire synagogue. In the end, both Jewish and Christian leaders were asked to take an oath renewing their allegiance to the provisions of the Pact of 'Umar.

CIVIL WARS AND CENTRALIZING REGIMES

The major polities of the Mediterranean all underwent serious dynastic crises as ruling elites and individual rulers struggled for power in a changing social and economic landscape. In Egypt a series of destructive factional struggles over the sultanate and the changes to Mamluk government introduced by al-Nasir Muhammad brought a new group of Mamluk sultans to power. In the western Mediterranean, Nasrid Granada and Catalonia also suffered through dynastic and successional strife, eventually leading to Castilian dominance on the Iberian peninsula. In north-central Italy, Venice, Milan, and Florence expanded their territorial reach at the expense of their neighbors. In Byzantium the Palaiologian dynasty established by Michael was challenged by John Kantakouzenos, combining elite factional struggle with social and religious dissent. The Ottomans initially benefited from Byzantine disorder but were soon embroiled in civil wars of their own.

The Mamluk sultan al-Nasir Muhammad, who attained the sultanate for the third time in 1310 and ruled through 1341, made significant changes to Mamluk traditions in order to stabilize his position. The sons of mamluks, born as Muslims, were initially not permitted to serve as soldiers themselves and were thus blocked from the upper echelons of power. Under al-Nasir, himself not of slave origin, some sons of prominent mamluks were allowed to serve in the army. He rewarded his mamluks with material plenty rather than treating them with the stringent discipline characteristic of earlier regimes, thereby undermining his dynasty's military capacity. Al-Nasir and his family also wove a web of kinship through marriage, and

his own household and harem were enormous. Al-Nasir's extensive public and private patronage projects—irrigation systems, government buildings, mosques, and new palaces for his emirs, wives, and slaves—bolstered the image of his royal authority, although royal expenditure far exceeded revenues. After the death of al-Nasir, the sultanate entered a period of political instability in which the throne passed in rapid succession between 12 of his descendants and real power rested with the emirs of the dominant factions.

A new period of Mamluk rule, the Circassian regime, ended the intense factional struggle after al-Nasir's death and brought a form of bilateral negotiation to Mamluk factions. In 1382, a mamluk named al-Malik al-Zahir Barquq, of Circassian origin, seized power. The move reflected the increasing number of mamluks drawn from the Black Sea region and the falling number of ethnic Turks. The Circassian Mamluks also ended the earlier regime's dynastic attitude to the sultanate, returning power to a group of veterans who, from the 1420s, were divided into two main factions that negotiated to divide up resources and offices. As a result, the sultan's dependence on the oligarchy of senior mamluks increased significantly.

The Mamluk elite, stationed in urban centers during long periods of peace and faced with dropping revenues from landholdings, became increasingly involved in commerce during the fifteenth century, to the detriment of both European and Karimi merchants. As state intervention in private enterprise grew, merchants were compelled to buy commodities like wood, iron, sug-

Exterior of the citadel of the Mosque of Sultan al-Nasir Muhammad in Cairo, built 1318–35. *Photo: James Morris / Art Resource, NY*

ar, and beans from government agents. In the 1420s, Sultan Sayf-ad-Din Barsbay imposed a government monopoly on the spice trade that passed through the Red Sea, restricting and eventually dissolving the Karimi cartel which had previously dominated that trade. European merchants in Alexandria were compelled to buy spices from government agents in fixed quantities and prices. Barsbay also undertook military actions against Catalan and Genoese pirates to protect Mamluk trade and launched three campaigns against Cyprus because it was a haven for these pirates. In 1426, Mamluk forces conquered the island and reduced its Lusignan king to a tribute-paying vassal.

Despite this victory over Cyprus, the Egyptian economic system was in a deep decline by the fifteenth century. Post-plague depopulation was exacerbated by a lack of maintenance of the irrigation systems that were essential to the agricultural productivity of the countryside. Impoverished farmers deserted the land and swelled the numbers of the urban poor, and land revenues for the elite dropped dramatically. There was also technological stagnation, so while the textile industry in Europe benefited from new methods of production, the sultans' desire to keep the status quo meant that these innovations were not adopted in Egypt. The Mamluk army rejected the use of firearms as well, which would eventually put them at a disadvantage in their growing rivalry with the Ottomans in the later fifteenth and sixteenth centuries.

The two polities that dominated eastern Iberia, Nasrid Granada and the kingdom of Aragon-Catalonia, were both riven by internal strife in the fifteenth century. Members of the ruling dynasty of Granada replaced one another rapidly between 1417 and 1454: there were five different monarchs during this time, although one of the five, Muhammad IX, ruled for 27 of those 35 years, providing more continuity than it would seem at first glance. Aragon-Catalonia's dynastic troubles began in 1410, when the house of Barcelona died out with King Martin. After a two-year interregnum during which five different contenders vied for power, the 1412 Compromise of Caspe put Martin's nephew Ferdinand, of the Castilian Trastámara dynasty, on the throne. This choice caused difficulties and resentment with Catalan political elites, who were used to a more contractual and negotiated relationship with the monarchy.

A process of political centralization was under way in the factitious and factionalized city-states of northern Italy. By about 1380 communal governments were on the wane, and most Italian cities were ruled by a lord or signore. Both princely states like Milan and republican states like Venice and Florence embarked on campaigns of expansion against their neighbors. Giangaleazzo Visconti of Milan had ambitions to reestablish the ancient Lombard kingdom, and he conquered the cities of the Po valley, and set his sights on Bologna, Pisa, and Siena. His troops were aiming at Florence when he suddenly died in 1402. The Florentines then seized the opportunity to expand their own state, taking the port cities of Pisa (1406) and Livorno (1421). Venice also saw an opportunity to expand its rule onto the Italian peninsula, taking Vicenza, Verona, and Padua and reaching north to Friuli in the 1420s. A severe succession crisis in Hungary, in addition to the cessation of hostilities with Genoa in 1381, offered the Venetian Republic a chance to reassert control in Dalmatia, and between 1409 and 1420 the Venetian flag was raised in almost all of the port cities and islands of the eastern Adriatic coast. In contrast, Genoa was beset by civil strife and came under foreign rule several times.

The new regional states of northern Italy were characterized by rising levels of taxation and borrowing in order to finance their expensive military campaigns, which were increasingly conducted by paid mercenary captains. The leaders of these states, concerned about their own legitimacy and right to rule, also spent huge sums of money on artistic and cultural endeavors. One of the most lavish patrons of art, architecture, and literature was Alfonso of Aragon, whose stated ambition was to restore the Roman Empire in the Mediterranean. Alfonso inherited the kingdom of Aragon-Catalonia from his father, Ferdinand; in 1421 he accepted Queen Joanna II of Naples's offer to make him her heir. Joanna later changed her mind, naming René of Anjou as her successor, and when she died, in 1435, there was open warfare between the two contenders. Genoa, afraid that Aragonese victory would sever their commercial connections in favor of Catalan rivals, supported René's claim and inflicted a major naval defeat on Alfonso, destroying his fleet and capturing the king and his whole entourage. Alfonso, who was turned over to the prince of Milan, snatched victory from the jaws of defeat by charming his way out of captivity. Over the next seven years, Alfonso's forces systematically conquered the towns and lands of southern Italy, ending with the successful 1442 siege of Naples.

Alfonso's imperial vision placed Mediterranean expansion ahead of his Iberian domains. He remained in Naples until his death, in 1458, leaving his wife, Maria of Castile, to rule Aragon as his regent. In Naples he confirmed the landowning aristocracy's authority over their estates and those who lived on them, ensuring their support for his rule with generous grants of offices and titles. Alfonso used his literary and artistic patronage to create a court culture that communicated his princely legitimacy in Italian style. He repaired and rebuilt the capital city, paved roads, and reopened the university. His policies offered benefits to Catalan merchants, who entered markets previously dominated by Florentines. Alfonso envisioned the economic integration of all his territories—seeing industrial development in Iberia while Sicily, Sardinia, and Naples were to develop their agricultural potential, with an enlarged Catalan fleet communicating between all of them. Alfonso's vision did not last after his death, when his Neapolitan territories went to his illegitimate son Ferdinand and his Aragonese and Sicilian holdings went to his son John II, who almost immediately faced a serious rebellion in Catalonia.

The Catalan Civil War (1462–72) brought together two types of rebellions, elite civil war and popular revolt and protest. Barcelona's elites were divided into two factions—the Busca, generally composed of merchants and artisans, were opposed to the Biga, patrician commercial oligarchs who resisted royal efforts at centralization. In 1453 the Busca party, with royal support, won a dominant position in city government, but in 1460 the antiroyalist Biga party regained control. This struggle between factionalized municipal elites intertwined with increasingly sharp peasant agitation for the abolition of serfdom. By 1462 the peasants were in open revolt against their landlords but supported King John II against the rebellious municipal elites, who claimed that he had not respected Catalan customs and privileges. During the decade of bitter fighting that followed, the peasants mounted a successful and well-organized revolt that resulted in the abolition of serfdom in Catalonia. The Biga faction turned to René of Anjou as an alternate candidate for the throne, but King John and his supporters outlasted the rebels, and by 1472 the rebellion was over.

There is no doubt that the war severely damaged Barcelona's commercial power and contributed to Catalonia's economic woes. Historians disagree on the extent to which the war caused economic decline or contributed to an ongoing trend, but the outcome was a crippled economy. A second result of the Catalan Civil War was the kingdom's subordination to Castile. In 1469, John II's son Ferdinand married the Castilian princess Isabel, a partnership that would lead to the union of Castile and Aragon. Despite formal guarantees that the two kingdoms would remain legally separate, Ferdinand and Isabel's joint rule created the beginnings of a unified Spanish kingdom and ended Aragon-Catalonia's existence as an independent kingdom.

TRANSITIONS IN THE EASTERN MEDITERRANEAN

In Byzantium, dynastic strife twice roiled the political order, from 1321 to 1328 and again from 1341 to 1354. This political division came at a moment when increasingly powerful and well-organized neighbors—Serbia to the north and the Ottomans to the east—threatened Byzantine territory. In 1321 the heir apparent to the empire, Andronikos III, tried to have his mistress's lover murdered, but the hired assassins instead killed his younger brother, Prince Manuel, causing their father to die of shock and sorrow. The reigning emperor, Andronikos II, disinherited his grandson, and the two went to war. Both contenders relied on foreign troops, bringing the Bulgarians and Serbs into the struggle. Andronikos III eventually became co-emperor and forced his grandfather's abdication, but the war weakened the government and damaged the economy.

Byzantium's second civil war spread beyond dynastic strife over the imperial throne and involved social unrest and struggle between the landed aristocracy and the merchants, bankers, and common people. The immediate cause of the war was a power struggle between John Kantakouzenos, a wealthy aristocrat who served as an imperial adviser and the commander in chief of the army, and supporters of the young Palaiologian emperor John V. In 1341, Kantakouzenos declared himself emperor, opening a destructive civil war in which the aristocracy supported Kantakouzenos while the people supported John V. Both sides relied on foreign mercenary troops who exploited the chaos to their own advantage. Kantakouzenos formed a close alliance with Ottoman forces and married his daughter Theodora to the Ottoman sultan, Orhan, in 1346. Kantakouzenos won the first round of hostilities and entered Constantinople in triumph in 1347, just in time for the first outbreak of the plague. The struggle between the Kantakouzenoi and Palaiologi broke out into open warfare twice more before John V's eventual victory, in 1357, but in the meantime the empire's agricultural and commercial foundations had been severely damaged, its treasury depleted, and its populace impoverished.

In the mid-fourteenth century, the Byzantines and Ottomans had become closely tied through a half-century of diplomatic and marital connections, as well as through military struggle. In 1352, the Byzantine emperor gave a group of Turks a fortress on the European side of the Dardanelles, and two years later, Ottoman forces took the city of Gallipoli when a major earthquake destroyed its walls. With this, the Ottomans gained a bridgehead onto the European side of the straits, and they began a systematic invasion and settlement of Byzantine Thrace. Until recently there has been comparatively little research on how plague affected Ottoman state and society in the medieval era, although some scholars have suggested that the massive depopulation of the Balkans and Anatolia was instrumental in the Ottomans' ability to dominate the region in the 1350s. By the late 1360s, the main fortifications and countryside were all under Ottoman control including the key city of Edirne (formerly Adrianople), where the Ottomans established a second capital.

Both Ottoman and Byzantine rulers faced internal divisions and challenges to their rule. In the Byzantine case, the elite, and even the imperial family, was divided over whether to pursue a strategy of alliance with the Ottomans or to look to the west for help. John V alternately pursued both strategies: he married his daughter to an Ottoman prince but also turned to Latin Europe for aid: little was forthcoming, and in desperation he traveled to Rome in 1369, personally accepted the Catholic faith, and publicly submitted to the pope on the steps of St. Peter's Basilica. John V's younger son, Manuel, who supported an aggressive anti-Ottoman strategy, set up an independent court in Thessalonica, a city of great intellectual and artistic importance in the Byzantine world. Ottoman succession policies also caused internal strife: only one of the sultan's sons could take his place, not necessarily the firstborn, which led to much competition. In the 1370s, John V's son Andronikos rebelled against his father and allied with Savci, son of the Ottoman sultan Murad I, who also hoped to depose his father. John V had recently signed a treaty making him Murad's vassal, and the Byzantine emperor and Ottoman sultan joined forces to repress their sons' rebellions.

At the same time that Ottoman forces continued to expand in the Christian Balkans, they exerted pressure against other Muslim Turkish principalities in Anatolia. Murad used marital alliances and diplomacy to extend Ottoman influence toward the southern Anatolian coast, employing Christian troops to fight against the rival Karaman emirate. In 1389, Murad turned back toward Europe to confront an alliance of Serbians and Bosnians resisting Ottoman encroachment. His Ottoman army met a combined Serb-Bosnian force led by Prince Lazar of Serbia at Kosovo in 1389. The battlefield, referred to as the "Field of Blackbirds," became the site of a massive slaughter on both sides; when the battle ended, the Ottomans

were victorious, but both sovereigns were dead, Murad assassinated by a Serbian spy and Lazar captured and decapitated. Serbia became a vassal state of the Ottomans, and Murad's son Bayezid took the reins of power. Shortly thereafter, John V also died and was replaced by his son Manuel, bringing new leadership to the Byzantine Empire.

The uneasy Byzantine-Ottoman coexistence turned to open warfare in the 1390s. In the spring of 1394, Bayezid began a siege of Constantinople and continued the Balkan campaigns, taking Bulgaria in 1393 and the Peloponnese in 1394. A joint French-Hungarian crusading army set out to oppose the Ottomans but suffered a serious defeat at Nicopolis in 1396, leaving Constantinople to its own devices. It was not crusaders from the west but Turco-Mongols from the east who cut short this phase of Ottoman expansion. Bayezid met Khan Timur-lenk (Tamerlane) in battle at Ankara in 1402, and the outcome was disastrous for the Ottomans. Bayezid was captured and died the following year, leading to a period of intense dynastic and civil strife between rival candidates to the throne that combined with widespread social upheaval lasting for a decade.

As it grew, the Ottoman state developed social, military, and political institutions that afforded it the strength and resilience to survive this period of interregnum. The Ottomans adopted strategies of accommodation toward its primarily Christian subject population. Both Christians and Jews were obligated to pay a special head tax, but the Ottomans interpreted Islamic law so that these taxes could be collected from communities as a lump sum, often significantly less than the tithes and labor services imposed by previous rulers. In return for these payments, the Ottomans offered religious and cultural autonomy, drawing on relatively tolerant and inclusive Central Asian and Islamic traditions. Some subjects, particularly the Turks in eastern Anatolia, resisted state centralization. Population resettlement (*sürgün*) brought tribesmen from the east into the Ottoman Balkans, both removing a source of disorder from the eastern frontier and injecting a source of military and economic strength into the Balkans. Beginning in the 1330s, the Ottomans also built charitable institutions called imarets, roughly equivalent to soup kitchens, which acted as a settlement mechanism in the provinces. The Ottoman military establishment depended on two main institutions, a levy on Christian populations in the Balkans (*devshirme*) and land grants in return for service (the timar system). The devshirme formed the backbone of the janissary corps, who, like mamluks, were taken at a young age, converted to Islam, and given a rigorous military training.

By 1413, Mehmed I emerged from a vicious struggle with his brothers to take the throne and reestablish the Ottoman state. He first restored Ottoman supremacy over the beyliks of Anatolia, defeating the emirate of Aydin with help from the Genoese of Chios and the Hospitallers of Rhodes. Mehmed then faced a 1416 revolt led by Sheikh Bedreddin, the Balkan-born son of a mixed marriage between a Muslim judge and the daughter of a Byzantine governor. Bedreddin had studied theology as well as Sufi mysticism in Cairo and Konya, and he preached a syncretic doctrine that advocated for the common ownership of all material goods as well as the importance of close relationships with Christians for salvation. Bedreddin's antitax message resonated with people impoverished by more than a decade of civil war and dislocated by the rapid social, political, and economic changes sweeping the region; his religious emphasis on the "oneness of all being" gained him followers in the influential Sufi community. Bedreddin's followers were defeated in western Anatolia, and he was publicly executed in Macedonia in 1420.

By the time Cyriac of Ancona arrived in the Ottoman capital of Edirne in 1429, many of the characteristic institutions of the Ottoman state were in place. Sultan Murad II, who took the throne in 1421, overcame a challenge to his rule by a relative and briefly besieged Constantinople in 1422. Although he spent much of the next 20 years locked into a power struggle for supremacy in the Balkans with Hungary and Venice, Murad II generally preferred peace to war, and he was surrounded by a group of high officials who promoted a vision of the Ottoman state modeled on Islamic tradition and with an economy based on trade, crafts, and agriculture. Others among Murad's advisers argued against tolerance or accommodation toward their Christian neighbors, promoting policies of war and conquest. Like the Ottomans, the Byzantine elite was divided over foreign policy, one faction advocating military strength and cooperation with western Christians while another saw Byzantium's salvation in accommodation with the Ottomans. The Byzantine emperor attempted to walk a line between these two policies, outwardly submitting to Ottoman supremacy while actively pursuing aid from the west and implementing defensive strategies.

By the 1430s, Ottoman conquest had shorn most Byzantine territory away from Constantinople, leaving the city with almost no hinterland. Desperate, Emperor John VIII was willing to consider a union with the Latin church in return for military aid from western Europe. His father, Manuel, perhaps thinking of earlier failed attempts at union, had advised him to use the promise of union only as a diplomatic tool, writing that "as far as this synod is concerned, continue to study and plan it, especially when you need to frighten the impious. But do not bring it about." John was running out of options, and in 1437, Pope Eugenius agreed to host a church council in Italy to discuss the theological issues at stake. John and a contingent of Byzantine ambassadors and theologians traveled first to Ferrara and then to Florence, where Latin and Greek theologians debated the use of leavened or unleavened bread in communion services, the Latin doctrine of purgatory, and the issue of papal supremacy. In the end the Byzantine delegation was pressured to compromise by their urgent need for military assistance against the Ottomans. In 1439 the Roman pope, the Byzantine emperor, and the patriarch of Constantinople signed an agreement formally ending more than three centuries of division between the Latin and Greek Orthodox churches. John and the Byzantine delegation were met with anger and resistance from Constantinople's clergy and people on their return, but John's bold move did result in some military aid.

Murad II, apparently exhausted by decades of warfare and in hopes of avoiding a bloody succession battle, in 1444 made the unprecedented move of abdicating in favor of his 12-year-old son, Mehmed II. Almost immediately the Ottomans were confronted with several threats, including a crusading coalition of mostly Hungarian, Polish, and Serbian troops and the Albanian frontier lord George Castriot, better known as Skanderbeg, who seized the fortress of Croia (Kruja) and led Albanian resistance to Ottoman encroachment for the next two decades, relying on Venetian, papal, and Neapolitan support. Murad was called out of retirement to lead the Ottoman forces, which crushed the Christians at the battle of Varna in November 1444. Several more Ottoman victories in the Balkans and Greece followed. The constant warfare that characterized Murad's reign accelerated his reliance on the janissary corps and pushed him to build a navy as well.

When Mehmed II assumed the throne for the second time in 1451, it did not take the new sultan long to fix his sights on Constantinople. Mehmed needed a military victory to signal his hold on power, and Constantinople had a strong symbolic value within Islamic and Turkish traditions as well as among Christians. Mehmed ordered the rapid construction of a fortress north of the city walls to block naval aid from reaching Constantinople and commissioned an enormous cannon for the assault on the city. Murad's engineers reportedly learned the most advanced techniques of cannon technology from a renegade Hungarian Christian. Emperor Constantine XI frantically called for aid from Europe, but in April 1453, when Mehmed and his armies arrived at the city walls, only a few thousand Latins had volunteered to aid in Constantinople's defense. After two months of relentless bombardment, the land walls were in tatters, and on May 29, Ottoman troops assaulted the ruined defenses and poured into the city.

The Ottoman conquest of Constantinople signaled a permanent shift in the balance of power in the eastern Mediterranean. The city's fall was clearly tragic from a Byzantine point of view: the last remnants of the Byzantine state, in the Morea (Peloponnese) and in Trebizond, were conquered in 1460–61, ending the empire's existence. From the Ottoman viewpoint, the conquest reunited the capital city with its hinterlands and completed the transformation of the Ottoman state from a frontier polity to a powerful and centralized state with claims to imperial status. While the pope and many Latin Christian writers bemoaned Constantinople's loss, Genoese and Venetian merchants were quick to come to economic terms with the new rulers. The Genoese at Pera maintained a formal neutrality during the siege and survived as a Latin merchant community under Ottoman control, while the Venetians signed a 1454 treaty that offered them a settlement and commercial privileges.

In the second half of the fifteenth century, states and dynasties across the Mediterranean expanded their realms by expanding or conquering their neighbors. The unification of Castile and Aragon in 1469 joined much of the western Mediterranean into a single system of federated kingdoms. In the east, Venice held the Adriatic coast of the Balkans and faced the Ottoman state across a porous and unruly frontier zone. The armies and navies of these expanding states clashed on occasion, but their diplomats also negotiated accords, their merchants exchanged goods, and their scholars debated and learned from one another. It is this creative and complex mix of cultures that created a Mediterranean Renaissance.

CHAPTER EIGHT

The Renaissance Bazaar

In 1479, as part of the negotiations to end a 16-year war with Venice, Sultan Mehmed II requested that the Venetian senate send a painter, a sculptor, a bronzeworker, a maker of chiming clocks, and an expert in the manufacture of clear glass to his court in Istanbul. This was not the sultan's first such request, he had previously solicited artists, craftsmen, and architects from other Italian states, including Florence and Rimini. In response, the senate dispatched the most prominent Venetian painter of the day, Gentile Bellini, who resided in Istanbul for two years and produced a number of works (many now lost) for his new patron. The most significant of these is the famous portrait of Mehmed as a Renaissance prince, shown in a three-quarter view, framed by an arch and seated behind a balcony draped in a richly ornamented textile. On either side of the arch are three crowns, possibly depicting Mehmed's three realms of Greece, Trebizond, and Asia. The painting relies on a shared vocabulary of power and legitimation that would have been immediately recognizable throughout the Mediterranean.

Mehmed's portrait fits into a larger pattern of cultural interests and strategies that he pursued after his conquest of Constantinople in 1453. He actively patronized artists, craftsmen, and intellectuals from Italy, Persia, and his own empire as he embarked on an ambitious program of urban renewal in the city itself. Mehmed's interest in the Romano-Byzantine past and his participation in an elite culture of ostentatious display made him a sought-after patron for both Christians and Muslims. Mehmed's self-fashioning as a Renaissance prince has caught the attention of scholars because in many ways his actions seem to fit into a larger pattern of "Renaissance" culture.

Since the nineteenth century, the concept, significance, parameters, and utility of the concept of the Renaissance have been a matter of great debate among scholars. In its narrowest sense, the term Renaissance has been used to refer to a revival of classical forms and ideas in the vibrant culture of late medieval Italy; speaking more broadly, the term defines a cultural resurgence or historical era encompassing the two or three centuries between the Middle Ages and the modern era, roughly 1400–1600. Many scholars have forcefully criticized the concept of the Renaissance, pointing to its focus on elite male culture, its ignoring of medieval precedents, and its Italian bias. On this last issue, one of the most insightful strands of recent scholarly study has convincingly shown that cross-cultural Mediterranean exchanges, and broader global connections, played a decisive role in shaping Renaissance culture. It is, in short, no longer possible to think of the Renaissance as a narrow, Italian phenomenon.

Easy generalizations about the Ottoman sultans as Renaissance princes are complicated by the strategies of Mehmed's son and successor, Bayezid II, who, after his father's death, sold many of the paintings his father had commissioned. Bayezid apparently took Islam's strictures against figurative art to heart, at least initially, as he tried to distinguish himself from his father with whom he had had serious differences. This initial impetus did not last, however, as a 1505 Ottoman inventory of the imperial palace lists both European and "heathen" objects, that is items bearing figural representations. In addition, Bayezid followed in his father's footsteps in the ongoing transformation of Istanbul into an imperial capital, and he continued to patronize Italian artists and architects, including Leonardo da Vinci and Michelangelo.

Mehmed's patronage of Italian artists and his son's initial rejection of the practice highlight the need to consider the Renaissance in a context of Mediterranean cross-cultural exchange, but they also show the complexity of doing so. The cultural flowering of the Renaissance owed a great deal to its broader Mediterranean connections, but the impact of this exchange cannot simply be measured by identifying products, styles, or ideas that the "West" acquired from the "East" (or vice versa). Rather it is to be found in the deliberate and creative assimilation and adaptation of diverse traditions that led to the cultural dynamism of the late medieval and early modern Mediterranean. In this way, the Renaissance provides an interesting parallel with the cultural efflorescence of Iberian convivencia, which some scholars have ascribed to the intense interaction between Christians, Jews, and Muslims. It is possible to view the Renaissance as a similar era of vigorous exchange between diverse religious and cultural traditions that spurred a range of creative responses. This is evident in shifting patterns of exchange in luxury goods, both imported and locally produced; in shared patronage practices that sought to signal social standing and legitimate political rule; and finally, in the resuscitation and vibrant exchange and adaptation of ideas drawn from a shared Greco-Roman, and to a lesser extent Arabic, classical tradition.

During the thirteenth and fourteenth centuries, Italian merchants were the chief intermediaries in the Levantine trade, though Catalan merchants also occupied an important position. They exported mostly raw materials such as timber, slaves, and wool and in return imported luxury and other goods from the east. This dominance of cross-Mediterranean networks of exchange continued into the fifteenth century; indeed, following a series of wars with Genoa in the latter decades of the fourteenth century and the disruption of Catalan commerce due to internal political turmoil, Venice's share of the Levantine trade grew from 40% to 60% by 1450. This gave the city significant leverage: for example, in the 1430s, collective pressure from Venetian merchants forced the Mamluks to reduce commodity prices they had recently raised.

Spices remained the core commodity in this trade and, as such, exemplify the growing integration of the Old World. They were produced in Indonesia, India, and China and then transported to the coast of India. There they were sold to Arab merchants, who carried them overland through the Himalayas, or more commonly by sea through the Persian Gulf or the Red Sea, to the Levant, where Italian merchants then purchased and shipped them to Italy and from there throughout the peninsula and into the north. While many spices were imported, pepper was far and away the most popular: around 1400 it represented 75% of Venice's total spice imports. The profits derived from the Levantine trade were fantastic: in 1423 the Venetian doge Tommaso Mocenigo reported that 10 million ducats annually were invested in it, with an astounding 40% return on investment. By the end of the fifteenth century, despite the era's political disruptions, both the scale and the profits of the spice trade had grown even larger. When the Portuguese entered into the equation following Vasco da Gama's discovery of the cape route around Africa to the Indies in 1497–98, there were fears in the Levant and Venice that the supply of spices would be cut off. However, following an initial disruption in the first decades of the sixteenth century, the trade revived by midcentury.

Although spices were an integral part of Mediterranean trade, there has often been a tendency to highlight them at the expense of the many other commodities and goods that made up a large proportion of commerce, and to ignore the western Mediterranean in favor of the eastern half of the sea. So, for instance, although Genoa was muscled out of the spice trade after the end of the Veneto-Genoese wars in 1381, it remained a maritime power with one of the sea's largest fleets and occupied an important place in trade in the central and western Mediterranean. The city also continued to be an important economic player in the eastern Mediterranean, maintaining a vibrant trade in slaves, grain, wine, alum, cloth, metals, and other products with the Ottomans, and its merchant colony at Pera, across the Golden Horn from Constantinople, remained one of the city's largest until its conquest. Catalan merchants dominated the western Mediterranean trade until the mid-fifteenth century; their trade in the Levant ebbed and flowed, though it remained at a lower level overall compared to Italian competitors. In the sixteenth century, alongside the spice trade, Italian, Catalan, and French merchants traded in cotton, raw silk, grain, cloth, jewels, and other commodities; indeed, this traffic expanded considerably in the final decades of the century. Growing numbers of Ottoman Greek, Jewish, Slavic, and Armenian merchants also entered the fray during the sixteenth century, as did northern Europeans: first French traders, primarily from Marseilles, but by the end of the century, English and Dutch merchants. In short, Mediterranean trade during this period was multifaceted, multicentered, and in constant flux.

The demand for luxury items in the Mediterranean trade was driven by elite appetites for opulent and rare goods, which were used for public displays of wealth as well as private pleasure. This phenomenon has been particularly well studied in Italy, where the expanding class of merchants in the late fourteenth and fifteenth centuries had more disposable wealth, which they wanted to expend on objects that announced their economic and social status. Urban culture in particular valued grace and pleasure in domestic settings. Some of this new taste for decorative domestic objects was imported by merchants returning from long residences abroad, where they had experienced the refined lifestyle of eastern Mediterranean elites. Venetian merchants often spent years living abroad in the commercial centers of the Levant, buying and selling silk, spices, and textiles. Inventories of merchants' homes in Damascus, for example, show that they lived *alla moresca*, that is, in the local style, and possessed all sorts of local decorative arts in their homes. Upon returning to Venice, merchants filled their homes in a similarly rich fashion, with rugs from Egypt or Persia, ceramics and bed coverings from Istanbul, Persian marquetry, and perfumes and spices from throughout the east. Inventories of elite households in Crete and elsewhere in the Mediterranean show similar tastes in luxuries.

As the expanding European elite's demand for luxury goods increased, manufacturers responded by augmenting their homegrown industries. In Italy the textile industry experienced notable growth, and entrepreneurs developed or expanded other industries, such as glass and ceramics, which competed with products from the east, first in domestic markets and then on an international scale. These new producers imitated, borrowed, and transformed Islamic artisanal and decorative traditions, which were in great demand. Ottoman craftsmen in turn imitated Italian technologies and artistic styles, creating multidirectional patterns of trade and a fluid circulation of artistic influences. The shared repertoire of stylistic motifs gave goods broad appeal to potential customers throughout the Mediterranean and also encouraged the rise of local industries employed in producing imitations. These cross-cultural influences can be seen clearly in the easily transportable decorative arts—textiles, carpets, leatherwork, ceramics, metalwork, and glass—although they certainly left their mark in paintings and architecture as well.

The complex interplay of technical and stylistic exchanges and markets can be seen in the so-called arts of fire: glass and ceramics. For glass, the obvious example is Venice. The Venetian glass industry's roots date to before 1000, and it has been suggested that Jewish artisans from the Levant may have played a role in its founding. From very early on, Venetian glassworkers borrowed extensively from Islamic styles. Beginning in the thirteenth century their techniques came under the strong influence of the more advanced Byzantine and Syrian glass industries, and they were equally dependent on Syrian ash and broken glass as raw materials in the manufacturing process. In 1291, Venice's glass furnaces were transferred to the island of Murano because of concerns about fire, and in subsequent centuries the industry experienced notable growth. The account book of the fifteenth-century Venetian merchant Giacomo Badoer, for example, shows him exporting large quantities of Murano glass to Byzantine Constantinople. The Venetian glass industry experienced another growth spurt after 1460, when its chief Syrian competitors were destroyed by the Timurids.

By the sixteenth century, Venice's glass manufacturing had surpassed its medieval masters and rivals and had become the largest and most innovative in the Mediterranean. Venetian glassworkers were producing much larger quantities of glass, crystal, mirrors, and other products that were exported throughout the eastern Mediterranean and beyond. Many items, such as mosque lamps, were designed specifically for majority-Muslim markets like Egypt and Syria, where some 20% of all Venetian production was shipped. Islamic-inspired styles were in great demand in the domestic market as well. By the latter part of the century, the Ottoman market was importing large quantities of Venetian product—including glass for 24,000 pairs of spectacles in one 1540 shipment and 900 lamps for a new mosque in 1569. Venetian glass beads also became an important part of the trans-Saharan trade. Venice's artisans produced both generic products for a variety of Mediterranean, and specifically Islamic, markets and custom-made objects for wealthy patrons, including high Ottoman officials. They adapted their output to the demands of an international luxury market and were thus interested in learning about the customs and forms of that market. Similar to the way Venice's industry had early on benefited from links to Syrian and Byzantine producers, Venetian techniques and styles were appropriated and adapted in Spain, primarily in Catalonia and Castile. The Spanish glassmakers built on preexisting Iberian traditions rooted in the Islamic period as well as knowledge provided by immigrant Venetian artisans. To complete the circle, glassware produced in Spain was sold in Italy and well beyond.

As for ceramics, Spanish lusterware, with its tin-glazed finish and blue and gold Hispano-Moresque design, was broadly popular; one scholar has described the demand for lusterware as a phenomenon of fifteenth-century taste. In the fourteenth century, the center of production shifted from Málaga in the Muslim south to Valencia, where Mudéjar artisans brought their trade secrets and ornamental styles. They were commissioned by Florentine commercial agents to produce dishes and other items emblazoned with families' coats of arms, the display of which was popular among Florence's elites. Beyond custom orders, there was a wider market for ready-made objects that were also highly valued.

Because of its popularity, Spanish lusterware had a decisive influence on Italian Renaissance maiolica (tin-glazed earthenware), particularly in important ceramic centers like Deruta and Gubbio where the technique was being used by the mid-fifteenth century, if not earlier. By 1500 the Italian ceramic industry had surpassed Spain's and dominated the European market for several centuries to come. With clear stylistic links to the Islamic world of both the eastern and western Mediterranean, Italian artists expanded their palette of glazes to include purple, green, orange, yellow, and a brilliant red that was learned from the famed Ottoman potters of Iznik.

Despite the burgeoning domestic industry and its growing exports, ceramics continued to be imported from both Spain and Ottoman lands, and Italian potters closely copied these styles in response to local demand. Iznik pottery grew in popularity over the course of the sixteenth century. Its tiles were in great demand for imperial Ottoman mosque projects, and they were also highly sought after by European customers who commissioned personalized works and often offered higher prices than those fixed by the sultans. This demand led to widespread copying and even counterfeiting. In Venice it stimulated a domestic industry that produced items decorated in the characteristic blue and white arabesque style of Iznik. The Iznik style also strongly influenced the later sixteenth-century porcelain workshop established by the Medici in Florence, and there is evidence that Ottoman artisans provided direct technical assistance to this initiative. Although stylistic influence went primarily east to west, Italian ornamentation also influenced Ottoman pottery.

Other examples of this dynamic abound. Textiles represent a central component of Mediterranean exchange in which goods, techniques, and styles flowed from multiple centers in numerous directions. For instance, silks, velvets, and brocades from Bursa and Damascus reached Europe as items of trade and diplomatic gifts, and they were used for everything from synagogue curtains to royal wardrobes to Catholic vestments. Demand for patterned silks imported from the Islamic world inspired a creative response in the Italian textile industry, spurring its expansion and contributing not only to Italian textiles' success in European entrepôts but also to growing demand across the Mediterranean. Indeed, in the fifteenth century, Italian fabrics came to dominate the market because of technological, artistic, and economic innovations. They were in especial demand in the Ottoman court, known as the Porte, which purchased or received as gifts large quantities of Venetian silk and velvet, which were made into ceremonial garments for the imperial elite. Cross-fertilization between production centers was common: Ottoman textile designers incorporated typically Italian motifs such as the crown into their silks, while Venetian workshops that catered to the Ottoman market produced cloth that closely mimicked Ottoman silks and damasks. Similarly, Italian cloth techniques and styles, which were introduced by Genoese craftsmen, became widespread in Spain, particularly in Catalonia, where the cloth trade was a mainstay.

Throughout the late medieval and early modern periods, artisans from across the region worked to feed the growing appetite for domestic luxury items. There is also evidence of "marketing" products through deliberate attempts to influence tastes and therefore increase demand for certain items. One way this was done was through the exchange of gifts, which was an essential component of Mediterranean diplomacy. In 1473, for example, the Mamluk sultan Qaitbay sent the Venetian doge presents of porcelain and muslin cloth; his ambassadors in Florence in 1487 offered textiles, exotic animals (including a giraffe), and porcelain as gifts. This was not a random choice, as the Mamluks were trying to promote porcelain, a new luxury good that was starting to arrive in Egypt from China. Similarly, in 1483, Bayezid II presented the Venetian ambassador with three types of velvet that were beginning to be produced locally. For their part, Venetian ambassadors made extensive use of diplomatic gifts, particularly glass and luxurious cloths, two of the city's chief manufactures, which seem to have primed the Ottoman court's purchase of large quantities of both commodities. This culture of diplomatic gift exchange created what has been described as a Mediterranean "community of taste."

An excellent and quite literal example of these communities of taste was the expansion of coffee consumption. Indigenous to Ethiopia and Yemen, coffee drinking spread slowly, first into the Arabian peninsula then to Mamluk Egypt by the early sixteenth century. The first coffeehouses in Istanbul were opened by midcentury and became meeting places for "pleasure seekers and idlers, and . . . men of letters and literati." Coffee was being traded in Hungary by 1579 and in Venice by 1638, where it quickly became popular; a century later there were over 200 coffeehouses in the city. The coffee trade even compensated to a degree for transformations in the spice trade caused by the Portuguese incursion into the Indian Ocean.

As coffee drinking proliferated, debates over it became common. Muslim clerics came out strongly against both the drink, which they considered an intoxicant, and coffeehouses, which were the "refuge of Satan" and "dens of sedition." Both Mamluk and Ottoman authorities attempted repeatedly and unsuccessfully to ban the beverage. It raised concerns among Jewish religious officials as well: when a rabbi in Egypt was asked whether Jews could drink coffee prepared by a gentile, he saw no problem with the drink per se but was strongly opposed to Jews consuming it in company with gentiles in coffeehouses. Another new beverage introduced into the Mediterranean from the New World via Spain, chocolate, elicited similar controversy among Spanish clerics regarding both its consumption by women and whether it could be drunk during Lent.

INTELLECTUAL DISCOURSES

To understand the Renaissance bazaar it is essential to remember that the legacy of classical Greek and Roman antiquity was a touchstone for its heirs, regardless of their religious or political persuasion. Classical ideas and models profoundly informed all parts of the Mediterranean throughout the fifteenth and sixteenth centuries. In Italy this reverence for the past was particularly intense because of the rich and omnipresent vestiges of antiquity and the peninsula's intimate association with this history. So it is no surprise that fourteenth-century Italy was home to the rise of humanism, a multifaceted intellectual movement that responded to what was exaggeratedly perceived as the sterility of the medieval intellectual world, in particular scholasticism. Humanists venerated classical Rome and Greece and believed that through a careful study of the history, language, philosophy, and literature of antiquity, they could derive tools to obtain an accurate understanding of the past that could relate to the questions and issues of their own day.

Education was a central pillar of humanism; indeed, the term is derived from the *studia humanitatis*, or liberal arts, which were the core of the humanist curriculum. If humanists initially focused their gaze on the Latin and the Roman past, their attention quickly expanded to Greece as well. Refugees from the troubles convulsing the Byzantine Empire in its final century were at the forefront of both the teaching of Greek language and the introduction of Greek literature to Italian humanists. The study of Greek was under way in Florence and Venice already in the late fourteenth century; in 1397 the Byzantine scholar and diplomat Manuel Chrysoloras was appointed to the first European chair of Greek at the University of Florence. The study of Greek letters led to a revival of Plato, conspicuous in the work of the humanist Marsilio Ficino and the ethereal art of Botticelli. Lorenzo the Magnificent, who fancied himself a philosopher and poet, patronized a Platonic school in Florence in the latter decades of the fifteenth century.

In Venice, Plutarch, Plato, and the Greek fathers were translated either by Venetian or Byzantine scholars, and individuals collected libraries of texts, such as the humanist and cardinal Domenico Grimani, who owned 392 Greek manuscripts. The most significant example, however, was the donation to the republic of more than 1,000 rare Greek manuscripts that the Byzantine scholar and prelate Basilios Bessarion had spirited out of Constantinople before its fall, which became the core of the city's famous Marciana Library. The culmination of this cross-cultural circulation in classical Greek texts was the project of the great Venetian printer Aldus Mantius to publish all the classical Latin and Greek texts in portable editions.

While humanists' intellectual interests and activities ranged broadly, one area of particular fascination to many, which has often been overlooked, was Islam. Humanists produced over 400 texts on Islam, significantly more than on other themes traditionally associated with the movement, such as nobility, education, or the dignity of humanity. In the buildup to and aftermath of 1453, some humanists depicted the Ottomans as new barbarians bent on the destruction of civilization. A recurring humanist motif was the threat presented by the "Turkish menace" and the quixotic dream of organizing a crusade to regain Istanbul. This strand of humanism is particularly apparent in the work of the Italian scholar and ecclesiastic Aeneas Silvius Piccolomini, who in 1458 became Pope Pius II. Following the fall of Constantinople, he wrote Pope Nicholas V, "But who can doubt that the Turks will vent their wrath upon the churches of God? I grieve that the world's most famous temple, Hagia Sofia, will be destroyed or defiled. I grieve that countless basilicas

of the saints, marvels of architecture, will fall in ruins or be subjected to the defilements of Muhammad. What can I say about the books without number there which are not yet known in Italy? Alas, how many names of great men will now perish? This will be a second death to Homer and a second destruction of Plato."

In contrast to Piccolomini's despair, Nicolò Sagundino, a Greek subject of Venice who was part of the 1454 peace delegation, described Mehmed II as a formidable foe—intelligent, driven, and commander of a strong, well-organized realm and military system. Sagundino portrayed Mehmed as inspired by classical culture: "He has particularly chosen to emulate Alexander of Macedon and Gaius Caesar, whose deeds he has arranged to be translated into his own language . . . He is determined to challenge their fame and he seems to be ardently inspired by their glory and praises." But Sagundino also emphasized that Mehmed was "inflamed against Christians" and determined to win the reputation of an Alexander or a Caesar through conquering Italy: "Everything is being prepared [by Mehmed] to assault Italy, . . . to this end he directs and aspires all of his thoughts, to this he bends all of his

Map of Italy, from Francesco Berlinghieri, Septe Giornate della Geographia (1482). Biblioteca Laurenziana, Florence. Photo: Alinari / Art Resource, NY

THE MEDITERRANEAN WORLD

decisions." As these examples suggest, humanism as a movement was diverse and adaptable, and humanists were not monolithic in their response to Islam. If some historians depicted Ottomans as cruel and barbarous, others portrayed Mamluks, Timurids, and "Saracen" Arabs as "good" Muslims.

In addition to Greek and Latin, humanists became increasingly interested in other Mediterranean languages and cultural traditions, including Hebrew and Arabic. One of the most influential scholars of the late fifteenth century, Giovanni Pico Della Mirandola, was a proponent of philosophical and religious syncretism and held that all knowledge from all times and places contained "precious nuggets of universal truth" and was all part of God's broad revelation to humanity. He wrote, "Surely it is the part of a narrow mind to have confined itself within a single Porch or Academy," and so in addition to classical Greek and Roman sources, he applied his humanistic lens to Jewish and Muslim texts. One of the key ideas of his most famous work, *Oration on the Dignity of Man*, is the unity of all learning—Islamic, Jewish, and Christian—as an essential component of the divine revelation. In addition to Greek and Latin texts, European collectors avidly sought important Hebrew, Arabic, and Ottoman works, which scholars such as Pietro della Valle were often engaged to collect during their Mediterranean travels.

The Mediterranean intellectual exchange was not a one-way street. Mehmed II possessed an expanding library of Greek and Latin texts, and he commissioned translations of important works and was tutored in classical geography and philosophy by the polymath and former Byzantine imperial official George Amiroutzes. While some scholars have exaggeratedly claimed that Mehmed surrounded himself with humanists, there is no question that they were a presence in his court. Some so-called philo-Turkish humanists, such as Giovanni Stefano Emiliano, offered their services in the hopes of winning the sultan's patronage. At the behest of his master, the Italian mercenary and nobleman Sigismondo Malatesta, Roberto Valturio sent Mehmed a copy of his *De re militari*, filled with exquisite illuminations. The Greek refugee Francesco Filelfo wrote a flattering poem to the sultan, and his son Giovanmario devoted three of the four chapters of his epic poem *Amyris* to praising Mehmed's conquest of Constantinople. In 1465 the humanist George Trapezountios (George of Trebizond) addressed a series of flattering letters to the sultan that went so far as to claim that Mehmed, like a new Alexander the Great, was anointed by God to restore peace to world. He also prepared a Latin translation of Ptolemy's astronomical treatise *Almagest* for Mehmed.

The trans-Mediterranean character of humanism is evident in the case of the Florentine humanist and statesman Francesco Berlinghieri, who in 1482 published *Geographia*. The book was based on the famous work of the classical geographer Ptolemy, the first copy of which had been brought to Florence from Constantinople in 1400. Berlinghieri sent a copy of the book with a dedication to Mehmed; when he learned of the sultan's death, he sent copies to two of Mehmed's sons who were vying for the throne. Ptolemy represented a common point of reference and part of the Mediterranean's shared classical intellectual legacy; several versions existed in pre-sixteenth century Ottoman collections, and Mehmed II commissioned an Arabic translation by George Amiroutzes. In contrast to their Christian counterparts, medieval Muslim geographers had expanded significantly on and corrected Ptolemy's classical base, and these changes were often ignored by Renaissance cartographers. Nevertheless, the *Geographia* circulated among elites who shared an interest in classical geography, and it illustrates the sustained conversation between communities of authors, printers, and readers that ranged across the fifteenth-century Mediterranean.

As this suggests, the humanist revival of classical learning was not strictly a Christian or European phenomenon. Several generations of scholarship have decisively demonstrated humanism's deep medieval roots, and scholars of Islam have pointed to analogous precedents beginning already in the tenth century in the Muslim Mediterranean. There are intriguing parallels, for example, between the sonnets of the father of Italian humanism, Francis Petrarch, and the rhyming couplets of the Arabic poetic form the ghazal. Another common genre of humanist writing, political-advice literature such as Machiavelli's *The Prince*, has close parallels to an extensive body of sixteenth-century Arabic, Persian, and Ottoman literature, such as Mustafa Ali's famous *Counsel for Sultans* (1581). This literature arose not necessarily through the direct transmission of texts but rather was inspired by comparable demands among evolving Mediterranean states. In the same period, converts to Islam composed narratives that engaged theological debates over correct rituals and questions of scriptural authority and salvation in making their case for the superiority of Islam, which exhibited humanist sensibilities in terms of textual criticism, the mastery of scriptural languages, and insistence on the primacy of original sources in religious debates.

While long a matter of scholarly disputation, it is now clear that Jewish intellectuals also engaged in the humanist program, though this was done on their own terms and not as part of some quest to achieve an "idyllic cultural symbiosis." In Italy, Jewish intellectuals and preachers emphatically embraced classical texts, called for studying the bible in the context of gentile and Jewish literature, analyzed texts from the Jewish tradition from a humanistic philological perspective, composed classically inflected history and poetry, and engaged with the humanist ideal of the well-rounded *homo universalis* (universal or Renaissance man), termed *hakham kolel* in Hebrew. The idea of creating a university was also broached: the Torah, Hebrew language, and Jewish philosophy were to be studied alongside classical philosophy, Latin, and a range of other topics. Jewish humanists often wrote in Hebrew but also composed works in Italian to engage Christian readers. Just as among Christians, Italian Jews engaged in heated debates about the relationship of new humanist ideas and approaches to established paradigms. Jewish humanist activity was not limited to Italy; humanism had been imported into Iberian Jewish intellectual discourse through Aragonese Naples before the expulsion. The Sephardi diaspora introduced humanism into Ottoman lands, and there were strong intellectual connections and vigorous debates between Jewish communities in Italy and the Ottoman Empire.

Jewish and Christian scholars engaged in productive exchanges on Hebrew language and kabbalah; indeed, Christian humanists were from quite early on interested in Hebrew because of serious concerns regarding the reliability of the Latin Vulgate translation of the bible and the degree to which it adhered to its original textual sources. To address this and other questions, the Florentine humanist and politician Giannozzo Manetti immersed himself in the study of Hebrew with Jews and Jewish converts to Christianity, collected Hebrew manuscripts that would form the core of the Vatican collection, and translated the Psalms and other biblical texts into Hebrew in Naples between 1455 and 1458. Pico della Mirandola's views of human potential were also informed by Muslim ideas filtered through several Jewish interlocutors.

There are many other examples of interregional intellectual exchange and flows of knowledge in the Mediterranean. These include the Ethiopian Coptic Christian scholar and diplomat Saga Za'ab, who traveled in Portugal in 1527, where he was received with suspicion because of doubts about Ethiopian religious practices such as circumcision, which were viewed seen as potentially Muslim or Jewish. Saga Za'ab ably defended his Christian bona fides while in Lisbon, and several years later he prepared a defense of his faith as part of an ongoing dialogue with several Portuguese humanists and scholars, including Damião de Góis, a close friend of the great Dutch humanist Erasmus. Another emblematic figure was the Syrian Orthodox scribe Moses of Mardin, who taught Syriac in Rome in the mid-sixteenth century and played a central role in the growing interest in Syriac language and texts. He was also instrumental in the printing of a Syriac New Testament.

The Moroccan al-Hasan ibn Muhammad al-Wazzan, or Leo Africanus, baptized by Pope Leo X in 1520, was a unique and important participant in this Mediterranean republic of letters. He lived in Rome for many years and engaged with humanist circles there. He prepared many works, including his hefty and influential *Cosmography and Geography of Africa*, which was first published in Italian in 1550, in Venice. The work treats African geography, economy, culture, weather, flora and fauna, and religion; in Europe it was considered the authoritative work on Africa for over two centuries.

An important aspect of intellectual exchange in the early modern Mediterranean, which was linked to the growing influence of humanism, was the circulation of texts. The rise of printing, of course, had a profound effect. From the early sixteenth century on, scholars, entrepreneurs, and ecclesiastics were engaged in a range of ambitious and innovative printing projects uniquely tied to the Mediterranean's multilingual environment. They published influential books in an array of languages, which were intended primarily for export into the eastern half of the sea.

Italy, in particular Venice, was the center of Mediterranean-language publishing in the sixteenth century, though Rome became increasingly important in the second half of the century. One of the most innovative printing houses of the time was the Aldine Press, founded in 1495 by the great scholar and printer Aldus Mantius, who migrated to Venice from near Rome. The press specialized in publishing Greek works in the original language, including editions of Aristotle and Galen, and in 35 years over 90 Greek first editions were published. Venice was also the chief hub of printing in other non-Latin languages such as Hebrew, Cyrillic, and Glagolithic for the Slavic-speaking market. The first book in Armenian was published Venice in 1512, and the city remained the epicenter of Armenian publishing for over two centuries. The first book in Albanian was also published there in 1555.

In addition, Italy was the most important early center of Hebrew printing: Jewish printers were active in Rome in the 1460s, but by the early sixteenth century, with the rise of its Jewish community, Venice superseded Rome. Numerous Jewish presses were active in the city, and Christian publishers also fed the Jewish market, including Daniel Bomberg, who specialized in Hebrew language books and, between 1520 and 1523, accomplished the monumental task of printing the first complete edition of the Talmud. The output of Hebrew-language presses in general was primarily directed toward Jewish readers, but it also found a growing market among the community of non-Jewish scholars interested in Hebrew texts.

The sixteenth century also saw a flourishing of Arabic-language publishing: one of the earliest works was printed in Granada at the start of the sixteenth century for use in catechizing the Moriscos. A book of Christian prayers was published in Fano in Italy in 1514, and in 1537 a Venetian firm published the first edition of the Qur'an in Arabic, though it was filled with errors and was a commercial failure. In 1565 an Arabic catechism aimed at Lebanese Maronite Christians was printed in Rome, and in 1584, with papal dispensation and Medici support, Giovan Battista Raimondi established the Typographia Medicea Linguarum Externarum to print Christian texts in eastern languages. Over the next three decades this press published gospels, a grammar, scientific works, and classical texts in Arabic, including a translation of the bible. Presses printing in Arabic also existed in Palermo, Padua, Paris, and Milan, which published with a clear view to exportation to the Islamic world.

Early modern Turkish-language print culture presents an interesting parallel to Arabic printing. In 1485, Bayezid II banned printed books in Arabic and Turkish in the Ottoman Empire, though printing in other languages was permitted. His motivations are a matter of debate among scholars, but they were probably based on a belief that the mechanical reproduction of sacred texts was inappropriate; moreover, there was opposition from powerful and entrenched scribes and copyists, not to mention the difficulty of faithfully and accurately producing the complex written languages of the Islamic world in a way that could compete with the beautiful tradition of Muslim calligraphy. Whatever the reasons, Bayezid's decree was reiterated in 1515 by Selim I, who declared that "occupying oneself with the science of printing is punishable by death."

This position created a void that entrepreneurs elsewhere eagerly filled. In 1559 a heart-shaped world map with an extensive commentary in Ottoman on European explorations, an astute contemporary political overview, and a discussion of recent Ottoman territorial gains, was prepared in Venice in the workshop of the Venetian printer and entrepreneur, Marcantonio Giustiniani. Attributed to a fictitious Tuni-

sian cartographer, Tunuslu Hacı Ahmed, the pioneering map was intended for sale to a literate Ottoman audience that shared in the general fascination of the day for the latest geographical knowledge. A decade later, Giustiniani launched a commercial enterprise to supply Turkish language texts to the Ottomans, though it was not until 1588 that several Italian merchants were authorized by Murad III to market books in Arabic, Persian, or Turkish. The first Turkish language press was established in Istanbul in 1727 by Ibrahim Muteferrika and published 17 works over the next 15 years.

Printing in the Ottoman Empire existed long before 1727, however. Armenian-language publishing began in Istanbul in 1567

A Complete and Perfect Map Describing the Whole World (Venice, 1559–60 [printed 1795]). Attributed to Tunuslu Hacı Ahmed, the map was in reality created in the workshop of the Venetian printer and entrepreneur Marcantonio Giustiniani for sale in Istanbul. *Courtesy of the John Carter Brown Library at Brown University*

when an Armenian delegate to Rome returned with type from Venice and published several books. The first book printed in an Arab country was likely a psalter published in a Lebanese convent in 1610. Nicodemus Metaxas, a graduate of Oxford, established a Greek-language press in Istanbul in 1627, but it lasted less than a year because of the religious controversy that his few publications elicited.

The earliest and by far most significant example of printing in the Ottoman Empire was that of the Jews. The diaspora of Jews from Iberia and other European centers turned the Ottoman Empire into one of the most important centers of Jewish printing in the sixteenth century. Istanbul's first Hebrew-language press was established by two Spanish exiles, David and Samuel Ibn Nahmias, perhaps as early as 1493, though there is some debate on this date. Two decades later, in 1512, a press was established in Salonica (formerly Thessalonica), with type brought from Portugal. The most important Jewish press was that of the Soncino family, refugees from Germany who initially settled in Italy near Mantua before moving to Naples; they then went to Salonica and finally settled in Istanbul in 1530. There they produced numerous editions in Hebrew and Ladino. In all, more than 100 books were published in Ottoman territory during the sixteenth century, including prayer books, rabbinical responsa, kabbalist writings, literature, and the Mishnah. Iberian Jewish printers also briefly established themselves in Fez after the expulsion, before moving on to Italy and Holland. The circulation of Jewish publications, particularly in Ladino, played an important role in the development of a Sephardic koine that linked, however loosely, various branches of the Mediterranean Jewish diaspora.

While Spain lagged slightly in the development of printing, it was nonetheless the site of one of the great early works of both humanist scholarship and printing, the six-volume polyglot bible, or *Complutensian Polyglot*. Begun in 1502 at the University of Alcalá and not published until 1522, the project's aim was to prepare a scholarly edition of the bible in all four of its original languages — Greek, Hebrew, Chaldean, and Latin. This leviathan task was carried out by a diverse cross-section of humanist scholars from across the Mediterranean — including three Spanish Jewish conversos, an Old Christian Spaniard, and an immigrant from Greece. The team was assembled by a seemingly unlikely patron, the primate and chief inquisitor of Spain, Cardinal Francisco Jiménez Cisneros, who was also a great patron of humanistic studies. While for Cisneros the bible represented a means to enlighten clergy by giving them access to "pure" sources of religion, it was also a significant accomplishment for Spanish humanism and early printing. In the brief interlude between the invention of printing and the expulsion, Jewish publishing also became well established in the Iberian peninsula; one scholar has called printing perhaps the greatest cultural innovation of the Sephardim. The first Hebrew book published in Spain was in 1476, in Guadalajara, and by the following decade presses were active in Hijar, Zamora, and Lisbon.

Printing exerted a powerful and entirely new influence on the exchange of information in the early modern Mediterranean, amply attested to in the appearance of books in collections throughout the region, such as the library of a sixteenth-

A page from the *Complutensian Polyglot Bible* (Alcalá, 1522), from the first chapter of Genesis, with text in Greek, Hebrew, Chaldean and Latin. *Biblioteca Nacional, Madrid. Photo: Album / Art Resource, NY*

century Cretan collector that included Dante, Boccaccio, Aretino, Ficino, and Bembo, as well as classical Greek and Roman authors. Printing, however, has often been focused on at the expense of other sources of and modes for the circulation of knowledge. For example, though it has long been argued that the failure to embrace printing set the Ottomans apart from Europe, a new generation of communication studies has decentralized printing's importance and shown how oral and scribal forms coexisted alongside the printed word and played a central role in the circulation of ideas and information. This was true of the early modern world generally, not just the Ottoman Empire. As a result of the ongoing verbal nature of culture, there was a vibrant network of news and communications, both oral and manuscript, that crisscrossed the Mediterranean and dwarfed printed texts in quantity and popular impact. This took the form of diplomatic dispatches, letters, and

Ottoman astronomer Taqi al-Din Muhammad ibn Maruf at work in his observatorium in Istanbul. From Seyyid Lokman *Shāhanshāhnāma* (Book of the King of Kings) (Istanbul, 1581–82). *Topkapi Palace Museum, Istanbul.* Photo: Art Resource, NY

the famous *avvisi*; these handwritten newsletters were precursors to the newspaper and were closely associated with the vibrant news centers of Rome and Venice, but they both contained and conveyed news from throughout the region. This network interconnected with the intensive oral culture that characterized Mediterranean ports and central squares.

A subset of the larger Mediterranean intellectual exchange centered on science. While the rich and varied medieval cross-cultural scientific dialogue has received extensive treatment, its continuation during the Renaissance has attracted less attention. In the same way, the ongoing importance of European links with the Islamic world in the scientific advances of the era has also been ignored. As one scholar has noted, science "has always been a transnational activity," and the early modern Mediterranean continued to be a zone of mutual scientific exchange and embrace.

Astronomy, considered the queen of the sciences and at the forefront of the scientific revolution, illustrates the complex interplay and interdependence between Muslim and Christian practitioners during the Renaissance. Islamic astronomers from the ninth to the sixteenth centuries were actively and imaginatively engaged in correcting and expanding on the received views of classical antiquity such as those of Ptolemy. Their results were circulated into the Latin west via translations and other methods, and they had a significant impact. For instance, many of the novel mathematical techniques at the heart of the great astronomer Nicolaus Copernicus's theories and calculations were identical to the work of Islamic astronomers such as Nasir al-Din al-Tusi and Ibn al-Shatir, who labored in the preceding centuries; Copernicus's unique innovation was to use this foundation to shift from a geocentric to a heliocentric conception of the solar system. Another example of the influence of al-Tusi is the existence of an Arabic copy of his work in the possession of the French scholar Guillaume Postel, full of Latin annotations, which became the source of a series of lectures he delivered at the Collège de France.

In the same vein, Postel's contemporary, the distinguished Ottoman astronomer Taqi al-Din Muhammad ibn Maruf, relied on a Latin copy of Ptolemy, and perhaps other works, which he accessed in part through the use of an Italian multilingual dictionary. Taqi al-Din became the chief astronomer of Murad III and founded the short-lived Istanbul observatory in 1579. Building on a robust Islamic astronomical tradition, his calculations were known to the Danish astronomer Tycho Brahe, who prized them because of their superior precision, which surpassed both his own computations and those of Copernicus.

This Ottoman astronomical tradition had roots reaching back to Mehmed II, who, as part of his imperial agenda, also invited intellectuals and craftsmen from Persia to his court. One of the most notable was the astronomer Ali Kusci, who was appointed the keeper of an observatory attached to Hagia Sophia and was given a large stipend. His library inspired Taqi al-Din and other Ottoman astronomers who in turn influenced the course of astronomical research in the sixteenth century. Jewish scholars and astronomers in the Ottoman Empire, because of their experience in both eastern and western astronomical traditions, also played an important mediating role in this scientific dialogue. For instance, Taqi al-Din was assisted in his work by a Salonican Jew, David the Mathematician.

A more mundane, but no less important, example of this scientific interchange is the circulation of scientific instruments. Astrolabes, for instance, were the most sophisticated calculating machines of their day and were used for a variety of navigational and mathematic computations. During the Middle Ages they reached Italy and other northern countries from the Muslim world, which initially was their sole source. Eventually, however, European producers were able to master the manufacture of these precision instruments. Another scientific innovation of the era, the telescope, was dispersed in the opposite direction, though the optical knowledge behind its design was heavily indebted to Arabic science.

As science forged new boundaries and scholars asserted their right to explain the world in ways at variance with traditional religious narratives, tensions developed, particularly with ecclesiastical officials and institutions, both Muslim and Christian. For more than two decades the Pisan polymath Galileo Galilei was famously enmeshed in a series of controversies with ecclesiastical authorities (but also, it must be said, with other scholars) over his revolutionary ideas, particularly but not solely associated with heliocentrism. This culminated in his well-known face-off with Pope Urban VIII and the Roman inquisition, which in 1633 resulted in the banning of some of his works and Galileo being placed under house arrest until his death, in 1642, at age 77. Galileo had a parallel antecedent in the brief history of the Istanbul observatory, which was dismantled in 1581, very shortly after its construction, when religious officials accused the astronomers of using magic and attributed the outbreak of an epidemic and other disasters to their hubristic scientific activities.

While connection and exchanges played an important role in the early modern Mediterranean, by the seventeenth century the scientific and technological distance within the Mediterranean was expanding. If the Islamic world had been the scientific torchbearer and Christian Europe the acolyte during the Middle Ages, the early modern period saw these roles gradually but fundamentally reversed, with significant long-term implications for both.

An area of mutual influence that had some of the direst consequences for the region's inhabitants was military technology. Both the Ottoman and the Habsburg polities have been described as gunpowder empires because of their use of new weapons technologies. This notion is not particularly useful, both because most states in the era were using gunpowder weapons and because the limitations of the technology, particularly in its earliest centuries, made it of limited strategic importance. Nonetheless, there is no question that gunpowder weapons and other new technologies already had begun to alter the military landscape throughout the Mediterranean in the fifteenth century. In terms of military technology and technique, the Ottomans were early and imaginative adopters: at Mohács, in 1526, for example, they had perhaps 300 cannon to the Hungarians' 85. Over the course of the century, the Ottomans kept pace with technological and logistical developments; indeed, in sapping and mining they led out, and organizationally their large standing army and its elaborate provisioning system set them apart. This innovativeness and openness to new ideas and technologies made the Ottoman military if not superior, as many contemporaries and some modern scholars have held, then at the very least the equal of its rivals, well into the seventeenth century.

The consistent movement of matériel, men, and technology characterized the early modern Mediterranean. Skilled gun founders and blacksmiths were in high

demand, and the opportunities presented by Ottoman enthusiasm for new military technologies made the empire a magnet for innovators and their ideas. In the same way, knowledge of the principles behind the novel defensive structures known as the *trace italienne*, developed in this period by Venice and others to counter gunpowder weapons, was circulated broadly by itinerant military engineers who offered their expertise to the highest bidder. Though officials tried to prevent it, there was an active contraband trade in military matériel, too: for instance, in the 1460s, gunpowder, bombards, and other military armaments were shipped from Ancona to Istanbul, and Italian-produced matchlocks are amply represented in Ottoman weapon collections. There was also a licit trade in arms. Venice was supplying the Persians with advanced weapons for use in their wars against the Ottomans by 1473. The Venetians and the Ottomans both assisted the Mamluks in their struggle against the Portuguese in the early sixteenth century: Venice provided cannon and expert shipbuilders, while the sultans sent raw materials in short supply in Egypt, marine soldiers, gun founders, and the experienced naval commander Kemal Reis.

Parallel to the transfer of technology, the late medieval and early mod-

Example of new style of trace italienne fortification on an islet at the entrance of Souda Bay, Crete. From Olfert Dapper, *Naukeurige Beschryving der Eilanden, in de Archipel der Middelantsche Zee* (Amsterdam: Wolfgangh, Waesbergen, Boom, Someren, and Goethals, 1688). Aikaterini Laskaridis Foundation (www.travelogues.gr)

ern Mediterranean was characterized by a significant movement of military specialists of all sorts. There was a regular stream of workers with specialized military and industrial skills beating a path from Venice (particularly from its famous arsenal) and its maritime state to Istanbul to offer their services. Greek shipbuilders and sailors played a central role throughout the eastern Mediterranean, in the Ottoman fleet in particular. The highly technical manufacture of cannon led to a great degree of mobility for experts who sold their knowledge regardless of political or religious persuasion. In Istanbul, Ottoman and Persian blacksmiths; Armenian and Greek miners; and Bosnian, Serbian, Ottoman, Italian, German, French, English, and Dutch founders and engineers created an ideal setting for technological dialogue.

Early modern militaries were international organizations. Philip II's armies included English, Irish, German, Italian, and Spanish men. Venice's frontier fortresses were manned by many non-Catholic mercenaries from Muslim and Protestant areas, whom officials zealously defended from inquisitional attempts to enforce religious conformity. The Ottomans recruited soldiers from throughout their vast empire, along with many non-Ottoman mercenaries and technicians, including Tatars, Circassians, Moldavians, Wallachians, Transylvanians, Poles, and French. This military migration was not limited to simple soldiers; ambitious or impoverished noblemen from Italy and Dalmatia offered their services to rulers throughout the region, and quite indiscriminately; many of the chief Ottoman military men of the age fit this bill, such as the famous Sicilian renegade Cigalazade Yusuf Sinan Pasha, who became admiral of the Ottoman fleet and commander of the army. The thousands of rowers necessary to propel the galleys that remained the mainstay of naval warfare for much of this period included men from throughout the region and well beyond, who served either voluntarily or, more often as demand for their services grew after 1500, involuntarily as slaves or convicts.

PATRONAGE AND POWER

A final aspect of the Renaissance bazaar, illustrated by the acquisitions of Mehmed II, was the Mediterranean elites' and rulers' shared culture of ostentatious display as a means of representing and projecting power. This was displayed through a range of media, including painting, tapestries, medals, and, in particular, architecture, which was considered the purest and most noble of the arts. Renaissance rulers in some ways considered a legacy of architectural magnificence as important as either wealth or military victories. Rulers seeking legitimacy and reputation commissioned large public and private structures and engaged in grandiose urban projects. The age saw the rise of a new architectural and decorative language with a common vocabulary that drew on classical models. Italy was at the forefront of this new classicism; however, this is not the story of Italian diffusion but rather one of multiple centers all drawing on shared veneration for Greco-Roman tradition, adapted and applied in uniquely different ways, whether in El Escorial, the Alhambra, the Louvre, St. Peter's, or the Süleymaniye.

One of the prime examples of this phenomenon began in earnest after 1460 with the transformation of Constantinople into Istanbul by its Ottoman rulers, who selectively appropriated a classical, Byzantine, and Islamic vocabulary in reenvisioning their new imperial capital. Because of the many connections between the Ottoman court and its Italian contemporaries, Renaissance notions of structuring the urban environment played a key role in this project. This is apparent in the city's rapidly evolving holy landscape. Before 1453, Ottoman mosque architecture had generally referenced the styles and iconography of powerful Muslim neighbors such as the Timurids, Mamluks, and Mongols. The conquest presented a panoply of new possibilities and inspirations.

When Mehmed entered Constantinople, he was struck, as one Ottoman official described, by "its great size, its grandeur and beauty, its teeming population, its loveliness, and the costliness of its churches and public buildings and of the private houses." The most important of these was Hagia Sophia, Emperor Justinian's monumental sixth-century church, the masterpiece of Byzantine architecture whose massive dome to Procopius seemed "suspended from heaven" and which awed Mehmed when he first saw it. He followed tradition and transformed Hagia Sophia (as well as many lesser Byzantine churches) into a mosque. This conversion consisted primarily of removing the crosses and bells (the extensive mosaics were left untouched until the eighteenth century) and introducing traditional Islamic decorative elements such as a minbar, mihrab, and minarets. The structure itself remained fundamentally unchanged and became the model for the great mosques that would come to fill Istanbul's skyline over the next 150 years.

Hagia Sophia's influence is apparent in the first major mosque that Mehmed had constructed within Istanbul's city walls, Fatih Cami (Conqueror's Mosque), built between 1463 and 1470, and destroyed in an earthquake in 1766. Generally attributed to Atik Sinan, who is believed to have been a Greek janissary taken in the devshirme, Fatih Cami was the first imperial mosque erected in the capital, and it remained the largest and most important for a century. In addition to the mosque proper, the extensive complex incorporated a bath, library, hospital, hospice, caravanserai, and eight madrasas. Fatih Cami blended Islamic and Ottoman architectural traditions with Roman, Byzantine, and Italian Renaissance concepts, illustrating the hybrid fusion of the new Ottoman architecture. The dome, tympanum arches, and other elements harked back to Hagia Sophia, and key features and dimensions of the complex were strikingly similar to the Ospedale Maggiore in Milan, which was designed by the influential Florentine architect Antonio Filarete and begun in 1456 for his patron the duke of Milan, Francesco Sforza. Filarete's architectural and urbanistic theories, which with those of Leon Battista Alberti were the most influential in fifteenth-century Italy, were informed by Byzantine notions filtered through the Constantinople-born humanist Francesco Filelfo, who remained deeply connected to his birth city following the Ottoman conquest. There is strong evidence that Filarete himself traveled to Istanbul seeking Mehmed's patronage in 1465, during the construction of the Ospedale, and in this way direct-

ly influenced Fatih Cami and other projects in the city, and in turn was influenced by what he saw in Istanbul.

Fatih Cami (Conqueror's Mosque), the first imperial mosque constructed in Istanbul (1463–70). It blended Islamic and Ottoman architectural traditions with Roman, Byzantine, and Italian Renaissance concepts, and is the first example of the hybrid fusion of the new Ottoman architecture. Detail from Melchior Lorck, *Prospect of Constantinople* (1583) (PK-P-BPL 1758/13). *Leiden University Library*

Whether Filarete ended up in the Ottoman capital or not, architectural and artistic cross-pollination proliferated throughout the Mediterranean in the post-conquest period. Mehmed's patronage of Bellini is the most famous, but certainly not the only, example. Mehmed also wooed the Florentine architect and sculptor Michelozzo, who like Filarete was an apprentice of the great Florentine artist Lorenzo Ghiberti and whose Mediterranean projects included work in Cyprus and on the famed walls of Ston in southern Dalmatia. A parallel to Bellini was Mehmed's court artist, Sinan Beg, a renegade, perhaps from Italy, who appears to have been trained in portraiture by a Ragusan artist and was further exposed to artistic developments in Italy when he was sent there as a cultural ambassador, at the same time that Bellini was in Istanbul. In turn Sinan Beg passed on his synthetic Italo-Ottoman style to his pupils.

Ottoman sultans were key parts of the broader patronage network of Italian artists and, like their European contemporaries, saw in them a means to articulate and accentuate their power and status. For instance, in 1503, Leonardo da Vinci, describing himself as "your obedient ser-

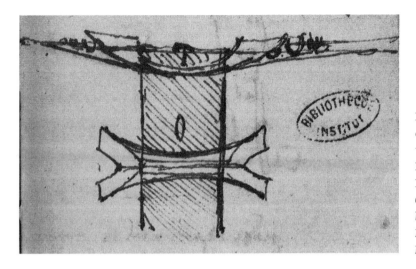

Leonardo da Vinci, design for bridge over the Golden Horn, Istanbul, 1502 (Paris Manuscript L, Folio 66r). *Bibliothèque de l'Institut de France, Paris. Photo: RMN Art Resource, NY*

vant," was in communication with Bayezid II to construct a bridge across the Golden Horn. Leonardo had likely heard that the sultan was looking for an Italian engineer during the visit of several Ottoman ambassadors to Rome. He sketched out an innovative and beautiful, but impracticable, scheme for a masonry bridge 350 meters long, with a single arch 240 meters long and so high "that a ship under full sail could sail underneath." Several years later, the sultan invited Michelangelo to submit a design for the Golden Horn bridge, and a decade later Selim I made a second attempt to lure the great artist to Istanbul. This widespread and consistent practice of Ottoman sultans patronizing Italian craftsmen continued throughout the sixteenth century.

Similar practices can be observed among other Renaissance princes. For instance, Francis I of France employed culture as a means to expand his power and reputation both within his kingdom vis-à-vis his nobility and on the international front. As part of this program he pursued many Italian artists, inviting them to France and commissioning them to produce works of art. His greatest coup, and confirmation of the international demand for Italian artists and artisans, was luring Leonardo da Vinci to Amboise near Francis's favorite royal château, where he spent his final years, from 1516 to 1519. Other Italians followed, including Andrea del Sarto, Primaticcio, and Benvenuto Cellini. A major part of Francis's cultural program centered on the reconstruction of the medieval Louvre palace and his hunting lodge at Fontainebleau according to Renaissance principles, for which many Italian artisans were employed.

The rulers of newly united Spain employed a similar approach to legitimating and strengthening their rule through the patronage of artists steeped in the classicizing style first associated with Renaissance Italy. This is evident in Emperor Charles V's commissions of paintings, literature, and architecture, in particular his palace in the Alhambra complex in Granada, which is considered the first and most

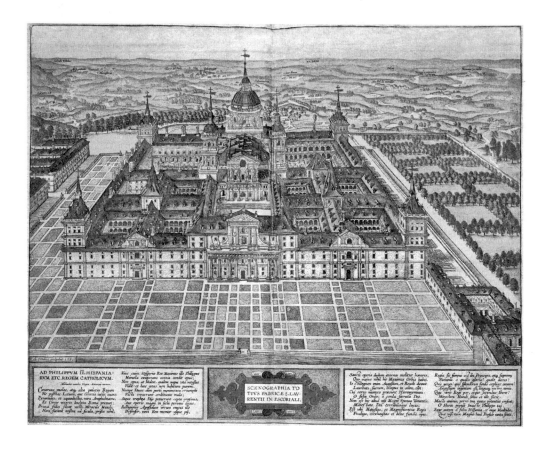

important Renaissance building in Spain and the major architectural symbol of its patron's reign. It was designed by Pedro Machuca, a painter who, like many Spanish artists of the day, worked and studied in Italy. He was in Rome from 1515 to 1520, where he was exposed to the city's ancient ruins and imbibed the classicism of Raphael, Michelangelo, and Giulio Romano. The influence of Italian Renaissance architecture, and in particular the great architect Donato Bramante, is evident in both Machuca's conception of the building and its classical architectural language. Though never completed, the Palace of Charles V tangibly and strikingly articulated his growing sense of association with ancient imperial Rome and proclaimed that Spain, like Italy, was a worthy center of the Renaissance classical revival. Constructed on the grounds of the last Spanish Muslim outpost, it also served as a powerful statement to Charles's restive subjects of both the power of Spain's new Habsburg rulers and the emperor's commitment to defending his realm against any threat, particularly from Islamic lands.

Abraham Ortelius, El Escorial, in Theatrum Orbis Terrarum (Antwerp, 1603). Photo: Alfredo Dagli Orti / Art Resource, NY

In his will, Charles V directed his son, Philip II, to construct a "dynastic pantheon" to house the remains of Spain's rulers, but certainly also as another expression of the legitimacy of Habsburg rule. When he came to the throne in 1556, Philip expanded on his father's original idea when he

202   *THE MEDITERRANEAN WORLD*

conceived of El Escorial. Begun in 1563, it was to be a combination palace, mausoleum, administrative building, and monastery. Philip instructed his architects to construct the complex in the "unadorned style" associated with Italian Renaissance architecture, in contrast to the much more ornate plateresque style common in Spain to that point. The end result represents the epitome of Italian Renaissance architectural classicism in Spain. The palace's initial architect, Juan Bautista de Toledo, had lived in Rome for many years and was deeply engaged with the Vitruvian classicism of the day. In fact, he had been Michelangelo's adviser for a time on the construction of St. Peter's, and the dome of El Escorial recalls that of the basilica in scale and grandeur. Other clear precedents include Bramante's Tempietto in San Pietro in Montorio, Filarete's Ospedale Maggiore, and, indirectly, several structures in Istanbul. The plans for the palace were presented for review to the Academy of Florence, headed by Giorgio Vasari, and in addition, the great classicist architect Andrea Palladio submitted plans for the monastery church at the center of the complex. Juan de Toledo died in 1567, before much work on the structure had been completed. He was replaced for a time by an Italian, Giovanni Battista Castello, before Juan de Herrera, his apprentice and a humanist and mathematician, took over. Upon completion, in 1584, at the massive cost of 5 million ducats, the complex was known as the eighth wonder of the world.

El Escorial was intended to serve as a monumental expression of the piety of Spain's Habsburg rulers, and of the wealth and power of their expanding global empire. It also articulated Philip's profound religiosity and asceticism in its simplicity and unadorned prospect. The royal quarters are small, plainly furnished, and communicate directly with the altar of the basilica, suggesting the ascetic retreat of a monk, similar to that of the Augustinians housed in the attached monastery, rather than the quarters of the ruler of the largest empire of the day. By burying his father and family under the basilica's main altar, a space usually reserved for saints, they became holy relics, conveying political continuity and legitimacy, as well as divine approval for Philip's rule. With its size, its classical stylistic genealogy, and its pervasive religious symbolism, El Escorial expresses the image of an imperial Catholic monarch, a new Constantine, the model universal Christian emperor. This linkage is made even more explicit in a painting in El Escorial by El Greco, *The Dream of Philip II*, in which the king gazes up at the letters IHS, *in hoc signo* (by this sign), which are the words that Constantine saw in his famous vision before the fourth-century battle at the Milvian bridge.

In examining these architectural and artistic connections, it is important to emphasize their multicentered, dialectical nature. There is a tendency, as we have seen in the discussion of material cultural exchanges, to view this process as one-sided, flowing primarily in one direction. Indeed, there has been a scholarly tendency to focus on the elusive prey of influences, and to see one piece or another of this equation as a passive wellspring of contacts, objects, monuments, and sources of inspiration rather than developing a more complex, multidirectional model of cultural interaction. As the essential work of Gulru Necipoğlu on the sixteenth-century

El Greco (Domenikos Theotokopoulos), *Dream of Philip II* (1579). *Real Monasterio del Escorial, Spain.*
Photo: Art Resource, NY

oeuvre of the greatest Ottoman architect, Sinan, amply illustrates, there was a much richer and more multifaceted reality at play in the early modern Mediterranean. Necipoğlu locates Sinan's constructions in their Ottoman social and religious contexts, understanding them as a conversation with architectural influences outside the empire's borders, including but not limited to those of the Italian Renaissance. She also places his work within the same context as the concurrent reconstruction of St. Peter's in Rome, an approach that allows her to move past interpretations of cross-cultural "borrowing" or "copying" of stylistic and architectural elements. Rather, she sees the simultaneous projects of urban renewal and domed, central-plan sanctuaries in Rome and Istanbul as proof of the popes' and the sultans' similar programs for asserting imperial and spiritual hegemony, and the analogous ways both drew on a shared Romano-Byzantine past and its recent Renaissance revival.

Architects and artists working in both centers drew on these sources for inspiration in a variety of ways, and were in dialogue with each other either directly through travel or indirectly through the circulation of architectural knowledge by way of eyewitness descriptions, architectural treatises, prints, and plans that were exchanged by travelers, merchants, and diplomats. Michelangelo, for instance, may have obtained information on Hagia Sophia and Ottoman dome construction through diplomatic and architectural contacts. In the same vein, it has been suggested that Luciano Laurana, Duke Federico of Urbino's Dalmatian architect, was directed to emulate Mehmed's transformation of Istanbul, and in particular his opulent new palace Topkapı Sarayı, in his redesign of Federico's Palazzo Ducale. This interchange is also noticeable in several fifteenth-century architectural plans in Istanbul that show a conflation of European and Islamic conventions of architectural drawing, suggesting links between Ottoman and Italian architects. The results of this integrated architectural Mediterranean can be seen in monuments as diverse as Michelangelo's St. Peter's Basilica in Rome, Palladio's Il Redentore in Venice, and Sinan's Süleymaniye Mosque in Istanbul, all of which bear witness to the interconnected character of the Mediterranean during the late medieval and early modern periods.

CHAPTER NINE

Mediterranean Empires

Habsburg, Venetian, and Ottoman

D uring the winter of 1543–44, visitors to the French city of Toulon on the Mediterranean coast were met with an unexpected sight. More than 30,000 soldiers and sailors from the 200 ships of the Ottoman fleet anchored in the bay swarmed the streets of the city. This was not an invading force; the Ottoman fleet was wintering in Toulon with the permission of King Francis I. The reason for this unprecedented situation was that the king and Sultan Süleyman I intended to undertake a joint venture to retake the North African town of Tunis in the spring. During the Ottomans' sojourn, they were provided with provisions, the port's cathedral was converted into a mosque, and the call to prayer echoed over the city each day. As one contemporary commented, "To see Toulon, one might imagine oneself at Constantinople." The French, fearing that the presence of a massive fleet might disrupt the city, evacuated many of the inhabitants, especially women and children. However, the Ottoman forces were by all accounts well behaved. As one French observer noted, "Everyone pursu[ed] his business with the greatest order and justice . . . never did an army live in stricter and more orderly fashion than that one." On its surface this event seems unimaginable, even surreal. Yet these sorts of collaborations were common in the early modern Mediterranean, and in fact most of the region's powers at one time or another allied with each other indiscriminately across religious lines.

The period from the second half of the fifteenth to the sixteenth century was a time of adaptation and consolidation among the chief Mediterranean polities — the Habsburg, Ottoman, and Venetian empires — in terms of not only geography but also institutional structures. In terming them *empires*, it is important to make qualifications. First, despite their political heft, these were not the only actors in the

region; rather, the Mediterranean should be conceived of as a fluid patchwork of centers and shifting allegiances. Second, these empires were composite states incorporating broad and often disparate regions and comprising significant cultural and religious diversity. Their rulers grappled with imprinting their sovereignty and preserving their empires, at the same time looking for ways to expand their power through conflict or, as in Toulon, cooperation.

THE OTTOMAN EMPIRE

The conquest of Constantinople in 1453 marked a key turning point in the fortunes of the House of Osman. The next 100 years saw dramatic changes in the empire, its structures and institutions. In the immediate years following the conquest, Mehmed II worked to consolidate his rule, but only briefly. In 1456 he attempted unsuccessfully to take Belgrade; from 1463 to 1479 he was engaged in a conflict with Venice that resulted in the acquisition of a number of Venice's Greek and Albanian possessions. He expanded Ottoman power in the Black Sea with the conquest of Trebizond in 1461 and Crimea in 1475. In 1480 he besieged Rhodes, unsuccessfully, and in the same year his forces attacked Otranto and established the first Ottoman toehold in southern Italy.

Ottoman fleet wintering in French Port of Toulon in 1543. From Matrakçı Nasuh, Süleymanname (Mss Hazine 1608, c. 1545). Topkapi Museum, Istanbul. Photo: Gianni Dagli Orti / Art Resource, NY

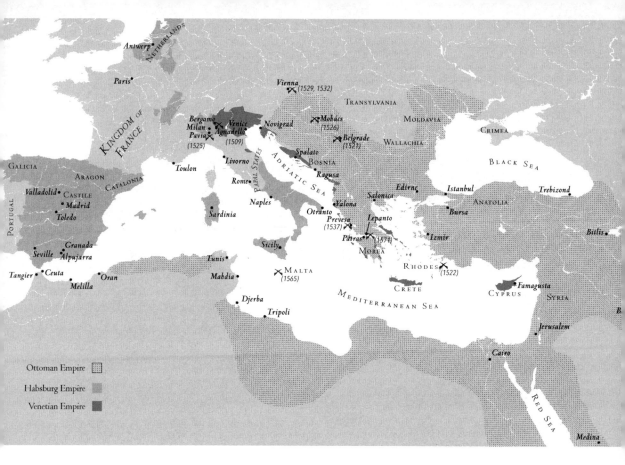

Early Modern
Empires

Whether this was simply an act of opportunity or an integral part of Mehmed's strategic vision of crafting a new Ottoman Roman empire, the foray was cut short by his death, in 1481.

While Ottoman expansion has often been explained simplistically in terms of gazi, or holy war, scholars now emphasize economic and political over purely religious intentionality, though all were certainly factors. Ottoman expansion was driven by a competition for markets and a desire to control sources of economic revenue, rather than simple territorial conquests by a one-dimensional society of soldiers motivated by a warrior ethos. A late-fifteenth-century handbook advised sultans to "look with favor on the merchants . . . for through their trading the land becomes prosperous, . . . through them, the excellent fame of the Sultan is carried to surrounding lands." This is apparent in the case of Istanbul: Immediately following the conquest, Mehmed took a census of the property of the Genoese inhabitants of Istanbul's international quarter of Galata, guaranteed their security, and granted them generous legal, tax, and commercial privileges in return for several minor concessions. After the first Veneto-Ottoman War (1463–79), he issued similarly generous terms to his former foes.

The most significant Ottoman territorial acquisition after Istanbul came in 1516 and was partly driven by commercial considerations. Mehmed's grandson, Selim I, came to the throne in 1512 after forcing his father, Bayezid II, to abdicate. The continuous expansion of the empire that characterized Mehmed's rule had slowed under Bayezid: he consolidated Ottoman control of the Morea in a second war with Venice (1499–1503) and put down rebellions in the east that flared in the wake of the rise of Safavid Iran in 1501. Selim, however, renewed Ottoman expansion in earnest, most notably with the conquest of Mamluk Syria and Egypt.

A variety of factors informed Selim's campaign. The prestige of becoming ruler and protector of Islam's most holy sites and shrines—Jerusalem, Mecca, and Medina—certainly played a role. The rise of the Shia Safavids and the threat that they would ally with the Mamluks was also a concern. A final motivation was the Portuguese presence in the Indian Ocean, dating to Vasco da Gama's 1497–98 discovery of the cape route. Manuel I of Portugal, the "grocer king," was intent on monopolizing the spice trade, and since the defense of this lucrative commercial activity was a primary Ottoman objective, the sultans provided the Mamluks with technical and material assistance. This proved only minimally effectual, however, because of the Mamluks' lack of a naval background and inexperience with the new gunpowder technologies, which certainly influenced the Ottoman decision to attack their fellow Sunni Muslims in 1516.

It took barely six months for the centuries-old Mamluk sultanate to collapse, in part because of the Ottomans' effective use of artillery against the more traditional Mamluk cavalry and generally weakened military structure. The conquest brought immense prestige to the Ottomans, doubled the size of their empire, and solidified their status as the preeminent Islamic power. Egypt was the most populous Ottoman province (Cairo alone numbered 150,000 people) and provided a valuable new source of manpower for Ottoman campaigns. It was also the empire's wealthiest province: its annual tribute exceeded all other regions, and its legendary agricultural fertility made it an imperial breadbasket that helped provision the empire, in particular the rapidly expanding imperial capital.

The incorporation of Egypt into the empire was not without challenges. There was a significant population transfer as Ottoman soldiers and bureaucrats settled in the new province and Egyptian craftspeople and religious scholars relocated to Istanbul. Inevitably, there were cultural misunderstandings: many Ottomans considered the Egyptians unruly, dishonest, and second-class citizens, while some Egyptians viewed the Ottomans as their intellectual and religious inferiors. Over time, however, these views evolved as rulers and ruled adapted to each other and as the commercial and political benefits that came with Ottoman rule became apparent.

The height of Ottoman power in the Mediterranean was unquestionably achieved during the reign of the most famous successor of Mehmed II, Süleyman the Magnificent. Born in Trebizond in 1494, he came to the throne in 1520 and ruled until 1566, the longest reign of any sultan. Under his leadership the empire experienced a new wave of expansion and inaugurated significant legal, institutional, and cultural changes. Where Selim had focused his attention on the declining Mamluks in the south and the rising Safavids and Portuguese in the east, Süleyman turned his attention westward during the first decades of his reign. This was due not only

Süleyman I the Magnificent and his Venetian crown. From a 1535 engraving by Agostino Veneziano. © *The Metropolitan Museum of Art.* Photo: Art Resource, NY

to the logistical challenges he faced in expanding Ottoman power in the Indian Ocean but also to the failure of the Portuguese to completely cut off the spice trade, which made this a less pressing issue. Another motivation for the turn west was the expanding Mediterranean presence of Süleyman's chief European rival, the Habsburg emperor, Charles V.

In fairly rapid succession, Süleyman initiated a series of campaigns that expanded his empire deep into Christian Europe. In 1521 he conquered Belgrade, and in 1522, Rhodes, both of which his great-grandfather, Mehmed II, had failed to take. In 1526 he led an army of 50,000 into Hungary and at Mohács routed its last king, Louis II, who drowned while attempting to flee the field of battle. In the following years Transylvania and Moldavia became tributary states, and Buda was captured. In 1529 and again in 1532, Süleyman unsuccessfully attacked Austria with massive armies, an act of tremendous logistical complexity given the great distances involved.

Following a Habsburg raid on Ottoman Morea that exposed the limitations of the Ottoman fleet, Süleyman shifted his attention to the Mediterranean and in 1534 invited the famed corsair captain Hayreddin Barbarossa to become grand admiral of the Ottoman fleet. "Pirate-entrepreneurs" like Barbarossa, who was born on the Greek island of Lesbos around 1466, had emerged in response to the extension of Habsburg power in the western Mediterranean and had entered into alliances with threatened North African rulers. For the Ottomans, the infusion of matériel and naval experience that Barbarossa brought made the primarily land-focused empire into a sea power competing for naval and commercial superiority in the Mediterranean. This important shift meant that for much of the next century and a half, conflict in the Mediterranean would play out on the sea. This was evident four years later when a combined Spanish, Venetian, and papal fleet was defeated at Prevesa, on the western coast of Greece, by a much smaller Ottoman fleet. Further campaigns at sea also proved successful, until the siege of Malta, in 1565, when fewer than 10,000 defenders held off an Ottoman force two to four times larger.

Süleyman's turn to the west and to the sea was not exclusive; after an initial interlude, he returned his attention to affairs on the eastern borders of the empire. Against the Portuguese, he had ships constructed in the Red Sea, captained by commanders with experience in the Mediterranean. They were unable to drive the interlopers from the Indian Ocean but did help prevent the Portuguese from completely dominating the spice trade. He also mounted two major campaigns against the Safavids. In 1533, his brilliant grand vizier, Ibrahim Pasha, was given command of an army that in the span of a year conquered Bitlis, Tabriz, and Baghdad, bringing Iraq under direct Ottoman control. A second offensive in 1548 produced few results. Just as on the western front, distance and other logistical issues made it difficult to expand the empire beyond certain distant boundaries. This was acknowledged in the 1555 Treaty of Amasya which established the border between the Safavids and Ottomans and marked the end of hostilities for a generation. While his zeal for campaigning waned somewhat in his final years, when Süleyman died, in 1566, he was in his tent in Hungary at the head of his army on the thirteenth major military campaign of his long and storied life.

In addition to the projection of Ottoman power, the empire also underwent important innovations and adaptations following the conquest of Constantinople. The reign of Mehmed II marked a turning point in the Ottoman evolution from principality to empire; indeed, by conquering Byzantium, the Ottomans saw themselves as having inherited the legacy of Rome. Mehmed styled himself as the new Caesar of the Romans (*Kayser-i-Rûm*) and embraced a Byzantine style of government that held Istanbul up as the new Rome and favored it economically and politically over all other cities in the empire. The city experienced a dramatic revival and expansion under its new rulers and came to be viewed, as one poet described it, as the "birthplace and school of famous men, the nursery of many nations."

The new Ottoman imperial system focused intensely on the person of the sultan, who was to be isolated and elevated from a tribal chieftain to an imperial icon. At the end of his reign, Mehmed issued the *Kanunname*, or Code of Laws, which supplanted previous unwritten customary practices and laid out in detail the organizational structure of the Ottoman state and the ceremonial order of the palace. A central element of the new model held that the sultan, who until then had appeared frequently in public, should be secluded from his subjects and the empire's ruling elite. This was inherited from both Islamic and Byzantine practices. Physical and human barriers were erected to remove the sultans from regular intercourse with the outside world, which made them unapproachable, all-powerful figure-heads whose power was manifest in their "splendid isolation."

The stage for this political theater was the new imperial palace, Topkapı Sarayı, which Mehmed began constructing immediately after the conquest. The palace was divided into three courtyards. The first was open to the public. The second was generally limited to the governing elite and was where the divan, or imperial council, met and ambassadors were received. The third and innermost court, the Abode of Felicity, was the sultan's private domain, accessible to very few people and from which its inhabitants almost never exited. The palace school was here as well, with its hundreds of carefully selected boys and young men, drawn from the devshirme, who were being trained for government service by their white eunuch guards and teachers.

The controversial practice of devshirme, or the levy of youths, was another component of the classical Ottoman state. After its beginnings on the Balkan frontier, the devshirme was practiced irregularly and on a varying scale depending on needs. On average, perhaps 3,000 youths were conscripted annually; up until 1500 they were all Balkan Christians, though eventually youth from Anatolia were also included. The objective of the devshirme was to ensure that the sultan possessed a loyal pool of officials and a devoted professional army. The system proved quite effective in assimilating elements of the diverse empire into an imperial ruling elite, and it served as a powerful centralizing tool. Although some recruits resisted, others were eagerly put forward by their families, as the devshirme represented the possibility of great social and economic mobility. Though they were supposed to be "without root and without ties," because they were generally recruited in their teens, boys of the levy retained strong links to their families and places of birth. For instance, the influential sixteenth-century grand vizier Mehmed Sokullu constructed a bridge in his Bosnian hometown and was patron to family members and local Christian and Muslim institutions.

Another much-misunderstood component of the evolving imperial system, and a central feature of the palace complex, was the harem. During the sixteenth century it numbered about 150 women. Notwithstanding the voyeuristic fantasies of many European observers, few of these women were actual concubines of the sultan. The majority of them were educated and performed duties within the harem or were married out to male members of the ruling elite to link them even more closely to the imperial household. Another myth of the harem holds that its women were powerless because of their seclusion, but in fact the opposite is true. As the sultans became increasingly isolated in the later sixteenth century, women in the harem

A Janissary officer
recruiting devshirme
youths for Sultan
Suleyman I. From Ali
Amir Beg Shirwani,
Süleymanname (Mss
Hazine 1517, f.31v, 1558).
*Topkapi Palace Museum,
Istanbul / Bridgeman
Images*

gained power because of their unique and regular access to the ruler, which almost none of even the highest male officials enjoyed. Women were often important actors in political matters, such as Nurbanu, favorite of Selim II, who played a key role in the 1573 peace following the battle of Lepanto. Wealthy and influential harem women also patronized important public building projects and charitable works. Hürrem Sultan (known in Europe as Roxelana), Süleyman's powerful wife, spearheaded the construction of a complex in Istanbul that included a mosque, several schools, a soup kitchen, a women's hospital, and a bathhouse.

Yet another important aspect of the consolidation of power by the Ottoman rul-

FORMA TIBI LAVDĀDA QVIDEM MORESQ. POLITI
BARBARA SED CRVDVM PECTORA VIRVS HABĒT

ROSSA SOLY MANNI VXOR

PHILTRA DOCET TROGILLA CIBIS MISCEDAQ. VINO
SOLA VT DILECTO TV POTIARE VIRŌ .

Theodor de Bry,
*Hürrem Sultan or
Roxelana, in Vitae
et icones svltanorvm
Tvrcicorvm*
(Frankfurt, 1596).
*Courtesy of Beinecke
Rare Book and
Manuscript Library,
Yale University*

ers was their growing assumption of religious authority. Selim I received the symbolic cloak of the caliphate following his conquest of Egypt in 1517 (or at least subsequent Ottoman historians claimed he did) and assumed the titles of Servant and Protector of the Holy Cities of Mecca and Medina, which had previously been claimed by the Egyptian Mamluks. Süleyman's chief adviser on religious law, the grand mufti Ebussuud Effendi, declared that the House of Osman had the exclusive right to the caliphate, which made its head the universal sovereign over all Muslims. Some scholars, particularly Arabs, rejected this as a power grab, in part because the Ottoman sultans did not come from the tribe of the Prophet. Nonetheless, the sultans regularly claimed this authority as the head of all Islam and took it on themselves to intervene on behalf of Muslims in Russia, Spain, and elsewhere, as well as ensuring the security of the haj.

Despite these overt religious actions, inclusiveness and openness to diversity remained hallmarks of Ottoman rule. In contrast to the vision of the Ottomans as absolute despotic rulers that many contemporaries held, the sultans were quite flexible in ruling over the diverse parts of their vast empire. For instance, tax-collecting policies in Hungary and other areas were adapted to local practices, rather than according to strict Islamic principles, which required a head tax from all non-Muslims. In Transylvania, Wallachia, and Moldavia, instead of establishing direct rule, the Ottomans opted for a tributary relationship. Some of the Arab lands conquered by Selim were granted relative autonomy, and many customary laws and practices were left intact. In Egypt, while the Ottomans occupied all the province's chief military and administrative positions, they avoided interfering unnecessarily in religious life. In the case of their Greek subjects, the sultans became the most important patrons and defenders of Orthodoxy.

Ottoman lands also served as a generally safe haven for Jews. Jews, who had suffered under the Byzantine emperors, saw their circumstances improve significantly under Ottoman rule. Following the expulsion from Spain, the Ottomans actively encouraged Sephardic Jews to settle throughout their empire. While no firm statistics exist, it appears that thousands of Iberian Jews migrated to Patras, Edirne, Bursa, and especially Salonica, which came to be known as the "the Jerusalem of the Balkans." Ottoman officials encouraged many Sephardim to settle in Adriatic ports to help them expand commercially: in Valona, refugees from Spain and Italy numbered 527 households, or one-third of the population, by 1520 and dominated the city's long-distance trade for much of the sixteenth century, before resettling in Ragusa (Dubrovnik), Novigrad, and Spalato (Split).

Mehmed's imperial model was expanded by Süleyman, who was very conscious of developing and projecting an image of himself as a wise, just, powerful, cultured ruler, as well as a military genius. To this end he patronized poets, scholars, and court historians who composed beautifully illuminated histories of the dynasty. The most prolific sixteenth-century historian was Seyyid Lokman, who described the sultan as "a mine of talent, a quarry of abundance and munificence; he had no equal in grace and charm; he was free from vanity and arrogance." Süleyman envisioned himself as the heir to great classical rulers of Persia, Rome, and Greece, as well as a worthy rival to contemporary Habsburg and papal claimants for that honor. He adopted classical symbols that had little resonance in Islamic or central Asian culture, such as sitting on an elevated throne (rather than cross-legged on a divan as was the practice of his predecessors), holding a scepter, and wearing a magnificent crown.

This appeal to the legacy of Rome was especially apparent in Süleyman's use of architecture. He was patron to Koca Mimar Sinan Agha, a military engineer who became the chief Ottoman architect and is considered by some as the greatest architect of the sixteenth century. Among his many creations during his long life, the Selimiye and Süleymaniye mosque complexes are Sinan's masterpieces and some of the finest representatives of the architectural culture shared by both Ottoman

and Italian patrons, particularly sixteenth-century sultans and popes, who embraced classical, Byzantine, and Renaissance models to assert "imperial and spiritual hegemony." So successful was Süleyman in his image manufacturing that following his death, in 1566, his heirs suffered unfairly in comparison, and the myth of Ottoman decline from a Süleymanic ideal became widespread.

HABSBURG SPAIN

The marriage of Isabel of Castile and Ferdinand of Aragon, in 1469, brought with it the merger of the two most powerful Christian kingdoms in Spain. It also marked a crucial stage in their united kingdom's accession to the status of one of the great Mediterranean, and eventually global, powers. The two sovereigns made several administrative and military reforms and innovations that served to strengthen their power, often at the expense of traditional noble and ecclesiastical forces. They also were able to increase tax receipts significantly; in Castile, for example, revenues grew from under 1 million reals in 1474 to 26 million by 1504. The union of Castile and Aragon under Ferdinand and Isabel

Melchior Lorck,
Süleymaniye
mosque (1570).
© Trustees of the
British Museum

THE MEDITERRANEAN WORLD

marked the first step in the unification of Spain, but it is important to remember that unification was not inevitable; it took decades in the case of Aragon and Castile, and even longer as other components of the kingdom were brought into the royal fold, often in fits and starts. A decisive moment in this process, of course, was the conquest of the last bastion of Muslim Spain, the emirate of Granada, in 1492. With the acquisition of Granada, Ferdinand and Isabel were now in a position to cast their attention more broadly beyond the Iberian peninsula to Europe, the Mediterranean, and points well beyond. The year 1492 also marks, of course, the famous voyage of Christopher Columbus, which quite literally opened up a whole new world and would have a profound impact on the kingdom's fortunes.

Sixteenth-century Spanish history is dominated by two great sovereigns: Charles V, who ruled from 1516 until his voluntary abdication in 1556, and his son, Philip II, who reigned from 1556 until his death in 1598. Charles was the grandson of Ferdinand and Isabel, through their daughter Juana, who in 1506 had married Philip of Habsburg, heir to Austria and the Low Countries. Following the death of Isabel in 1504 and Ferdinand in 1516, Charles, as archduke of Austria, inherited their throne, becoming the first Habsburg ruler of Spain; two years later he was elected

Holy Roman emperor. He thus became the hereditary ruler of Burgundy, the Low Countries, the Holy Roman Empire, and the kingdom of Spain, with its expanding global empire.

As ruler over such a large and disparate empire, Charles lived an itinerant life that he described as "one long journey." Indeed, one of every four days of his entire reign were spent on the road: he made ten expeditions to the Netherlands, nine to Germany, seven to Italy, six to Spain, four to France, and two each to England and North Africa. Because of this constant movement, Charles was considered an "absentee monarch" in Spain, despite the fact that he spent more time there, 17 total years, including seven in one stretch, than in any other part of his empire. But he was also absent from the peninsula more than anywhere else, most notably during the final 14 years of his rule. These absences were the source of deep discontent among his subjects, which at times flared into open opposition.

Charles's travels were necessary to try to hold together what was quite a fragile edifice. The collection of states that he ruled over, though termed an empire, was more like a confederation. Its diverse territories were independent of each other and did not conceive of themselves as part of larger whole with reciprocal obligations; rather, their concerns were chiefly local. To the degree that they were united, it was in the person of their sovereign and the taxes that they each paid to him at varying rates. Charles's titles, rights, and duties varied from realm to realm. There were no common institutions or representative bodies that linked his various dominions, so he and a small body of advisers had to improvise. As he could not be present to personally rule the many parts of his realm, Charles appointed regents and viceroys to administer them in his place.

A large part of Charles's itinerancy was occasioned by war. During almost every year of his long reign, he was engaged in some conflict somewhere in his extensive dominions. This was not part of some grand strategy for regional or world domination; rather, it was situationally reactionary and adaptive, heavily informed by Charles's sense of personal reputation and dynastic self-interest. He and his heir, Philip, regularly resorted to a neo-crusading rhetoric and claimed that their hope was for peace among Christians and war against the Ottomans, but the reality was a bit more nuanced. The Habsburg-Ottoman rivalry was certainly an important focus of both Charles's and Philip's designs, but war with fellow Christians occupied significantly more of their attention and treasure. Charles's reign, for instance, was dominated by the Italian Wars, which he inherited from Ferdinand and Isabel. They began in 1494 and lasted until the treaty of Cateau-Cambrésis brought them to a close in 1559. This conflict, which Charles considered his highest priority, saw Habsburg Spain and its Valois French antagonist engaged in a battle for control of the peninsula, at the expense of the five chief Italian regional states—Naples, Rome, Milan, Venice, and Florence—and for dominance in Europe more generally. The Italian Wars were only part of a broader Habsburg-Valois rivalry that played out on multiple stages and involved at one time or another all the chief European powers, including the Ottomans.

Spanish potentates had long held a stake in Italy. The Aragonese had ruled Sicily and Sardinia since the late thirteenth century and had been directly involved in Neapolitan affairs since the mid-fifteenth century. Alfonso I had conquered Naples in 1442 and lived there and ruled his realm until his death, in 1458, whereupon his illegitimate son Ferrante assumed the throne. Ferrante's death, in 1494, and questions of who had legitimate claim to the throne sparked the outbreak of the Italian Wars. It was not until 1503, following a series of military victories over Louis XII's forces, that Ferdinand was able to assert his claim to Naples and take definitive possession of the city, which remained under Spanish rule for the next 200 years. Naples became the center of Habsburg power in the Italian peninsula, and Italy became a laboratory for Spanish imperial practices. Spain's influence was further solidified in 1535 when Milan devolved to Charles. These territorial acquisitions, combined with well-placed dynastic marriages, the subjugation of the papacy, and the definitive defeat of French aspirations, made Spain the dominant power in Italy from midcentury. That dominance had important implications for both: Italian art, music, drama, and religious ideas profoundly affected Spain, which in turn was a major patron and political and economic influence in Italy.

As Holy Roman emperor, Charles was also deeply engaged in northern European affairs, particularly in Germany, which continually deflected his attention from the Mediterranean. The dominant issue there was the Protestant reform that erupted in 1517 when Martin Luther posted his celebrated 95 theses in Wittenberg. Despite his attempts to mediate the split, most notably at the Diet of Worms, in 1521, Charles faced increasing popular and aristocratic opposition. The Peasants' War (1524–25) produced horrific violence, with perhaps a third of the 300,000 rebel peasants losing their lives. This was followed in 1531 by the creation of the Schmalkaldic League by German Lutheran princes for defense against Charles and the empire's Roman Catholic estates. Its ongoing actions against the established church and throne led to open warfare in 1546–47: Charles successfully snuffed out the revolt, but not Protestantism. In the Netherlands, several years prior, high taxes led to the uprising of Ghent in 1539, which Charles personally put down in 1540.

While the primary focus of Charles's political and military efforts was on Italy, Spain, Germany, and other Christian parts of Europe, the Ottoman Empire also occupied his attention. Charles saw himself as the political leader of Christendom and the bulwark against the expansion of Islam. He aspired to continue the neo-crusader vision of his predecessors by conquering and Christianizing North Africa, where Spanish and Portuguese outposts such as Tangier, Ceuta, Melilla, Oran, and Tripoli were established beginning in the early fifteenth century. Habsburg rivalry with the Ottomans was accentuated following the loss of Hungary to Süleyman, in 1526, and the siege of Vienna in 1529. Charles's singular success came at Tunis, in 1535, when an allied fleet under the Genoese admiral Andrea Doria numbering more than 400 vessels and 30,000 soldiers, the largest naval expedition mounted to date, defeated the Ottomans under the command of Hayreddin Barbarossa in the scorching summer heat. This success was tempered, in short order, however, when another allied fleet, this time including Venetian forces, was soundly defeated by Barbarossa at Prevesa in 1538.

By midcentury, Charles had exhausted his seemingly endless reserves of energy. In 1555 he began to withdraw from political affairs, and in realization of the impossibility of a single man ruling a global empire, he divided his realm into two. To his brother, Ferdinand I of Austria, he gave the hereditary Habsburg lands in eastern Europe and the title of Holy Roman emperor. His son, Philip, received the bulk of his empire, including Spain, Italy, the Netherlands, and his global possessions. Though related by blood and history, the Spanish and German Habsburgs generally functioned independently of each other following Charles's abdication.

Like his father, Philip II was almost continually at war; indeed, he spent nearly 150 million ducats on military affairs over the course of his 40-year reign. The result was massive debt, but Spain also became the preponderant power in Europe as its French rivals slipped into civil war during the so-called Wars of Religion following the death of Henry II, in 1559. In the Mediterranean, Philip's political and military balance sheet was decidedly more complex.

In 1560 the Habsburgs suffered their most ignominious defeat at the hands of the Ottomans when a fleet of some 90 ships and 12,000 men was trapped at the Tunisian island of Djerba. Half the ships were sunk, and 10,000 men were taken captive and marched through the streets of Istanbul. The scale of the defeat was unprecedented, and it stunned Philip's court and all of Europe. Following a series of smaller setbacks in the next two years, Philip was convinced that he needed to focus seriously on reforming his position in the Mediterranean. Over the course of the next decade he invested heavily in building up the fleet, until it was four times larger than Charles's fleet had ever been. This buildup set the stage for his greatest triumph, at Lepanto in 1571.

Despite this victory, by the middle of Philip's reign it had become clear to him that defeating the Ottomans was not to be achieved, at least not in the short term. As a result in 1581 the Habsburgs and the Ottomans did the seemingly unthinkable and signed a peace treaty. Philip was partly motivated to seek a truce because of serious challenges in other parts of his empire, in particular the decades-long Dutch revolt. Charles had ceded the Netherlands to Philip in 1555, and from the outset his rule there was fraught with difficulties. One of the chief of these was that within a few years of his accession, Philip left the north for Spain, never to return. Tensions boiled over in 1566 when mobs of Calvinists went on a rampage in the major cities of the Netherlands, destroying images and desecrating churches. Philip responded in 1567 by sending an army of 10,000 under the duke of Alba, whose iron hand and haughty character made him extremely unpopular.

The revolt quickly became linked to broader rivalries, including in the Mediterranean. In 1569 the Dutch secretly sought and were offered Ottoman support for their cause, and the rallying cry of the Dutch mercenary naval force known as the Sea Beggars was "better a Turk than a Papist." The savage 1576 sack of Antwerp by mutinous Spanish soldiers catalyzed the Dutch, resulting in the Pacification of

Ghent, in which both rebellious and loyalist provinces asserted their united opposition to the Spanish occupation and persecution of Protestantism. The revolt festered for the entirety of Philip's reign and well into the seventeenth century, with tremendous violence and suffering, loss of human life, and expenditure of treasure. In the final analysis, the human cost is unknown, but the rulers of Spain expended over 200 million ducats in the Netherlands, almost double what was collected from its American colonies in the same period. The revolt also prevented Philip from focusing his full attention on the Mediterranean and the Ottomans, as he may have preferred.

Beyond warfare, an essential aspect of the Habsburgs' consolidation of power in Spain was related to its religious minorities. The fragile but long-lived convivencia of the Middle Ages began to disintegrate in the late fourteenth century, as the position of Spain's Muslims and Jews eroded significantly during the final stages of the Reconquista. A decisive step in this transformation was the permission granted to Ferdinand and Isabel by the papacy in 1480 to reestablish an inquisition to bring order and a degree of religious uniformity to their lands. The initial target was the conversos, the one-third of the Jewish population who had converted to Christianity following the pogroms of 1391. Conversos were singled out because of their perceived nonconformity and suspicion that they were continuing to practice Judaism secretly, though there is good evidence that by the time the inquisition was established many conversos had embraced their new faith. In the sixteenth century, Jews continued to attract attention, but Protestants, converted Muslims (Moriscos), witches, and those accused of sexual deviancy became the preferred targets of the inquisition.

The Spanish inquisition has been the source of much fascination and misinformation; the reality, however, was significantly more complex. For example, there was not a single inquisitional structure but rather significant diversity in what was prosecuted and how inquisition was implemented in the various regions of Spain, its empire, and other parts of Roman Catholic Europe where inquisitions were also established. In Venice, for example, the inquisition was closely supervised by a lay governmental magistracy that strongly influenced the court's functioning. While certainly a tool of religious conformity, Spain's various inquisitions also served as a means to defend the favored social and economic position of "old Christians" against incursions by "new Christian" conversos and Moriscos. Inquisitorial courts were not all-powerful, nor were they able to control every aspect of life where they were established. Recent research has emphasized their institutional failings and sporadic effectiveness.

Secrecy, fear, torture, and violence all were undisputedly characteristics of inquisition and brought untold suffering to the thousands who fell afoul of it. Scholars, however, have shown that Mediterranean inquisitions were more restrained in the use of violence than is commonly believed. Inquisitorial courts were not arbitrary chambers of horrors; instead, they labored under very specific and strict guidelines. Although horrific examples of torture certainly exist, torture was only used in

Pedro Berruguete,
*Saint Dominic Guzmán
Presiding over an
Auto-da-fé* (1493–99).
*Museo Nacional del
Prado, Madrid. Photo:
Scala / Art Resource*

cases involving heresy, which in Spain represented 42% of the total, and its application fluctuated over time. Before 1500, inquisitors almost never resorted to torture, while during the sixteenth-century it was used in 25–30% of eligible heresy cases, and overall in perhaps 15% of cases. In Venice, torture was used in only 2–3% of all cases. Execution was also less common than generally assumed. During the most intense period in Spain, from 1480 to 1530, perhaps 2,000 people were put to death, and of the 44,674 cases tried between 1540 and 1700, less than 2% (826) resulted in executions. In Venice, of the more than 1,500 cases prosecuted from 1541 to 1592, the death penalty was imposed 14 times; in comparison, the city's secular courts put 168 people to death over the course of the entire sixteenth century. The most common punishment imposed by inquisitions was a public ceremony of penance, the auto-da-fé. While this revisionist scholarship complicates our understanding of the institution, it should not deny the suffering and terror of the tens of thousands who appeared in the inquisitors' courts throughout the early modern period.

The Treaty of Granada in 1492 was another critical moment in Ferdinand and Isabel's attempts to manage their kingdom's religious and cultural diversity. The treaty guaranteed specific political, cultural, and religious rights to Muslim and Jewish subjects; however, almost immediately the sovereigns began to disregard its stipulations. In March 1492 they issued a decree that gave all their Jewish subjects four months to either convert or depart the kingdom. The ostensible motivation was the "great damage . . . being done to Christians by the contact, conversation, and communication they have had and have with Jews . . . [who] always seek by all possible means to subvert faithful Christians and take them away from our holy Catholic faith." In reality, Spain's Jews and Muslims, despite the shared history and culture of the peninsula's diverse religious communities, were perceived by some as a threat to the dream of a united, Christian kingdom, an idea that was especially dear to Isabel. There was also certainly an economic aspect to the decision, as many stood to benefit from the confiscation of Jewish property, though Jewish wealth has been greatly exaggerated, and this was not the chief motivation. In the end, the objective of the decree was to eliminate a religion, not a people.

Estimates of Jews living in Spain in 1492 are hotly debated and have ranged between 200,000 and more than 400,000. Recent scholarship has suggested that Jewish numbers had fallen greatly from their fourteenth-century height, and that at most there were 80,000 to 125,000 Jews, out of a population of 5.2 million in 1492. To this number we must add perhaps 225,000 conversos and their descendants. Of the total number of Jews in 1492, 25,000 to 50,000 converted and stayed in Spain, and perhaps 80,000 went into exile. Many moved to Christian lands, including areas under Spanish rule, with Portugal attracting large numbers until they were expelled from there as well in 1497. Others went to North Africa, Italy, and Ottoman lands. Perhaps as many as 20% of those expelled soon returned to Spain and accepted conversion. While the conversos who remained continued to experience profound suspicion and persecution, by the middle of the sixteenth century, many had assimilated sufficiently to achieve important political and ecclesiastical positions, particularly in the Jesuit order. Despite these revisions to the traditional narrative of the Jewish expulsion, it is the scale of the expulsion and the attendant suffering for Jews who left and those who converted and remained that sets the Spanish experience apart from previous similar, but much smaller, events in other parts of Europe.

In comparison to the Jews, Spain's Mudéjar (Muslim) minority was spared for a few years longer, until 1499, when Granada's Muslims revolted in response to increasingly aggressive attempts to coerce them into conversion. The uprising was quickly suppressed, but it provided a pretext to implement the crown's objective of religious uniformity. Over the next 25 years all of Spain's Muslims were faced with the choice of conversion or exile. Some fled, but most had little choice but to convert in order to preserve their property and livelihoods, which they did in huge public ceremonies.

The issue of the newly converted Moriscos, or "little Moors," became one of "the nodal issues" that would occupy Spain's rulers for more than a century. In comparison to the Jews, there were many more Moriscos: they likely numbered 300,000–330,000, or more than 6% of the total population. In addition, Moriscos were concentrated in certain regions, such as Granada and Valencia, where they represented 30–50% of the total population and played an integral economic role.

Doubts about the Moriscos' coerced conversion arose quickly. In 1526 an assembly of clerics in Granada concluded that in order to achieve true conversion and complete assimilation, all forms of Morisco particularism had to be effaced. Many political and religious authorities viewed Muslim-inflected "deviant customs" as contaminating the Moriscos, and as evidence of an insincere and incomplete conversion, which in turn prevented the creation of a unified community. By suppressing cultural practices, such as the use of Arabic, dress, song and dance, hygiene, and foodways, it was believed that Morisco ties to their Islamic past would be broken, thus facilitating their complete and sincere assimilation into Christian Spanish society. This represented a significant shift from the position that had been advanced in the years after 1492 by many clerics, including the archbishop of Granada, Hernando de Talavera, who advocated for a strategy of integrating, rather than effacing, Morisco cultural practices.

When this cultural cleansing finally began to be widely implemented in the 1560s, it led to a second major Morisco uprising, the Alpujarras revolt, which ultimately set the stage for their expulsion in the early seventeenth century. The crackdown by ecclesiastical and political authorities was based on the assumption that Morisco cultural practices were outward manifestations of a crypto-Muslim identity, and that Morisco resistance was primarily religiously motivated. While political and religious authorities attempted to define Christian orthodoxy and heterodoxy in increasingly restrictive terms, determining when Moriscos consciously acted with religious or political intentionality is problematic since the actions for which they were being prosecuted were common, routine acts, usually performed with no consideration of their symbolic or religious meaning. There is evidence that the Moriscos were in fact assimilating and that they and Old Christians might have coexisted had political and religious authorities not intervened.

Beyond coercive actions, the Habsburgs utilized other, softer means to consolidate their power. Charles V and his advisers orchestrated a vast propaganda campaign with the objective of crafting a favorable image of his policies and of him as leader of Christendom. This included artists, most famously Titian, whose masterful equestrian portrait of Charles in full armor provides a window into both the

emperor's power and his solitude. As in the Ottoman Empire, official historians were also engaged to provide laudatory chronicles of Charles's military
endeavors, particularly against the Ottomans.

One of the ways that Philip II consolidated and rationalized his power
was by creating a new capital city. In 1561 he decided to transfer his semi-
itinerant court from Toledo to the small town of Madrid. The city was not a
natural capital; it suffered from extremes of heat and cold (nine months of
winter and three months of hell, as the saying goes), lacked natural resources, and was located in a vast arid tableland far from trade routes, with no
access to the sea. The king's motivations were primarily political: he hoped
to weaken the power of more established, larger cities with entrenched interests, such as Toledo, Valladolid, and Seville, and thus accentuate his own
power. Madrid's central geographical position within the peninsula was also
attractive.

The transfer of the court transformed Madrid from a sleepy town of
8,000 in 1561 to a bustling city of 80,000 by century's end. Part of this transformation was driven by the relocation of nobles, clergy, and diplomats. The
city also attracted large numbers of craftsmen, artists, and architects from
throughout Europe, but especially Italy and the Netherlands, who came to
help transform Madrid into a worthy capital. One of the most notable projects was the construction, beginning in 1563, of the new palace outside of
Madrid, El Escorial (see chapter 8).

Moriscos dancing
la Zambra traditional
dance with typical
costumes and
instruments, in
Christoph Weiditz,
Trachtenbuch
(1530/1540).
*Germanisches
Nationalmuseum,
Nürnberg*

VENICE: CITY AND EMPIRE

Titian, *Emperor Charles V at Mühlberg* (1548). Museo del Prado, Madrid. Gianni Dagli Orti Art Resource, NY

For Venice, 1450 to 1570 was a time of significant change and adaptation in its relations to the other, expanding powers in the Mediterranean. During the period of Ottoman ascendancy, the Venetians had navigated the shifting political shoals quite successfully by generally adopting a position of neutrality, which allowed them to consolidate their hold over the rich Levantine trade and to continue to reap its fantastic profits. During the final siege of Constantinople, however, the large Venetian contingent there, against explicit instructions from

Venice, actively participated in the city's defense. As punishment, the Ottomans executed the community's head for being a "breaker of the peace," along with several other Venetians, and many others were imprisoned.

This setback proved temporary; already by 1454, Venice had signed a new treaty with Mehmed that granted favorable terms that were essentially unchanged from those enjoyed during the Byzantine era. The situation in the Levant had altered permanently, however, and with this Venice's standing was transformed, too. Mehmed recognized the short-term importance of Venice's commercial role, which led to his generous terms, but at the same time he was intent on ultimately weakening the city both politically and economically. This policy, combined with competition from old and new rivals, gradually eroded Venice's position.

Over the course of the next 50 years, Venice and the Ottomans went to war twice. In the first instance, from 1463 to 1479, Venice's rulers were motivated by a "most lively fervor" and a misplaced optimism in their ability to confront the sultan. The folly of this position was driven home by the great cost of the war in terms of treasure and land, and by Venice's complete failure to obtain any of its objectives. In the second war, in 1499, the Venetians were much more reluctant to break the peace, and with good reason as the results ended up the same—tremendous expenditures and significant territorial losses in the Adriatic and the Aegean.

By the cessation of hostilities, in 1503, Venice had come to the realization that its position in the Mediterranean had been permanently altered. The Ottoman challenge was accompanied by news that made the city "dead with fear"; the Portuguese were in India and threatening the spice trade, the republic's commercial lifeblood. The loss of that trade, according to one contemporary, "was more important to the Venetian state than the Turkish war, and than any other war that might occur." Aware of their own weakness vis-à-vis Ottoman military might, and recognizing that the Ottomans were key to reviving the spice trade, the policy of Venice's rulers after 1503 was one of nonalignment and neutrality, buttressed by a formidable diplomatic corps and a strong defensive military force. This stance proved reasonably successful: after 20 years of hostilities in the 50 previous years, over the next 135 years Venice avoided open conflict with the Ottomans except for two brief interludes, 1537–40 and 1570–73.

Despite its reduced standing, Venice remained economically and culturally vibrant, as well as politically relevant in Mediterranean affairs. In large part because of Ottoman actions in the Indian Ocean, the spice trade revived by midcentury, albeit only temporarily, while both the city of Venice and its *terraferma* state on the Italian mainland proved adaptable to changing economic conditions. The city was an important cultural capital, home to great artists, publishers, architects, musicians, scholars, scientists, and literary figures. It was a highly innovative and adaptive leader in the burgeoning practice of diplomacy, which its rulers rightly understood to be a pillar of the city's survival and relevance in a Mediterranean in which it lived between "the anvil of the Habsburgs and the hammer of the Turks." While Venice maintained resident ambassadors in all the chief courts of Europe, it devoted special attention and resources to the embassy in Istanbul, which was considered its most important diplomatic posting. Venetian diplomacy was supplemented by a noteworthy investment in military infrastructure, including the extensive reworking of its maritime *stato da mar* defenses according to the most modern techniques and the maintenance of a large fleet of warships produced in the arsenal, the largest industrial complex in the Mediterranean and Europe, which ensured Venice's continued naval relevancy.

Venice's challenges did not just come from the east. After the fall of the Byzantine Empire, in 1454, the regional states of Italy, which had been in almost uninterrupted conflict in the century after the outbreak of the plague, declared a cessation of hostilities at the Peace of Lodi, in part inspired by the quixotic hope of a united Christian crusade to regain Istanbul. Though the crusade never materialized, Lodi ushered in a period of relative calm within the peninsula that endured until the end of the century. The descent of Charles VIII of France into Italy in 1494, which the great historian Francesco Guicciardini labeled "the beginning of the years of misfortune," signaled the start of the Italian Wars and the permanent disruption of the peninsula's political order.

For Venice, the most powerful of the Italian states, the most dramatic moment occurred in the War of the League of Cambrai (1508–16), during which a shifting coalition of foes and allies, including the papacy, France, Spain, England, and the other chief Italian regional states, allied to present the greatest threat to the republic since the wars with Genoa in the late fourteenth century. The low point came in the catastrophic defeat at Agnadello in 1509, when Venice's terraferma state (which had been gradually acquired during the previous 150 years) effectively disintegrated. By the cessation of hostilities in 1516, however, Venice had regained all its lost possessions on the Italian mainland, which it would preserve generally unchanged until the end of the republic, in 1797. In contrast, Venice's stato da mar experienced significant losses, though these were spread out over the final centuries of the republic and were punctuated by the occasional reacquisition of lost territory, particularly during the Veneto-Ottoman war of 1684–99. Notwithstanding this generally positive outcome, Venice's conflicts in the century after the fall of Constantinople definitively revealed a city that had become a second-rate power both in a peninsula that was increasingly dominated by the Habsburgs and in a Mediterranean largely dominated by the Ottomans.

Despite the territorial losses to the Ottomans in the east and the temporary threat to the terraferma from the west, the sixteenth-century Venetian Empire still stretched from Bergamo in northern Italy to the islands of Crete and Cyprus in the eastern Mediterranean. The city was a magnet, as one observer put it, like " 'a tiny dot on a great sphere' toward which all the civilizations of the Mediterranean converge." Its inhabitants included significant communities of Armenians, Greeks, Slavs, Germans, and many Italians from throughout the peninsula. All told, non-Venetians numbered perhaps 20,000 out of a total population of 100,000–110,000 in 1500.

An influx of Jews in the first decades of the sixteenth century resulted in one of the most significant additions to the city's diverse population. Though small num-

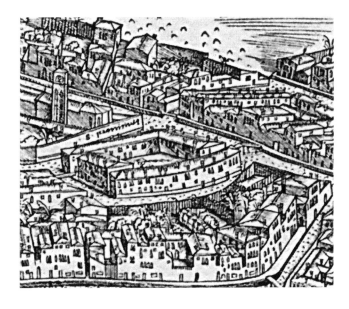

Detail of the Venetian ghetto, c.
1500, from Jacopo de' Barbari,
Grande Pianta Prospettica (c. 1500).
Private Collection/Bridgeman Images

bers of Jews had resided in Venice and on the mainland for at least two centuries, in 1513 Venice granted a five-year charter to the university (or community) of Jews, permitting them to reside in the city. By 1600 that group numbered 2,000–3,000 individuals. The community that eventually evolved from this initial act was not monolithic: the Jews divided themselves into three groups—German (which included Italians), Levantine (Ottoman), and Ponentine (Iberian). Their charter had to be renewed regularly, and although there were debates about their presence in the city and even attempts to revoke their legal standing, the Jews remained a continuous presence in, and vital component of, Venetian society from 1516 to World War II.

The chief reason that Venice's rulers issued the charter was to take advantage of the moneylending and pawnbrokering services of certain leading figures in the Jewish community, though as their numbers grew, Jews' economic activities became increasingly diversified, particularly in international commerce but also printing and other areas. Jews had been forbidden to participate in the Levantine trade in the Middle Ages, but by the sixteenth century the evolving commercial situation led the rulers of Venice and other Italian cities to compete for the services of important Jewish merchants, granting them special charters and commercial privileges usually reserved for patricians and citizens. Commercial and political expediency were at the heart of Veneto-Jewish relations, which were at times characterized by hostility and misunderstanding, evidenced most famously in Shakespeare's *Merchant of Venice*, but probably more often by cautious interaction and even cooperation.

The central stipulation in the charter restricted Jewish residence to a specific sector of the city, called the ghetto. The name most likely comes from the Venetian word for metal casting, which had been practiced in the area before the Jews' arrival. The ghetto was a small island surrounded by canals: its inhabitants were locked in every night and kept under guard, though it was relatively easy to slip in and out unnoticed. While the notion of a ghetto has come to possess highly negative connotations, the attitude of early modern Jews toward the ghetto was more ambiguous. The ghetto segregated Jews and created a regime of inferiority that was intended to protect Christians from the polluting influence of Jewish infidels, yet by physically setting them apart, the ghetto helped quell anxieties about the Jewish presence in the city, and the charter granted them a legal standing with certain privileges. Ultimately, the experiment was largely successful, as Venice experienced few traces of overt anti-Jewish violence .

In response to the formalization of its presence, the Venetian Jewish community grew rapidly, to the point that it overflowed its narrow confines, as the ghetto became the most densely populated area of the city. This growth was fed in large part by Sephardic Jews who began to trickle into the city over the course of the decades after their expulsion from Spain. They were drawn by the legal status and recognition that Venice offered, as well as by the city's close links to the eastern Mediterranean and the Ottoman Empire. By midcentury the Ponentine had become the most populous of the three Jewish groups, with the largest and richest synagogue of the eight located in the ghetto.

In addition to the diverse population within the lagoon, Venice ruled over an extensive mainland state in northern Italy and a highly diverse population in its eastern Mediterranean stato da mar. Venice's subjects included an array of Italians, Istrians, Dalmatians, Slavs, Albanians, Montenegrins, and Greeks. This latter group was the largest minority population in the empire. In 1550 almost 20% of the empire's total population was Greek, about 480,000 people, making Venice the Christian state with the largest Greek population. The challenges of ruling over this cultural farrago ranged from linguistic to religious and cultural issues.

In governing its empire on the mainland and throughout the eastern Mediterranean, Venice's officials and institutions generally ruled with a fairly light hand. Local political, legal, social, and economic structures and practices were largely preserved and respected, as were variations between subject cities and regions. A wide array of Venetian officials were dispatched throughout the empire to administer and represent the interests of the metropole, but rather than supplanting local elites and institutions, they generally worked closely with them. There was no single, centrally dictated approach applied to every subject polity. This was particularly true in the period before Cambrai; in the later decades of the sixteenth century, the center's intrusion on the periphery through expanded magistracies and other structures gradually increased in areas related to military affairs, defense, and provisioning but also crime and local politics and administration. Overall, though, Venice's subjects enjoyed a fair degree of autonomy and local control.

During a time of intense religious strife in much of Europe, Venice was generally successful in preserving a level of stability and tolerance, despite its great cultural diversity. This was a result of Venice's adaptability in ruling over a diverse polity and its willingness to accommodate cultural heterogeneity. Venice made no effort, for instance, to impose linguistic uniformity, in contrast to the zealous persecution of the Arabic language in Habsburg Spain; indeed, the republic maintained an elaborate and effective network of interpreters to facilitate multilingual communications. As for religion, where Venetian officials previously had attempted in some areas to prevent their Greek subjects from worshiping according to the Orthodox rite, from 1550 on they defended the community's religious rights, even in the face of post-Tridentine attempts by the papacy and other ecclesiastical entities to impose religious conformity. This unintrusive approach was in general characteristic of large and diverse early modern composite states and was well adapted to their limited capacity to assert dominion over expansive, heterogeneous realms that spread across the Mediterranean and beyond.

COMMON FRIENDS, COMMON ENEMIES

Despite the often heated rhetoric, the seemingly intractable divisions between Christian and Muslim states actually were quite malleable. Throughout the early modern period almost all the chief European powers attempted to collaborate at varying levels with the Ottomans as a means to strengthen their positions within intra-European rivalries. For example, Elizabeth I of England, in defiance of canon law, sold the Ottomans arms and raw materials like lead and iron that could be used to manufacture weapons. These dealings were kept quiet to prevent public, particularly Catholic, opposition to dealing with what one contemporary critic decried as "the cruel and dreadful tirante and enemie of our faithe the Great Turke." The general attitude was most clearly articulated by the Venetians, who after they broke ranks with their Christian allies and signed a separate peace with the Ottomans following the battle of Lepanto, declared, "First we are Venetians, then Christians."

The most notable example of collaboration, however, was between the kingdom of France and the Ottoman Empire. During the sixteenth century the French and Ottoman rulers found common ground in their shared concern over rapidly expanding Habsburg power. The roots of the Franco-Ottoman alliance dated back to the devastating defeat Francis I suffered at the hands of the Charles V's forces during the Italian Wars at the battle of Pavia in 1525, when the French king was taken captive. This defeat, combined with the desertion of the Genoese fleet to Habsburg service in 1528, which greatly undercut French naval power, was the catalyst for making common cause in a 1536 treaty. In Süleyman, Francis found a willing ally who shared "a common desire" to ensure "that the domain of the emperor is not great."

The alliance between the Most Christian King of France and the Caliph of Islam, though shocking to many contemporaries, produced relatively few results. Plans for a joint assault on Italy, with the French attacking in the north and the Ottomans the south, foundered when Francis, without Süleyman's knowledge, concluded a ten-year truce with Charles in 1537. In subsequent years, however, Franco-Ottoman cooperation reached new heights. French galleys reinforced the Ottoman fleet in 1537, and together they plundered the Catalan and Calabrian coasts. In 1543, Süleyman put the Ottoman fleet at Francis's disposal, and the French ambassador sailed with it from Istanbul and participated in a raid on Italy. A joint Franco-Ottoman fleet also sacked Habsburg Nice before wintering in Toulon in preparation for another joint venture to retake Tunis, which never materialized. Despite the fact that most European powers flirted with the Ottomans, because of their long open relationship the French were decried as "true Turks" and the "Turks of the West" for their "unholy alliance" with the sultans. Overall, France, which underwent significant political challenges during the sixteenth century, probably benefited more from the alliance than did the Ottomans.

As part of their anti-Habsburg efforts, the Ottoman sultans also supported European Protestants from as early as 1530. The sultans followed religious developments in Europe closely and saw the Protestant movement as another means to weaken their chief rivals by keeping Europe divided. In 1552, Süleyman tried to incite Protestant German princes against the pope and emperor on the eve of his own planned invasion, and Selim offered military support to the Protestant foes of Philip II during the Dutch revolt and suggested similarities between Islam and reformed Christianity, such as strict monotheism and opposition to idolatry. The Ottomans supported the French Huguenots and were outraged at news of the Saint Bartholomew's Day massacre of Protestants in 1572, and Calvinism found a fertile ground among the sultans' Christian subjects in Hungary and Transylvania, both of which became Protestant strongholds. Some scholars have argued, in fact, that Ottoman pressure distracted the Habsburgs and the papacy sufficiently that it created a space in which the nascent Protestant movement could take root without bearing the full brunt of papal and imperial opposition.

While some in Europe were convinced that the sultans had "as objective the monarchy of all the world and the destruction of Christendom," in reality Ottoman military efforts were focused primarily against fellow Muslim rulers in Egypt, North Africa, and particularly Iran, whose Shia Safavid rulers represented the most serious challenge to Ottoman power and influence in the region. In recognition of this, from 1500 all the major European powers at one time or another attempted to establish alliances with the Safavids against their common Ottoman enemy (or ally, depending on the ever-changing political winds). The Portuguese were the first to initiate direct relations, and following their 1507 capture of the strategic island of Hormuz in the Persian Gulf, they entered into an alliance with Shah Ismail I against the Ottomans. This ultimately benefited the Portuguese more than the Safavids, though the former provided men and cannon to Shah Tahmasp during Süleyman's second invasion of Persia in 1548. Other European powers similarly attempted to collaborate with the Persians against the Ottomans and, occasionally, against each other. At the end of the century, Pope Clement VIII sent an envoy in the vain hope of converting Shah Abbas I, or at the very least of pursuing joint action against "the unceasing and most hostile enemy the Turks." Despite attempts on both sides, none of these initiatives bore fruit because of logistical difficulties in coordinating efforts and constantly shifting political tides.

The century following the fall of the Byzantine Empire was marked by widespread conflict throughout the Mediterranean that was less about religion or clashing visions of civilization than about political and economic rivalries. During the sixteenth century, though alliances changed with dizzying regularity and complexity, at their core, many of the chief conflicts — Vienna, Tunis, Algiers, Prevesa — were clashes between the two dominant regional dynasties, the Ottomans and Habsburgs, as they struggled for the upper hand in the Mediterranean. The most memorable of these confrontations was the great galley battle at Lepanto.

The precipitating cause of the conflict was the Ottoman attack on the Venetian island of Cyprus in July 1570 and the yearlong siege of the city of Famagusta. This led Venice to break with its long-standing policy of neutrality and to form a league with the Habsburgs and the papacy in the desperate hope of preserving its shrinking presence in the eastern Mediterranean. On October 7, 1571, the naval forces of the combatants met amid a group of islands off the western coast of Greece, about 40 miles from the town of Lepanto. Arrayed along a battle line several miles long, the Christian armada numbered more than 300 vessels and about 80,000 men, while the Ottoman fleet counted 250 ships and perhaps 90,000 men.

The fighting was intense but brief; the entire action lasted only three hours and ended in total triumph for the Holy League. The key to the victory was the deployment in the vanguard of Venice's galleasses, a hybrid ship with oars and sails and 50 small guns, which wreaked havoc on the Ottoman lines. The battle devolved into hand-to-hand combat, and the carnage was immense. The balance sheet showed 110 Ottoman ships sunk or destroyed, 130 captured, 35,000 men killed or wounded, 3,000 prisoners captured, and almost 15,000 slaves freed from the Ottoman galleys. The Christian fleet, in contrast, lost 10 galleys and suffered 20,000 casualties.

One participant in the battle, the great Spanish writer Cervantes, described the Christian victory as "the most noble and memorable event that past centuries have seen or future generations can ever hope to witness." In Europe the triumph was acclaimed in music, verse, song, commemorative medals, and paintings, and the celebrations continued through the carnival season of the following year. In Venice, debtors were freed from prison, the Rialto was draped in blue cloth, and stores had "Closed because of the Death of the Turks" written on them. The day of the battle was designated as the feast of Santa Maria della Vittoria, and monumental depictions by Veronese and Vicentino were commissioned for the Doge's Palace. There was a sense among many that Lepanto marked the end of the myth of Ottoman invincibility and the turning of the tide of the sultans' centuries-long advance.

For Ottomans the shock of Lepanto was profound. One observer held that no greater disaster had occurred since the creation of the world and the construction of the first ship by Noah. Chroniclers were unanimous in concluding that the defeat was intended as a warning from Allah to Muslims for their sins. At the same time, the official reaction was anything but despair. Selim is reputed to have said that "the infidels only singed my beard," while his grand vizier, Mehmed Sokullu, asserted that "the Ottoman state is so powerful, if an order was issued to cast anchors from

Martin Rota, *Battle of Lepanto* (1572). *Photo: Suark / Art Resource, NY*

silver, to make rigging from silk, and to cut the sails from satin, it could be carried out for the entire fleet."

In many ways the Ottoman assessment ended up being most accurate. Almost immediately following the victory, Venice sued for a separate peace. Venice's primary objective in breaking with its tradition of neutrality had been to save Cyprus, but with the island's loss just days prior to Lepanto, Venice lost its feigned zeal for the Holy League, preferring instead to protect its remaining Mediterranean possessions and revive its valuable trade relations with the Ottomans. For his part, Philip was distracted by the revolt in the Netherlands, and though Pope Pius V tried to rally the members of the league, his efforts "could not revive a cadaver." Venice's resolve for peace was strengthened when the Ottomans quickly rebuilt their fleet and with it recaptured Tunis in 1574. If Lepanto did not destroy Ottoman power in the Mediterranean, it did deflect Selim's plans to besiege Crete, allowing Venice to hold the island for another century. It also marked the beginning of a new stage in Mediterranean warfare, in which corsairs and surrogates of both the Ottomans and the Habsburgs would contest their rivalry at sea, with Venice regularly caught in the middle.

CHAPTER TEN

Life on the Frontier

Migration and Conversion, Piracy and Slaves

D uring the middle of the night of April 7, 1596, a group of 40 men slipped into the great Ottoman fortress of Clissa (Klis) through an opening in the massive walls that was used to discard garbage. The fortress was a few miles from the Venetian commercial town of Spalato, located on the Dalmatian coast of the eastern Adriatic Sea. The few guards who defended it were asleep, allowing the infiltrators to slip in without detection. They lay in wait quietly until just before daybreak, and then "having three times invoked the help of Jesus," they burst out of their hiding place, planted a flag with the crucifix, and began massacring the fortress's defenders and inhabitants. With relative ease, they took possession of this linchpin of the Ottoman frontier defenses in the region.

On its surface the celebrated capture of the fortress of Clissa in 1596 seems another example of the sort of religious rivalry and violence that was endemic to the Veneto-Ottoman-Habsburg frontier that converged in Dalmatia—a clear example, in other words, of the clash of civilizations. However, when we dig a bit deeper, the story becomes decidedly more complex. The assault on the fortress was planned by Giovanni Alberti, who was a Spalatine noble, a Christian, and a Venetian subject. Some of his key conspirators, however, were Ottoman subjects, including several brothers and a minor official in the fortress, all of whom were Muslim. Even though they draped their actions in a veil of religion, economic despair and political dissatisfaction with both Ottoman and Venetian rule, as much as anything, seem to have been their motivation. A large contingent of Uskoks, border raiders from throughout the region nominally in Habsburg service and whom both Venetians and Ottomans considered bandits, also played an important role. And the papacy was active in at the very least encouraging the attack. Far from supporting the conquest of the

fortress, Alberti's Venetian lords were furious about what had happened, and they collaborated closely with local Ottoman officials in ensuring its timely restitution.

As this incident highlights, the early modern Mediterranean was a space of numerous frontiers: political, physical, and cultural. The predominance of the nation-state paradigm over the past century has profoundly marked our conceptions of geographical space; we envision the world in terms of clearly delineated and defended political boundaries. The reality in premodern times was much more diverse and fluid. In comparison to the frontiers of the medieval Mediterranean, in the early modern period increasingly powerful empires declared their sovereignty over wide swaths of the region and attempted to implement more centralized and unified administrative structures. Despite these efforts, however, a real tension existed between the centripetal objectives of empire and the centrifugal realities of life on distant peripheries.

The Dalmatian coastal setting of the attack on Clissa provides some sense of life on the Mediterranean borderlands. Despite repeated efforts to clearly delineate political borders in the region, such lines generally held minimal significance and were crossed easily as Ottoman, Habsburg, and Venetian subjects mingled freely on both sides of the border. For instance, the region's transhumant Vlachs constantly crisscrossed the frontier as they herded their cattle, Venetian subjects worked Ottoman fields and ground their wheat in Ottoman mills, and Ottoman subjects routinely pastured animals on Venetian lands. Families owned or rented lands on both sides of the border, and family members were often subjects of separate rulers and incorporated both Muslim and Christian practices. Friendship and cross-border marriages were so common that Christian officials warned such "familiarity presents an occasion for many sins." As a result of these connections, it is not surprising that religious and political differences were often trumped by a shared local culture, language, and sociability that transcended political boundaries.

Dalmatia had an integrated economy centered on cross-border trade: fairs attracted merchants from throughout the region who moved freely across the border. Venetians exported salt, cloth, oil, and spices; Ottoman traders provided wax, timber, silk, mohair, and hides. More importantly, they also supplied cattle, cheese, honey, and grain for the Venetian coastal enclaves, which could not produce enough to feed themselves. The post-Lepanto period saw a significant increase in trade in Spalato when Ottoman and Venetian entrepreneurs, led by the Jewish merchant Daniel Rodriga, collaborated to develop the port as the terminus of the overland trade routes from Istanbul.

Dalmatian religious boundaries were also fluid: Christians were the overall majority throughout the region, with pockets of Muslims and Jews. Conversions were common, though disproportionally from Christianity to Islam, which beckoned with opportunities for social and economic advancement for the increasingly isolated and marginalized inhabitants of Venetian Dalmatia. Religious distinctions were blurred, and there were many shared popular beliefs and practices, in part because common folk received limited instruction in their faiths due to the persistent shortage of clerics. Muslim converts continued to read the Gospels, drank wine during Ramadan, made offerings to Christian saints, and held that Muhammad was the Holy Spirit. Places of pilgrimage were venerated and shared, and Muslim and Christian clerics consulted on common concerns.

Notwithstanding the close links that cut across the frontier, there were also frequent disruptions in the region. Animals were regularly rustled, a shadow economy in contraband thrived, and kidnappings and murders were not unknown. This violence was rarely religiously or politically motivated; rather, it was more often indiscriminate banditry and criminal activity. Indeed, Ottoman and Venetian local officials regularly cooperated to preserve the peace in the borderlands in order to facilitate trade and avoid unwanted conflicts, as the rulers of both empires explicitly ordered their representatives in the region to do.

As life in early modern Dalmatia demonstrates, the frontiers of the Mediterranean were often imprecise and regularly breached, and as a result, the daily experience in these liminal regions possessed a unique character. Episodes of violence such as the seizure of the fortress of Clissa did occur, but they were exceptions to the more common reality of cooperation and exchange. Where descriptions of the Mediterranean have often emphasized religious, political, and cultural divisions, the premodern sea was a highly connected space characterized by cultural mixing, porous and malleable borders, and intense circulation of goods, ideas, and peoples.

DEFINING AND MAPPING FRONTIERS

The early modern era was a time of significant dialogue, both philosophical and pragmatic, on the nature and functioning of political society. Institutional structures and administrative practices, as well as theoretical conceptions of governance, were undergoing significant change. Associated with these transformations, the notion of states as clearly delineated geographical entities, whatever their composition and character, also began to be broadly established. Despite, or, perhaps better, in response to, the ambiguity of frontiers and the unruliness of life there, early modern polities became interested in more clearly demarcating their borders.

The Veneto-Ottoman political boundary, for example, was a matter of ongoing dispute from the late fourteenth century onward. In 1479–80, following a decade and a half of hostilities, an Ottoman official traveled to the Venetian-held Peloponnese coastal town of Nauplion (Nafplio) to try to determine the new border. Local officials, elderly inhabitants, and tax records were consulted, and the confines were marked based on these data and on features such as mountains, wells, and fortresses. Throughout the sixteenth and seventeenth centuries lack of clarity over the Balkan frontier led to a series of joint Venetian and Ottoman delegations that worked together on the ground for months to identify the border. Where physical features were unavailable, it was marked by crosses or crescents carved into trees or boulders, heaps of rocks, or small stone pyramids. Along their northern frontier, the Ottomans did the same with representatives of the kingdom of Poland-Lithuania, using both natural and built features and, where neither existed, erecting mounds of earth to indicate the border.

The liquid frontiers of the Mediterranean were perhaps even more important. The sea was of course not a neutral space; it served important political and economic ends and was thus the focus of endless rivalries. The Adriatic, for example, was considered Venetian space, not only by Venice but also by the Ottomans and Habsburgs, who demanded that the Venetians ensure the security of shipping in the region. Marking borders in the water presented unique challenges. Liquid territory could be demarcated by islands, towns, and especially fortresses constructed in strategic locations. Corfu, for instance, was considered the key to the Adriatic and was defended by two mighty Venetian fortresses. Navies functioned as mobile markers; following their conquest of the Aegean, the Ottomans asserted their somewhat tenuous hold on this distant edge of the empire by sending an annual naval expedition, often commanded by the admiral of the fleet, to travel through the region to collect taxes and confirm ongoing Ottoman sovereignty over the land and the sea. Venice maintained two separate contingents of galleys to patrol the Adriatic and the sea-lanes of the Aegean, and the Spanish similarly docked fleets in the Iberian peninsula, on Sicily, and at Naples that regularly cruised the central and western Mediterranean to defend the sea-lanes and imprint Spain's political claims.

Attempts to mark political territory were part of an overall growth in interest in maps. The early modern era was the first great age of cartography, experiencing what has been described as a "map boom." As new worlds were discovered and familiar ones explored, a veritable explosion of maps for both artistic and practical purposes ensued. Geography became a means to understand and articulate difference, as well as to inscribe power.

Maps were generated as tools of administration. Venice was precocious in using maps for administrative purposes; in the fifteenth century, Venetians already were creating maps to clarify ambassadorial reports, situate defensive fortresses, resolve property disputes, and define borders. Venetian magistracies, such as the Rural Land Office and the Office of Border Commissioners, generated a growing body of maps for bureaucratic purposes, such as the 1538 mapping of the frontier between Venetian and Habsburg German territories. In the same vein, in late-sixteenth-century Naples, Mario Cartaro, the official cartographer of the Spanish viceroy, produced a remarkable series of maps of the kingdom and its provinces. Philip II commissioned several cartographers, beginning with Pedro de Esquivel, to produce highly detailed scale maps of Spain and its territories for use in administering the far-flung empire.

The growth in geographic curiosity was mirrored in the Ottoman Empire. Part of this involved the translation or reworking of classic works from the grand tradition of Arabic geographies in response to new interests and exigencies. In the sixteenth century, Ottoman cartographers also began to produce important geographical works. The most famous of these was the world map produced by the Ottoman mariner Piri Reis in 1513 and expanded a decade later. The work is notable for its inclusion of information on the new world, one of the earliest surviving maps to do so. Selim I used Piri Reis's famous map to plan Ottoman military expansion in the Indian Ocean; indeed, military ends were an important driver in the growth of cartography. The Ottomans also desired to keep up with expanding European geographical knowledge; held in the sultan's palace was a highly secret map by the Portuguese court cartographer, Pedro Reinal, showing Magellan's circumnavigation of the globe. Also notable was Mehmed Ashik's *Menāzirü'l-Avālim* (The Vantage Points of the Worlds, 1597), the standard Ottoman geographical reference throughout the seventeenth century, whose over 1,000 pages represent the definitive Turkish-language synthesis of Arabic geographical learning.

MIGRATION AND MOVEMENT

The early modern era was a highly mobile age, and this was particularly true of the Mediterranean. For many years scholars thought that the sea functioned as a barrier to movement, forcing its inhabitants to remain fixed in one place. More recent scholarship, however, has demonstrated that Mediterranean peoples were very mobile and that the sea's "liquid landscape" facilitated rather than blocked travel. In fact, mobility was deeply rooted in the collective mentality of the region, and as historians Peregrine Horden and Nicholas Purcell have shown, relative proximity and ease of travel were central to the seaborne connectivity between various microregions that was one of the Mediterranean's distinguishing characteristics.

The reasons behind this mobility were varied: labor mobility, including trade, shipping, agriculture, pastoralism, fishing, and soldiering, was a primary motivation for many. Natural occurrences such as drought, famine, disease, or earthquake drove many migrants. Political and military events could also influence migration and population patterns. For instance, peasants throughout the Mediterranean often expressed their dissatisfaction with their feet by fleeing Christian rule for Ottoman. Movement in the opposite direction also occurred, though with less frequency.

We get some sense of the breadth of motivations behind this mobility in examining the eastern Mediterranean Greek cultural zone. During the early modern period, the Greeks were highly mobile, and Venice was a major destination. The Greek cardinal Basilios Bessarion described the city as "almost another Byzantium." The fall of the Byzantine Empire, in 1453, propelled many Greek immigrants to the lagoon, and this, combined with migration from its own Greek colonies, gave Venice the largest Orthodox population in all of western Europe, totaling perhaps 5,000–6,000 in 1600. Greeks worked in a variety of Venetian industries, including shipbuilding and printing, and as merchants, shopkeepers, and sailors. Most settled in the Castello neighborhood, where, in 1513, Venice granted them permission to construct a church, San Giorgio dei Greci.

Mediterranean migration made for diverse urban centers. In Venice, for instance, it has been estimated that foreigners numbered 15,000–20,000 of a total population of perhaps 110,000. These individuals and families came primarily from the eastern Mediterranean—Dalmatia, Albania, Greece—but also from points farther to the east, including Russia, Georgia, and Hungary. Many came from the Italian mainland as well. Some Muslims were included in this figure; most were in the city transitorily, as merchants, diplomats, or travelers, and in 1621, in response to their large numbers, Venetian authorities opened an institution, the *fondaco dei turchi*, to house and sequester Ottomans temporarily resident in the city. Other subjects of the sultan were in the city more permanently: between 1590 and 1670 approximately 1,000 Muslims, many of whom were domestic slaves in Venetian patrician households, passed through the Catechumen House, an institution that existed to ease the transition of converts into Venetian and Christian society. Over half came from the Ottoman Balkans; another quarter divided evenly between North Africa and the Ottoman Greek islands. There were also many Ottoman galley slaves in the Venetian fleet at any given time.

Istanbul was another magnet for immigration, on a decidedly larger scale than Venice. The combination of religious pogroms in parts of Europe and the relative religious tolerance of Islam made Ottoman lands attractive to displaced Jews from across Europe. Mehmed II and his successors pursued a policy intended to

Caravanserai on a pilgrim route to Mecca. From a 1588 Ottoman manuscript illustration.
Topkapi Museum, Istanbul. Photo: Gianni Dagli Orti Art Resource, NY

Pilgrims engaging in typical devotional activites around a saint's tomb in the Story of Saint Stephen by fourteenth-century Italian artist Bernardo Daddi. *Vatican Pinacoteca. Photo: Scala / Art Resource*

The interior of Hagia Sophia, Istanbul. *Photo: Album/Art Resource, NY*

The mosque at Cordoba has an elaborately decorated prayer niche (mihrab) surrounded by geometric stucco decoration, mosiacs, and reused Roman marble columns. *Photo: Album/Art Resource, NY*

The Dome of the Rock, commissioned by the Ummayads and completed in 691; the mosaic decoration and marble column and panels continue inside. *Photo: SEF/Art Resource, NY*

The exterior of St. Mark's Basilica in Venice is decorated with reused marble columns, Byzantine-style mosaics, and Islamic window screens. *Photo: Monique O'Connell*

Lusterware bowl from fifteenth-century Valencia showing a three-masted sailing ship in a cobalt blue drawing. *Photo: bpk, Berlin/Museum fuer Islamische Kunst/Georg Niedermeiser/Art Resource, NY*

Galley and nef at anchor in Vittore Carpaccio's painting Arrival of the Ambassadors (1497–98) from the Scenes from the Life of St. Ursula. *Accademia Venice. Photo: Alfredo Dagli Orti/Art Resource, NY*

Naval scene with a warship and a castle in the background. From a 1592 Ottoman manuscript illustration by Nakkas Osman. *Topkapi Palace Museum, Istanbul.*
Photo: Werner Forman / Art Resource, NY

A variety of Mediterranean War galleys drawn up for battle. From the seventeenth-century Le Memorie turchesche (Turkish reminiscences), Codex Cicogna 1971. *Museo Correr, Venice. Photo: Alfredo Dagli Orti/ Art Resource, NY*

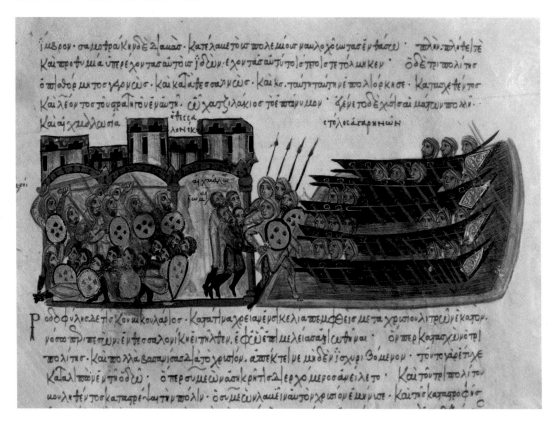

Invaders leading a group of war captives out of Thessalonica and onto boats. *Biblioteca Nacional, Madrid. Photo: Album/Art Resource, NY*

This thirteenth-century mosaic on the Trinitarian Church of San Tommaso in Formis, Rome, shows Christ between a black and a white freed slave, reflecting the order's mission of redeeming captives. *Photo: Celeste McNamara*

Madonna and child, flanked by the emperors Justinian offering a model of Hagia Sophia and Constantine with a model of the city. From a sixth-century mosaic inside Hagia Sophia, Istanbul. *Photo: Erich Lessing/Art Resource, NY*

Süleymaniye Mosque, designed by Sinan, is the largest mosque in Istanbul. From Seyyid Lokman, Tārīkh-i Sulṭān Sulaymān (History of Sultan Süleyman, 1579). © *The Trustees of the Chester Beatty Library, Dublin/Bridgeman Images*

Made of Almohad silk for a Castilian queen, this pillowcase has an Arabic (Kufic) inscription surrounding two central figures. ©Patrimonio Nacional, Spain

Mamluk carpet from Cairo, sixteenth century. *Museum fuer Angewandte Kunst, Frankfurt.*
Photo: Erich Lessing/Art Resource, NY

Roger II of Sicily's coronation robe is made of Byzantine silk and edged with an Arabic (Kufic) inscription. *Kunsthistorisches Museum, Vienna. Photo: Erich Lessing/Art Resource, NY*

A mid-fourteenth-century Mamluk mosque lamp, found in Egypt, decorated with the name of Sultan Barquq. *Musée du Louvre, Paris. © RMN-Grand Palais / Art Resource, NY*

An eleventh-century ivory casket made for a Taifa king, turned into a reliquary for the Burgos Cathedral by application of enamel angels. *Photo: Album / Art Resource, NY*

Hispano-Moresque-ware dish with a luster finish, probably from Valencia. *Musée du Louvre, Paris. © RMN-Grand Palais / Art Resource, NY*

Iznik tile panel, Anatolia, Ottoman, c. 1575. *Victoria and Albert Museum, London.*
Photo: V&A Images, London/Art Resource, NY

In a fifteenth-century painting by Gentile Bellini, Mehmed II is framed by a classical arch and a highly decorated and bejeweled rug. © *National Gallery, London/Art Resource, NY*

Sinan Beg, an Ottoman court artist, painted this fifteenth-century image of Mehmed II smelling a rose. *Topkapi Palace Museum, Istanbul. Photo: Werner Forman/Art Resource, NY*

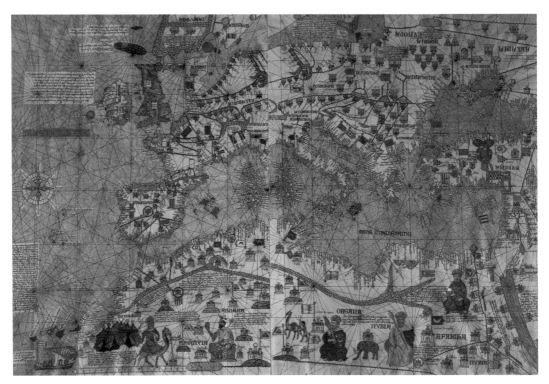

Abraham Cresques, detail from the Catalan Atlas (Majorca, 1375). *Bibliothèque nationale de France, Paris. Photo: Album / Art Resource, NY*

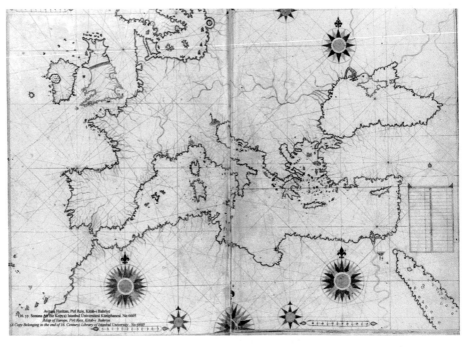

Piri Reis, map of Istanbul and Galata, from the Kitab-ı Bahriye (Book of Navigation), Istanbul, sixteenth century. *Courtesy of Sächsische Landesbibliothek — Staats- und Universitätsbibliothek Dresden / Deutsche Fotothek*

attract Jewish immigrants to Ottoman lands by promising them sanctuary from the more dangerous realms of western Christendom. A famous fifteenth-century letter from a refugee rabbi, Isaac Sarfati, optimistically encouraged European Jews to migrate to the Ottoman Empire with the promise that "every man may dwell at peace under his own vine and fig tree." After their expulsion from Iberia, Bayezid II invited Jewish refugees to settle in the city as a means of strengthening its economy, a strategy that proved successful as Jews came to occupy important positions in commerce and other economic sectors. By 1600 more Jews lived in the Ottoman Empire than any other contemporary polity, and in Istanbul they made up perhaps 10% of the total population. Similarly, numerous Greeks, both Ottoman and Venetian subjects, migrated to Istanbul, pushed by the difficult economic situation on many of the Greek islands and pulled by the hope of finding gainful employment especially as woolworkers, as seamen, and as laborers in the capital's shipbuilding trades, where Greeks, particularly from Crete, may have composed a majority of the workforce.

A dramatic mixing of peoples was characteristic of all Mediterranean port cities. Marseilles, for example, was known for its diverse population, especially Italians who dominated large-scale trade. French immigration to the Iberian peninsula was also extensive; a 1669 estimate placed the total number of French immigrants in Spain at 200,000. So numerous were French workers in Zaragoza that a visiting French cardinal found that "everyone" spoke his language. In Madrid, perhaps 40,000 French artisans, masons, and retailers filled the city.

Migration transformed the Mediterranean's more rural and less populous areas, too. Emigration to urban centers could profoundly affect local populations. The island of Milos, for example, experienced a dramatic population decrease in the eighteenth century as a result of piracy, malaria, and a devastating earthquake. Migrants settled in rural areas as well; late medieval migrations saw the establishment of over 50 Albanian and several Croatian enclaves in southern Italy, and early modern Spanish agriculture was heavily dependent on French peasant labor. Famine and environmental factors drove many from the countryside toward Mediterranean urban centers: in the late 1580s perhaps 4,000 desperate peasants entered Rome in a single day in search of food. Similarly, Madrid was a magnet for the subsistence-driven migration of large numbers of peasants from the countryside of northern Spain.

While much migration was permanent, seasonal movements of people were common as well. In Sicily, peasants, artisans, and others traveled to work temporarily in the island's sugar industry to supplement their incomes. In 1571, 2,000 seasonal workers came to prune vines in the region of Marseilles. Similarly, livestock raisers in the Balkans migrated seasonally with their animals between highlands and lowlands. In Spain, *jornaleros* (migrant workers) were numerous, perhaps as high as 60% of all rural families in Castile in the 1570s. In Extremadura, peasant farmers planted their own fields then went to Andalusia to work in grain, olive, and grape production because, as one observer wrote, "most of the people are poor." So widespread was this practice that it was difficult to collect taxes in the region. Labor was in such demand in La Mancha that grain farmers recruited workers from northern Spain to bring in the harvest. Women participated in this intensive period of labor, though usually they came from within the region. More commonly, women migrated from rural areas to urban centers to work in domestic service. This was only temporary for many young women, who eventually returned to their villages to marry. Turnover thus was very high, upward of 35% annually in early modern Cuenca, for example.

While much of the circulation of peoples was voluntary, or at least motivated by desperation, forced migrations were also an important part of Mediterranean mobility. The Ottomans at times had recourse to a policy of mass, state-organized resettlement (*sürgün*) to revive underpopulated regions of their expanding empire, to jumpstart economic growth, and to resettle recalcitrant communities. Following the conquest of Constantinople, Mehmed II implemented extensive reengineering of the population to transform the city into a worthy imperial capital and to revive its economy. He offered favorable conditions, including free housing, to attract Greeks from the Morea, Izmir, and Trebizond; Jews from Salonica; Armenians from Tokat, Amasya, and Kayseri; and ethnic Turks from Anatolia. Voluntary displacement was not entirely successful, and people were forcibly moved based on their qualifications in industry or commerce. This policy of forced resettlement endured: after the conquest of Cyprus in 1571, Muslim farmers and nomads were transferred from Anatolia, not primarily, it appears, to dilute the Greek population of the island but rather to reinvigorate its economy after years of neglect under Venetian rule.

The rulers of Spain utilized a similar policy in dealing with its Jewish and Muslim minority populations. After over a century of persecution, in 1492 Ferdinand and Isabel expelled all of Spain's remaining Jews, who had at one time been the largest population in Europe, which led to massive suffering and resettlement throughout the Mediterranean. This was followed on an even larger scale by the internal resettlement and eventual expulsion of Spain's Moriscos. In the 1570s, following the revolt of the Alpujarras, fearing that the Morisco population of his kingdom might act as an Ottoman fifth column, Philip II had Moriscos from coastal regions evicted them from their homes and forcibly relocated in small groups throughout the northern and central interior of Spain. The second act of this tragedy occurred in 1599 when the Spanish Council of State ordered the expulsion of all Moriscos from the kingdom. The operation did not begin until 1609, when 300,000 people were driven out, with most migrating to North Africa, Morocco, and other Ottoman territories, including a significant community in Istanbul. The impact of the Morisco expulsion on Spain was significant. In Valencia in 1638 almost half of the 453 Morisco villages remained empty, and Aragon lost 15% of its population. Fertile regions that the Moriscos had farmed returned to nature, and some of the Christian nobility in Aragon and other affected regions were impoverished by the depopulation of their lands. Many parts of Spain remained unproductive and underpopulated for decades after the expulsion.

Related to early modern Mediterranean mobility and connectivity was the widespread phenomenon of slavery, which touched all aspects of life in the region. Because of the scale of the Atlantic slave trade, its centrality to the American experience, and its extensive historiography, there has been a tendency to think of slavery primarily in the racial terms that dominated that context and to overlook the important place of slavery in the early modern Mediterranean, or to see it as more benign and transitory in relationship to its Atlantic counterpart. Mediterranean slavery, however, shared many of the same brutal characteristics and had a profound and lasting effect on the region. Into the mid-seventeenth century it was of much greater concern, at least in Europe, than Atlantic slavery, and echoes of the fears of the slave raids that plagued and haunted the region endure to this day. To be sure, there were significant differences: in contrast to the Mediterranean, American slaves were transported to a dramatically alien setting far from their homes, with no chance to maintain contact with their families and no opportunity to regain their freedom. These differences, however, should not overshadow the trauma and suffering of Mediterranean slavery.

Compared to the 11–12 million individuals transported across the Atlantic, the scale of Mediterranean slavery was significantly smaller, though actual totals have been a matter of some debate. One scholar has estimated that between 1500 and 1800, 3 million slaves were taken, with Christians outnumbering Muslims two to one; another has suggested a figure of 4–5 million, with an average of 300,000 slaves in chains at any given time. These figures are based on a variety of archival sources and informed estimates. For example, we have numbers such as the 20,000 Christian slaves that Charles V freed in 1535 when he conquered Tunis or the 5,000 Muslims taken in a Portuguese raid on Morocco. At the battle of Lepanto, 3,000 Muslims were taken captive, and over 15,000 Christian slaves were liberated from the Ottoman galleys. In Istanbul the total number of slaves was 60,000 in 1568 and 100,000 by 1609, or approximately one-fifth of the city's population. Part of the challenge in counting slaves is the diverse spectrum of slaveries in the region, from institutional slavery in the Ottoman *kul* system to household slavery in Italy and Spain to the more familiar galley slavery of the Barbary bagnios.

The number of slaves was not static either; it ebbed and flowed, particularly in response to periods of warfare. Overall, there was a surge in Mediterranean slavery (in comparison to smaller medieval totals) that began around 1500 and lasted until 1800, though with significant tapering after 1700. Notable spikes accompanied periods of conflict, such as following Lepanto and during the intense corsair activity of the first half of the seventeenth century. There was a constant demand for new slaves because of the 25% annual attrition rate through conversion and escape, as well as mortality. Death claimed 15–17% of slaves each year, in line with the rates identified for the West Indies.

As in earlier periods, the Mediterranean's many slaves resulted from a wide range of sources and activities. Historically, the majority of slaves in the Ottoman

Empire were captives of war. In the Mediterranean the endemic corsair activity at sea and on land was a significant source of slaves for both Christian and Muslim masters. Crimean Tatars in the Black Sea steppe and African traders from sub-Saharan regions also provided chattel for the sea's many slave emporia. Another source was the devshirme, or child levy, which extracted a limited number of boys from Christian Balkan villages to provide the largest slaveholder in the Ottoman Empire, the sultan, with a constant supply of personal slaves. Because of their education and access to power, however, the experiences of these kul slaves of the sultan differed dramatically from that of other Mediterranean slaves; indeed, many scholars do not even include them in the same category.

Slaves came from throughout the Mediterranean basin and beyond. Many were captured along the coasts and on the islands of the sea, with Spain and Italy the chief source of Christian slaves. Others came from northern Europe: a 1626 source counted 1,200 English captives in Salé. Around the same time, three vessels from Tripoli with 200 seamen, including many English renegades, captured 400 inhabitants of Iceland. When the Spanish occupied Tripoli in 1510, over 10,000 captives were taken. In the Ottoman Empire, many Circassians from the Caucasus region, particularly women, were captured by Tatars and sold into slavery. One study of Spanish enslaved between 1575 and 1769 found that many were captured on land or in immediate coastal waters while engaged in agriculture and fishing.

Mediterranean slavery was not racial, but there were numerous black African slaves throughout the region during the early modern period in comparison to the Middle Ages. While much has been written about the African slave trade within the Atlantic context, the trans-Saharan trade was one of Africa's main outlets for black slaves. Women occupied a preponderant position in this component of the Mediterranean slave trade; they were especially sought after for domestic work, which was in great demand. Africans were captured in slave raids in sub-Saharan regions such as Sudan, western Africa, and the Sahel and sold in regional slave markets to African traders, who then marched the unfortunates across the Sahara in extremely harsh conditions to the major slave centers of North Africa: Algeria, Tunisia, Libya, Egypt, and Morocco. From there they were shipped throughout the Mediterranean, to the Ottoman Aegean, the Levant, and the Balkans. Many were also enslaved in Christian parts of Europe, including perhaps 700,000 to 800,000 in Spain and Portugal alone. Overall, it has been estimated that between 1400 and 1800, 2.4 million African slaves were forcibly transported along these slave-trading routes.

In another contrast with medieval slavery, states, rather than individuals, were the primary holders of slaves in the early modern era. This is because many slaves were destined to serve as the human engines of the Mediterranean's galleys, some of which required between 200 and 300 rowers. In 1673, for instance, it was reported that 2,000 Muslims rowed on French galleys. On Christian galleys, on average less than a quarter of rowers were Muslim (the remainder were convicts and freemen), in order to discourage rebellions. Thus, the eight Spanish galleys of Sicily contained 1,413 rowers, 629 of whom were Muslim. Slaves were also employed in public-works

Spanish galley slaves carrying barrels, 1529. From a German costume book by Christophe Weiditz. *Biblioteca Nacional, Madrid.* Photo: Album / Art Resource, NY

projects including bridges, fortifications, and a variety of building complexes. In Naples almost 400 Muslim slaves worked from 1753 to the end of the century on the royal palace in Caserta. Moulay Ismail, the Alaouite ruler of Morocco from 1672 to 1727, constructed his massive palace complex in Meknes (intended to rival Louis XIV's Versailles) and other projects with thousands of Christian slave laborers, who were obtained through his systematized program of corsairing.

Slaves labored in many other sectors as well. They worked as guards, porters, miners, masons, scribes, and musicians. They also worked in agriculture, particularly in Morocco, though in comparison to Atlantic slavery their numbers were much smaller because of the paucity of large agricultural estates in much of the region. Many women, but also some men, served as domestic slaves, stewards, gardeners, wet nurses, laundresses, maids, and cooks.

While significant attention has been devoted to Christians enslaved by Muslim masters, the reverse phenomenon has until recently been largely overlooked. In part this is because Christian Europeans held that Islam was solely responsible for the inhumane practice of slavery. It is now clear that Christians were fully involved in the Mediterranean slave trade; that slavery in Christendom did not end during the Renaissance, as was long thought, but rather continued and expanded throughout the early modern period; and that Christians enslaved large numbers of Muslims. Slavery was, in short, a Mediterranean, not just a Muslim, phenomenon.

In Livorno in 1689, for example, there were 859 Muslim slaves; between a quarter and a third came from the eastern Ottoman Empire—Anatolia, the Aegean, the Balkans, and Egypt—with the remainder from the Maghreb, particularly Algeria. During the eighteenth century, papal galleys regularly captured anywhere from 60 to 160 Muslims annually; similar quantities were snared by the fleets of Naples, Tuscany, and Genoa in the same period. When Napoleon conquered Malta in 1798, he liberated 2,000 Muslim slaves. In the eighteenth century, when the heyday of Mediterranean slavery had long passed, there were still between 2,000 and 3,000 Muslim slaves in Italy, and they may have outnumbered Italian slaves in Muslim hands.

There is significant debate over the treatment of slaves throughout the Mediterranean, with some scholars hyperbolically describing their conditions as approaching those of Nazi concentration camps or Soviet gulags. Others have argued that Muslims enslaved in Europe were treated more harshly than Christians in parts of the Islamic world. While slavery was inherently dehumanizing and brutal, it is extremely difficult to definitively address the question of the treatment of slaves given the limitations of our historical sources.

Among Europeans, views of the severity of slave conditions grew out of a new genre of literature, the slave narrative, which became popular as the number of slaves increased. These accounts invariably present a litany of the harsh living and working conditions and inhumane treatment that slaves received at the hands of their Muslim masters. For instance, the former slave John Rawlins detailed the brutality he claimed was used against new slaves to coerce them to convert: "They commonly lay them on their bellies, beating them so long till they bleed at the nose and mouth: and if yet they [the slaves] continue constant, then they strike the teeth out of their heads, pinch them by their tongues, and use many other sorts of tortures."

Beyond such acts of extreme brutality, the everyday lives of slaves, particularly on the galleys, were often extremely harsh, and death rates were high. Rowers were chained to their positions and prodded with the lash to row for long periods in cramped, unsanitary conditions, often during blistering summer heat. The title of an anonymous seventeenth-century galley slave's account, "Summary of the Infernal Life of the Galley," seems fitting. When in port, slaves were housed in bagnios in equally unpleasant conditions. Food was simple: oarsmen on papal galleys received 30 ounces of biscuit accompanied by a fava bean or rice soup. The soup was provided daily in the winter and three times a week during "the time of navigation," mid-May to mid-November. During periods of intense effort, giving chase or in battle, this might be supplemented with some wine or other additional food.

While slavery was a miserable state and many slaves experienced horrible conditions, sensationalistic accounts need to be placed into a more nuanced context. As one scholar has argued, it is essential to distinguish between "history" and "hysteria," that is, between what captives and others with a stake in exaggerating the severity of their conditions reported and what actually happened. Though coercion undergirded all slavery, unrestrained violence was not always the norm. Slaves represented property with significant economic value, thus slave dealers and owners had a vested interest in maximizing the return on their investments' utility and longevity. Thus, prudent owners sought to maintain slaves' value by minimizing their exposure to physical injury or undue psychological stress. In addition, in Ottoman lands, custom, religion, and sultanic law constrained Muslim owners toward benevolence, and the Qur'an recommended that slaves be shown kindness.

Members of religious orders working to free slaves in Algiers acknowledged that slaves' conditions were not unrelentingly brutal. They were permitted "to attend the churches, to frequent the saintly sacraments and in holy days the owners send them to carry out the obligation of Christians, they do not force anyone to leave the Christian religion, they treat them uniformly well, and if one of them complains to the governor about his owner mistreating him, they punish him and make [the owner] sell [the slave] to another." In Meknes, despite often-harsh working conditions, Moulay Ismail allowed slaves to construct a church, monastery, and infirmary.

In Livorno, new Muslim galley slaves were given two suits of white clothing, shoes, and a beret, and new clothes were distributed annually. Onboard medical assistance was provided, and when necessary, slaves were removed to hospitals, such as the one Cosimo III had constructed in the late seventeenth century. Some even went to mineral baths. When in port, Livornese slaves worshiped in a mosque constructed for them, were led in prayer by an imam, and had a kadi whom they elected to resolve their differences and represent their collective interests.

Slaves were not always confined to bagnios; in fact, they regularly circulated in the streets of port cities with a good degree of liberty. Many engaged in small-scale commercial and artisanal activities. In Livorno, oarsmen could pay to free themselves from the rigors of the galley, and many established small enterprises in the port area. Some had shops or sold goods from carts near the port; others worked as barbers; still others went about town selling water or working as porters. Papal slaves made baskets, marquetry, and hats, which they sold to raise money, while others opened coffeehouses and tobacco shops. Barbary slaves sold wine, cheese, and other foodstuffs or distilled and sold brandy. Others earned income from sewing and mending clothing, and even composing poems.

In the Maghreb, slave conditions were closely associated with the treatment that Muslim slaves received in Christian lands. If rulers there received news of mistreatment or forced conversions, they often increased the burdens and even violence against their own slaves as a means to coerce Christian rulers into improving the conditions of slaves under their control. Slaves were able to communicate with family and officials in their homelands, and their correspondence could influence their conditions and the negotiations for their redemption. For example, slaves in Livorno wrote letters complaining of their poor treatment, which directly affected ongoing negotiations to redeem Christian slaves in Algiers.

No real effort was made to convert slaves held by Christians, in part to avoid similar efforts in Muslim lands but also because a converted slave could expect to be treated more humanely. There were clear regulations that mandated better food and clothing for converts. Conversions did occur, and some slaves perceived baptism as a way to free themselves, or at least to improve their conditions, though this did not necessarily occur. Conversion certainly did not lead to liberation for either Muslim or Christian slaves, despite widespread, desperate hopes to the contrary. Institutions such as the Opera Pia de' Turchi Battezati in Genoa and catechumen houses in many other towns existed to facilitate the transition to Christianity. In the

final tally, however, compared to Christians who embraced Islam, relatively few Muslim slaves converted to Christianity, perhaps 1–2%.

Priests of the Trinitarian Order, negotiating the ransom of Christian slaves on the Barbary coast, seventeenth century. From Pere Dan, *Histoire de Barbarie et de ses corsaires* (Paris, 1637). *Photo: Art Resource, NY*

One of the ways Mediterranean slavery differed significantly from Atlantic slavery was that it did not always represent a life sentence or the sort of social death that has been identified with slavery in other contexts. Many Mediterranean slaves ultimately were able to regain their freedom: they might achieve this by escaping, converting, being manumitted, purchasing or earning their freedom, or being redeemed. During the early modern era, elaborate structures evolved to facilitate the redemption of slaves. Christian efforts were centered on the two medieval religious orders, the Order of the Most Holy Trinity for the Redemption of the Captives (Trinitarians) and Order of Our Lady of Mercy and the Redemption of the Captives (Mercedarians), which were established to free slaves taken during the Crusades. These orders continued to play an important role in slave redemptions, particularly in the western Mediterranean. They proved incapable, however, of dealing with the great rise in slave numbers in the early modern period, and as a result new

248   THE MEDITERRANEAN WORLD

redemptionist initiatives arose. This effort has been described as "one of the major social movements of the early modern Mediterranean world."

Institutions to supplement these religious orders were established, tasked specifically with addressing the burgeoning slave issue. The first of these was the Real Casa Santa della Redentione de' Cattivi, founded by the Spanish viceroy of Naples in 1548 to provide a state institution dedicated to raising funds to free the growing number of slaves from the city. It was followed by similar bodies in Bologna, Palermo, and Genoa. The most important new institution was Rome's Opera Pia del Riscatto, established in 1581 by Gregory XIII, which had affiliated groups in towns and cities throughout Italy. Similar institutions were established in other parts of Europe, including the Sklavenkassen of Hamburg and Lubeck and the Monte della Redenzione of Malta.

In Venice the redemption of slaves was overseen by a government board of three noblemen, the Magistratura sopra gli Ospidali e Luoghi Pii. Besides coordinating the liberation of Venetian captives, their duties also included publicizing the plight of slaves by placing donation boxes in Venetian churches and encouraging preachers to mention them in their sermons (this was also done in Spain). In addition to this state agency, a lay confraternity was established in the church of Santa Maria Formosa in 1604 "to benefit the souls of and to help the poor and unhappy slaves."

These institutions were all charged with redeeming slaves in Muslim hands. They were responsible for raising funds to purchase slaves' freedom and for the logistics of securing their liberty. Oftentimes families were expected to supplement institutional funds before a slave could be liberated. There was a hierarchy that redeemers relied on to decide whom to liberate. First in line were slaves who were citizens or subjects or had been taken in the service of the city or state they represented. Women and children were to be liberated before men, as they were considered more likely either to be dishonored sexually or to convert to Islam if they remained in servitude for too long.

Roman Catholics were not the only captives in the Mediterranean: Protestants, Orthodox, and Jews were also enslaved. For example, many Jewish slaves were held in Malta—in the mid-seventeenth century there were at least 220—and they were required to wear a yellow badge on their caps. In response to this situation, Jews in Livorno, following their duty to free coreligionists held in captivity, established their own confraternity for the redemption of slaves.

While most scholarship has focused on the liberation of Christian slaves of Muslim masters, redemption was also a concern in the Islamic world. Freeing enslaved Muslims whose faith and virtue might be in danger was a religious duty required of all believers, but especially Muslim potentates. It was considered a pious act to liberate a slave: a hadith holds that the deliverer of a Muslim captive from Christian hands would be spared the fires of hell. In contrast to Christian practices, however, there were no institutions devoted specifically to the redemption of Muslim slaves; instead, the issue was confronted in a more piecemeal fashion. In Algeria, for example, the Deys were concerned about the number and condition of their enslaved subjects. The matter was confronted through diplomatic missions, correspondence with Christian rulers and envoys, and in treaties signed with Christian powers, all directed toward improving the conditions of Algerian slaves and arranging their repatriation.

Ottoman sultans also intervened to free their enslaved subjects. The release of individuals captured during seventeenth- and eighteenth-century hostilities was usually built into the treaties that ended these conflicts. The women of the harem were also involved in redeeming Muslim slaves who often, though not always, belonged to influential families. For instance, encouraged by the harem women, Murad III refused to renew France's capitulations until two Ottoman girls who had been captured, converted, married, and had become ladies-in-waiting to Catherine de' Medici were released. The Ottomans also tended to favor slave exchanges over purchases, as in the 1590 trade of 29 Muslim slaves in Malta for six knights of the order. Non-officials, such as Sufi merchants, also became involved in slave redemptions. Pious bequests and income from waqf charitable trusts provided funds to pay for the redemption of enslaved Muslims, and alms to free slaves were collected in mosques.

In many instances it was the slaves themselves who negotiated and financed their own liberation, paid for with funds they had been able to earn and save over the years. Friends and family members also might treat and pay for the release of enslaved relatives. In these instances, freelance brokers and other intermediaries were often retained to negotiate the release. Many Jewish merchants were involved in this activity, often working on commission of perhaps 15% of the total ransom.

Redemption efforts had the unintended effect of incentivizing slave taking, creating an "economy of ransom" that represented a profitable element of the early modern Mediterranean financial system. The price to purchase freedom depended on supply and demand and the status of the slave; in the seventeenth century it ranged from 100 to 350 scudi. Because of the serious labor shortages that most Mediterranean fleets regularly faced, naval forces were often reluctant to free galley slaves unless they were old or sick. In the case of domestic slaves, manumission was somewhat more common. Islam viewed slavery as a temporary state; thus, the freeing of slaves was encouraged as an act of charity. The Islamic system of limited service contracts allowed slaves to work independently and keep their earnings so as to be able to ransom themselves after a contractually determined period. Many urban craftsmen retained slaves on these terms. While they might occasionally manumit Muslim captives, Christians seem to have been on the whole less likely to free their slaves.

CORSAIRS

Intertwined with slavery, and indeed inseparable from it, was the activity of the region's many pirates and corsairs. Corsairs (or privateers) acted under the auspices and authorization, if not always the direct control, of a political entity. Pirates (or freebooters) acted independently and outside all political authority and controls, though the distinction between the two was often hazy as corsairs could act as pirates and vice versa as opportunity permitted. More legitimate military actors also often operated opportunistically in ways indistinguishable from pirates and corsairs, which was considered part of the "tradition of the sea." As Fernand Braudel described it, piracy in whatever form was quite simply "another form of aggression, preying on men, ships, towns, villages, flocks; it meant eating the food of others in order to remain strong."

The period of the late sixteenth and seventeenth centuries was the "Age of the Corsair" in the Mediterranean, and part of a wider, global phenomenon of piracy. The most intense period of corsair activity (called the *corso* by contemporaries) was from 1580 to 1620, arising at least initially in response to the relative vacuum of naval power that occurred in the aftermath of Lepanto, when the Habsburg-Ottoman rivalry cooled and the rulers of both empires shifted their attention from the Mediterranean. Pirates from the Balkans and corsairs from Livorno and Malta took advantage of this situation to flood the eastern Mediterranean. Following a military uprising in Tunisia in 1591, the Ottoman Porte adopted a decentralized method of rule over the three Maghreb provinces of Tripoli, Tunis, and Algiers, which were each granted the status of a privileged province, or regency. They were allowed to maintain their own fleets and exempted from remitting any of their revenues to Istanbul, in return for waging corso against Christian enemies of the sultan and providing galleys for his occasional naval campaigns. After 1700, corsair activity tapered off dramatically in the Mediterranean, though it endured in a diminished state into the first decade of the nineteenth century.

The great centers of the early modern corso were the same as its centers of slavery: Malta, Livorno, Algiers, Tunis, Tripoli, and Salé. Of these, Algiers was perhaps the most infamous. The city's existence and growth were directly tied to the corso: it grew from 20,000 to 50,000 or more inhabitants over the course of the sixteenth century, with slaves totaling perhaps 15,000 in 1600. As much as 25% of the economically active population of Algiers may have been involved in corsairing at its height. The scale of Algerian activity is also evident in the expansion of its fleet: in 1580 there were 60 ships of various sizes involved in the corso; by 1620 there were over 100. During the heyday of corsairing, Algiers was a cosmopolitan center that attracted migrants, both forced and voluntary, from throughout the Mediterranean and Europe, including several thousand Jews and many Moriscos, following their expulsion from Spain. The corsairs themselves were a diverse lot; in 1588, for instance, 19 of 34 corsair captains in Algeria were renegades. Most came from the Mediterranean, but many came from farther afield as well, such as the Dutch renegade Simon Danser, who was the most famous Algerian corsair at the end of the sixteenth century.

Corsairing was not, of course, strictly a Muslim activity. Christians were actively engaged as well, though this is an often less acknowledged aspect of the story. The predominant Christian corsairs during the early modern period were the Knights of St. John of the Order of Malta, and the Knights of St. Stephen, based in Livorno, though the naval forces of most Italian states were also actively involved, as were the French and Spanish. The Order of St. Stephen was founded in 1562 by Cosimo I de' Medici, duke of Florence, supported by the papacy, and quickly became feared for its knights' exploits, so much so that their patron became known as the "terror of the Ottomans, scourge of the Turks, fright of the Moors."

The capital of Christian corsair activity, however, was situated at the crossroads of the Mediterranean on the small island of Malta. The Knights Hospitaller, as they had been known since medieval times, were expelled from Rhodes following the siege of 1522 and were given the island of Malta by Charles V in 1530. There were approximately 500 members who were charged with guarding Christian waters, and they considered corsairing the most effective way to accomplish this duty. Initially their focus was on North Africa, but after Lepanto the knights turned their attention to the eastern Mediterranean. Malta's fleet was relatively small, growing from five galleys in 1596 to eight in 1685. In addition to the official fleet, however, about 14 private corsair entrepreneurs were licensed annually. They paid 10% of their prize to the grand master of the order and divided the remainder among investors, the captain, and the crew. Maltese slaving, both public and private, brought in perhaps 120,000 to 150,000 piastres in the mid-seventeenth century, though it appears that the costs outweighed the income, at least in the case of the Hospitallers.

Piracy was not limited to the great corsair centers of the Mediterranean. In the post-Lepanto period, English pirates increasingly plied the waters of the western Mediterranean and played an important role in the rise of the Barbary regencies of the Maghreb. They also wreaked havoc on the rich shipping in the Levant and the Aegean. Piracy was practiced on a more local scale, too. Small fishing and cargo boats in the coastal waters of Spain, Albania, Sardinia, and the Greek coast and islands moonlighted in occasional acts of petty piracy or harried small-scale shipping in localized areas.

The effect of the corso on Mediterranean life was profound. For the inhabitants of its islands and coastal areas, as well as for merchants and travelers, a culture of fear loomed over the age. In response to this threat large swaths of the Spanish coastline were deserted. Christian corsair raids on North Africa grew so common that people inhabiting coastal areas lived in "perpetual dread" of being captured. The psychological impact of the combination of corsairing and captivity is suggested by an Arabic poem composed in the wake of an attack on the coast of Morocco that enslaved over 5,000 people: "Mothers were separated from their children, and husband from wife / Their tears streamed down their cheeks, for the loss of those they loved / The veil was taken away from the virgin, revealing all her beauty and charm / And the enemy stared at her beauty, while her tears accompanied her moans."

Political officials tried different methods to cut into corsair activities. During the reign of Philip III, walls were constructed along the Spanish coast and fleets were organized to defend exposed or vital areas. In Spain, Italy, and Malta, authorities erected watchtowers and other defensive structures to protect defenseless coastal populations from slaving raids. The Spanish viceroys constructed over 500 such towers along the coasts and islands of southern Italy, including 137, or one approximately every 5 miles, in Sicily. For their part, the Ottomans attempted to protect the islands of the Aegean and the coasts of the Morea with regular patrols of vessels from its fleet.

The impact of corsairs on Mediterranean shipping and commerce was far-reaching: between 1606 and 1609, Algerian corsairs captured 466 English and Scottish ships, over 100 Dutch ships between 1618 and 1620, and 80 French merchant vessels from 1628 to 1634. Braudel estimated that in the period 1592–1609 on average 138 to 166 vessels were captured annually, divided equally between Muslim and Christian pirates and corsairs. In 1605 a single ship loaded with spices that was captured while traveling from Alexandria yielded spoils valued at 150,000 crowns. Scholars have pointed to the extensive corsair activity of the era not only as proof of the ongoing vibrancy of Mediterranean trade—where there are no merchants, there are no corsairs—but also as a reaction to losses caused by the growing commercial ascendancy of northern Europe.

The fundamental character of the Mediterranean's "corsairing industry" was economic. Corsairs were violent adventurers, but they were also entrepreneurs. This is evident in the case of Tunis. In contrast to Algiers, where corsairing was a state monopoly, in Tunis the corsair economy was a complex system involving multiple actors—ship captains, ship owners, crews, local businessmen who supplied the fleet, and the state. The commodities they dealt in included the ships themselves, the merchandise they carried, and especially the slaves they captured, who could be sold or redeemed. The spoils of the corso produced power, wealth, and social status among many of its participants, not the least the regency's deys, who took a 10% cut of all booty. In Tunis corsair wealth could be seen in the architecture of its newly constructed opulent palaces, the lavish lifestyle of their owners, and the city's cosmopolitan milieu.

While an important component of the economy, corsairing never fully eclipsed trade in the regencies, and as the former contracted in the later seventeenth century, the latter expanded in terms of both goods shipped within the empire and grain carried to France, England, and other European states. There is growing evidence that agriculture and handicrafts were more important elements of the economies of the chief corsair centers than piracy and slave trading, and that interactions between the Barbary regencies and their Christian neighbors to the north were characterized more often by commerce than conflict.

Although it has been commonplace to see corsairing as part of a broader unholy war between Islam and Christianity, the reality was much more complex. Christians regularly preyed on other Christians: Orthodox were captured by Latin-rite corsairs who justified their actions with flimsy accusations that their coreligionists collaborated with Muslim merchants and officials. Venetian and French corsairs looted Christian ships and assaulted the coasts of Naples and Sicily, and Christians, particularly in Calabria, served as guides for Muslim corsairs who enslaved their neighbors as a means of carrying out vendetta. Similarly, Muslims enslaved individuals from groups perceived as apostate or "bad" Muslims, such as during the Ottoman-Safavid hostilities, when Iranian Shia were classed as non-Muslims and enslaved in large numbers by Sunni Ottomans. Black Muslims from the Sudan, whose transition to and embrace of Islam were considered incomplete and therefore suspect, were often enslaved by fellow Muslims as well.

RENEGADES

Closely linked to the epidemic of corsairing and slavery in the early modern Mediterranean was the phenomenon of the renegades. For contemporaries, a renegade was an individual who had "rebelled against the faith" and embraced a new religious community. The period from 1500 to 1650 was the golden age of the renegade: in 1496 the German traveler Arnold von Harff reported that the Mamluk sultans of Egypt had 15,000 renegades in their service, and a century later, Diego de Häedo estimated that renegades constituted almost half of Algiers's population of 50,000. While such figures are clearly impressionistic, most scholars agree that the "hemorrhage" of women and men from Christianity in this period numbered into the hundreds of thousands. As we have seen, there were also many Muslims and Jews who converted to Christianity, particularly in Spain, but in other areas as well, albeit on a smaller scale.

The majority of Christian renegades came from throughout the Mediterranean, especially the Balkans, the Greek islands, and the Iberian and Italian peninsulas; many, however, came from more distant lands: a 1612 publication mentioned English, Dutch, Scandinavian, Russian, Bulgarian, and German renegades, among many others in Algiers. Men outnumbered women. More renegades came from lower socioeconomic strata, but nobles, wealthy merchants, skilled artisans, lawyers, engineers, and important political and military leaders converted as well.

Conversion and slavery were closely linked: in Algiers between 1609 and 1619, a quarter of the 8,000 slaves taken, "despairing of liberty," converted to Islam. The most common justification for conversion made by renegades seeking readmittance to their birth communities of faith was, as Paul Rycaut described, the "menaces and fear" to which they were subjected. Penitents who appeared before the region's inquisitions almost universally claimed that their conversions had been coerced with violence, and that to preserve their lives they had converted outwardly, though they insisted that they had preserved their true religious faith within their hearts. Christian, Muslim, and Jewish authorities all considered masking inner belief with outward profession and practice as an acceptable response to the dangers of the age. In Islam this was called *taqiyya*; in Christianity, nicodemism. Individuals who claimed coercion were almost always welcomed back into their birth faith with minimal inquiry or penance.

The question of coerced conversions is a fraught one. Both Muslim and Christian scripture and tradition inveighed against the practice; indeed, the Qur'an famously states there should be "no compulsion in religion." However, such conversions did occur. In the Ottoman Empire, the primary source of involuntary conversions was the devshirme. Occasionally, sultans pursued policies that encouraged conversion, but a solid body of evidence has demonstrated that such conversions were quite uncommon in general, despite deeply held traditions to the contrary in Balkan areas formerly under Ottoman rule. Coerced conversions were in fact more common in Christian lands: the most notable instances were those of the hundreds of thousands of Muslim and Jewish subjects of the Spanish crown. In a parallel example from the same time period, and motivated by a similar objective of using religious homogeneity to assert power over the new Safavid state, Shah Ismail I decreed Shia Islam the state religion and compelled all Persians and Sunni clerics in his realm to embrace Shiism. Over the course of the next two centuries, his heirs proved willing to use violence against Sunni, Christian, and Jew to achieve this end.

In reality, many, probably most, conversions were voluntary. Some individuals converted to escape personal complications, to start a new life, or simply in search of adventure. Cynical Christians believed that men converted because of fevered expectations of an exotic, permissive Muslim sexual world of "harems, odalisques, eunuchs, and sodomy." Other converts to Islam were driven by socioeconomic considerations: contemporaries believed that the Ottoman world opened opportunities for social advancement, regardless of one's birth. Many converts were merchants, artisans, and sailors, drawn especially to Ottoman urban centers looking to improve their financial circumstances. Not surprisingly, times of extreme economic crisis and political turmoil saw increases in conversions.

Individual conversions were the norm, but larger groups occasionally converted en masse. Five entire Maronite villages in Syria converted to Islam collectively, and as did two groups totaling 1,400 men, women, and children from Cosenza in Calabria. This latter episode was inspired by the people's inability "to tolerate the government of the Spanish in those parts." And in perhaps the most curious case of group conversion, on Chios some 300 Christians publicly embraced Islam, with the approval of their Jesuit pastors, though in secret they continued to live as Christians. Given the prominence of dissimulation, crypto-Muslim and Christian groups and individuals were not uncommon. Another well-known instance of group conversion was that of a group of 200 French mercenaries defending a Habsburg frontier garrison in Hungary, who defected collectively in 1600, in part because their pay was months in arrears. Military defections were not uncommon, in fact: many soldiers in Spain's Algerian citadels of Oran and Mers el-Kébir fled to the lands of Islamic rulers because of debts, poverty, hunger, boredom, isolation, and the general rigors and discipline of military life. A Seville court found that in a 12-year span, some 500 soldiers had fled the forts due to their "extreme penuriousness." Some abandoned their outposts as a calculated gambit: as Ottoman soldiers, they could earn enough to pay off debts and return to Iberia, where they could obtain absolution from the inquisition, rather than serving their sentences in Spain's frontier fortresses. Others fled in the hope that as slaves they might be liberated by the redemptionist orders.

Muslim conversions to Christianity, while significantly less frequent, were not unknown. Ottoman merchants trading in Venice sometimes converted and claimed their principals' goods. In one case that attracted significant attention, the beglerbeg (governor) of Syria converted in fear after a protracted confrontation with the grand vizier. Muslim slaves on Christian galleys and slave women in domestic settings were prime sources of converts. Group conversions from Islam to Christianity were not unknown either: in the sixteenth century, 70 janissaries and their families fled to Crete and converted.

There are also many examples of intrareligious conversions: after the Ottoman conquest of the Balkans, many Roman Catholics converted to Orthodoxy because of its favored status in the empire. Latin-rite missionary orders proselytized extensively among Christians in Lebanon, Syria, and Egypt, with some success. The conversions of these eastern Christians had much in common with conversions to Islam: the converts were often in difficult familial, social, or economic situations, and conversion presented a means to escape. Movement between Muslim sects occurred as well: in one instance, a Persian ambassador to Istanbul renounced Shiism in favor of the Ottomans' Sunnism. The Safavid rulers of Iran also sent missionaries to proselytize Sunni Ottomans.

Because conversion was so common in the early modern Mediterranean, there was widespread suspicion of renegades, as indeed there often was of other nonconformists and individuals who did not easily fit into established religious categories. The English traveler Thomas Sherley described renegades as "for the most parte roagues, & the skumme of people, . . . villanes and atheists," while an Ottoman official said of renegades, "A pig still remains a pig, even if they do cut off its tail." Jews similarly suspected the motivations of converts, as suggested by the saying, "Beware of Proselytes to the tenth Generation."

Although practical economic, social, and political catalysts for conversion were common, we should not overlook religious conversions that originated not in some profound spiritual transformation but rather in embracing a new set of ritual and cultural practices. Conviction, if it occurred, followed later and grew out of a process of socialization and communal engagement. This is evident in the examples of renegades who resisted attempts to coerce them into returning to their birth faiths. One convert, who was recaptured by Christians and refused to reconcile, described himself as initially having accepted Islam without reflection, but having gradually come to embrace his new faith as he acquired "a true knowledge" of it. His wish was that God would allow his "last hour to be spent in the same faith." In another instance an Irish renegade was captured by Christian corsairs and enslaved on Spanish and French galleys for 30 years before being redeemed and returning to Algiers. He was viewed by his fellow Muslims as "a very pious man and a great zealot" for having resisted tremendous pressure to abandon Islam. He declared that "God had delivered him out of a hell upon earth" in Christendom and had returned him to an Islamic "heaven upon earth." In yet another instance, Francisco Cola Sapon, who lived as a Muslim for 25 years, during his appearance before the inquisition in Sicily mocked holy images, refused to confess because he considered priests "deceivers-of-the-world," and declared that "the sect of the Turks was better than that of the Christians, [and] that Muhammad was a saint."

As the examples of the renegades suggest, the religious world of the early modern Mediterranean was malleable and nuanced, and less monolithic and antagonistic than has often been depicted. Recent scholarship has identified widespread evidence from throughout the region of the much more fluid and interconfessional character of religious belief and practice among the sea's diverse communities of Jews, Muslims, and Christians.

The long-neglected work of F. W. Hasluck, published in the early twentieth century, was precocious in this area. He showed that Muslims and Christians shared devotion to many urban and rural sanctuaries and cult sites that were "transferred from Christianity to Islam." For instance, the Orthodox monastery of Mileševa in Serbia attracted Muslim and Jewish pilgrims who often offered more alms than their Christian counterparts. In Istanbul the Latin-rite church of San Antonio Abbate attracted "a universal and indistinct crowd" of all sects, drawn by its purported healing powers. Muslims regularly slept in the church, washed in and drank the holy waters of its well, brought offerings to the monks, listened to their preaching, and received blessings from them, all in the hope of being made well. When such healings occurred, word spread rapidly, solidifying the church's miraculous reputation throughout the city. In Lebanon, Christians and Muslims similarly slept in a protected spot on Mount Carmel in the belief that doing so they would be cured. Muslims, Druzes, Jews, and Christians of various sects also slept in the grotto of St. Elie al-Khadir, sacrificed goats, and were watched over by a saint's statue.

Everyday cultic activities often transcended religious frontiers as well. In Bulgaria, for example, Muslims observed Christian rituals, revered Christian saints, carved the cross on their bread and displayed it on their door frames, and kept holy water obtained from village priests. Bosnian Muslims similarly embraced Christian festivals and saints and incorporated Islamic, Christian, and pagan elements into their birth and wedding rituals. Muslims regularly baptized their infants, in the belief that it would protect them against leprosy, and because they assumed it must possess some value, "otherwise it would never have been instituted." This appropriation is evident in the case of a Muslim woman healed by a Catholic priest. Her coreligionists justified her receiving these blessings, saying that the saint fulfilled their prayers "because he had been a Muslim, . . . and had believed in Muhammad."

Intra-Christian theological divisions between Latin-rite and Orthodox were similarly imprecise; indeed, ecclesiastical officials reported that "simple people" could not comprehend the differences between them. On Corfu people attended services indiscriminately and confessed and paid alms to clergy from both sects. On Naxos the island's Orthodox inhabitants participated in Corpus Christi solemnities at the Latin-rite cathedral and paved the roads around it with their prostrate bodies so that the Roman Catholic archbishop's feet never touched the ground. The motivation was the belief that in doing so they might avoid death or other trials in the coming year. In Spain, Christian religious practice was a "free mixture" of tradition, superstition, and imprecise dogma, which provided "an immense range of cultural and devotional options." Muslims and Christians shared popular beliefs in Bible tales, "demons and angels, heaven and hell," and women from both religions joined in venerating Mary.

Scholars have similarly shown that millenarian expectations of religious renewal were broadly shared among Muslim, Christian, and Jewish communities across the medieval and early modern Mediterranean. These collective concerns intensified following the conquest of Constantinople, and in the sixteenth century apocalyptic expectations reached a high point. Süleyman the Magnificent was identified by many as the Mahdi, or rightly guided one, who would initiate an Islamic religious revival and return peace and justice to a world in chaos. After becoming Holy Roman emperor in 1519, Charles V was in similar fashion seen as fulfilling prophecies of a Christian "world emperor," who would be the savior and redeemer of Christendom against its various internal and external enemies.

A final aspect of this fluid religious world was the widely held popular belief that the differences between the Mediterranean's religions were fundamentally insignificant. As the Spanish converso Juan del Prado asserted, "All men are entitled to redemption, each in virtue of his own religion—Jew, Muslim, and Christian are entitled to eternal happiness." Menocchio, the miller from Carlo Ginzburg's well-known history *The Cheese and the Worms*, argued before the inquisition that ultimately took his life, that "God has given the Holy Spirit to all, to Christians, to Turks, and to Jews; and he considers them all dear, and they are all saved in the same manner." In the Granada countryside in the 1620s, a woman of Muslim origin similarly stated that a "Muslim can be saved in his faith as the Jew can in his."

This view was widely shared, and it was accompanied by significant imprecision and a basic unawareness of theological differences between faith traditions; in fact, observers regularly commented on the "confused Notions and Precepts of Religion" throughout the region. For instance, a Jewish woman made the confused claim that "Jesus Christ was the same person as Moses, son of Queen Esther." Another common notion was that of a Catalan peasant, who asserted that "there is no heaven, purgatory, or hell; at the end we all have to end up in the same place; the bad will go to the same place as the good and the good will go to the same place as the bad." Yet another declared that "he does not believe in heaven or hell, and God feeds the Muslims and heretics just the same as he feeds the Christians."

Ecclesiastical leaders of all stripes struggled at times to negotiate and manage this fluid reality. The distinct divisions that scholars and theologians, both Christian and Muslim, drew between their respective faiths were much more flexible in practice and overlapped in the minds of the masses. Saints could be venerated as Christian or their religious identity adapted to popular beliefs, and in either case divine favor might be obtained. This imprecision, even indifference, about distinctions between religious communities, distinctions that have often been asserted to be the essence of premodern identities, underlines again the ever-shifting nature of life on the frontiers of the early modern Mediterranean.

CHAPTER ELEVEN

Mediterranean Transformations

In 1581, while posted to the Kurdish city of Van in the far eastern reaches of the Ottoman Empire, Mustafa Ali Gelibolulu, an important bureaucrat and intellectual, began composing one of his most influential works, a treatise entitled *Counsel for Sultans*. In it he argued that the once mighty Ottoman state had deviated from the practices that were the foundation of its greatness and had been enfeebled by the venality and ignorance of its ruling elite, who were negligent in their administration of the empire. Ali also daringly chided the sultan himself, decrying his failure to supervise his officials and to maintain control over the empire while living "isolated behind a curtain."

Ali's work was widely imitated and enjoyed a long popularity among Ottoman intellectuals; indeed, it was the first example of the *nasihatname*, a genre of advice literature influenced by the traditional Islamic "mirror for princes." Nasihatname writers suggested both causes and remedies for what they perceived as key factors in the decline of the Ottoman state from its apex during the reign of Süleyman the Magnificent. Seventeenth-century writers such as Koçu Bey (known as the Ottoman Montesquieu for his sharp analysis) or Katip Çelebi pointed to weak and distant rulers, overly strong viziers, and the increased role of women in the rule of the empire as evidence of encroaching Ottoman weakness. Ali and his intellectual progeny had a deep impact on modern historiography as well, as scholars long accepted at face value their vision of Ottoman decline. In many ways these Ottoman observers have their intellectual doppelgängers in Spain's *arbitristas*, political writers such as Fernández de Navarrete and Lope de Deza who in the same period began addressing what they perceived as Spain's economic, political, and moral decline from an earlier, vaguely defined, and much-debated "Golden Age."

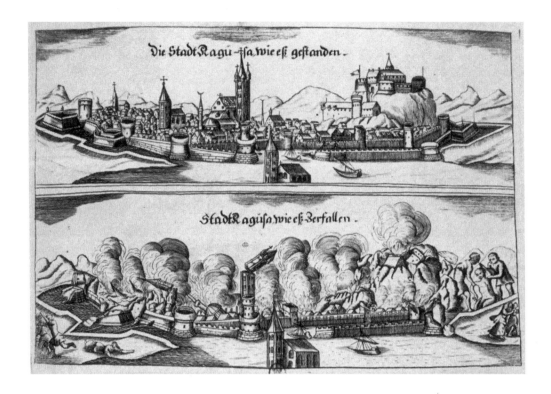

Die Stadt Ragu-sa wie eß geftanden.

Stadt Ragusa wie eß Zerfallen.

Ragusa (Dubrovnik) before and after the earthquake of 1667. From a copper engraving, Germany, c. 1667. National Information Service for Earthquake Engineering, PEER-NISEE, University of California, Berkeley

In many ways contemporary scholars have appropriated these Spanish and Ottoman critics' portrayal of this period, particularly the "long" seventeenth century (approximately 1590–1715), as an era of crisis. Since the 1950s historians have described the age as a time of marked global instability, characterized by economic turmoil, social revolt, political upheaval, subsistence shortfalls, endemic warfare, and military transformation; more recently they have added significant climatic change to the list of the age's woes. In the Mediterranean, according to this narrative, the era was one of widespread decline in almost every meaningful sector: Venice's economy contracted due to the collapse of the spice trade; weak rulers deviated the Ottoman Empire from its classical political structures and expansionist policy and set it on the path to becoming the sick man of Europe; and Spain wavered politically and economically because of its inability to adapt to changing global conditions and to the weight of its massive empire.

The reality in such a richly diverse region is, not surprisingly, a great deal more complex than this narrative of decline permits. Mediterranean polities and people made serious attempts to adapt to the challenges and opportunities that they faced in a variety of innovative ways. Because we know that ultimately the center of power shifted north and west, toward the Atlantic, we need to be cautious in not projecting this transformation backward. While the Mediterranean underwent significant and deep

THE MEDITERRANEAN WORLD

transformations, we should not ignore the very tangible ways it remained a vibrant, adaptive region for much of the early modern period.

THE ENVIRONMENT

While it is problematic to generalize global climatic trends, there is now ample evidence that the early modern centuries were generally cooler. The so-called Little Ice Age that began in the 1560s was intensified following the eruption of Mt. Huaynaputina in Peru in 1600. This cooling trend endured until 1710, with the period after 1680 characterized by extreme cold in many areas, with attendant harvest failures and famine.

This general global trend had significant implications for the early modern Mediterranean. Crete, for example, between 1548 and 1648 experienced 25 years of drought and 21 years of exceptional winters marked by intense cold, excessive rain, and even snow, which delayed planting until the late spring. These extremes hurt grain, grape, and olive harvests, as well as animal herds. The Ottoman Empire was especially hard hit by climate-related changes, including recurring harsh winters, spring droughts, and attendant harvest failures and shortages. The 1590s saw the worst drought in the Mediterranean in 600 years, which was accompanied by a severe outbreak of disease that killed large numbers of sheep and cattle in the Balkans and Anatolia. These environmental challenges were exacerbated by demographic pressure caused by the doubling of the empire's population over the course of the sixteenth century.

Natural disasters also took their toll. Ragusa experienced over a half dozen significant earthquakes in this period, the most destructive of which destroyed much of the city in 1667, killing perhaps a third of its population and devastating the city's already straitened economic fortunes. In Sicily in 1693 "an earthquake so horrible and ghastly that the soil undulated like the waves of a stormy sea, and the mountains danced as if drunk" destroyed the city of Noto and "in one miserable moment kill[ed] more than a thousand people." Cities and towns stretching from Messina in the east to Palermo in the west were seriously damaged; many were rebuilt in the eighteenth century in stunning late-baroque style. Volcanic activity also surged in this period: after a long silence, Vesuvius erupted in 1631, with half a dozen subsequent eruptions before 1800.

Natural disruptions were accentuated by human activity. The issue of deforestation, for instance, has been much debated by scholars. It was long argued that shipbuilding, construction, and other overuse led to widespread deforestation in the Mediterranean. In the case of Venice, however, recent research has shown that officials aggressively preserved forests on the Italian mainland to provide raw materials for the city's nautical needs. The French instituted similar state management of forests in the mid-sixteenth century. In Spain it was long held that the peninsula's forests were systematically decimated to provide ever-increasing pastureland for Merino sheep. In addition, some scholars have argued that the Spanish had a "proverbial hatred of trees" that led to indifference and the failure to establish policies of preservation or reforestation. In fact, royal forest protection ordinances reached a high point in the sixteenth century under Charles V and Philip II, who has been described as "one of the first ecological rulers," though these rules had limited effect until a 1748 naval forest ordinance was passed belatedly. More significant was the cultivation of oak groves that were used in the cork industry and to provide pasture for pigs used to produce Spain's famous cured hams. Northern European naval powers even turned to the Mediterranean for wood supplies in the eighteenth century, which indicates the need for a more nuanced understanding of deforestation in the region.

In comparison to the Atlantic and northern Europe, the Mediterranean had fairly limited quantities of another natural resource, fish. Tuna was fished in the Bosporus, Sicily, North Africa, Andalusia, and the Algarve; dried squid and octopus in the Greek archipelago; and sardines and anchovies in Provence. Barrels of salted tuna were regularly shipped up the East African coast from Lagos to the Mediterranean to fulfill demand. Demand for Mediterranean coral grew rapidly in the seventeenth century, which led to the depletion of fisheries along the North African coast by the beginning of the next century. Notions of preservation existed from the Middle Ages in Marseilles, where fishing guilds regulated fishing schedules and grounds, which helped avoid fishery depletion.

One major transformation of the era was the introduction of new crops from the Americas, which had a significant impact on agriculture and diets. Broadly speaking, maize and potatoes were the most important. Maize first appeared in the western Mediterranean in Morocco and Spain in the sixteenth century, then spread to Egypt and Italy and by the early seventeenth century reached the Balkans and Anatolia. It caught on quite rapidly because it was well adapted to the region's dry summers and was easily integrated into the existing irrigation infrastructure. Maize flourished in the Mediterranean's mountainous areas, where it produced significantly higher yields than wheat or barley and made survival somewhat easier. The potato was adopted more slowly and not as widely: it was most popular in Iberia and only made a slight imprint in more arid Morocco and Anatolia.

The impact of maize (and to a lesser extent potatoes) is evident in the Alpujarras region of Spain. By adapting maize cultivation, peasants were able to feed themselves on less arable land than when they depended solely on wheat and barley. This in turn resulted in the abandonment of less-productive higher-altitude fields. By the late eighteenth century maize was the chief crop in some areas, which contributed to population increases as well. In the Rif region of northern Morocco, the seventeenth-century introduction of maize allowed its Berber inhabitants to produce more food, which contributed to demographic growth and in turn led to increased clearing of forest. This process suggests the complex interdependency of environmental factors in the Mediterranean.

In Italy maize cultivation spread rapidly: In the Veneto, it was introduced in the sixteenth century and, in the form of polenta, came to play an important role in peasant diets, particularly during times of famine. Maize was less common in Venice proper, especially on the tables of the rich, who considered it primarily animal fodder. In the seventeenth century it spread to Lombardy, Emilia Romagna, and farther south. By the eighteenth century maize had replaced minor cereals such as sorghum and millet, and in certain areas it had become the primary food source, with a resultant rise in serious vitamin deficiencies and pellagra.

DEMOGRAPHY

While we lack complete demographic data for the early modern Mediterranean as a whole, solid data from some regions provide a broad sense of the situation. These figures are a byproduct of expanding state bureaucracies and allow us a much more complete picture than is possible for earlier centuries. The data show that far from declining, Mediterranean population grew at a dramatic pace in the sixteenth century before stabilizing and holding in the seventeenth and eighteenth centuries. Of course there were significant local variations that complicate this general pattern.

Population in the Mediterranean doubled during the sixteenth century, reaching perhaps 70 million by 1570. Malta's population, for example, rose from 25,000 in 1530 to almost 52,000 by 1632, remained constant throughout the century, then almost doubled again to 91,000 by the end of the eighteenth century. The population of the Ottoman Empire in 1520 was 12–12.5 million; by 1580 it was 30–35 million, with urban growth outstripping rural, in part because of the explosion of Istanbul into one of the largest cities in the world, with over a half a million inhabitants. During the eighteenth century Ottoman population declined, slipping from one-sixth to one-tenth of western Europe's total. On the Barbary Coast, Algiers's population shrank from 125,000 in 1570 (including perhaps 25,000 slaves and 8,000–9,000 Jews) to 100,000 in 1700, before falling to 30,000 by the early nineteenth century.

Nationalist historiography long held that Greek lands under Ottoman rule experienced dramatic depopulation, a result, it was assumed, of the sultans' oppressive rule. In fact quite the opposite was true; many areas, including the Greek mainland and islands, experienced significant growth during Ottoman times. The western Cyclades grew from 532 households in 1570 to 1,300 by 1735, and the population of Kythera (Kíthira) expanded from 1,850 individuals in 1545 to almost 7,500 by the end of the eighteenth century. The same phenomenon is apparent in areas not under Ottoman suzerainty, such as Venetian Crete, where the population soared from 160,000 in 1571 to 287,000 in 1644.

Italy experienced slower demographic growth: by 1500 pre-plague levels had been surpassed, with population totaling perhaps 11 million. That figure reached 12 million by 1600 before dipping to 11 million in the aftermath of the devastating plagues of the early seventeenth century, then surging once again to 13 million by 1700. Many major cities remained at their same population levels or increased slightly. Venice's population, for example, from 1550 to 1800 hovered between

140,000 and 160,000, with occasional spikes and drops, making it consistently the second-largest city in Italy, after Naples, and among the top ten in Europe. Regional cities such as Cremona, Pavia, and Ferrara, however, lost 20–40% of their populations. In Sicily, Palermo and Messina doubled in size in the sixteenth century, and overall population grew by 50% in the eighteenth century, though this growth was focused primarily in urban centers.

Spain presents an altogether different story: its "fewness of people" compared to other regions, particularly its arch rival France, was a cause for ongoing concern. Historians estimate Spain's population at approximately 4.7 million in 1534 and 6.6 million in 1591, followed by a plague-induced dip to 4.5 million in 1631 before rebounding in the early eighteenth century and reaching over 10 million by 1800. In addition to warfare and disease, Spain's expulsion of the Moriscos and conversos certainly had an impact; the over 300,000 Moriscos exiled in the first decade of the seventeenth century represented perhaps 5% of the total population. Spain's aggressive imperial agenda also affected demography, with an average of 4,000 individuals, disproportionately young men, setting out to seek their fortunes in the colonies every year in the sixteenth and seventeenth centuries.

If overall population increased in the early modern period, some areas of the Mediterranean experienced decreases. Corsair activity, for example, had an effect on certain Greek islands and other coastal areas. The Aegean island of Milos faced serious demographic decline in the eighteenth century, in part due to economic challenges brought on by the decline in corsair activity, on which the island's economy had been highly dependent, and in part because of volcanic activity, which gave rise to pulmonary maladies, an increase in swamps, and a shortage of potable water. Migration caused demographic decline in some rural settings, as people moved to more vibrant urban areas. Following the battle of Lepanto, the population of Venetian Dalmatia, the traditional source of many of the sailors in the republic's fleet, declined precipitously, with some villages being completely abandoned. In Spain the increasing burden of taxation to finance burgeoning imperial costs combined with traditional tithes, rents, and fees to create a nearly unbearable situation for rural peasants, which in turn led to an exodus from the countryside. Exploitation of scarce resources also led to the depopulation of Mediterranean mountain regions.

DISEASE AND FAMINE

Closely related to questions of demography and Mediterranean decline is the issue of disease and the role it may have played in the population transformations of this era. The richly diverse ecosystems of the sea, together with its intense networks of interchange, created a situation ripe for the rapid circulation of a diverse array of diseases. Trade, war, and empire were vectors for the spread of disease, thus the Mediterranean, with its links to Africa, Asia, and the Atlantic, was a clearinghouse for maladies of all sorts.

Malaria, for instance, was endemic to many parts of the region, and it ebbed and flowed in response to a complex set of environmental and human factors. The term comes from the Italian *mal aria*, or bad air, and derived from the belief that miasmas from marshes and swamps produced the disease; the actual cause is a parasite transferred by female mosquitoes. Outbreaks could be devastating: in 1602, for example, 40,000 people died from the disease in Italy alone. The era's climate change reduced the impact of malaria in some areas, at least for a time. In other areas, human-influenced environmental degradation partly offset this: in Sicily, for instance, deforestation caused soil erosion, which led to the silting up and disruption of the island's rivers. These conditions produced regular flooding with the attendant expansion of marshlands in previously fertile valleys, which caused a proliferation of mosquitoes and increased outbreaks of malaria. Similarly, on the Ottoman island of Milos the population declined significantly in the eighteenth century due to the spread of malaria caused in part by negligence in maintaining existing water-drainage systems.

Another disease endemic to many parts of the sea was typhus, which is characterized by high fever, delirium, body aches, and rash, and was propagated by lice and fleas that thrived in the squalor of the day. In the Iberian peninsula, typhus, or *tabardillos*, first appeared in the late fifteenth century and caused significant loss of life. In Cuenca it was perhaps the chief cause of high levels of mortality: major outbreaks occurred in 1606, 1631, 1710, 1735, and 1804. Epidemics occurred every few years in Italy as well, often during periods of escalated warfare and their accompanying circulation of soldiers. Smallpox was another disease endemic to the Mediterranean that took many lives, particularly in times of pandemic, such as the outbreak of 1614. Anatolian and Greek peasant women developed the practice of injecting small pieces of smallpox scab into the skin to counter the disease, well before vaccination became general medical practice elsewhere.

Though these and other diseases combined may have caused more deaths, plague remained endemic to the Mediterranean and ravaged it regularly throughout the early modern period. Major outbreaks occurred in Italy in 1575–77 (which wiped out half the population of Messina), in 1629–31, and again in 1656. In Venice over 46,000 died in the 1575–77 outbreak, and approximately the same number perished from July 1630 to October 1631, combined with 24,000 who fled the city on two days in August 1630. Perhaps half the populations of Mantua, Milan, Padua, and Verona died in the 1629–31 plague, which overall cost 1.1 million lives in Italy alone. The great plague of 1656 in Naples killed two-thirds of the city's population, which numbered perhaps 240,000–270,000 people, while an outbreak in Malta in 1675 killed almost 9,000, about 15% of the total population.

In Spain, as in other parts of the Mediterranean, surges in plague were at times localized, such as that in Andalusia in 1676–85, though more widespread outbreaks also occurred, as in the plague of 1596–1602, which killed perhaps a half million people across Spain. The peninsula was spared any serious outbreaks for a generation, until Málaga and Andalusia lost 20,000 people in four months in 1637. The last major visitation of the plague in Spain was in 1678 and was introduced by sailors

VUE DE L'HOSTEL DE VILLE DE MARSEILLE ET D'UNE PARTIE DU PORT

returning from the Algerian city of Oran. In total, perhaps a million Spanish died from the plague in the seventeenth century.

These severe outbreaks notwithstanding, by the seventeenth century the plague's grip on the Mediterranean was loosening somewhat. Possible explanations for why have ranged from the gradual waning of the traditional Eurasian trade routes (though this assumes that plague came only from the east, when in fact there is evidence of reservoirs of the disease throughout the Mediterranean), climate change, and the effectiveness of attempts to control the disease. Political responses predicated on the assumption that people and goods in movement were responsible for the spread of disease did become more systematic in certain parts of the Mediterranean in this period. Venetian officials throughout the *stato da mar*, for example, issued bills of health to ships and travelers that certified that their point of departure was plague-free. These documents eased travel and were necessary to avoid protracted time in one of the growing number of quarantines, or *lazaretti*, in the region.

The first such structure was constructed in 1423 on the small island of Santa Maria di Nazareth in Venice (the name *lazaretto* is a corruption of Nazareth), though the practice of quarantine, if not the actual edifice, had been established previously in Ragusa. Based on contemporary ideas about the nature and spread of the plague, ships arriving from the eastern Mediterranean were impounded for 40 days, scrubbed, and fumigated; the crew and passengers went ashore and were isolated; and the cargo was unloaded and exposed to the sun and fumigated. Over the next centuries the practice spread throughout the Mediterranean to Naples, Corfu, Spalato, Palermo, Valencia, Livorno, Marseilles, Trieste, and Genoa.

Jean Rigaud, *View of the Town Hall and Part of the Port of Marseilles during the Plague Outbreak of 1720. Chateaux de Versailles et de Trianon. © RMN-Grand Palais / Art Resource, NY*

THE MEDITERRANEAN WORLD

As for overland transportation, the Habsburgs' *cordon sanitaire* attempted to achieve the same objective. Established in the eighteenth century, it was a swath 10–20 miles wide and 1,200 miles long that stretched across the Balkans and consisted of a permanent line of sentry posts that attempted to prevent individuals who had not undergone quarantine from entering Habsburg territory. In Venetian Spalato, quarantine was also imposed on overland caravans that arrived in the city from Istanbul.

The construction or expansion of quarantines throughout the early modern period was a response both to growing political will and capacity to control and surveil, but also to expanding commercial activity throughout the region. Quarantines were transnational institutions: just as trade routes, which were the primary vector for the spread of disease, transcended political boundaries, so too health bureaus and quarantines communicated regularly and collaborated extensively to try and prevent the spread of disease.

Quarantine was generally not practiced in predominantly Islamic sectors of the Mediterranean until the establishment of a maritime lazaretto in Tunisia in 1784–85. The Ottomans did not formally implement quarantines until the nineteenth century, and they did not appear in Algeria until after the 1830 French conquest. One exception was Chios, which preserved its pre-Ottoman practice of quarantine following the island's 1566 conquest. The reasons for this reticence have been extensively debated, with explanations ranging from differing Muslim medical views on disease to theological fatalism to the notion that the faithful had a responsibility to care for, not abandon or isolate, the sick.

Although no formal, permanent system was established, Ottomans and Muslims more generally were not fatalistic in accepting disease as the will of Allah. Both imperial and local officials implemented a variety of piecemeal, temporary procedures during disease outbreaks to control its spread. In 1579, for instance, the sultan ordered the governor of Alexandria to prevent merchants and pilgrims from traveling by ship to Istanbul. Similarly, in Trebizond local officials isolated sick individuals, and other walled cities attempted to limit entrance to control the spread of disease.

Beginning in the second half of the sixteenth century the Ottomans instituted initiatives to control and fight plague epidemics, particularly in Istanbul. During outbreaks, deaths were tracked carefully, special burial protocols were instituted, and preventive measures related to urban hygiene and planning were implemented. Regulations were promulgated ordering street cleaning and paving as well as garbage disposal. Similar directives were issued in provincial areas such as Adana and Mecca. Provision of a clean water supply to the capital was also addressed, and the construction of fountains and public baths throughout the city, and indeed the empire, was a common pious act. Numerous hospitals were also established in Istanbul and other parts of the empire as well, and the sixteenth-century creation of a medical school in the great Süleymaniye complex, though the only such institution in the empire, was an important step in formal attempts to provide and regulate medical treatment. The bulk of physicians in the Ottoman Empire, however, and in fact throughout the Mediterranean and Europe, were not trained in medical schools but through apprenticeships with established practitioners.

The budding institutionalized response to disease proved reasonably effective: by the end of the seventeenth century plague outbreaks at least were minimized. In the eighteenth century there were only two major episodes of plague, the most notable in Marseilles in 1720 when the disease spread from the quarantine into the city and killed 60,000 of the 100,000 inhabitants, though it was prevented from spreading farther by the complete isolation of the city for four years by the French crown. We should be cautious, however, in attributing too much significance or success to these efforts as it is quite clear that quarantines were limited in their ability to force compliance and were regularly and widely subverted. Thus, plague outbreaks continued, though on a reduced scale.

Closely related to disease was famine. Hunger preoccupied the collective imagination during the early modern era and was a persistent feature across the Mediterranean. In the last decades of the fifteenth century, over 15% of all harvests in the region failed. Famine was a persistent problem in sixteenth-century Venice and in Bologna, where recurring shortfalls between 1587 and 1595 caused the population to plummet from 72,000 to 59,000. Between 1375 and 1791, Florence experienced 111 years of famine and only 16 "very good" harvests.

Just as with disease, early modern rulers devoted significant resources to ensuring a reliable, sufficient food supply. While these efforts had roots in the Middle Ages, during the early modern period they became increasingly centralized and rationalized. This was motivated by both humane and practical impulses, as hunger was frequently the cause of disorder, particularly bread riots, which were often initiated by women. In sixteenth-century Rome the papacy played a central role in the city's provisioning through the magistracy of the Annona, which administered all aspects of the city's grain supply, from purchase from the farmer to storage in the city's granaries in Trastevere to production by millers and bakers.

The Ottoman Empire had even larger and more complex provisioning institutions, developed to ensure a reliable food supply for the empire, and particularly its massive capital. Distribution was the key issue, as the empire generally produced enough for its needs. The grand vizier was responsible for food supply, and as in Rome, officials oversaw every stage of grain production. Farmers received seed loans, tax rebates, and even tax amnesty in bad years. Officials also controlled exports to ensure that the empire's provisioning needs were met first. They also set and enforced food prices: in Istanbul the chief kadi was charged with this task, as well as patrolling the market and administering fines. Public silos in Istanbul received more than 300 shiploads of barley annually, and a state-administered flour exchange provided for the city's bakers, who were required to keep a month's supply of flour on site.

Besides overseeing the supply of food, particularly bread, another concern of Mediterranean rulers was controlling the export of limited food resources. Despite

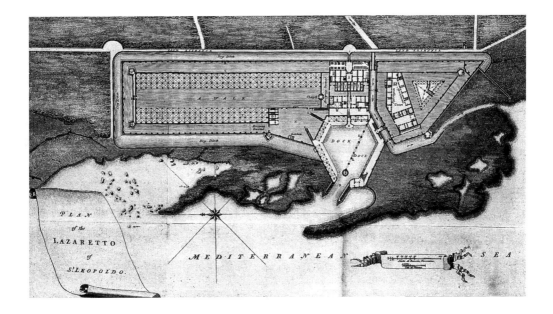

Milan's regular surplus of grain and livestock, the dukes tried to restrict exports by banning markets held along its frontiers, and they constructed an extensive canal system largely to funnel grain produced in the countryside to the center. In Spanish Naples, civic officials limited cereal exports and fixed food prices, but incidents of popular unrest led the crown in 1562 to establish an office, the Grassiero, administered by a crown functionary, to oversee this critical process. In 1555 the Ottomans banned almost all exports of grain and other foodstuffs, though as everywhere in the Mediterranean a massive contraband trade thrived.

ECONOMY

The economic balance sheet of the early modern Mediterranean is quite complicated, not the least because it is difficult to generalize about the sea's diverse parts and polities over such an extended stretch of time. That said, in broad terms the economy experienced a phase of ongoing growth and vibrancy in the sixteenth century, and even into the seventeenth, before entering into a period of significant change. In this latter stage certain sectors of the economy were in retreat, but a broader internal and external perspective reveals a much more dynamic and richly complex situation than is often acknowledged. There is no question that the early modern Mediterranean economy changed dramatically; however, instead of a paradigm of decline, it is more accurate to think of the period as one of adaptation, diversification, and transformation.

For many years it was believed that Mediterranean economic decline

Plan for the lazaretto of San Leopoldo in Livorno. From John Howard, *An Account of the Principal Lazarettos in Europe* (Warrington, 1789). *Wellcome Library, London*

began in the early sixteenth century in response to the rise of the Ottomans, the disruption of the spice trade by the Portuguese, and a commercial shift toward the Atlantic occasioned by the discoveries of Columbus. It is now quite clear that throughout the century the economy remained robust in most sectors. The Mediterranean spice trade revived by midcentury and only really began to ebb in the seventeenth century. In Italy, agriculture, commerce, and industry continued to thrive. Venetian nobles who bought up estates on the mainland, for example, made improvements that turned swampland into arable fields. Institutional landowners in Florence such as the Ospedale Maggiore undertook similar activities. In fact, at the start of the seventeenth century, northern Italy was one of richest and most industrialized areas in the Mediterranean and Europe, and Venice was its most advanced city, a leader in the era's few real industries: textiles, shipbuilding, and glass. Textiles such as Neapolitan silk and Venetian wool reached their highest levels of output after 1600. In Spain the Segovia wool industry went from producing 3,000 cloths annually at the start of the century to 16,000 by its end; Cordoba produced around the same number, making both cities among the top centers of woolen production. Málaga's silk trade expanded substantially, until 1568 when it was disrupted by the revolt and relocation of the Moriscos, while Spanish shipbuilding remained strong into the late seventeenth century.

The first signs of trouble appeared on the horizon at the end of the sixteenth century in some places and by the first decades of the seventeenth in others. It is important to emphasize, however, that the economic troubles that roiled the Mediterranean were part of the much wider global crisis. This was the product of a variety of factors, including environmental changes, agricultural disruptions, demographic decline, and endemic and increasingly costly warfare. Another factor was the massive influx of American silver through Spain, which had begun in the later sixteenth century, and profoundly affected the region. The Ottomans, for example, had confronted silver shortages before but were unprepared (as were other states) to deal with a silver surplus. Thus, the decision in 1584 to devalue the asper by 10% unleashed a severe financial crisis. The empire was flooded by cheap American silver, which crowded out other commodities, and the exchange rate rose from 60 to 200 aspers per Venetian ducat. This economic upheaval in turn produced significant social and political turmoil.

The extent of the economic retreat of the seventeenth century is evident in a variety of sectors. Genoese silk looms declined from 8,000 in 1570 to 2,500 in 1670. In Milan they dropped from 3,000 in 1605 to 600 in 1625, and from 70 wool manufacturers in 1620 to 15 in 1640. In Venice, soap cauldrons fell from 40 to 7, and output from 13 to 2.5 million pounds. In southern Italy, the famous velvet and damask industry of Catanzaro near Naples disappeared completely. Florentine wool producers shrank from 152 in 1561 to 84 in 1616. In Spain, Segovia went from having 600 wool looms in 1580 to 300 by 1650. Silk production in Bursa and wool production in Salonica also experienced significant reductions, though these were more a result of political turmoil caused by the massive Celali popular revolt, which spread throughout Anatolia beginning in the last decade of the sixteenth century and for a time threatened the Ottoman Empire's very existence.

The dominant historical narrative for a long time held that Mediterranean polities and economies were unable, perhaps even unwilling, to respond to the crisis. Yet there are many examples of people and institutions confronting the era's challenges rationally and successfully, such as in Venice. While some Venetian industries were slow to adapt to changing economic conditions, others proved much more flexible. One example is the glass industry: at the end of the sixteenth century 40 furnaces "worked continually day and night" producing large quantities of glass that were exported throughout Europe and the Mediterranean. In the seventeenth and eighteenth centuries, competition within guilds over prices and manufacturing processes produced new strategies, such as shifting from the manufacture of luxury glass to inexpensive glass beads and employing many women workers. These led to a doubling of production. Venice's silk industry also adjusted production techniques, adopting new commercial strategies and employing cheaper female labor.

Another form of innovation was reducing labor costs by shifting production to rural areas, which offered lower wages and less guild regulation, as well as a ready supply of raw materials and natural resources. Ceramic production, for instance, thrived in part because producers moved from traditional centers in Venice and Padua to the foothills of Vicenza and Bassano where raw materials were more readily available. Venice's *terraferma* became a pillar of its economy and was one of the most lively industrial regions in Europe. Northern Italy was a leader in relocating production to rural areas, and the practice eventually spread to the rest of Europe. In Genoa, 80% of silk looms were rural by 1675, and we see similar shifts from urban to rural production in the Ottoman Empire.

Similar adaptability is apparent in Mediterranean wool production. Pastoralism historically had been a vital component of the Mediterranean economy, and this continued during the early modern period. Major producers included Anatolia, southwestern France, southern Italy, the Maghreb, the Balkans, and especially Spain. Wool was Castile's principal export and was managed by La Mesta, the powerful sheep-owners association. It was long held that transhumant herding impeded Spanish economic development, though now it is recognized that it was ideally adapted to the Iberian environment and ultimately beneficial to Spain's economy, and that agriculture and manufacturing were not elbowed out by herding's success.

Like other sectors of the economy during the seventeenth century, Spanish wool production dropped significantly from its sixteenth-century high of 3,000 tons annually before rebounding after 1670. By the eighteenth century, Castile alone was exporting some 5,000 tons of fine raw wool annually. This had a ripple effect to other industries linked to wool production in Spain and elsewhere in the Mediterranean. In fact, although Mediterranean woolen industries were especially hard hit in the economic downturn, demand remained strong among regional textile producers in Florence and Venice, Provence, and Salonica; in the carpet industry in Syria, Anatolia, and Iraq; and among hand-loom weavers in northern Europe through much of the eighteenth century. We see an almost identical pattern in another important wool-producing region, Naples, which raised 1–4 million sheep annually.

International trade remained a central—indeed, emblematic—component of the Mediterranean economy during the early modern era. Although there were significant changes to the commercial landscape in the period, and ultimately the center of trade shifted to the Atlantic, we should neither exaggerate nor telescope this process. In the case of Spain, for instance, there is the notion of the "treason of the bourgeoisie," which holds that Spanish merchants abandoned entrepreneurial values for aristocratic ones and invested in land so as to join the aristocracy. There is no question that merchants did change their business models; however, these were rational, profit-maximizing decisions in response to changing economic realities. In the seventeenth century, commerce along Spain's Mediterranean coast increased substantially in response to blossoming trade with France, and the ports and cities in the region experienced significant growth, particularly Barcelona, which expanded from 30,000 inhabitants in 1717 to 100,000 in 1818. While regional trade was an important component of their commerce, Catalan merchants also engaged in trade with the Americas, Italy, France, and Russia. Exports of Málaga wine and raisins increased over 100% in the first decades of the eighteenth century, evidence of the rapid expansion of export-oriented agriculture and trade. Mallorca similarly exported large quantities of olive oil.

In Venice a similar narrative developed, equating the sapping of the empire's vitality with a turn away from Mediterranean commerce. Historically, international trade, particularly with the Levant, was the foundation of Venetian wealth and power and was monopolized by the ruling elite. Beginning in the fifteenth century, however, Venice's patricians began shifting from maritime trade to land investments on the Italian terraferma. Contemporaries worried that this shift was destroying the maritime foundations of Venetian wealth and its patricians' very identity. Around 1500, Girolamo Priuli described the mainland as "a malignant tumor sucking the maritime vitality that had made Venice great," and subsequent historical analyses often located Venetian decline in this same process. While overall international commerce experienced a reduction during the sixteenth century and Venice lost the monopoly over the east-west trade it had enjoyed in the fifteenth century, advances in other areas of the economy made up for the loss, and this adjustment represents not the abandonment of some essential Venetian commercial character but rather an example of rational, and ultimately successful, diversification. Another aspect of Venice's adaptation was the gradual shift of its port away from international to regional trade, a trend mirrored in other Mediterranean ports.

Venice's experience suggests that historians should avoid privileging international trade over regional commerce when evaluating long-term commercial changes. In much of the Ottoman Empire, for example, while merchants participated consistently and successfully in international trade throughout the early modern period, the primary focus of the Ottoman market was imperial and internal. The objective was to ensure that the empire, and in particular the capital, was provided with necessary, basic commodities and that the military was well equipped. Exports had the potential to deprive the command economy of needed goods, resulting in higher prices and potential social unrest and political instability. Thus, internal needs dictated policy while international trade remained ancillary, and the Ottoman system of centralized provisioning functioned remarkably well. Another aspect of this command economy was price controls imposed by the kadis on commodities such as olive oil, grain, cheese, flax, silk, and animal skins to ensure they were available at reasonable prices.

The nature of the Ottoman imperial economy is evident in Egypt and Syria, both of which allegedly experienced a severe decline as a result of the Ottoman conquest and the expansion of northern European trade in the region. In fact the incorporation of these two rich regions into the empire's vast internal market and the introduction of imperial administrative structures and personnel functioned as a catalyst for a commercial boom that began in the sixteenth century. Both benefited from the rapid growth of coffee consumption in the empire and its eventual spread into Europe. In Egypt around 1700, commerce with the east represented 36% of all trade, intra-imperial trade 50%, and trade with Europe just 14%. Western economic domination began only after 1750, when this internal imperial market was penetrated and compromised. Similarly, after Tunisia's entry into the Ottoman sphere of influence, in 1574, red woolen caps produced by local artisans began to be exported throughout the empire in large numbers, which continued into the nineteenth century.

A key aspect of the changing face of the Mediterranean economy was the appearance of new commercial competitors. France, in 1536, England, in 1581, and finally the Netherlands, in 1612, were all granted limited reciprocal commercial privileges, known as capitulations, by the Ottoman sultans, guaranteeing them favorable trade conditions throughout the empire. These were part of an ongoing attempt by the Ottomans to weaken the Venetian hold on Mediterranean trade, and they proved quite successful. Over the course of the latter quarter of the sixteenth century and the first half of the seventeenth, these new competitors conquered much of the Mediterranean trade in traditional products through aggressive marketing practices and the introduction of new products and markets. By 1636, England possessed 40% of the Levantine trade, the French 26%, the Dutch 8%, and Venice a still respectable but much diminished 26%.

English merchants initially traded light, cheap cloth worn by the poor, called kersey, which did not compete directly with high-quality Venetian cloth. In the seventeenth century, however, the English introduced new fabrics with the express purpose of challenging Venetian fine woolens, and they proved successful in cutting into Venice's portion of the Mediterranean cloth trade. Indeed, competitors copied the Venetian trademark of the lion of St. Mark, which assured high quality, with attendant high prices, and passed off cheap imitations as Venetian. In the Ottoman Empire, the fortunes of the Bursa silk industry rose and fell based on northern European demand. When European demand was high, Anatolian raw silk was exported and the Bursa silk industry struggled to acquire raw materials. When European demand was low, the local industry revived. Similarly, as the English call for raw wool and imports of English finished cloth increased in the mid-seventeenth century, the Salonica wool industry experienced a significant decline.

The entry of northern competitors into the Mediterranean had a significant impact on their home economies. For example, the expansion of trade in Marseilles followed directly on the heels of the granting of France's capitulations. The rise of England as a commercial and industrial center likewise rested on its expansion into the Mediterranean and its success against its trade rivals there. This led to a fivefold increase in English woolen production from 1600 to 1640, which damaged Venice's wool industry considerably.

While the commercial center ultimately shifted from the Mediterranean to the Atlantic, well into the seventeenth century, the sea remained the focus of trade. In 1650, for instance, the Mediterranean was the single largest destination for English exports, with 48% of the total, compared to 9% being traded to the Americas. For Amsterdam and London, it was their success in the Mediterranean, not their exploitation of the Atlantic, as yet a relatively insignificant market, that was the source of their expansion.

A final factor in the changing Mediterranean economy, and another example of openness to innovation and adaptation, was the rise of new commercial centers at the end of the sixteenth century that capitalized on the evolving economic conditions. Chief among these were Livorno and Izmir, which came to symbolize Mediterranean trade in their era just as Genoa and Venice had during an earlier time. The Medici rulers of Florence proved particularly innovative in proactively confronting changing realities through their development of a new port in Livorno. The city was constructed almost from scratch in the late sixteenth century along the malaria ridden coastline near Pisa with heavy investment by Duke Ferdinand I, who was eager to revive Tuscan maritime trade, which the silting of Pisa's riverine harbor had effectively paralyzed. From its inception, Livorno was envisioned as a multicultural community. Once it was established, foreign merchants from throughout the Mediterranean, regardless of religion, were lured by incentives that included low tax rates and even exemptions, the right of free and public religious practice, and provisions against discrimination. The Medici aggressively promoted Livorno as a free port where transit trade was not taxed and foreign merchants paid reduced duties. Jews especially were encouraged to settle in Tuscany generally, and in Pisa and Livorno in particular, and the Medici dukes facilitated their economic activities. The investment was a huge success. By 1600 the population had grown from 500 to 3,000; in 1642 it reached 12,000; and by 1689 more than 20,000 Jews, Greeks, Dutch, English, Armenians, and Italians inhabited the cosmopolitan emporium known as "the ideal city and the homeland of all." Livorno went from receiving 200 ships in 1592–93 to 2,500 in 1609–10, on the way to becoming Europe's chief silk market.

Where Livorno was a project of the Medici dukes, Izmir evolved in the seven-

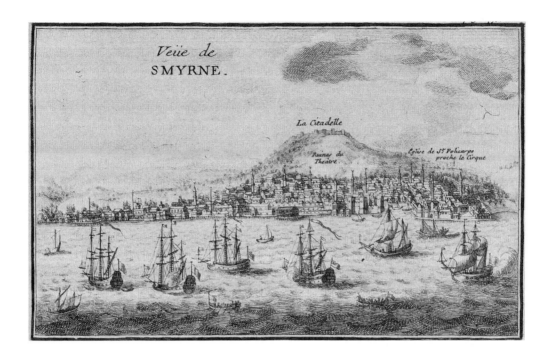

View of Smirne (Izmir). From Joseph Pitton de Tournefort, *Relation d'un Voyage du Levant*, Vol. 2 (Paris: Imprimerie Royale, 1717). Aikaterini Laskaridis Foundation (*www.travelogues.gr*)

teenth century into the dominant port in western Anatolia in a more organic fashion. It grew in response to increasing demand for Anatolian products and attempts by northern European traders to break into the region's markets by finding novel product niches, such as cotton, and alternatives to existing caravan routes. Izmir's expansion also was a response to a certain weakening of Istanbul's ability to hold the region within the imperial provisioning system. Faced with new commercial options, local officials were freer to strike deals without interference from the center.

Across the Mediterranean, people responded to the shifting economic winds. Genoa moved away from Levantine trade toward finance and became a major banking center to Spain, which in the sixteenth century grew increasingly dependent on Genoese creditors, especially after Philip II's 1557 bankruptcy. Genoa reigned as the financial capital of Europe until at least the Spanish bankruptcy of 1627. On Crete, when international wine exports dried up in the seventeenth century, the economy became much more diversified and the focus of trade shifted to a more regional eastern Mediterranean market.

In the final analysis, the Mediterranean economy in the early modern period demonstrated ongoing vitality and adaptability. Following a strong sixteenth century, the global seventeenth-century crisis had an acute impact, but merchants, artisans, and politicians adapted to its transformations with reasonable success. By the latter half of the century the economy was rebounding, and in many areas economic levels of the previous century had by 1700 been regained or even surpassed. If some regions like Venice were unchanged in absolute terms, others had begun to decline more clearly. What plainly had altered was the region's relative economic standing in relation to Atlantic economies, which were at least three times that of Venice and even higher in comparison to other parts of the Mediterranean.

TRAVEL AND LITERATURE

Despite its changing fortunes, the Mediterranean remained the focus of ever-increasing interest among travelers, writers, and artists. The burgeoning travel literature of the age, a product of both the rise of printing and growing connectivity, testifies to the region's pull on the imagination. The Mediterranean had always enticed travelers, often attracted by its holy sites, but beginning in the sixteenth century it drew many more who spilled a great deal of ink describing every aspect of their experience. For example, from 1492 to 1630 in France alone, easily four times more books were published on the Ottoman Empire than on the Americas. Venice was especially important in the transmission of information about the Ottoman world, and as a result an extensive range of histories, plays, chronicles, ambassadorial reports, prophecies, and travel narratives on the Ottomans and Islam began to be published there and in other centers.

One of the most famous early examples of this growing body of travel literature was the account of Nicolas de Nicolay, the royal geographer to King Henry II, who accompanied the French ambassador to the Porte in 1551. Upon his return he authored an influential travel narrative on the Ottoman Empire, *Les navigations, pérégrinations, et voyages faits en la Turquie* (Navigations, Peregrinations, and Voyages in Turkey), published in France in 1568 and translated into English, Dutch, German, and Italian over the next two decades. Nicolay described his lengthy voyage to the Ottoman capital, the city and its ancient and contemporary monuments, the organization of Ottoman government, and Islam, as well as noting many everyday aspects of life, such as foodways and other cultural customs. The volume was accompanied by numerous woodcuts that illuminated scenes of life in the Ottoman capital. Just as Nicolay's observations would be recycled repeatedly by subsequent travelers, so too these images were republished and repurposed for years to come.

Costume books and images of the Mediterranean world also enjoyed a growing popularity. Artists traveled in the region, often as members of diplomatic entourages, and they produced (or if necessary invented) depictions of individuals, landscapes, and everyday scenes there. Travelers could also purchase images produced by local Ottoman artists who relied on stock figures and scenes. These were often sold individually, like postcards, and then gathered together, labeled and described in personalized costume books. Images of "Turks" also became familiar decorations on the walls of houses across Europe.

Women, too, became active participants in this Mediterranean republic of letters in the later seventeenth century. One of the most influential travel narratives

Donna Turca, engraving of an Ottoman woman. From Nicolas de Nicolay, *Le Navigationi et viaggi, fatti nella Turchia* (Venice, 1580). *Aikaterini Laskaridis Foundation (www. travelogues.gr)*

was that of Lady Mary Wortley Montagu, who in 1716, at age 27, accompanied her husband, the newly appointed English ambassador, to the Ottoman Empire on a months-long journey across land and sea to Istanbul. Over the course of her travels and her two-year residency in the city, she wrote a series of letters to correspondents in England describing her experiences and impressions. Of particular interest are her descriptions of cloistered Ottoman women, whose lives had only been imagined in a voyeuristic fashion in the accounts of earlier male travelers. Similarly, in 1691 the French noblewoman and noted writer Madame d'Aulnoy composed an engaging and detailed account of her travels in Spain, which represents one of the most important early modern accounts of that land.

A new type of literature that gained in popularity in conjunction with the rise of

John Hall, *Lady Mary Wortley Montagu Visits the Sultana Hafiten* (1765). © Victoria and Albert Museum, London

travel writing and the great sixteenth-century expansion of corsairing was the captivity narrative. This genre described in excruciating, often exaggerated, language the experiences of the Mediterranean's slaves; a common element was lurid descriptions of what were depicted as their violent and libidinous Muslim masters. These details allowed captives to shape their narratives to meet the expectations of audiences at home and, more importantly, to emphasize that they had preserved their honor and faith while in captivity. Works such as *A True Account of the Captivity of Thomas Phelps* (1685) or Joseph Pitts's 1704 narrative often went through multiple editions and were widely popular. Women's captivity narratives, such as the Dutch book *Wonderbaarlyke en merkwaardige gevallen van een twaalfjarige slavernij, van een vroupersoon. Genaemt Maria ter Meetelen, woonagtig tot Medenblik* (Miraculous and Remarkable Events of Twelve Years Slavery, of a Woman, Called Maria ter Mee-telen from Medenblik, 1748), were less common.

Perhaps the most influential body of work within the broad category of captivity literature is that of the Spanish poet, author, and playwright Miguel de Cervantes. Cervantes was born in 1547 near Madrid, and as a young man he participated in the War of the Holy League, receiving several wounds at Lepanto. In 1575, while returning to Spain, he was captured by corsairs off the Catalan coast and taken to Algiers where he was enslaved for five years. This experience had a profound effect on Cervantes, and his subsequent works were infused with images of captivity. His play *Los tratos de Argel* (The Traffic of Algiers) is a heavily autobiographical and cathartic evocation of his experience as a slave, as is his 1615 play *Los banios de Argel* (The Bagnios of Algiers). His masterpiece *Don Quixote* also weaves in themes such as slavery and conversion, drawn from his Mediterranean adventures and travails. One recent scholar has suggested that Cervantes's greatness is inextricably inter-twined with both the traumatic and defining experience of his Algerian captivity.

The sea was a recurring presence on other stages of the era. This is certainly evident in Shakespeare's oeuvre: of 38 total plays, 21 are set in the Mediterranean, including some of his most famous works, such as *The Merchant of Venice* and *Othello*. In these plays, Shakespeare looks at the complex interplay of Christians, Jews, and Muslims in Venice and other Mediterranean settings and addresses issues such as conversion, cross-cultural love, and honor. Also popular were so-called Turk plays, such as George Peele's *Soliman and Perseda* (1590) or Philip Massinger's tragicomedy *The Renegado* (1623). From 1580 to 1630 dozens of such plays were staged, suggesting the anxious interest the English had for Islam and Islamic pow-er. This fascination was fed by recurring encounters with Muslims through trade, slavery, and diplomacy, which directly exposed many English for the first time to this Mediterranean world. Such curiosity was not limited to England; similar stories were fashionable on French and Italian stages, such as Jean Desmares's *Roxelana* (1643) or Prospero Bonarelli's *Il Solimano* (1619).

Historians long argued that the Islamic world was fundamentally uninterested in Christian Europe; however, more recent scholarship has seriously undercut this view. Though not as numerous as European travelers, there were nonetheless Arab and Ottoman diplomats, merchants, ecclesiastics, jurists, spies, and slaves who ven-tured into the "lands of the Christians," as well as to Asia, India, Africa, and even the Americas. They were neither indifferent to nor ignorant of the world around them; indeed, no one devoted more written attention to the Europeans than the Otto-mans, and in particular Arab travelers and writers. They wrote firsthand descrip-tions of peoples and customs, and of the geography and ethnography of the lands they visited. These voices have been ignored in part because of a tendency to con-fine travel literature rather narrowly to works that fit easily into European models. While such examples do exist, Ottoman and Arab views are more often found in a wide range of other types of sources such as correspondence, verse, histories, and religious writings.

One work that qualifies as the early modern analogue to Ibn Battuta's monumental medieval narrative, is the 10-volume *Seyahatnâme* (Book of Travels), penned by the great Ottoman traveler Evliya Çelebi. Born in 1611 in Istanbul, Evliya set out in 1640 on a series of voyages that would occupy the next 40 years of his life. He traveled the length and breadth of the Ottoman Empire and well beyond before his death in 1684 or 1685. A rich and complex blend of his own empirical observations and numerous geographical sources, combined with a dose of imagination and invention, Evliya's *Seyahatnâme* is considered one of the seventeenth century's most monumental examples of travel narrative.

The large early modern output of European works on Islam, Arabs, and the Ottoman Empire deeply informs one of the most influential books on the Mediterranean, and a canonical text in cultural studies, Edward Saïd's *Orientalism* (1978). Saïd argues that historically the West both set itself off from and defined itself against its binary opposite or Other, "the Orient," by which he means primarily the Islamic Near East. In his interpretation, this process of "othering" began in the late eighteenth century and was deeply informed by the ways in which the West manufactured and perpetuated a representation or image of the Orient through literary and visual media. This was not simply an act of cultural hegemony, Saïd contends; rather, Orientalism, or the act of representing Islam, was a means by which the West politically dominated and attempted to transform the East: "The relationship between Occident and Orient is a relationship of power, of domination, of varying degrees of a complex hegemony."

While highly influential, a generation of scholars has challenged many aspects of Saïd's orientalist model. They have shown, for example, that what Saïd saw as a phenomenon situated primarily in the post-Napoleonic nineteenth century in fact had deep roots in the medieval and early modern eras, periods in which Europeans were far from dominating the Islamic world but actually were deeply intimidated by Muslim corsairs and Ottoman sultans. They have argued against Saïd's reductive model of a monolithic East and West and have shown that both Christians and Muslims were highly diverse communities, and that members of both groups had not a single but rather a range of complex views of each other. Such views were not timeless or unchanging either but, on the contrary, ebbed and flowed in relation to time and context. Saïd's critics have also shown that western observers did not simply represent an imagined oriental other but were often able to portray diverse cultures in a reasonably accurate and informed fashion. Indeed, there was an expanding demand for accurate information about the Ottomans, Arabs, and Islam, and the early modern surge in ethnographic works was both a response to this demand and an expression of a growing fascination. Finally, rather than conceiving of the Mediterranean as cleaved into intractable blocs or civilizations, recent scholarship has emphasized the rich network of connections and interaction that linked east and west, Muslim, Jew, and Christian.

The fascination with the Mediterranean evidenced in the tremendous output dedicated to it in the early modern era was mirrored by a growing interest in traveling there. As a result, many parts of the region became integral stops on the Grand Tour. The Grand Tour was a cultural rite of passage among European elites, in which they undertook an extended journey, often lasting two or three years, to visit the chief political and cultural centers of the day. This educational pilgrimage introduced participants into European cosmopolitan culture and functioned as a type of finishing school to round out their classical educations. Travelers carried Greek and Roman authors in hand and were accompanied by a tutor, or cicerone, who served as their guide and instructor. The roots of the Grand Tour date back at least to the sixteenth century when it was common for patrician young men from Venice to travel to European capitals as part of their entry into political life. In the seventeenth century this practice spread to northern Europe, particularly England, reaching its apogee during the eighteenth century.

The Mediterranean represented the final and most anticipated stage of the Grand Tour: as the English writer Samuel Johnson observed, "The grand object of all travel is to see the shores of the Mediterranean. All our religion, almost all our law, almost all our arts, almost all that sets us above the savages, has come to us from the shores of the Mediterranean." A typical itinerary began in France, passed through other northern continental areas, and might include Spain. More adventurous travelers ventured farther afield, to Greece, Istanbul, and the Holy Land. The ultimate destination, however, was Italy, which exercised an almost magical effect on travelers. The English traveler Charles Thompson in 1744 wrote that he was "impatiently desirous of viewing a country so famous in history, which once gave laws to the world; which is at present the great school of music and painting, contains the noblest productions of statuary and architecture, and abounds with cabinets of rarities, and collections of all kinds of antiquities." Typical stops included Venice, Florence, and Sicily, and many travelers ventured to Naples to see Vesuvius, particularly after it flared back to life in the seventeenth century, as well as Pompeii, which attracted widespread fascination after its rediscovery in 1755. Of course, Rome represented perhaps the most anticipated stop on the circuit because of its rich classical archaeological heritage and religious significance.

The impact of the grand tour is evident in the experience of Johann Wolfgang Goethe, who traveled to Italy in 1786–88 during a midlife crisis and had what he described as a rebirth. "In Rome I have found myself for the first time," he wrote, and his Italian sojourn had a lasting influence on his personal, intellectual, and artistic development, which he recounted in his famous travel narrative, *Italienische Reise* (Italian Journey), published in 1816–17. While Italy and the Mediterranean continued to attract the gaze of foreign travelers in the nineteenth century, they came increasingly to see them as emblems of what they perceived as the decline and degradation of once-great cultures that had fallen on hard times.

CHAPTER TWELVE

The Waning of the Early Modern Mediterranean

I n 1802 the great English Romantic poet William Wordsworth, in response to the tumultuous political transformations of his age, composed what is considered by many to be one of his finest works, a short dirge entitled "On the Extinction of the Venetian Republic."

> Once did she hold the gorgeous East in fee;
> And was the safeguard of the West: the worth
> Of Venice did not fall below her birth,
> Venice, the eldest Child of Liberty.
> She was a maiden City, bright and free;
> No guile seduced, no force could violate;
> And, when she took unto herself a mate,
> She must espouse the everlasting Sea.
> And what if she had seen those glories fade,
> Those titles vanish, and that strength decay;
> Yet shall some tribute of regret be paid
> When her long life hath reach'd its final day:
> Men are we, and must grieve when even the Shade
> Of that which once was great is pass'd away.

As the title implies, the sonnet was occasioned by the abrupt collapse of the over-1,000-year-old republic barely five years previous at the hand of the French Revolutionary Army. Though Wordsworth had never set foot in Venice, its demise had a profound effect on him, as well as on many of his contemporaries. Despite Venice's reduced place in the political and economic landscape of the eighteenth century, for Wordsworth, Byron, and others, the fall of Venice from its status as a powerful and wealthy Mediterranean empire to foreign subjugation and serving as a pawn in the political rivalries of the great powers was shocking and unexpected. It marked a troubling rupture with the past and a harbinger of the changes that would buffet the Mediterranean during the dramatic upheavals and transformations of the nineteenth century. If the period 1600–1750 was one of adaptation and adjustment, then by the final decades of the eighteenth century the status of the Mediterranean in comparison to other regions had changed in fundamental ways. New players entered into the power politics of the sea; the reverberations of the French Revolution were felt throughout the region; the balance of power, particularly in historically important Mediterranean centers such as Venice, Malta, Spain, Rome, and Egypt, shifted dramatically; and institutions such as slavery and corsairing were transformed.

RUSSIA

A new player in the Mediterranean was Tsarist Russia. Russian influence in the region had been increasing since the mid-sixteenth century, when Ivan the Terrible and the Ottomans had come to blows over Ottoman attempts to construct a canal linking the Don and Volga rivers. But with the waning of Safavid power at the end of the seventeenth century and Peter the Great's military expansion, conflict flared up again. The Ottoman-Russian rivalry would occupy center stage in Mediterranean affairs over the course of the eighteenth century. Indeed, the two empires would clash repeatedly into the early twentieth century.

Many factors fed into this rivalry, but the chief issue was control of the Bosporus and the Dardanelles, the straits that linked the Mediterranean to the Black Sea. As Russia began to emerge as a maritime power in the Black Sea in the eighteenth century, and as its grain production in the region expanded, access to and control over the sea's only portal became a critical issue. There were other motivations, too, including Russian aspirations for territorial expansion and regional power, as well as religious matters. These were evident in the so-called "Greek project" of the 1780s, in which Catherine the Great envisioned the overthrow of Ottoman and Muslim power in the region and the reestablishment of the Christian Byzantine Empire in Istanbul, though now with a Russian ruler on the throne.

Following a series of minor confrontations, war broke out between the Ottomans and Russians in 1768. This marked the first in a series of conflicts that greatly eroded Ottoman power and territorial holdings on its northern frontier. The Treaty of Küçük Kaynarca in 1774 ended this round of hostilities. Crimea briefly gained its independence after 300 years of Ottoman rule, before being annexed by Russia in 1783. For the first time Russia secured control of a portion of the Black Sea coast and extracted the right to establish consuls throughout the Ottoman Empire and for its ships to pass freely through the Dardanelles and Bosporus into the open Mediterranean. Russia also was granted a protectorate over all Orthodox Ottoman subjects,

and it received an enormous indemnity of 7.5 million aspers. From 1787 to 1792 hostilities flared once more, this time with Austria allied alongside Russia, and again the Ottomans came up in the losers column.

In addition to military expansion, the Russians also represented a growing commercial presence in the Mediterranean. In 1796, Catherine the Great established the free port of Odessa, which quickly became an important trade center. By the first years of the nineteenth century large quantities of oil, wine, and wool from Greece, Spain, and Italy were passing through its port. Because of the key role played by Italians in the new city's economic and cultural life, Odessa was known as "the last Italian Black Sea colony." In exchange for these goods, Russia exported grain valued at over 5 million rubles from the Black Sea into the Mediterranean and beyond.

Adriaan Schoonebeek, Siege of the Ottoman Fortress of Azov in July 1696 by Russian Forces led by Peter the Great (1700). State Hermitage Museum, St. Petersburg. Photo: HIP / Art Resource, NY

NAPOLEON

Other political transformations in the Mediterranean were set in motion by the actions of Napoleon Bonaparte. In the span of a decade his influence disrupted and significantly transformed Italy, Spain, and

THE MEDITERRANEAN WORLD

the Ottoman Empire. Born in 1769 in Corsica, Napoleon was a man of the Mediterranean. Corsica had long been under Genoese suzerainty, but following a
revolt, the island passed to France in the year of Napoleon's birth. As a result, he
grew up a French subject and attended a French military school for impoverished
sons of the nobility. He came of age during the French Revolution and rapidly rose
through the ranks in the new republic's armies. Thanks to a combination of skill,
luck, and patronage, at the age of 27, when France went on the offensive against
its European enemies, he was given command over the Italian campaign, which
marked the beginning of a meteoric rise to power, followed by an equally dramatic
fall, all in the space of 20 years.

In March 1796, Napoleon took a ragtag army of 40,000 soldiers and descended
into Italy. He quickly defeated the Austrian armies that confronted him in Pied-
mont and Lombardy and pursued them eastward into Venetian territory. Venice's
rulers tried unsuccessfully to preserve the city's historic neutrality. The French
arrived at the lagoon in May and demanded that the government be dissolved and a
democratic council established. With no real military option available to them, and
fearful that they might lose their valuable mainland estates and that the fate of the
French aristocracy might await them, the members of the Venetian Grand Council
voted that body, and the millennial republic, out of existence on May 12, 1797.

With this action, Venice and its former territories became a bargaining chip
for the great powers of Europe, and they were passed back and forth in a series of
increasingly humiliating treaties. Napoleon reorganized the political map of Italy
repeatedly, creating several republics, before grandiose visions of himself as a new
Charlemagne led him to declare himself king in 1805 and to divide the peninsula
among family members. During these trying times, Venice was systematically looted by its foreign rulers, its economy collapsed, the center of Adriatic trade shifted to
Trieste, and the Venetian ruling elite entered into sharp demographic and economic
decline. One hundred palaces and almost as many churches were also destroyed as
Venice's new rulers transformed the physiognomy of the city.

The fall of Venice had a domino effect on the eastern Mediterranean as well. In
1797, Venice still possessed a number of Istrian, Dalmatian, and Albanian coastal
towns, as well as several Greek mainland enclaves and islands, most notably Corfu.
With the collapse of the republic, the status of these remaining territories was cast
into doubt. In the case of Corfu, fearing that the Russians would move into the void,
a French fleet took possession of the island in mid-1797. Over the next decade and a
half, Corfu was shunted between Venetian, French, and Russo-Ottoman rule before
becoming a British protectorate in 1815.

Napoleon's unanticipated success in the Italian campaign deeply influenced
him—"In Italy," he stated, "I realized I was a superior being and conceived the
ambition of performing great things"—and set the stage for his most audacious
Mediterranean adventure, the conquest of Egypt. When he returned to Paris in
late 1797, he was welcomed as a conquering hero and was tapped to lead a cross-
channel invasion of France's chief European rival, Great Britain. Rather than

undertake a dangerous direct assault on a powerful enemy defending its home territory, Napoleon proposed that the expedition be redirected to Egypt. He argued that this would allow France to weaken Britain's valuable Levantine trade with its connections to Asia, undercut the British position in the Mediterranean, and create a French empire able to challenge Britain's global political and economic might. Beyond these political motivations, Napoleon conceived of the Egyptian campaign as a way to accrue reputation to himself: "We must go to the Orient," he insisted. "It is there that great glory has always been gained." The campaign, however, proved to be an unmitigated failure, which nevertheless paradoxically enhanced Napoleon's reputation and led to his elevation to the summit of French political power.

The French expedition to Egypt further upended the rapidly evolving situation in the Mediterranean. On July 1, 1798, the French fleet of almost 400 vessels and 50,000 men, landed near Alexandria. While still nominally under the sultans' rule, Ottoman authority in Egypt had been compromised by the reinvigorated Mamluks in the last half century. Indeed, Napoleon made the unbelievable claim that he and his men were Muslims who had come to liberate the Egyptians from Mamluk tyranny.

Over the next weeks the French advanced systematically up the Nile, facing minimal resistance but suffering from the harsh conditions. According to one participant, "Soldiers were dying in the sand from lack of water and food; the intense heat forced them to abandon their booty; and many others, tired of suffering, simply blew their brains out." On July 21, the French decisively defeated the Mamluks at Cairo in what was dubbed the battle of the Pyramids. This victory was followed by a serious setback on August 1, when British admiral Horatio Nelson destroyed the French fleet in the port of Abu Qir, effectively stranding Napoleon's army. An early 1799 invasion of Syria to forestall an Ottoman counterattack likewise proved a catastrophic failure, with thousands of French casualties, many of whom died during a plague outbreak.

Ultimately, the French lacked the resources to occupy anything more than Cairo and the delta, and even then their hold was tenuous at best. In August 1799, after a year in Egypt, Napoleon abandoned his army and secretly returned to France to organize the coup d'état that brought him to power. Two years later, the Ottomans allied with the British to defeat the few remaining French in Egypt. This marked the end of Napoleon's Egyptian folly, which cost him between 10,000 and 15,000 men and immense treasure. On the other side of the ledger, there are no accurate statistics for the number of Egyptians killed or the economic impact of the French invasion.

Though scholars have suggested that the brief French occupation marked the beginning of the modern era in Egypt, the reality is that this interlude had a relatively minor impact in terms of any lasting reforms. The campaign did, however, disrupt the regional political order. Following the French expulsion, a young Albanian military officer in the sultan's army, Muhammad Ali, took advantage of the unstable situation to usurp the Ottomans' greatly reduced authority in Egypt and to lay the foundations of independence. Napoleon's campaign also revealed structural weaknesses in the Ottoman state, which led other powers to seize

Antoine Jean Gros, *Napoleon Bonaparte before the Battle of the Pyramids, 21 July 1798* (1838). *Musée du Louvre, Paris.* © RMN-Grand Palais / Art Resource, NY

Ottoman territories and emboldened other parts of the empire, including Serbia (1817) and Greece (1828), to break free of Ottoman rule. By the same token, there is no doubt that the loss of Egypt played a role in bringing about the sweeping Tanzimat reforms that would begin in 1839 and breathe new life into the Ottoman Empire.

Napoleon's Mediterranean aspirations were not limited to Egypt. In 1807 he invaded the kingdom of Spain, whose political standing had been progressively undercut over the course of the eighteenth century. The process had been set in motion during the War of the Spanish Succession (1701–14), in which most of the powers of Europe maneuvered politically and militarily to decide the question of who would succeed the last Habsburg ruler of Spain, Charles II, who had died without an heir. While the precipitating cause was the succession question, the conflict was really over European hegemony, with Spain as a pawn in the machinations of other powers. The conflict was resolved with the Treaty of Utrecht in 1713, which saw Philip V of Bourbon recognized as king, in return for the division among vari-

Grande hazaña! Con muertos!

Francisco de Goya, *Grande hazaña! Con muertos!* (A heroic feat! With dead men!) from *The Disasters of War.* © *Trustees of the British Museum*

ous European rulers of significant Spanish territories in the Italian and Iberian peninsulas, the Netherlands, and the Americas.

Napoleon's invasion almost a century later, and the insertion of his oldest brother, Joseph, on the throne in 1808, once again subjected Spain to outside intervention in its affairs and made it largely a puppet in the political and military maneuverings of France and Great Britain. The Peninsular War, which dragged on until 1814, produced some of the bloodiest fighting of the Napoleonic wars. The French lost over a quarter million soldiers and expended 1 billion francs. Looking back, Napoleon traced his downfall to his "Spanish Ulcer," opining, "all my disasters can be traced back to this fatal knot." Spain suffered even more, with over 1 million dead, about 10% of the total population, and untold economic and social devastation. Politically, the Peninsular War led to significant changes within Iberia's polities and hastened the breakup of the Spanish and Portuguese empires, particularly in Latin America, in the subsequent years. The extreme violence and suffering that the extended conflict produced were recorded in a series of 82 horrifying prints by the great Spanish artist Francisco Goya entitled *The Disasters of War.*

CORSAIRS AND SLAVES

The political disruption created by Napoleon's incursions into the Mediterranean and the ongoing Anglo-French rivalry also affected the culture of slavery in the region. On the voyage to Egypt in 1798, the French fleet had halted in Malta long enough to seize the outpost from its rulers, the Knights of the Order of St. John. The island ought to have presented a more formidable challenge with the massive fortress at Valletta and its 1,500 canon. But internal dissension within the order, combined with generous French bribery, led to only a token single day of resistance, a striking contrast to the island's lengthy struggle against the Ottomans in the famed siege of 1565. Malta provided Napoleon with millions of francs of tribute and booty, a powerful, strategically situated naval base for the expedition to Egypt, and an opportunity to control the east-west Mediterranean sea-lanes and thus weaken British influence in the region. In abolishing the order and snuffing out its nearly 400-year rule of Malta, Napoleon also removed one of the most important actors in the Mediterranean slave trade.

The heyday of Mediterranean slavery had been the sixteenth and seventeenth centuries. Already by the late seventeenth century corsairing and slaving had begun to ebb, and this became even more pronounced after 1700. Slave numbers dropped from a total of perhaps 100,000 at any given time during the seventeenth century to under 10,000 in the eighteenth century. The exception to this precipitous drop came during the disruptions of the Napoleonic wars, when corsair activity experienced a momentary resurgence. In Algiers and Tunis, numbers doubled or even tripled in a few short years, before plummeting back to prewar levels.

The eighteenth-century decline in slavery was the product of a complex set of factors, including outbreaks of disease, the changing character of the Mediterranean economy, and a decline in warfare between its chief powers. Another factor was technological: the growing firepower of European fleets limited Maghreb corsair activity. After 1680, France and England compelled the Barbary regencies to respect their shipping, thus reducing potential targets to weaker powers such as Spain and several Italian and Scandinavian states. To protect their mercantile activity, these polities paid protection money in the form of tribute to the regencies. With the decline in Mediterranean slavery, tribute came to be one of the primary sources of income for the Barbary states, as most powers of the day calculated that payment was less expensive than the military alternative. In 1798, for example, Tripoli demanded 100,000 French francs from Sweden, plus an annual payment of 8,000 francs, in return for security for its shipping in the Mediterranean. When the Swedes refused, their ships became the target of attacks and hundreds of their subjects were enslaved. The issue was only resolved when Sweden agreed to pay 80,000 francs plus the annual tribute.

The experiences of the new United States offer another example of the changed Mediterranean landscape of slavery and privateering. In 1784, one year after the country achieved independence, and thus no longer enjoyed protection under British treaties, an American ship from Philadelphia, the *Betsey*, was captured by Moroccan corsairs who demanded that a tribute be paid to prevent similar future actions. This marked the opening salvo of the so-called Barbary wars, which would occupy the United States for 30 years as it struggled to defend its merchants and

to carve out a position for itself as an independent state. The undeclared war flared into open conflict twice, in the Tripolitan War of 1801–5 and the Algerine War of 1815–16.

The Tripolitan War was the first meaningful challenge that the new American president Thomas Jefferson faced following his election in 1801. The ruler of Tripoli, Yusuf Karamanlı, declared war on the United States when Jefferson refused to pay a tribute of $225,000. An American squadron was dispatched to the region in May, and open hostilities broke out in August. The conflict played out over the next four years, with several naval engagements, the blockade and bombardment of Tripoli, an American alliance with Naples, and overland actions by American forces, famously commemorated in the Marine Corps hymn. In 1805 a treaty was signed in which the United States paid $60,000 for the release of its prisoners of war and Tripoli waived all claims to tribute. It is an exaggeration to describe this as the first war on terror, as some have done, as trade, not religion, was the central issue. There is no doubt, however, that the conflict, which represented the United States' first real foreign military foray, was a defining moment for the young republic. For Tripoli the war marked a significant and symbolic defeat at the hands of a minor power that possessed only a small fleet, and it underlined the changed power dynamics in the Mediterranean and the diminution of the formerly influential Barbary states.

The changes in Mediterranean corsairing and slavery were accompanied by significant political transformation as well. The North African regencies in the eighteenth century, though still under nominal Ottoman lordship, came to act with increasing autonomy. They also experienced significant internal power struggles, as well as open hostilities between the regencies,

Bonvalet, *The Travels and Exploits of General Bonaparte* (early 1799), showing Napoleon at Malta, about to cross the Mediterranean to invade Egypt. *Musée Carnavalet, Paris. Photo: Gianni Dagli Orti / Art Resource, NY*

THE MEDITERRANEAN WORLD

particularly Tunisia and Algeria. Local officials turned these disruptions to their benefit. In 1701, for example, a janissary officer, Karamanlı Ahmed, became governor of Tripoli and in short order established a hereditary governorship, which was effectively independent of Ottoman control. In Tunisia, as the corso declined in the later seventeenth century and the Barbary regencies failed to diversify their economies sufficiently to remain competitive, political power shifted away from the European renegades who had ruled during the heyday of corsair activity. In Algeria, power came to be concentrated in the hands of a single official, the dey, which led to longer terms of office and greater stability.

COLLECTING THE MEDITERRANEAN

The changing political environment of the Mediterranean is also evident in matters of culture. Travelers to the region had always been interested in not only seeing but also owning a piece of its rich cultural heritage. In the sixteenth and seventeenth centuries, visitors sought classical talismans and relics as mementos of their travels and as evidence of their erudition and appreciation of the sea's ancient cultures. By the later eighteenth century this had taken on a decidedly different form. Collecting expanded in scale and began to take on the character of despoliation as individuals and officials from wealthier and more politically powerful areas of Europe took advantage of growing power imbalances to cart off quantities of valuable artifacts. The late eighteenth and early nineteenth centuries saw the wholesale exodus of cultural materials from Italy, Spain, and the Ottoman Empire. The looting of the Mediterranean by northern Europe was a way to connect with its storied past but also to possess and appropriate it for political ends.

This is evident in the well-known story of the Parthenon in Athens. Following the Ottoman conquest of the city in the mid-fifteenth century, the Acropolis was used as a fortress and the Parthenon, with its mosaics and frescoes painted over, functioned as a mosque for the garrison. In 1687, during the first war of the Morea, the building sustained serious damage when Venetian forces attempting to drive the Ottomans from Greece bombarded the Acropolis. A mortar shell penetrated the Parthenon's roof and exploded a store of gunpowder that had been cached there, causing extensive damage to the structure and its ornamentation. The Venetian commander, Francesco Morosini—in an attempt to emulate Doge Enrico Dandolo, who had looted Constantinople following the Fourth Crusade—then tried to remove some of the Parthenon's sculptures but only succeeded in smashing them. A hundred years later, the French ambassador to the Ottoman Empire, Comte de Choiseul-Goffier, acquired a few fragments of the Parthenon frieze.

The tragic tale culminated with Thomas Bruce, earl of Elgin and British ambassador to the Ottoman Empire from 1799 to 1802. Faced with Napoleon's invasion of Egypt, the Ottomans turned to Britain for support against the French. Bruce obtained a sultanic firman that permitted him to excavate around the Parthenon and make casts of its surviving frieze and statuary. Instead, over the course of a decade

VEDUTA DEL CAST: D'ACROPOLIS DALLA PARTE DI TRAMONTAN

The Destruction of the Parthenon, from Francesco Fanelli, Atene attica (Venice, 1707). Sächsische Landesbibliothek— Staats- und Universitätsbibliothek Dresden/Deutsche Fotothek

he sent all of the frieze that he considered worth preserving, about 75 meters, plus a number of statues and metopes, to London, doing irreparable damage to the temple in the process. The marbles, which Elgin had personally paid to excavate and transport, were sold to the British government in 1816 at a loss, even though Napoleon and other suitors offered more money.

The extraction of treasures of the Mediterranean past was perfected by Napoleon, who took cultural plundering to a unprecedented scale. As part of his dream of a united Europe under French rule, he envisioned gathering to Paris all the greatest works of art to be displayed in the Louvre (renamed the Napoleon Museum), the finest manuscripts to be stored in the Bibliothèque Nationale, and all Europe's documentary records to be housed in a new central archive. As a result, many priceless cultural treasures from the Mediterranean were seized and sent to the French capital. Following the conquest of Venice, for example, Napoleon declared that he would be "an Attila for the Venetian state" and set about plundering the city systematically. Some 25,000 paintings were carted off to Milan, the new capital of the kingdom of Italy, and to Paris. Veronese's monumental masterpieces *The Feast of the House of Levi* and *The Marriage Feast of Cana*, each painted for a Venetian monastery's refectory, were sent to the Louvre. In an act of retributive poetic justice, Napoleon also confiscated the four bronze horses of St. Mark's Basilica, which Venice had itself seized from Byzantine Constantinople in 1204.

Rome was similarly plundered: on a single day over 500 wagons loaded down with its greatest works of art set off for Paris, accompanied by strong popular protests. Napoleon also ordered that the entire Vatican archive be relocated to France.

THE MEDITERRANEAN WORLD

From 1810 to 1811 wagon trains carried over 100,000 volumes or bundles of documents over the Alps to Paris at the cost of 600,000 francs. After Napoleon's fall in 1815, two-thirds of the documents were returned, while the remainder were sold as scrap paper.

Cultural collecting also played a prominent role in the French conquest of Egypt. Napoleon's expeditionary force was accompanied by 167 scholars, scientists, and specialists who were tasked with recording the geography, botany, geology, and antiquities of Egypt. The result of these studies was the monumental *Déscription de l'Égypt*, published in 13 volumes from 1809 to 1828. Another cultural byproduct of the invasion was the 1802 description of his explorations of the upper and lower Nile by the French archaeologist, writer, and illustrator Dominique-Vivant Denon, which was the first systematic scholarly record of Egypt's antiquities and helped to ignite a European craze for all things Egyptian. Denon also convinced Napoleon to carry out a survey of Egyptian remains. The 1801 Treaty of Alexandria, which ended their occupation of Egypt, stipulated that the French were to "hand over all antiquities found by them." These included two small obelisks, several statues and sarcophagi, and, most famously, the Rosetta Stone, which was discovered by a French soldier and proved the key to deciphering the ancient Egyptian language. These and other antiquities that the French had collected were not returned to Egypt but were redirected to London, where they were first displayed in 1802 in the British Museum.

View of the Sphinx and the Second Pyramid, from Déscription de l'Égypte (Paris, 1809–28). © François Guenet / Art Resource, NY

As a symbol, the transfer of these antiquities from the Mediterranean to northern European capitals underscores the shift in power that had taken place over the course of the eighteenth century. To be sure, 1800 is an artificial endpoint; there was continuity amid the change of the decades on either side of this mark. But there is little question that the political transformations of the second half of the eighteenth century—with attendant social, environmental, and economic changes—altered some of the key characteristics of the early modern period and foreshadowed the very different reality that the Middle Sea would face in the brave new world of the nineteenth century.

As this book is aimed at the general reader rather than at scholars and experts, it was thought best to forgo extensive footnotes and references. Instead, we offer this guide to further reading for those who might be interested in exploring the issues, themes, and events discussed here. It should also be noted that just as the Mediterranean itself is a polyglot environment, scholarship relating to the Mediterranean is a multilingual affair, with important works in French, Italian, Spanish, Arabic, Turkish, German, Greek, Croatian, Albanian, and Hebrew. As the primary audience for this volume is the English-speaking public, the majority of the works included here are in English.

GENERAL REFERENCE

The seven volumes of the *New Cambridge Medieval History* (1995–2005) have been an invaluable reference and would be an excellent starting point for readers interested in more detailed accounts of the themes, institutions, and events presented in this book. See also the first two volumes of the *New Cambridge History of Islam*, ed. Chase Robinson (vol. 1, 2010) and Maribel Fierro (vol. 2, 2010), the first volume of the *Cambridge History of Egypt*, ed. Carl F. Petry (1998), *The Cambridge History of the Byzantine Empire c. 500–1492*, ed. Jonathan Shepard (2009); and the first three volumes of the *Cambridge History of Turkey*, ed. Kate Fleet and Suraiya Faroqhi (2006–12). Also useful is *The Oxford History of Byzantium*, ed. Cyril Mango (2002). The references below to primary source collections should not be taken to represent the latest or most authoritative scholarly editions of texts. They are simply an introductory list of some source collections that are both wide in scope, reliable in content, and generally easily available and accessible to nonspecialists.

INTRODUCTION

Abulafia, David. *The Great Sea: A Human History of the Mediterranean*. Oxford: Oxford University Press, 2011.

———, ed. *The Mediterranean in History*. Los Angeles: J. Paul Getty Museum, 2003.

———. "Mediterraneans." In *Rethinking the Mediterranean*, ed. W. V. Harris. Oxford: Oxford University Press, 2005.

Braudel, Fernand. *The Mediterranean and the Mediterranean World in the Age of Philip II*. New York: Harper & Row, 1972–73. Originally published as *Méditerranée et le monde méditerranéen à l'époque de Philippe II* (1949; 2nd ed., Paris: Colin, 1966).

Bulliet, Richard. *The Case for Islamo-Christian Civilization*. New York: Columbia University Press, 2006.

Fleet, Kate. "The Mediterranean." *Journal of Early Modern History* 6 (2002): 62–73.

Goitein, S. D. *A Mediterranean Society: The Jewish Communities of the Arab World as Portrayed in the Documents of the Cairo Geniza.* 6 vols. Berkeley: University of California Press, 1967–1983.

Herzfeld, Michael. "The Horns of the Mediterraneanist Dilemma." *American Ethnologist* 11 (1984): 439–54.

———. "Practical Mediterraneanism." In *Rethinking the Mediterranean*, ed. W. V. Harris. Oxford: Oxford University Press, 2005.

Hess, Andrew. *The Forgotten Frontier: A History of the Sixteenth-Century Ibero-African Frontier.* Chicago: University of Chicago Press, 1978.

Hodges, Richard, and David Whitehouse, eds. *Mohammed, Charlemagne, and the Origins of Europe: Archaeology and the Pirenne Thesis.* Ithaca, NY: Cornell University Press, 1983.

Horden, Peregrine, and Nicholas Purcell, *The Corrupting Sea: A Study of Mediterranean History.* Oxford: Blackwell Publishers, 2000.

Horden, Peregine, and Sharon Kinoshita, eds. *A Companion to Mediterranean History.* Oxford: Wiley Blackwell, 2014.

Huntington, Samuel. *The Clash of Civilizations and the Remaking of World Order.* New York: Simon and Schuster, 1996.

McCormick, Michael. *Origins of the European Economy: Communications and Commerce, A.D. 300–900.* Cambridge: Cambridge University Press, 2001.

Peters, Edward. "'Quid Nobis cum pelago'? The New Thassology and the Economic History of Europe." *Journal of Interdisciplinary History* 34 (2003): 49–61.

Pirenne, Henri. *Mohammed and Charlemagne.* Trans. Bernard Miall. New York: Barnes & Noble, 1939.

Purcell, Nicholas. "The Boundless Sea of Unlikeness? On Defining the Mediterranean." *Mediterranean Historical Review* 18, 2 (2003): 9–29.

Saïd, Edward. *Orientalism.* New York: Vintage Books, 1979.

Shaw, Brent D. "Challenging Braudel: A New Vision of the Mediterranean." *Journal of Roman Archaeology* 14 (2001): 419–53.

Tolan, John, Henry Laurens, and Gilles Veinstein. *Europe and the Islamic World: A History.* Princeton, NJ: Princeton University Press, 2013.

Wickham, Chris. *Framing the Early Middle Ages: Europe and the Mediterranean, 400–800.* Oxford: Oxford University Press, 2007.

ONE | THE WANING OF THE ROMAN MEDITERRANEAN

Brown, Peter. *The Rise of Western Christendom: Triumph and Diversity, 200–1000.* 2nd ed. Oxford: Wiley Blackwell, 2003.

Cameron, Averil. *The Mediterranean World in Late Antiquity.* 2nd ed. New York: Routledge, 2011.

Freeman, Charles. *Egypt, Greece, and Rome, Civilizations of the Ancient Mediterranean.* 2nd ed. Oxford: Oxford University Press, 2003.

Geary, Patrick. *The Myth of Nations: The Medieval Origins of Europe.* Princeton, NJ: Princeton University Press, 2002.

Goodman, Martin. *Rome and Jerusalem: The Clash of Ancient Civilizations.* New York: Knopf Press, 2007.

Levine, Lee I. *The Ancient Synagogue: The First Thousand Years.* New Haven: Yale University Press, 2000.

Winks, Robin, and Susan P. Mattern-Parkes. *The Ancient Mediterranean World: From the Stone Age to A.D. 600.* Oxford: Oxford University Press, 2004.

Berkey, Jonathan P. *The Formation of Islam: Religion and Society in the Near East, 600–1800.* Cambridge: Cambridge University Press, 2002.

Bonner, Michael. *Jihad in Islamic History: Doctrines and Practice.* Princeton, NJ: Princeton University Press, 2008.

Bosworth, C. E. *The Arabs, Byzantium, and Iran: Studies in Early Islamic History and Culture.* Surrey, UK: Ashgate Variorum, 1996.

Brett, Michael. *The Rise of the Fatimids: The World of the Mediterranean and the Middle East in the Tenth Century CE.* Leiden: Brill, 2000.

Collins, Roger. *Early Medieval Spain: Unity in Diversity, 400–1000.* 2nd ed. London: Macmillan, 1995.

Constable, Olivia Remie. *Medieval Iberia: Readings from Christian, Muslim, and Jewish Sources.* 2nd ed. Philadelphia: University of Pennsylvania Press, 2011.

Donner, Fred. *Muhammad and the Believers: At the Origins of Islam.* Cambridge, MA: Harvard University Press, 2010.

Gil, Moshe. *A History of Palestine 634–1099.* Trans. Ethel Broido. Cambridge: Cambridge University Press, 1992.

Haldon, John. "The End of Rome? The Transformation of the Eastern Empire in the 7th-8th Centuries." In *The Roman Empire in Context: Historical and Comparative Perspectives*, ed. Jóhann Árnason and Kurt Raaflaub. Oxford: Wiley-Blackwell, 2011.

———. *Warfare, State, and Society in the Byzantine World, 565–1204.* New York: Routledge, 1999.

Hawting, G. R. *The First Dynasty of Islam: The Umayyad Caliphate, 661–750.* 2nd ed. New York: Routledge, 2000.

Hoyland, Robert. *Seeing Islam as Others Saw It: A Survey and Evaluation of Christian, Jewish, and Zoroastrian Writings on Early Islam.* Princeton, NJ: Darwin Press, 1998.

Kaegi, Walter. *Byzantium and the Early Islamic Conquests.* Cambridge: Cambridge University Press, 1992.

Kennedy, Hugh. *The Prophet and the Age of the Caliphates: The Islamic Near East from the Sixth to the Eleventh Century.* 2nd ed. New York: Routledge, 2004.

Kreutz, Barbara. *Before the Normans: Southern Italy in the 9th and 10th Centuries.* Philadelphia: University of Pennsylvania Press, 1996.

Lewis, Bernard. *Islam: From the Prophet Muhammad to the Capture of Constantinople.* 2 vols. Oxford: Oxford University Press, 1987.

Metcalfe, Alex. *The Muslims of Medieval Italy.* Edinburgh: Edinburgh University Press, 2009.

Wasserstein, David. *The Rise and Fall of the Party-Kings: Politics and Society in Islamic Spain, 1002–1086.* Princeton, NJ: Princeton University Press, 1985.

Whittow, Mark. *The Making of Byzantium, 600–1025.* Berkeley: University of California Press, 1996.

THREE | CONNECTING AND DIVIDING EARLY MEDIEVAL
ECONOMIES AND CULTURES

Bloom, Jonathan. *Paper before Print: The History and Impact of Paper in the Islamic World.* New Haven: Yale University Press, 2001.

Brubaker, Leslie, and John Haldon. *Byzantium in the Iconoclast Era, c. 650–850: A History.* Cambridge: Cambridge University Press, 2011.

Cohen, Mark. *Under Crescent and Cross: The Jews in the Middle Ages.* 2nd ed. Princeton, NJ: Princeton University Press, 2008.

Constable, Olivia Remie. *Trade and Traders in Muslim Spain: The Commercial Realignment of the Iberian Peninsula, 900–1500.* Cambridge: Cambridge University Press, 1996.

Coope, Jessica. *The Martyrs of Cordoba: Community and Family Conflict in an Age of Mass Conversion.* Lincoln: University of Nebraska Press, 1995.

Fletcher, Richard. *Moorish Spain.* New York: Henry Holt, 1992.

Fowden, Elizabeth Key. "Sharing Holy Places." *Common Knowledge* 8, 1 (2002): 124–46.

Fynn, Paul. "Empire, Monotheism and Slavery in the Greater Mediterranean Region from Antiquity to the Early Modern Era." *Past and Present* 205 (2009): 3–40.

Glick, Thomas. *Islamic and Christian Spain in the Early Middle Ages.* Princeton, NJ: Princeton University Press, 1979.

Goitein, S. D. *Letters of Medieval Jewish Traders.* Princeton, NJ: Princeton University Press, 1973.

Griffith, Sidney H. *The Church in the Shadow of the Mosque.* Princeton, NJ: Princeton University Press, 2008.

Holo, Joshua. *Byzantine Jewry in the Mediterranean Economy.* Cambridge: Cambridge University Press, 2009.

Kennedy, Hugh. "From Polis to Madina: Urban Change in Late Antique and Early Islamic Syria." *Past and Present* 106 (1985): 3–27.

Khoury, Nuha N. N. "The Meaning of the Great Mosque of Cordoba in the Tenth Century." *Muqarnas* 13 (1996): 80–98.

Meri, Josef. *The Cult of Saints among Muslims and Jews in Medieval Syria.* Oxford: Oxford University Press, 2002.

Noble, Thomas F. X. *Images, Iconoclasm, and the Carolingians.* Philadelphia: University of Pennsylvania Press, 2009.

Rotman, Youval. *Byzantine Slavery and the Mediterranean World.* Trans. Jane Marie Todd. Cambridge, MA: Harvard University Press, 2009.

Shatzmiller, Maya. "Marriage, Family, and the Faith: Women's Conversion To Islam." *Journal of Family History* 21 (1996): 235–66.

Stillman, Norman. *Jews of Arab Lands: A History and Source Book.* Philadelphia: Jewish Publication Society, 1998.

Trombley, Frank. "The Arabs in Anatolia and the Islamic Law of War (Fiqh al-Jihād) (Seventh–Tenth Centuries)." *Al-Masaq* 16 (2004): 147–61.

Watson, Andrew. *Agricultural Innovation in the Early Islamic World: The Diffusion of Crops and Farming Techniques, 700–1100.* Cambridge: Cambridge University Press, 2008.

Wheatley, Paul. *The Places Where Men Pray Together: Cities in Islamic Lands, Seventh through the Tenth Centuries.* Chicago: University of Chicago Press, 2000.

FOUR | RESHAPING POLITICAL COMMUNITIES
CHRISTIAN AND MUSLIM HOLY WARS

Allen, S. J., and Emilie Amt, *The Crusades: A Reader.* Toronto: University of Toronto Press, 2003.

Catlos, Brian. *Infidel Kings and Unholy Warriors. Faith, Power, and Violence in the Age of Crusade and Jihad.* New York: Farrar, Straus & Giroux, 2014.

Christie, Niall. *Muslims and Crusaders: Christianity's Wars in the Middle East, 1095–1382, from the Islamic Sources.* London: Routledge, 2014.

Cobb, Paul M. *The Race for Paradise: An Islamic History of the Crusades*. Oxford: Oxford University Press, 2014.

Hillenbrand, Carole. *The Crusades: Islamic Perspectives*. Edinburgh: Edinburgh University Press, 2000.

Holt, P. M. *The Age of the Crusades: The Near East from the Eleventh Century to 1517*. New York: Longman, 1986.

Housley, Norman. *Contesting the Crusades*. Malden, MA: Blackwell, 2006.

Madden, Thomas. *The New Concise History of the Crusades*. New York: Rowman & Littlefield, 2006.

Mourad, Suleiman, and James E. Lindsay, "Ibn ʿAsakir and the Instensification and Reorientation of Sunni Jihad Ideology in Crusader Era Syria." In *Just Wars, Holy Wars, and Jihads: Christian, Jewish, and Muslim Encounters and Exchanges*, ed. Sohail H. Hashmi. Oxford: Oxford University Press, 2012.

O'Callaghan, Joseph. *Reconquest and Crusade in Medieval Spain*. Philadelphia: University of Pennsylvania Press, 2003.

Riley-Smith, Jonathan. *The Crusades: A History*. 2nd ed. New Haven: Yale University Press, 2005.

———. *The First Crusaders, 1095–1131*. Cambridge: Cambridge University Press, 1997.

———, ed. *The Oxford Illustrated History of the Crusades*. Oxford: Oxford University Press, 1995.

Tyerman, Christopher. *God's War: A New History of the Crusades*. Cambridge, MA: Belknap Press of Harvard University Press, 2006.

FIVE | CROSSING BOUNDARIES

MEDIEVAL FRONTIER SOCIETIES

Abulafia, David. *The Western Mediterranean Kingdoms, 1200–1500: The Struggle for Dominion*. New York: Longman, 1997.

Barber, Malcolm. *The Crusader States*. New Haven: Yale University Press, 2012.

Barton, Simon. "Traitors to the Faith? Christian Mercenaries in al-Andalus and the Maghreb, c.1100–1300." In *Medieval Spain: Culture, Conflict, and Coexistence: Studies in Honour of Angus MacKay*, ed. Roger Collins and Anthony Goodman. Houndmills, Basingstoke, UK: Palgrave Macmillan, 2002.

Beihammer, Alexander. "Defection across the Border of Islam and Christianity: Apostasy and Cross-Cultural Interaction in Byzantine Seljuk Relations." *Speculum* 86 (2011): 597–651.

Berkey, Jonathan. *The Transmission of Knowledge in Medieval Cairo: A Social History of Islamic Education*. Princeton, NJ: Princeton University Press, 1992.

Brodman, James. *Ransoming Captives in Crusader Spain: The Order of Merced on the Christian-Islamic Frontier*. Philadelphia: University of Pennsylania Press, 1986.

Burns, Robert I. "Christian-Islamic Confrontation in the West: The Thirteenth-Century Dream of Conversion." *American Historical Review* 74 (1975): 22–42.

Catlos, Brian. *Muslims of Medieval Latin Christendom, c. 1050–1614*. Cambridge: Cambridge University Press, 2014.

———. *The Victors and the Vanquished: Christians and Muslims of Catalonia and Aragon, 1050–1300*. Cambridge: Cambridge University Press, 2007.

Cobb, Paul M. *Usama ibn Munqidh: Warrior Poet of the Age of the Crusades*. London: Oneworld, 2005.

Dodds, Jerrilynn D., Maria Rosa Menocal, and Abigale Krasner Balbale. *The Arts of Intimacy: Christians, Jews, and Muslims in the Making of Castilian Culture*. New Haven: Yale University Press, 2008.

Ellenblum, Ronnie. *Frankish Rural Settlement in the Latin Kingdom of Jerusalem*. Cambridge: Cambridge University Press, 1998.

Folda, Jaroslav. *Crusader Art*. London: Lund Humphries, 2008.

Friedman, Yvonne. *Encounter between Enemies: Captivity and Ransom in the Latin Kingdom of Jerusalem*. Leiden: Brill, 2002.

Idel, Moshe. *Kabbalah in Italy, 1280–1510*. New Haven: Yale University Press, 2011.

Karamustafa, Ahmet T. *Sufism: The Formative Period*. Berkeley: University of California Press, 2007.

Kedar, Benjamin. *Crusade and Mission: European Approaches toward the Muslims*. Princeton, NJ: Princeton University Press, 1984.

Kinoshita, Sharon, and Jason Jacobs. "Ports of Call: Boccaccio's Alatiel in the Medieval Mediterranean." *Journal of Medieval and Early Modern Studies* 37 1 (2007): 163–95.

Mallette, Karla. *The Kingdom of Sicily, 1100–1250: A Literary History*. Philadelphia: University of Pennsylvania Press, 2005.

MacEvitt, Christopher. *The Crusades and the Christian World of the East: Rough Tolerance*. Philadelphia: University of Pennsylvania Press, 2008.

Powell, James, ed. *Muslims under Latin Rule, 1100–1300*. Princeton, NJ: Princeton University Press, 1990.

Ridder-Symoens, Hilde de, ed. *A History of the University in Europe*, Volume 1: *Universities in the Middle Ages*. Cambridge: Cambridge University Press, 2003.

Rodriguez, Jarbel. *Captives and their Saviors in the Medieval Crown of Aragon*. Washington, DC: Catholic University Press, 2007.

Strousma, Sarah. *Maimonides in His World: Portrait of a Mediterranean Thinker*. Princeton, NJ: Princeton University Press, 2011.

Usama ibn Munqidh. *The Book of Contemplation: Islam and the Crusades*. Ed. and trans. Paul M. Cobb. New York: Penguin, 2008.

Vryonis, Spyros. *The Decline of Medieval Hellenism in Asia Minor and the Process of Islamization from the Eleventh through the Fifteenth Century*. Berkeley: University of California Press, 1971.

SIX | COMMERCE, CONQUEST, AND TRAVEL

Abulafia, David. *A Mediterranean Emporium: The Catalan Kingdom of Majorca*. Cambridge: Cambridge University Press, 1994.

Abu-Lughod, Janet. *Before European Hegemony: The World System, 1250–1350*. Oxford: Oxford University Press, 1989.

Arbel, Benjamin. "Slave Trade and Slave Labor in Frankish Cyprus (1191–1571)." *Studies in Medieval and Renaissance History* 14 (1993): 149–93.

Ashtor, Eliyahu. *Levant Trade in the Later Middle Ages*. Princeton, NJ: Princeton University Press, 1983.

———. *A Social and Economic History of the Near East in the Middle Ages*. Berkeley: University of California Press, 1976.

Balard, Michel. *La Romanie génoise: XIIe début du XVe siècle*. Rome: École française de Rome, 1978.

Benjamin, Sandra, ed. *The World of Benjamin of Tudela: A Medieval Mediterranean Travelogue*. Cranbury, NJ: Fairleigh Dickinson University Press, 1995.

Blumenthal, Debra. *Enemies and Familiars. Slavery and Mastery in Fifteenth Century Valencia.* Ithaca, NY: Cornell University Press, 2009.

Borsch, Stuart J. *The Black Death in Egypt and England: A Comparative Study.* Austin: University of Texas Press, 2005.

Busch, Silvia Orvietani. *Medieval Mediterranean Ports: The Catalan and Tuscan Coasts, 1100–1235.* Leiden: Brill, 2001.

Constable, Olivia Remie. *Housing the Stranger in the Mediterranean World: Lodging, Trade, and Travel in Late Antiquity and the Middle Ages.* Cambridge: Cambridge University Press, 2003.

Dols, Michael. *The Black Death in the Middle East.* Princeton, NJ: Princeton University Press, 1977.

Dunn, Ross E. *The Adventures of Ibn Battuta, a Muslim Traveler of the Fourteenth Century.* Berkeley: University of California Press, 1989.

Epstein, Steven. *Genoa and the Genoese, 958–1528.* Chapel Hill: University of North Carolina Press, 1996.

Franceschi, Franco, Richard A. Goldthwaite, and Reinhold C. Mueller, eds. *Il Rinascimento Italiano e l'Europa,* vol 4: *Commercio e cultura mercantile.* Treviso: Fondazione Cassamarca, 2007.

Jacoby, David. *Commercial Exchange across the Mediterranean: Byzantium, the Crusader Levant, Egypt, and Italy.* Aldershot, UK: Ashgate, 2005.

Lopez, Robert S. *Benedetto Zaccaria: ammiraglio e mercante nella Genova del Duecento.* 1933. Reprint ed., Genoa: Fratelli Frilli, 2004.

——. *The Commercial Revolution of the Middle Ages, 950–1350.* Cambridge: Cambridge University Press, 1998.

Lopez, Robert S., and Irving Raymond, eds. *Medieval Trade in the Mediterranean World.* 1955. Reprint ed., New York: Columbia University Press, 2001.

McKee, Sally. "Domestic Slavery in Renaissance Italy." *Slavery and Abolition* 29, 3 (2008): 305–26.

Phillips, William D. *Slavery from Roman Times to the Early Transatlantic Trade.* Minneapolis: University of Minnesota Press, 1985.

Rouighi, Ramzi. *The Making of a Mediterranean Emirate: Ifriqiya and Its Andalusis, 1200–1400.* Philadelphia: University of Pennsylvania Press, 2011.

Reyerson, Katherine. *The Art of the Deal: Intermediaries of Trade in Medieval Montpellier.* Leiden: Brill, 2002.

Skinner, Patricia. *Medieval Amalfi and Its Diaspora, 800–1200.* Oxford: Oxford University Press, 2013.

Spufford, Peter. *Power and Profit: The Merchant in Medieval Europe.* New York: Thames & Hudson, 2002.

Tai, Emily Sohmer. "Marking Water: Piracy and Property in the Premodern West." In *Seascapes: Maritime Histories, Littoral Cultures, and Transoceanic Exchanges.* Ed. Jerry Bentley and Kären Wigen. Honolulu: University of Hawaii Press, 2007.

SEVEN | CRISIS AND CONSOLIDATION IN STATE AND SOCIETY

Belozerskaya, Marina. *To Wake the Dead: A Renaissance Merchant and the Birth of Archeology.* New York: W. W. Norton, 2009.

Cohen, Mark. "Jews in the Mamluk Environment: The Crisis of 1442 (a Geniza Study)." *Bulletin of the School of Oriental and African Studies* 47 (1984): 425–48.

Cohn, Samuel K. *Lust for Liberty: The Politics of Social Revolt in Medieval Europe, 1200–1425*. Cambridge, MA: Harvard University Press, 2006.

Finkel, Caroline. *Osman's Dream: The Story of the Ottoman Empire*. New York: Basic Books, 2005.

Freedman, Paul. *The Origins of Peasant Servitude in Medieval Catalonia*. Cambridge: Cambridge University Press, 1991.

Goffman, Daniel. *The Ottoman Empire and Early Modern Europe*. Cambridge: Cambridge University Press, 2002.

Harris, Jonathan. *The End of Byzantium*. New Haven: Yale University Press, 2010.

Imber, Colin. *The Ottoman Empire: The Structure of Power*. New York: Palgrave MacMillan, 2002.

Irwin, Robert. *The Middle East in the Middle Ages: The Early Mamluk Sultanate, 1250–1382*. Carbondale: Southern Illinois University Press, 1986.

Kafadar, Cemal. *Between Two Worlds: The Construction of the Ottoman State*. Berkeley: University of California Press, 1995.

Levanoni, Amalia. *A Turning Point in Mamluk History: The Third Reign of al-Nasir Muhammad ibn Qalawun, 1310–1341*. Leiden: Brill, 1995.

Nicol, Donald M. *The Last Centuries of Byzantium, 1261–1453*. 2nd ed. Cambridge: Cambridge University Press, 1993.

Ruiz, Teofilo F. *Spain's Century of Crisis: 1300–1474*. Oxford: Blackwell Publishing, 2007.

Ryder, Alan. *The Wreck of Catalonia: Civil War in the Fifteenth Century*. Oxford: Oxford University Press, 2007.

Zachariadou, Elizabeth. *Studies in Pre-Ottoman Turkey and the Ottomans*. Aldershot, UK: Ashgate Variorum, 2007.

EIGHT | THE RENAISSANCE BAZAAR

Ben-Zaken, Avner. *Cross-Cultural Scientific Exchanges in the Eastern Mediterranean, 1560–1660*. Baltimore: Johns Hopkins University Press, 2010.

Bisaha, Nancy. *Creating East and West: Renaissance Humanists and the Ottoman Turks*. Philadelphia: University of Pennsylvania Press, 2004.

Brotton, Jerry. *The Renaissance Bazaar: From the Silk Roads to Michelangelo*. Oxford: Oxford University Press, 2003.

Campbell, Caroline. *Bellini and the East*. New Haven: Yale University Press, 2005.

Carboni, Stefano. *Venice and the Islamic World, 828–1797*. New Haven: Yale University Press, 2007.

Darling, Linda T. "The Renaissance and the Middle East." In *A Companion to the Worlds of the Renaissance*, ed. Guido Ruggiero. Oxford: Blackwell, 2002.

Fleet, Kate. *European and Islamic Trade in the Early Ottoman State: The Merchants of Genoa and Turkey*. Cambridge: Cambridge University Press, 1999.

Jardine, Lisa, and Jerry Brotton. *Global Interests: Renaissance Art between East and West*. London: Reaktion Books, 2005.

Mack, Rosamund. *Bazaar to Piazza: Islamic Trade and Italian Art, 1300–1600*. Berkeley: University of California Press, 2002.

Meserve, Margaret. *Empires of Islam in Renaissance Historical Thought*. Cambridge, MA: Harvard University Press, 2008.

Necipoğlu, Gülru. *The Age of Sinan: Architectural Culture in the Ottoman Empire*. Princeton, NJ: Princeton University Press, 2005.

Hess, Catherine, Linda Komaroff, and George Saliba, eds. *The Arts of Fire: Islamic Influences on Glass and Ceramics of the Italian Renaissance*. Los Angeles: J. Paul Getty Museum, 2004.

Saliba, George. *Islamic Science and the Making of the European Renaissance*. Cambridge, MA: MIT Press, 2007.

Trivellato, Francesca. "Renaissance Italy and the Muslim Mediterranean in Recent Historical Works." *Journal of Modern History* 82 (2010): 127–55.

NINE | MEDITERRANEAN EMPIRES
HAPSBURGS, VENICE, AND THE OTTOMANS

Arbel, Benjamin. "Venice's Maritime Empire in the Early Modern Period." In *A Companion to Venetian History, 1400–1797*, ed. Eric R. Dursteler. Leiden: Brill, 2013.

Brummett, Palmira. *Ottoman Seapower and Levantine Diplomacy in the Age of Discovery*. Albany: State University of New York Press, 1993.

Capponi, Niccolò. *Victory of the West: The Great Christian-Muslim Clash at the Battle of Lepanto*. New York: Da Capo Press, 2006.

Chejne, Anwar G. *Islam and the West: The Moriscos*. Albany: State University of New York Press, 1983.

Coleman, David. *Creating Christian Granada*. Ithaca, NY: Cornell University Press, 2003.

Dandelet, Thomas. *The Renaissance of Empire in Early Modern Europe*. Cambridge: Cambridge University Press, 2014.

Dursteler, Eric R. *Venetians in Constantinople: Nation, Identity, and Coexistence in the Early Modern Mediterranean*. Baltimore: Johns Hopkins University Press, 2006.

Elliott, J. H. *Imperial Spain, 1469–1716*. 2nd ed. New York: Penguin, 2002.

Guilmartin, John F. *Gunpowder and Galleys: Changing Technology and Mediterranean Warfare at Sea in the 16th Century*. 2nd ed. London: Conway Maritime Press, 2003.

Hess, Andrew C. "The Battle of Lepanto and Its Place in Mediterranean History." *Past and Present* 57 (1972): 53–73.

Homza, Lu Ann. *The Spanish Inquisition, 1478–1614: An Anthology of Sources*. Indianapolis: Hackett, 2006.

İnalcik, Halil. "The Ottoman State: Economy and Society, 1300–1600." In *An Economic and Social History of the Ottoman Empire: 1300–1914*, ed. Halil İnalcik and Donald Quataert, vol. 1. Cambridge: Cambridge University Press, 1994.

Isom-Verhaaren, Christine. *Allies with the Infidel: The Ottoman and French Alliance in the Sixteenth Century*. London: I. B. Tauris, 2011.

Kamen, Henry. *Philip of Spain*. New Haven: Yale University Press, 1997.

———. *The Spanish Inquisition: A Historical Revision*. New Haven: Yale University Press, 1997.

Kunt, Metin, and Christine Woodhead. *Süleyman the Magnificent and His Age: The Ottoman Empire in the Early Modern World*. New York: Routledge, 2013.

Lane, Frederic C. *Venice, A Maritime Republic*. Baltimore: Johns Hopkins University Press, 1973.

Necipoğlu, Gülru. *Architecture, Ceremonial, and Power: The Topkapı Palace in the Fifteenth and Sixteenth Centuries*. Cambridge, MA: MIT Press, 1991.

O'Connell, Monique. *Men of Empire: Power and Negotiation in Venice's Maritime State*. Baltimore: Johns Hopkins University Press, 2009.

Parker, Geoffrey. *The Dutch Revolt*. London: Penguin, 2002.

Peirce, Leslie. *The Imperial Harem: Women and Sovereignty in the Ottoman Empire*. Oxford: Oxford University Press, 1993.

Perry, Mary Elizabeth. *The Handless Maiden: Moriscos and the Politics of Religion in Early Modern Spain*. Princeton, NJ: Princeton University Press, 2005.

Ravid, Benjamin, and Robert C. Davis, eds. *The Jews of Early Modern Venice*. Baltimore: Johns Hopkins University Press, 2001.

Root, Deborah. "Speaking Christian: Orthodoxy and Difference in Sixteenth-Century Spain." *Representation* 23 (1988): 118–34.

Tracy, James D. *Emperor Charles V, Impresario of War: Campaign Strategy, International Finance, and Domestic Politics*. Cambridge, MA: Cambridge University Press, 2002.

Vaughan, Dorothy M. *Europe and the Turk: A Pattern of Alliances, 1350–1700*. Liverpool: Liverpool University Press, 1954.

TEN | LIVING ON THE FRONTIER
INQUISITION, IDENTITY, AND CONVERSION

Bennassar, Bartolomé, and Lucile Bennassar. *Les chrétiens d'Allah: l'histoire extraordinaire des renégats, XVIe–XVIIe siècles*. Paris: Perrin, 1989.

Blumenthal, Debra. *Enemies and Familiars: Slavery and Mastery in Fifteenth-Century Valencia*. Ithaca, NY: Cornell University Press, 2009.

Bono, Salvatore. *Corsari nel Mediterraneo: cristiani e musulmani fra guerra, schiavitù e commercio*. Milan: Mondadori, 1993.

Casale, Giancarlo L. *The Ottoman Age of Exploration: Spices Maps and Conquest in the Sixteenth-Century Indian Ocean*. Oxford: Oxford University Press, 2010.

Davis, Natalie Zemon. *Trickster Travels: A Sixteenth-Century Muslim between Worlds*. New York: Hill & Wang, 2006.

Davis, Robert C. *Christian Slaves, Muslim Masters: White Slavery in the Mediterranean, the Barbary Coast, and Italy, 1500–1800*. New York: Palgrave, 2003.

———. *Holy War and Human Bondage: Tales of Christian-Muslim Slavery in the Early-Modern Mediterranean*. Westport, CT: Praeger, 2009.

Dursteler, Eric R. *Renegade Women: Gender, Identity, and Boundaries in the Early Modern Mediterranean*. Baltimore: Johns Hopkins University Press, 2011.

Faroqhi, Suraiya. *Subjects of the Sultan: Culture and Daily Life in the Ottoman Empire*. London: I. B. Tauris, 2007.

Friedman, Ellen. *Spanish Captives in North Africa in the Early Modern Age*. Madison: University of Wisconsin Press, 1983.

García-Arenal, Mercedes, and Gerard Wiegers. *A Man of Three Worlds: Samuel Pallache, a Moroccan Jew in Catholic and Protestant Europe*. Baltimore: Johns Hopkins University Press, 2003.

Harvey, L. P. *Muslims in Spain, 1500 to 1614*. Chicago: University of Chicago Press, 2006.

Kamen, Henry. "Strategies of Survival: Minority Cultures in the Western Mediterranean." In *Early Modern History and the Social Sciences: Testing the Limits of Braudel's Mediterranean*, ed. John A. Marino. Kirksville, MO: Truman State University Press, 2002.

Matar, Nabil. *Europe through Arab Eyes, 1578–1727*. New York: Columbia University Press, 2009.

———, ed. *In the Lands of the Christians: Arabic Travel Writing in the Seventeenth Century*. New York: Routledge, 2003.

Zilfi, Madeline C. *Women and Slavery in the Late Ottoman Empire: The Design of Difference*. Cambridge: Cambridge University Press, 2010.

Black, Jeremy. *Italy and the Grand Tour*. New Haven: Yale University Press, 2005.

Bulmuş, Birsen. *Plague, Quarantines, and Geopolitics in the Ottoman Empire*. Edinburgh: University of Edinburgh Press, 2012.

Casey, James. *Early Modern Spain: A Social History*. London: Routledge, 1999.

Dankoff, Robert. *An Ottoman Mentality : The World of Evliya Çelebi*. Leiden: Brill, 2004.

Garcés, María Antonia. *Cervantes in Algiers: A Captive's Tale*. Rev. ed. Nashville, TN: Vanderbilt University Press, 2005.

Goffman, Daniel. *Izmir and the Levantine World, 1550–1650*. Seattle: University of Washington Press, 1990.

Hanlon, Gregory. *Early Modern Italy, 1550–1800: Three Seasons in European History*. New York: Palgrave Macmillan, 2000.

Kagan, Frederick W., and Robin Higham, eds. *The Military History of Tsarist Russia*. New York: Palgrave Macmillan, 2008.

Lanaro, Paola. *At the Centre of the Old World: Trade and Manufacturing in Venice and the Venetian Mainland, 1400–1800*. Toronto: Centre for Reformation and Renaissance Studies, 2006.

Lewis, Bernard. *The Muslim Discovery of Europe*. New York: W. W. Norton, 1982.

McNeill, J. R. *The Mountains of the Mediterranean World: An Environmental History*. Cambridge: Cambridge University Press, 2003.

Murphey, Rhoads. "Provisioning Istanbul: The State and Subsistence in the Early Modern Middle East." *Food and Foodways* 2 (1988): 217–63.

Parker, Geoffrey. *Global Crisis: War, Climate, and Catastrophe in the Seventeenth Century*. New Haven: Yale University Press, 2013.

Phillips, Carla Rahn. "Time and Duration: A Model for the Economy of Early Modern Spain." *American Historical Review* 92 (1987): 531–62.

Rapp, Richard. "The Unmaking of the Mediterranean Trade Hegemony: International Trade Rivalry and the Commercial Revolution." *Journal of Economic History* 25 (1975): 499–525.

Saïd, Edward. *Orientalism*. New York: Vintage Books, 1978.

Sella, Domenico. *Italy in the Seventeenth Century*. London: Longman, 1997.

Shefer-Mossensohn, Miri. *Ottoman Medicine: Healing and Medical Institutions, 1500–1700*. Albany: State University of New York Press, 2009.

Tabak, Faruk. *The Waning of the Mediterranean: A Geohistorical Approach*. Baltimore: Johns Hopkins University Press, 2008.

Trivellato, Francesca. *The Familiarity of Strangers: The Sephardic Diaspora, Livorno, and Cross-Cultural Trade in the Early Modern Period*. New Haven: Yale University Press, 2009.

Varlik, Nukhet. "Disease and Empire: A History of Plague Epidemics in the Early Modern Ottoman Empire (1453–1600)." PhD diss., University of Chicago, 2008.

Vitkus, Daniel J. and Nabil Matar, eds. *Piracy, Slavery, and Redemption: Barbary Captivity Narratives from Early Modern England*. New York: Columbia University Press, 2001.

White, Sam. *The Climate of Rebellion in the Early Modern Ottoman Empire*. Cambridge: Cambridge University Press, 2011.

TWELVE | THE WANING OF THE EARLY MODERN MEDITERRANEAN

Aksan, Virgina H. *Ottoman Wars, 1700–1870: An Empire Besieged*. New York: Routledge, 2013.

Cole, Juan. *Napoleon's Egypt: Invading the Middle East*. New York: Palgrave Macmillan, 2007.

Esdaile, Charles J. *Fighting Napoleon: Guerrillas, Bandits, and Adventurers in Spain, 1808–1814*. New Haven: Yale University Press, 2004.

Faroqhi, Suraiya. *The Ottoman Empire and the World around It*. London: I. B. Tauris, 2006.

Fraser, Ronald. *Napoleon's Cursed War: Spanish Popular Resistance in the Peninsular War, 1808–1814*. London: Verso, 2008.

Gregory, Desmond. *Malta, Britain, and the European Powers, 1793–1815*. Cranbury, NJ: Fairleigh Dickinson University Press, 1996.

Hoock, Holger. *Empires of the Imagination: Politics, War and the Arts in the British World, 1750–1850*. London: Profile Books, 2010.

Jabartī, Abd al-Raḥmān. *Napoleon in Egypt: Al-Jabartī's Chronicle of the First Seven Months of the French Occupation*. Princeton, NJ: Markus Wiener Publishers, 2004.

Plant, Margaret. *Venice: Fragile City, 1797–1997*. New Haven: Yale University Press, 2002.

Strathern, Paul. *Napoleon in Egypt*. New York: Random House, 2007.

Whipple, A. B. C. *To the Shores of Tripoli: The Birth of the U.S. Navy and Marines*. Annapolis: Naval Institute Press, 1991.

Page numbers in *italics* refer to figures; *gallery* indicates the color insert following p. 240.

Catalonia, 42, 48, 101, 105, 107, 149, 159, 165; merchants from, 180–81, 182; plague in, 150, 162; political strife in, 168, 170

Catherine of Sinai, Saint, 70

Catherine the Great, 283, 284

Cellini, Benvenuto, 201

ceramics, 182–83, *gallery*

Cervantes, Miguel de, 233, 279

Charlemagne, 41–42

Charles of Anjou, 155–56

Charles V (king of Spain), 219–20, 243, 252; as patron, 201, 202; as ruler, 217–18, 224–25, 258

Charles VIII (king of France), 228

Christianity: bishops in, 23–25; Constantine and, 19–20; conversions from, 68, 254; conversions to, 66, 67, 111–12, 119, 166, 221, 255–56; Great Schism in Latin, 163; holy war ideas in, 87–91; and Islam, 34, 37, 38, 69, 110, 231–34; Lateran Councils in, 112, 113–14; and Latin language, 65–66; monasteries in, 22, 71–72; Nicene and non-Nicine forms of, 20, 29, 30; and Ottoman Empire, 174–75, 232; and paganism, 27–28; persecution of, 19, 51, 68; and pilgrimages, 20–21, 70, 87; Protestantism in, 219, 232; and religious images, 75–76, 77; and Roman Empire, 18, 19, 25–26; Rome-Constantinople division in, 34, 77, 99, 156, 176, 231, 256, 257; and saints, 55, 68, 69, 258; self-sacrifice and asceticism in, 21–22; shared identity with, 58–59, 70–71, 233; and slavery, 245

Chrysoloras, Manuel, 185

Cigalazade Yusuf Sinan Pasha, 198

Circassians, 169, 244

Cisneros, Francisco Jiménez, 192

cities, 52, 55, 57, 135–36, 274–75

Clement V (pope), 141, 158

Clement VI (pope), 141, 153

Clement VII (pope), 163

Clement VIII (pope), 232

climate, 48–49, 52, 132, 148, 261

Clissa (Klis), 235–36

coffee, 184

Cola di Rienzo, 162

Columbus, Christopher, 217

commerce and trade, 130–32, 269–76; Anatolia and, 138–39; Byzantine Empire and, 52, 58–59, 138; capitalism and, 131; cities created by, 9, 52, 57, 274–75; conflict and competition in, 139–42; glass industry and, 133, 181–82, 271; increasing demand for, 132–33, 139, 181–84, 262, 273–74; international vs. regional, 272–73; between Islamic and Christian worlds, 52, 56–58, 131–32, 140–41, 180–81; Jews and, 54, 59–60; for luxury items, 58–59, 133, 139, 181, 183–84; maritime, 39, 56, 133, 135, 272, 274; mediation with states and, 147; in post-Roman world, 28, 55–60; Renaissance and, 179–84; in Roman Empire, 16; silk road and, 148; in spices, 133, 180, 227, 270; textile industry and, 181, 183, 270, 271–72, 273–75; Venice and Genoa as centers of, 60, 131, 132, 133, 135–36, 137, 138, 139, 180, 181, 227, 272–73

Complutensian Polyglot, 192, *193*

Conrad of Montferrat, 97

Constans II (Byzantine emperor), 77

Constantine (Roman emperor), 19–20, *21*, 23

Constantine V (Byzantine emperor), 76

Constantine VII (Byzantine emperor), 63

Constantine XI (Byzantine emperor), 176

Constantinople, 12, 25, 35, 40, 42, 47, 58; buildings and architecture of, 30–31, 156, 199–200, *gallery*; Byzantine Empire and, 167, 176; Crusades and, 87–88, 93, 98–99, 100; as intellectual center, 63; luxury trade in, 58–59; monasteries of, 72, 156; Ottoman conquests of, 155, 174, 176–77, 207. *See also* Istanbul

conversion, in captivity, 115; to Christianity, 66, 67, 111, 119, 166, 221, 255–56; Christian views of, 111–12; coerced and voluntary, 254–55; to Islam, 66–67, 119, 254; and slavery, 247–48, 254

Copernicus, Nicolaus, 195

Copts, 28, 41, 72, 160, 168

Cordoba, 57, 58; Christians in, 68, 110; as cultural and intellectual center, 55, 61–62, 65; mosques in, 48, 61, 63, *gallery*; textile industry in, 270; Umayyad dynasty in, 42, 45, 46, 48, 49, 50, 67

Corfu, 55, 85, 238, 257, 285

Corrupting Sea, The (Horden and Purcell), 8–9

Ficino, Marsilio, 185

Filarete, Antonio, 199, 203

Filelfo, Francesco, 187, 199–200

Filelfo, Giovanmario, 187

fishing, 262

Florence, 133, 151, 162, 185, 274; economy of, 158, 182, 183, 270, 271; expansion of, 168, 170; famine in, *164*, 268

forest management, 261–62

France, 43, 218, 261, 273, 276; and Crusades, 102–3; under Napoleon, 284–88, 291–93; and Ottoman Empire, 231–32

Francis I (king of France), 201, 206, 231

Francis of Assisi, 111, *113*

Frederick I Barbarossa (Holy Roman emperor), 96–97, 125

Frederick II (Holy Roman emperor), 101, 102, 110, 124, 129

frontier societies: conversion and inquisition within, 110–122; defined, 106–7; individual and community lives in, 107–10; intellectual life in, 122–23

Fulcher of Chartres, 89, 116–17

Galen, 151

Galileo Galilei, 196

Genoa, 45, 150, 158, 171, 177, 180; as banking center, 275; silk production in, 270, 271; and slavery, 146, 247; struggle with Pisa by, 133, 137, 140; as trading center, 60, 131, 132, 133, 135–36, 137, 139, 180; Venice war with, 140, 148, 163, 171

geography, 187–88, 239

George of Antioch, 117

Gerard of Cremona, 124–25

Gerbert of Aurillac (Pope Sylvester II), 65

Ghazali, Abu Hamid al-, 92, 123

Ghiberti, Lorenzo, 200

Giangaleazzo Visconti, 170

Gibbon, Edward, 14

gift exchange, 184

Ginzburg, Carlo: *The Cheese and the Worms*, 258

Giotto, 158

Giustiniani, Marcantonio, 190–91

glass industry, 133, 181–82, 271, *gallery*

Godfrey of Bouillon, 88, 90

Goethe, Johann Wolfgang: *Italienische Reise*, 281

Góis, Damião de, 189

Goya, Francisco: *The Disasters of War*, 288, *290*

Granada, 50, 141, 160–61, 168, 170, 217; architecture of, 201–2; Christians in Muslim-controlled, 110, 117; massacre of Jews in, 79; Nasrid dynasty in, 101–2; plague in, 150, 151–52; population of, 110–11

Greece, 184–85, 263, 264; and Ottoman Empire, 176, 211, 263, 286–87; Parthenon in, 291

Greek language, 63, 65, 66, 192

Gregoras, Nikephoros, 151

Gregory I (pope), 27–28

Gregory II (pope), 77

Gregory VII (pope), 87

Gregory IX (pope), 111, 114

Gregory XI (pope), 165

Gregory XIII (pope), 249

Grimani, Domenico, 185

Guicciardini, Francesco, 228

Guiscard, Robert, 83–85

Guy of Lusingnan, 96, 97

Habsburgs, 216–25, 267

Hacı Ahmed, Tunuslu, 191

hadith, 38, 78, 249

Häedo, Diego de, 254

Hafsid dynasty, 119, 139, 141, 142

Hagia Sophia, 31, 156, 199, 205; illustrations, *157, gallery*

Hakem, al-, II (caliph of Cordoba), 62

Hakim, al- (Fatimid caliph-imam), 51, 117

Halevi, Judah, 123

Haram al-Sharif, 33–34

harems, 212–13, 250

Hasdai ibn Shaprut, 63, 67

Hasluck, F. W., 257

Hebrew language, 189, 190, 192

Henry VII (Holy Roman emperor), 158

heresy, 102, 112

Herrera, Juan de, 203

Hisham I (emir of Cordoba), 67–68

Holy Roman Empire, 41–42, 96–97, 102, 158, 218, 258

Hospitallers, 86, 90, 91, 140, 141, 252

Huguenots, 232

humanism, 184–89

Mediterranean studies, 7–10
Mediterranean term, 1
Mehmed I (Ottoman sultan), 175, 199, 207
Mehmed II (Ottoman sultan), 186–87,
    209–10, 227, 240–41, *gallery*; capture of
    Constantinople by, 176–77, 242; imperial
    system of, 211–12; as patron, 178, 179, 200
Melania the Elder, 22
Melania the Younger, 22–23
Melisande (queen of Jerusalem), 93, 128
Mercedarians, 115
mercenaries, 18, 43, 86, *121*, 159, 198, 255;
    Almohads' use of, 117, 119; Byzantine use
    of, 50, 83, 85
Mesopotamia, 35, 48, 58, 95, 100
Messina, *44*, 50, 84, 261, 264
Metaxas, Nicodemus, 192
Michael III (Byzantine emperor), 77
Michael VII Doukas (Byzantine emperor), 84
Michael VIII Palaiologos (Byzantine
    emperor), 100, 137, 156
Michelangelo, 179, 201, 202, 205
Michelozzo, 200
migration, 83, 240–42, 264. *See also*
    population mobility
Milan, 23, 168, 170, 218, 219, 269, 270
military specialists, 198
military technology, 196–97
millenarianism, 258
Mithras, 17
Mocenigo, Tommaso, 180
monasteries, 22, 23, 71–72
monetary system, 39, 135, 165, 270
Mongols, 103, 138, 140, 148, 150, 199
Montagu, Lady Mary Wortley, 276–77
Morocco, *121*, 130, 243, 244, 245
Morosini, Francesco, 291
Moses of Mardin, 189
Moulay Ismail, 245, 247
Muhammad (prophet), 33–35, 79
Muhammad Ali (viceroy of Egypt), 286
Muhammad V (sultan of Granada), 160
Muhammad IX (sultan of Granada), 170
Munastir, al- (Fatimid caliph-imam), 52
Murad I (Ottoman sultan), 173–74
Murad II (Ottoman sultan), 175, 176
Murad III (Ottoman sultan), 191, 195, 250
Mustafa Ali Gelibolulu: *Counsel for Sultans*,
    188, 259

Mustansir, al- (Fatimid caliph), 83, 94–95
Mu'awiya I (Umayyad caliph), 38
Mu'izz', al- (Fatimid caliph-imam), 46, 66
mysticism, 123–24

Naples, 43, 65, 171, 218, 245, 265, 290;
    Angevin rule in, 158, 165; economy of, 58,
    269, 272; Spanish control of, 219, 269
Napoleon Bonaparte, 245–46, 284–88;
    cultural plundering by, 292–93
Nasir, al- (Abbasid caliph), 98
Nasir Muhammad, al-, 168–69
Nasrid dynasty, 101–2, *161*
nation-state paradigm, 10, 236
natural disasters, 261
Nelson, Horatio, 286
Nero (Roman emperor), 18
Nestorius (patriarch of Constantinople), 25
Netherlands, 273; revolt against Spanish rule
    in, 219, 220–21, 234
newspapers, 193–94
Nicholas I (pope), 77
Nicholas II (pope), 83–84
Nicolas of Myra, 74
Nicolay, Nicolas de: *Les navigations,
    pérégrinations, et voyages faits en la
    Turquie*, 276
Nikephoros II Phokas (Byzantine emperor),
    47, 73
Nikephoros Phokas the Elder, 47
Niketas Choniates, 99
Nizam al-Mulk, 83, 88
Nizaris, 95
Normans, 81, 82, 83–85
Nur ad-Din (Nurredin), 94, 95
Nurbanu Sultan, 213

Odessa, 284
Odovacer, Flavius, 29
Orientalism (Saïd), 280
Orthodox Church, 29, 256; division between
    Rome and, 2, 77, 99, 156, 176, 257
Osman I (Ottoman sultan), 155, 159
Osman, Nakkas, *gallery*
Ostrogoths, 29–30
Ottoman Empire, 195, 198, 206, 207–16,
    242, 261; buildings in, 199–200, 212,
    215–16; and Byzantine Empire, 155,
    159, 168, 173–74, 175–76, 211; conquest

of Constantinople by, 155, 174, 176–77, 207; decline of, 259, 260; devshirme in, 212, *213*, 244, 254–55; diversity in, 174–75, 215; economy of, 182, 183, 268, 270, 273; expansion of, 155, 159, 207–11, 216; and France, 231–32; and Greece, 176, 211, 263, 286–87; harems in, 212–13, 250; Jews in, 174–75, 192, 215, 240–41; and Lepanto defeat, 233–34; medical and sanitary system in, 267; military technology of, 196–97; and Napoleon, 286–87; patronage networks in, 199–201; and corsairs, 252–53; printing of books in, 190, 191–92, 193; and Protestantism, 232; and Russia, 283–84; slaves in, 243–44, 250; and Spain, 218, 219–20; state structure of, 174–75, 211–12, 213–14; and Venice, 167, 177, 178, 182, 207, 209, 226–27, 233–34, 235–36, 237

Otto of Freising, 136

Pachominus, 22
paganism, 26–27
Palaiologian dynasty, 168, 172–73
Palermo, 84, 249, 264; Muslim rule in, 44, 46, 50, 55, 57, 61
Palestine. *See* Syria-Palestine
Palladio, Andrea, 203, 205
Pamplona, 43, 45
papacy, 25, 27–28, 98, 163
Parthenon, 291–92
patronage, artistic, 127–29, 178, 198–205, 224–25
Paul of Tarsus, 18
Peasants' War (1524–25), 219
Pechenegs, 52, 85
Peele, George: *Soliman and Perseda,* 279
Peninsular War (1807–14), 287
Peter I (king of Cyprus), 141
Peter III (king of Aragon), 156
Peter the Ceremonious, 165
Peter the Great, 283, *284*
Peter the Hermit, 87
Peter the Venerable, 112
Petrarch, Francesco, 154, 158, 188
Philip II (king of Spain), 198, 202–3, 217, 218, 225, 239, 242, 262; and Dutch revolt, 220–21, 234
Philip II Augustus (king of France), 96–97

Philip V of Bourbon (king of Spain), 287
Piccamiglio, Onofrio di, 142
Piccolomini, Aeneas Silvius (Pope Pius II), 185–86
Pico della Mirandola, Giovanni, 187, 189; *Oration on the Dignity of Man,* 187
pilgrimages, 20–21, 70–71, 87, 147, 148, 257, *gallery*
pirates and piracy, 43, 142, 250–54, 288–90; as economic enterprise, 143–44, 211, 253; impact of, 252, 253, 264; and slavery, 244, 253–54
Pirenne, Henri, 7–8, 55–56
Piri Reis, 16, 239, *gallery*
Pisa, 43, 89, 170, 274; and Genoa, 49, 87, 130, 133, 137, 140; merchants from, 52, 60, 90, 131, 132, 133, 135, 136, 139
Pitts, Joseph, 278
Pius V (pope), 234
Placidia, Galla, 12–13, 14
plague. *See* bubonic plague
Plato of Tivoli, 124
Pliny, 15
political centralization, 137, 170; and decentralization, 50, 52–53
Polo, Marco, 148
Polybius, 15
population mobility, 2, 136–37, 142–48, 239–42; in frontier societies, 116–17; Roman Empire and, 16, 18
Porphyry (bishop of Gaza), 26–27
Portugal, 180, 189, 197, 232, 270; Ottomans and, 209, 211
Postel, Guillaume, 195
Prado, Juan del, 258
Primaticcio, 201
printing and publishing, 189–94, 276
Priuli, Girolamo, 272
Proclus, 25
Protestantism, 219, 232
Ptolemy, 124, 187–88, 195
Pulcheria, Aelia, 12–13, 25

Qaitbay (Mamluk sultan), 184
quarantines, 266–67
Qur'an, 35, 37, 78, 79, 112, 667
Qutuz, al-Muzaffar, 103

Ragusa, 44, *260*, 261, 266

Vasari, Giorgio, 203
Vasco da Gama, 180, 209
Venice, 163, 183, 198, 226–31, 268, *gallery*;
    arsenal and weaponry of, 133, 197, 228;
    creation of, 42; and Crusades, 98, 100; as
    cultural center, 185, 227; decline of, 260,
    270, 282–83; Genoa wars with, 140, 148,
    163, 171; glass industry in, 133, 181–82,
    271; immigrants and foreigners living in,
    230, 240, 241; inquisition in, 221, 222, 223;
    Jews in, 228–30; Napoleon conquest of,
    285, 292; and Ottoman Empire, 167, 177,
    178, 182, 207, 209, 226–27, 233–34, 235–
    36, 237; plague in, 150, 265; population
    of, 230, 263–64; as publishing center,
    189–90, 276; and slave trade, 58, 146,
    249; territorial reach of, 168, 170–71, 228,
    238–39; as trading center, 60, 131, 137, 138,
    180, 181, 227, 272–73
Vienna, 210, 219
Vikings, 43
Villani, Giovanni, 132–33, 148
Visigoths, 12–14, 29, 31–32
von Harff, Arnold, 254

wages, 162, 271
War of Curzola (Korčula) (1293–99), 140

War of St. Sabas (1256–70), 140
War of the League of Cambrai (1508–16),
    228
War of the Spanish Succession (1701–14),
    287
Wifred "the Hairy" (count of Catalonia), 42
William II (king of Sicily), 129
William of Provence, 48
William of Rubruck, 148
William of Tyre, 128
Wittek, Paul, 159
women, 72, 125, 212–13, 242, 276–78; as
    slaves, 146, 244
Wordsworth, William, 282

Yazid II (Umayyad caliph), 76
Ya'qub ibn Killis, 67
Ystoria de Mahomet, 79
Yusuf I (sultan of Granada), 160

Zaccaria, Benedetto, 130, 137, 140, 142
Zaragoza, 49, 86, 91, 120, 162, 241
Zaryab, Ali ibn, 61
Zayyan ibn Mardanish, 101
Zengi, Imad ad-Din, 94
Zirid dynasty, 50, 51–52
Zohar, 123–24